THE NEW
AMERICAN
COMMENTARY

An Exegetical and Theological
Exposition of Holy Scripture

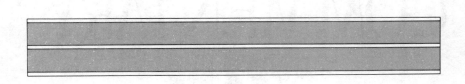

THE NEW
AMERICAN
COMMENTARY

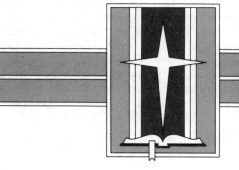

Volume
38

1, 2, 3 JOHN

Daniel L. Akin

BROADMAN
&HOLMAN
PUBLISHERS

Nashville, Tennessee

© 2001 • Broadman & Holman Publishers
All rights reserved
ISBN 0–8054–0138-5
Printed in the United States of America
04 03 02 01   4 3 2 1

To

my wife, Charlotte

and my sons,
Nathan, Jonathan, Paul, and Timothy

Editors' Preface

God's Word does not change. God's world, however, changes in every generation. These changes, in addition to new findings by scholars and a new variety of challenges to the gospel message, call for the church in each generation to interpret and apply God's Word for God's people. Thus, THE NEW AMERICAN COMMENTARY is introduced to bridge the twentieth and twenty-first centuries. This new series has been designed primarily to enable pastors, teachers, and students to read the Bible with clarity and proclaim it with power.

In one sense THE NEW AMERICAN COMMENTARY is not new, for it represents the continuation of a heritage rich in biblical and theological exposition. The title of this forty-volume set points to the continuity of this series with an important commentary project published at the end of the nineteenth century called AN AMERICAN COMMENTARY, edited by Alvah Hovey. The older series included, among other significant contributions, the outstanding volume on Matthew by John A. Broadus, from whom the publisher of the new series. Broadman Press, partly derives its name. The former series was authored and edited by scholars committed to the infallibility of Scripture, making it a solid foundation for the present project. In line with this heritage, all NAC authors affirm the divine inspiration, inerrancy, complete truthfulness, and full authority of the Bible. The perspective of the NAC is unapologetically confessional and rooted in the evangelical tradition.

Since a commentary is a fundamental tool for the expositor or teacher who seeks to interpret and apply Scripture in the church or classroom, the NAC focuses on communicating the theological structure and content of each biblical book. The writers seek to illuminate both the historical meaning and contemporary significance of Holy Scripture.

In its attempt to make a unique contribution to the Christian community, the NAC focuses on two concerns. First, the commentary emphasizes how each section of a book fits together so that the reader becomes aware of the theological unity of each book and of Scripture as a whole. The writers, however, remain aware of the Bible's inherently rich variety. Second, the NAC is produced with the conviction that the Bible primarily belongs to the church. We believe that scholarship and the academy provide an indispensable foundation for biblical understanding and the service of Christ, but the editors and authors of this series have attempted to communicate the findings of their research in a manner that will build up the whole body of Christ. Thus, the commentary concentrates on theological exegesis while providing practical, applicable exposition.

THE NEW AMERICAN COMMENTARY's theological focus enables

the reader to see the parts as well as the whole of Scripture. The biblical books vary in content, context, literary type, and style. In addition to this rich variety, the editors and authors recognize that the doctrinal emphasis and use of the biblical books differs in various places, contexts, and cultures among God's people. These factors, as well as other concerns, have led the editors to give freedom to the writers to wrestle with the issues raised by the scholarly community surrounding each book and to determine the appropriate shape and length of the introductory materials. Moreover, each writer has developed the structure of the commentary in a way best suited for expounding the basic structure and the meaning of the biblical books for our day. Generally, discussions relating to contemporary scholarship and technical points of grammar and syntax appear in the footnotes and not in the text of the commentary. This format allows pastors and interested laypersons, scholars and teachers, and serious college and seminary students to profit from the commentary at various levels. This approach has been employed because we believe that all Christians have the privilege and responsibility to read and seek to understand the Bible for themselves.

Consistent with the desire to produce a readable, up-to-date commentary, the editors selected the *New International Version* as the standard translation for the commentary series. The selection was made primarily because of the NIV's faithfulness to the original languages and its beautiful and readable style. The authors, however, have been given the liberty to differ at places from the NIV as they develop their own translations from the Greek and Hebrew texts.

The NAC reflects the vision and leadership of those who provide oversight for Broadman Press, who in 1987 called for a new commentary series that would evidence a commitment to the inerrancy of Scripture and a faithfulness to the classic Christian tradition. While the commentary adopts an "American" name, it should be noted some writers represent countries outside the United States, giving the commentary an international perspective. The diverse group of writers includes scholars, teachers, and administrators from almost twenty different colleges and seminaries, as well as pastors, missionaries, and a layperson.

The editors and writers hope that THE NEW AMERICAN COMMENTARY will be helpful and instructive for pastors and teachers, scholars and students, for men and women in the churches who study and teach God's Word in various settings. We trust that for editors, authors, and readers alike, the commentary will be used to build up the church, encourage obedience, and bring renewal to God's people. Above all, we pray that the NAC will bring glory and honor to our Lord who has graciously redeemed us and faithfully revealed himself to us in his Holy Word.

SOLI DEO GLORIA
The Editors

Author's Preface

Concerning the epistle of 1 John, Luther wrote: "Here the apostle … urges us to guard the Word and to love one another. Thus we shall never learn so much and be so perfect that need for the Word of God will not remain. For the devil never rests" (*LW*, 30:219).

In being granted the honor of writing this commentary in the NAC series, I have come to appreciate more than ever the wisdom of Luther's words. We must be tenacious in holding on to the Word of God, especially what it teaches about Christ, for all of our theology will emanate from what we think and believe about the Savior. We must also be faithful to love one another, especially those who are our brothers and sisters in Christ, and especially when we might not see eye to eye on particular issues of family life. To know the Savior and love the saints captures well the emphasis of the letters of John.

I wish to express special appreciation to several students, past and present, who made significant contributions to this commentary. I am grateful for the assistance of Pastor Tom Duke and his fine work on "propitiation." I want to thank Devin Hudson, Donnie Mathis, Ben Merkle, Randy Stinson, and Randall Tan, all outstanding students in the Ph.D. program at the Southern Baptist Theological Seminary in Louisville, Kentucky, for their excellent insights on matters of Greek exegesis. Their contribution was significant. Their gifts and skills far exceed my own, and I am singularly proud of each one.

No one has impacted my life as a minister more than my father in the ministry, Dr. Paige Patterson. I will always be thankful God allowed me the privilege of studying under and working alongside of him for many years. Dr. R. Albert Mohler, Jr. has been a friend, encourager, and model of scholarly excellence whom God has used to inspire me in the vein of 1 Pet 3:15. Dr. James Merritt is as dear a friend as anyone could ever hope to have, and not a day passes that I do not draw strength from our friendship.

Finally, I want to say thank you to my wife and hero, Charlotte, and my four sons: Nathan, Jonathan, Paul, and Timothy. No husband could want for a better wife, nor any Dad for better sons. Your love and support through the years has meant more to me than you will ever know. Any good God has accomplished in my life has, from the human side, been greatly shaped by you. I love you and pray I will never disappoint you.

In writing this commentary I can truly say I have come to love and adore even more our Lord Jesus. He is our advocate and atonement. What a Savior! It is my hope that above all he is pleased with this work and that it will be used by God to rightly exalt the one who showed us supremely the love of the Father for sinful humanity.

—Danny Aiken
Louisville, Kentucky

Abbreviations

Bible Books

Gen	Isa	Luke
Exod	Jer	John
Lev	Lam	Acts
Num	Ezek	Rom
Deut	Dan	1, 2 Cor
Josh	Hos	Gal
Judg	Joel	Eph
Ruth	Amos	Phil
1, 2 Sam	Obad	Col
1, 2 Kgs	Jonah	1, 2 Thess
1, 2 Chr	Mic	1, 2 Tim
Ezra	Nah	Titus
Neh	Hab	Phlm
Esth	Zeph	Heb
Job	Hag	Jas
Ps (pl. Pss)	Zech	1, 2 Pet
Prov	Mal	1, 2, 3 John
Eccl	Matt	Jude
Song	Mark	Rev

Apocrypha

Add Esth	*The Additions to the Book of Esther*
Bar	*Baruch*
Bel	*Bel and the Dragon*
1,2 Esdr	*1, 2 Esdras*
4 Ezra	*4 Ezra*
Jdt	*Judith*
Ep Jer	*Epistle of Jeremiah*
1,2,3,4 Mac	*1, 2, 3, 4 Maccabees*
Pr Azar	*Prayer of Azariah and the Song of the Three Jews*
Pr Man	*Prayer of Manasseh*
Sir	*Sirach, Ecclesiasticus*
Sus	*Susanna*
Tob	*Tobit*
Wis	*The Wisdom of Solomon*

Commonly Used Sources for New Testament Volumes

AB	Anchor Bible
ACNT	Augsburg Commentary on the New Testament
AGJU	Arbeiten zur Geschichte des antiken Judentums und des Urchristentums
AJBI	Annual of the Japanese Biblical Institute
AJT	*American Journal of Theology*
AJTh	*Asia Journal of Theology*
ANF	Ante-Nicene Fathers
ANQ	*Andover Newton Quarterly*
ATANT	Abhandlungen zur Theologie des Alten and Neuen Testaments
ATR	*Anglican Theological Review*
ATRSup	*Anglican Theological Review Supplemental Series*
AusBR	*Australian Biblical Review*
AUSS	*Andrews University Seminary Studies*
BAGD	W. Bauer, W. F. Arndt, F. W. Gingrich, and F. Danker, *Greek-English Lexicon of the New Testament*
BARev	*Biblical Archaeology Review*
BBR	*Bulletin for Biblical Research*
BDF	F. Blass, A. Debrunner, R. W. Funk, *A Greek Grammar of the New Testament*
BETL	Bibliotheca ephemeridum theologicarum lovaniensium
BETS	*Bulletin of the Evangelical Theological Society*
Bib	*Biblica*
BJRL	*Bulletin of the John Rylands Library*
BK	*Bibel und Kirche*
BLit	*Bibel und Liturgie*
BR	*Biblical Research*
BSac	*Bibliotheca Sacra*
BT	*The Bible Translator*
BTB	*Biblical Theology Bulletin*
BVC	*Bible et vie chrétienne*
BZ	*Biblische Zeitschrift*
BZNW	Beihefte zur ZAW
CBC	Cambridge Bible Commentary
CBQ	*Catholic Biblical Quarterly*
CCWJCW	Cambridge Commentaries on Writings of the Jewish and Christian World
CNTC	Calvin's New Testament Commentaries

CO	W. Baur, E. Cuntiz, and E. Reuss, *Ioannis Calvini opera quae supereunt omnia,* ed.
Conybeare	W. J. Conybeare and J. S. Howson, *The Life and Epistles of St. Paul*
CJT	*Canadian Journal of Theology*
CSR	*Christian Scholars' Review*
CTM	*Concordia Theologial Monthly*
CTQ	*Concordia Theological Quarterly*
CTR	*Criswell Theological Review*
Did.	*Didache*
DJD	Discoveries in the Judaean Desert
DNTT	*Dictionary of New Testament Theology*
DownRev	*Downside Review*
DSB	Daily Study Bible
EBC	Expositor's Bible Commentary
EDNT	*Exegetical Dictionary of the New Testament*
EGT	*The Expositor's Greek Testament*
EGNT	*Exegetical Greek New Testament*
EKKNT	Evangelisch-katholischer Kommentar zum Neuen Testament
ETC	English Translation and Commentary
ETL	*Ephemerides theologicae lovanienses*
ETR	*Etudes théologiques et religieuses*
ETS	Evangelical Theological Society
EvT	*Evangelische Theologie*
EvQ	*Evangelical Quarterly*
Exp	*Expositor*
ExpTim	*Expository Times*
FNT	*Filologia Neotestamentaria*
FRLANT	Forschungen zur Religion und Literatur des Alten und Neuen Testaments
GAGNT	M. Zerwick and M. Grosvenor, *A Grammatical Analysis of the Greek New Testament*
GNBC	Good News Bible Commentary
GSC	Griechischen christlichen Schriftsteller
GTJ	*Grace Theological Journal*
HBD	*Holman Bible Dictionary*
HDB	J. Hastings, *Dictionary of the Bible*
Her	Hermeneia
HNT	Handbuch zum Neuen Testament
HNTC	Harper's New Testament Commentaries

HeyJ	*Heythrop Journal*
HTKNT	Herders theologischer Kommentar zum Neuen Testament
HTR	*Harvard Theological Review*
HUCA	*Hebrew Union College Annual*
IB	*The Interpreter's Bible*
IBS	*Irish Biblical Studies*
ICC	International Critical Commentary
IDB	*Interpreter's Dictionary of the Bible*
IDBSup	Supplementary Volume to *IDB*
Int	*Interpretation*
INT	Interpretation: A Bible Commentary for Preaching and Teaching
ISBE	*International Standard Bible Encyclopedia*
JAAR	*Journal of the American Academy of Religion*
JANES	*Journal of Ancient Near Eastern Studies*
JAOS	*Journal of the American Oriental Society*
JBL	*Journal of Biblical Literature*
JES	*Journal of Ecumenical Studies*
JETS	*Journal of the Evangelical Theological Society*
JJS	*Journal of Jewish Studies*
JR	*Journal of Religion*
JRE	*Journal of Religious Ethics*
JRH	*Journal of Religious History*
JRS	*Journal of Roman Studies*
JSNT	*Journal for the Study of the New Testament*
JSOT	*Journal for the Study of the Old Testament*
JSS	*Journal of Semitic Studies*
JTS	*Journal of Theological Studies*
JTT	*Journal of Translation and Textlinguistics*
LB	*Linguistica Biblica*
LEC	Library of Early Christianity
LouvSt	*Louvain Studies*
LS	Liddel and Scott, *Greek-English Lexicon*
LTJ	*Lutheran Theological Journal*
LTP	*Laval théologique et philosophique*
LTQ	*Lexington Theological Quarterly*
LW	Luther's Works
LXX	Septuagint
MCNT	Meyer's Commentary on the New Testament
MDB	*Mercer Dictionary of the Bible*

MM	J. H. Moulton and G. Milligan, *The Vocabulary of the Greek Testament*
MNTC	Moffatt New Testament Commentary
MQR	*Mennonite Quarterly Review*
MT	Masoretic Text
NAB	New American Bible
NAC	New American Commentary
NASB	New American Standard Bible
NBD	*New Bible Dictionary*
NCB	New Century Bible
NCBC	New Century Bible Commentary
NEB	New English Bible
Neot	*Neotestamentica*
NICNT	New International Commentary on the New Testament
NIDNTT	*New International Dictionary of New Testament Theology*
NIGTC	New International Greek Testament Commentary
NIV	New International Version
NorTT	*Norsk Teologisk Tidsskrift*
NovT	*Novum Testamentum*
NovTSup	Novum Testamentum, Supplements
NPNF	Nicene and Post-Nicene Fathers
NRSV	New Revised Standard Version
NRT	*La nouvelle revue théologique*
NTD	Das Neue Testament Deutsch
NTI	D. Guthrie, *New Testament Introduction*
NTM	*The New Testament Message*
NTS	*New Testament Studies*
PC	Proclamation Commentaries
PEQ	*Palestine Exploration Quarterly*
PRS	*Perspectives in Religious Studies*
PSB	*Princeton Seminary Bulletin*
RB	*Revue biblique*
RelSRev	*Religious Studies Review*
ResQ	*Restoration Quarterly*
RevExp	*Review and Expositor*
RevQ	*Revue de Qumran*
RevThom	*Revue thomiste*
RHPR	*Revue d'histoire et de philosophie religieuses*
RSPT	*Revue des sciences philosophiques et théologiques*
RSR	*Recherches de science religieuse*

RSV	Revised Standard Version
RTP	*Revue de théologie et de philosophie*
RTR	*Reformed Theological Review*
SAB	*Sitzungsbericht der Preussischen Akademie der Wissenschaft zu Berlin*
SBJT	*Southern Baptist Journal of Theology*
SBLDS	SBL Dissertation Series
SBLMS	SBL Monograph Series
SBLSP	SBL Seminar Papers
SE	*Studia Evangelica*
SEAÛ	*Svensk exegetisk aΩrsbok*
SEAJT	*Southeast Asia Journal of Theology*
Sem	*Semitica*
SJT	*Scottish Journal of Theology*
SNTSMS	Society for New Testament Studies Monograph Series
SNTU	*Studien zum Neuen Testament und seiner Umwelt*
SPCK	Society for the Promotion of Christian Knowledge
ST	*Studia theologica*
Str-B	H. Strack and P. Billerbeck, *Kommentar zum Neuen Testament*
StudBib	Studia Biblica
SWJT	*Southwestern Journal of Theology*
TB	*Tyndale Bulletin*
TBC	Torch Bible Commentaries
TBT	*The Bible Today*
TCGNT	B. M. Metzger, *A Textual Commentary on the Greek New Testament*
TDNT	G. Kittel and G. Friedrich, eds., *Theological Dictionary of the New Testament*
TEV	Today's English Version
Theol	*Theology*
ThT	*Theology Today*
TLZ	*Theologische Literaturzeitung*
TNTC	Tyndale New Testament Commentaries
TRE	*Theologische Realenzyklopädie*
TrinJ	*Trinity Journal*
TRu	*Theologische Rundschau*
TS	*Theological Studies*
TSK	*Theologische Studien und Kritiken*
TTZ	*Trierer theologische Zeitschrift*
TU	Texte und Untersuchungen

Contents

1 John

──────── **INTRODUCTION** ────────

The epistles of John are something of an enigma when considered together. Few books of the New Testament are more loved, memorized, or quoted than 1 John. On the other hand one is hard pressed to find any books of Scripture more ignored and taught less than 2 and 3 John (the OT book of Obadiah and the NT book of Philemon might give them a challenge). Their brevity makes them easy to overlook, and it is not unusual to hear that nothing is lost if they are skipped over, since, after all, anything in them is

21

addressed in 1 John. This judgment, however, is too hasty. While the first epistle of John rightly occupies the primary position among the three, 2 and 3 John make their own unique and important contributions as well. To neglect them is to miss the more complete picture the Holy Spirit wished to paint when he moved the apostle to pen all three. M. Luther said of 1 John, "This is an outstanding epistle. ... It has John's style and manner of expression, so beautifully and gently does it picture Christ to us."[1] Many first year Greek students have cut their teeth on 1 John because of the simplicity of the grammar and vocabulary. In this context D. E. Hiebert notes:

> The forceful simplicity of its sentences, the note of finality behind its utterances, the marvelous blending of gentle love and deep-cutting sternness of its contents, and the majesty of its ungarnished thoughts have made 1 John a favorite with Christians everywhere. The plainness of language makes it intelligible to the simplest saint, while the profundity of its truths challenges the most accomplished scholar. Its grand theological revelations and its unwavering ethical demands have left their enduring impact upon the thought and life of the Christian Church. First John is indeed a singular, irreplaceable gem among the books of the New Testament.[2]

Concerning 2 and 3 John I would add: here we discover nuggets of gold that, when carefully mined, yield a small but valuable treasure that will better adorn the Lord's church with truth. If for no other reason than teaching the right (3 John) and wrong (2 John) use of Christian hospitality, these twin epistles have earned their right as part of the canonical Scriptures.

1. Authorship

Tradition has ascribed authorship of these three letters to the apostle John, son of Zebedee and the brother of James (cf. Mark 1:19–20). He is credited by many to have penned five books of the New Testament (also the Gospel of John and Revelation), though some doubts were raised in the early church concerning John's authorship of 2 and 3 John and Revelation. Strong similarities between 1 John and the Gospel of John argue for common authorship of these books. This same conclusion is reached when a comparison is made between 1 John and the latter two letters. It is instructive to note that no person other than John the apostle was ever suggested by the early church as the author of the first epistle. The same is not true of 2 and 3 John, though he was still the overwhelming choice, as will be explained below.

The authorship of the epistles of John is technically anonymous. The

---

[1] M. Luther, *Lectures on the First Epistle of St. John, LW* (St. Louis: Concordia, 1967), 30:219.
[2] D. E. Hiebert, *The Epistles of John* (Greenville: Bob Jones University Press, 1991), 1.

author of 2 and 3 John does identify himself as the elder (*hoᶜ presbúteros;* 2 John 1; 3 John 1), but he provides no personal name. First John contains no specific personal designation of any sort.

It is appropriate to examine both internal and external evidence. Our internal examination will give attention to the relationship of these letters, especially 1 John, to the Fourth Gospel. We then need to consider the relationship of 1 John to 2 and 3 John. External evidence will include the witness of the early church and also address the question of canonicity.

(1) Internal Evidence

The author of 1 John claims to be an eyewitness of Christ (1 John 1:1–3). In the prologue he emphasizes his sensory perception of Jesus, "the Word of life." This claim to eyewitness testimony has come under attack from modern scholars, with a number of them opting for a leader (or leaders) of a "Johannine Community," a second-generation Christian, as the author.[3] Such skepticism is unwarranted. The language in the prologue is direct and even striking in its avowal of eyewitness experience. C. Kruse points out that the author "writes as an individual, something which his repeated self-references in the first person singular indicate (2:1,7,8,12,13, 14,21,26; 5:13)."[4] Further, the author writes with an authoritative tone that is virtually apostolic. J. R. W. Stott notes this authority "is particularly evident in the 'I-you' passages and appears the more striking when viewed in contrast to the humble way in which he [the author] associates himself with his readers in some 'we' passages. There is nothing tentative or apologetic about what he writes. ... Dogmatic authority of the writer is seen particularly in his statements and commands."[5] It should be noted here that the title "elder" in 2 and 3 John would convey this same balance of authority

---

[3] See R. Bultmann, *The Johannine Epistles,* Her (Philadelphia: Fortress, 1973), 10; G. Strecker, *The Johannine Letters,* Her (Philadelphia: Fortress, 1996), xxxv–xlii; R. Brown, *The Community of the Beloved Disciple* (New York: Paulist, 1979); *The Epistles of John,* AB (New York: Doubleday, 1982), 95–96, 160, 163; R. Schnackenburg, *The Johannine Epistles* (New York: Crossroad, 1992), 41; R. A. Culpepper, *The Gospel and Letters of John* (Nashville: Abingdon, 1998), 42–61; *The Johannine School,* SBLDS 26 (Missoula, Mont.: Scholars Press, 1975). Brown and Culpepper, in particular, note the pioneering work of J. L. Martyn with regard to the "community hypothesis." Culpepper calls it "a trend-setting work" (*Gospel and Letters of John,* 43). See J. L. Martyn, *History and Theology in the Fourth Gospel* (1968; reprint, Nashville: Abingdon, 1979).

[4] C. Kruse, *The Letters of John,* The Pillar New Testament Commentary (Grand Rapids: Eerdmans, 2000), 9. R. Brown attempts to turn this evidence, saying, "The first person singular is relatively rare. ... A first person plural appears in 51 of 105 verses" (*Epistles of John,* 158). Kruse accurately weighs the evidence and notes, "While the author writes this letter as an individual, nevertheless, when he testifies to the eternal life proclaimed by and embodied in the incarnate Christ, he always associates himself with other firsthand witnesses" (p. 61).

[5] J. R. W. Stott, *The Letters of John,* rev. ed., TNTC (Grand Rapids: Eerdmans, 1988), 37–38.

and humility on the part of the author.

There is no compelling reason to deny that the author of 1 John was an eyewitness of the earthly Jesus. He was an individual who writes both with authority and humility to a people for whom he cares deeply and has a tender relationship.[6]

A comparison of 1 John and the Fourth Gospel reveals numerous similarities in theology, vocabulary, and syntax.[7] Note the revealing contrast or polarities in each: life and death, truth and falsehood, light and darkness, children of God and children of the devil, love and hate.

A. E. Brooke identifies no fewer than fifty-one parallel references in 1 John and the Gospel of John.[8] Similarities in soteriology also run throughout the books:

> In our unredeemed state we are "of the devil," who has sinned and lied and murdered "from the beginning" (1 John 3:8 / John 8:44); we are "from the world" (2:16; 4:5 / 8:23; 15:19). We therefore "sin" (3:4 / 8:34) and "have" sin (1:8 / 9:41), "walk in the darkness" (1:6; 2:11 / 8:12; 12:35) and are "dead" (3:14 / 5:25). God loved and sent His Son to be "the Savior of the World" (4:14 / 4:42) so that "we might live" (4:9 / 3:16). Believing in him or in his "name" (5:13 / 1:12), we pass from death to life (3:14 / 5:24). We "have life" (5:11,12 / 3:15,36; 20:31), for life is in the Son of God (5:11–12 / 1:4; 14:6). This is what it means to be "born of God" (2:29; 3:9; 5:4,18 / 1:13).[9]

The term *paraklētos* occurs only five times in Scripture, and all occurrences are in the Johannine corpus (John 14:16,26; 15:26; 16:7; 1 John 2:1). The word *monogenēs* as an expression of the Son's unique relationship to the Father occurs in John 1:14,18; 3:16,18, and 1 John 4:9. Hiebert correctly surmises: "This similarity between the two writings is all the more remarkable when it is remembered that the nature of the gospel is objective narrative, whereas the epistle is hortatory and polemical. The acceptance of a common authorship for these two writings greatly strengthens the evi-

---

[6] D. A. Carson, D. J. Moo, and L. Morris also recognize the authority of the author conveyed in all three letters and see this as evidence for apostolic authorship: "The most obvious explanation for this cross-congregational authority is that the author of these epistles was an apostle, since elders per se did not, so far as we know, enjoy such authority" (*An Introduction to the New Testament* [Grand Rapids: Zondervan, 1992], 450).

[7] Stott notes, "Even a superficial reading of the Gospel and the first letter reveals a striking similarity between the two both in subject matter and syntax. The general subjects treated are much the same" (*Letters of John*, 21).

[8] A. E. Brooke, *A Critical and Exegetical Commentary on the Johannine Epistles*, ICC (New York: Scribner's, 1912), ii–iv. See also R. Law, *The Tests of Life* (1914; reprint, Grand Rapids: Baker, 1979), 341–63 for an analysis of similarities and differences between 1 John and the Gospel of John.

[9] Carson, Moo, and Morris, *Introduction*, 447; also Stott, *Letters of John*, 21–23.

dence for the Johannine authorship of 1 John because tradition emphatically ascribes the Fourth Gospel to the Apostle John."[10]

Most scholars correctly affirm common authorship of the epistles of John.[11] Common milieu and vocabulary/parallel phrases is difficult if not impossible to overthrow; "(e.g., 'Jesus Christ has come in the flesh' [2 John 7 / 1 John 4:2]; 'deceiver' and 'antichrist' [2 John 7 / 2:23]; those who love and do good show that they are 'from God' [3 John 11 / 3:10; 4:4; 7]."[12] Stott adds in this context, "It is not necessary to marshal lengthy arguments for the common authorship of 2 and 3 John; it is almost self-evident."[13] He then surveys evidence similar to that noted above and states: "We conclude that both shorter letters were written by the same person, and that this person was also the author of the first letter, who, we have already argued, had previously composed the Fourth Gospel. ... It is impossible to study the Johannine problem if any one of these four writings is isolated."[14]

(2) External Evidence

The early church was consistent in ascribing the authorship of the Fourth Gospel and 1 John to the apostle John. This is an uncontested fact of history.[15] Possible allusions appear in (1) the *Didache* (ca. A.D. 90–120; 10:5–6 / 1 John 2:17); (2) Clement of Rome (ca. A.D. 96; *1 Clem.* 49:5; 50:3 / 1 John 2:5; 4:12,17,18); (3) the *Epistle of Barnabas* (ca. A.D. 130; 5:9–11; 12:10 / 1 John 4:2; 2 John 7); and (4) Polycarp (ca. A.D. 135; Phil 7:1 / 1 John 2:22; 4:2–3; 2 John 7).[16]

Papias, who knew John (and was born ca. A.D. 60), is the first person to make a specific reference to a Johannine letter as the work of the apostle

---

[10] Hiebert, *The Epistles of John,* 7. He goes on to survey objections to common authorship of 1 John and the Gospel of John (7–11) but finds these objections wanting. Where subtle and perhaps significant differences do appear, they do not outweigh the substantial evidence for common authorship. Carson, Moo, and Morris (*Introduction,* 448) rightly note in comparing the two books, "We should speak of complementarity of vision and thought, of differentiation in application, not of mutual contradiction." The variations in phrase we do discover actually argue for and suggest "common authorship rather than servile, or even intelligent, copying" (p. 449, quoting Brooke, *Johannine Epistles,* xvi). This is, in our judgment, a fair assessment of the evidence.

[11] I. H. Marshall, *The Epistles of John,* NICNT (Grand Rapids: Eerdmans, 1978), 31; G. Barker, *1 John,* EBC (Grand Rapids: Zondervan, 1981), 12:302.

[12] Carson, Moo, and Morris, *Introduction,* 449.

[13] Stott, *Letters of John,* 28.

[14] Ibid., 29.

[15] C. H. Talbert acknowledges that "the early Fathers regarded the author of 1 John and the Fourth Gospel as the same person, John, the Lord's disciple (Irenaeus, *Against Heresies* 3.11.7), the son of Zebedee (*Muratorian Fragment;* Jerome, *Illustrious Men* 9), the beloved disciple (Origen, so Eusebius 3.25.3)" (*Reading John* [New York: Crossroad, 1994], 5). Kruse produces, at length, the relevant historical texts that speak to this issue (*The Letters of John,* 11–14).

[16] Brooke, lii ff.; Carson, Moo, and Morris, *Introduction,* 446.

John in his *Exposition of Oracles of the Lord* (written ca. A.D. 130 and cited in Eusebius [*H.E.* 3.39.17]). Irenaeus (ca. A.D. 180) specifically makes reference to 1 and 2 John (*H.E.* 3.16.5; 3.16.8), and he clearly attributes both, as well as the Fourth Gospel, to the apostle John. In the same time period Clement of Alexandria writes of "the greater epistle" of John the apostle (see *Strom.* 2.15.66), an indication that (1) he believed John to be the apostle of 1 John and (2) he knew of at least one other letter of John. The evidence multiplies after this. Kruse concludes, "What is clear from these citations is that the early Christian tradition is unanimous in ascribing 1 John to John, the disciple and apostle of the Lord."[17]

External evidence for 2 and 3 John is not as early or strong as 1 John. This is probably because of their brevity and resulting limited circulation. Furthermore, a statement by Papias seems to imply the possibility of two Johns, the apostle John and the elder John (*H.E.* 3.39). Jerome reports that some believe the apostle penned 1 John whereas the elder penned 2 John and 3 John. Eusebius would use the statement by Papias to argue that the "elder John" wrote Revelation (which he disliked). However, the statement by Papias need not be interpreted as implying two Johns, and it seems that the better understanding is that they were one and the same person. The apostle John is the elder John. Both were appropriate designations for the last surviving member of Jesus Christ's disciples.[18]

Origen (ca. A.D. 250) is the first to mention all three letters, but Eusebius (*H.E.* 6.25.10) says "he does so in part to acknowledge that not everyone accepted the authenticity of 2 and 3 John."[19] Aside from the "elder John hypothesis," however, no one ever attributed 2 John and 3 John to anyone other than the apostle John. And, in spite of the questions occasionally raised in the early church, the obvious similarities in vocabulary, theme, and language have led most modern scholars to argue for common authorship of the epistles, even if they reject the apostle John as that common author.[20]

(3) Conclusion

Evidence both internal and external favors the view that the apostle John is the author of the three letters Christian tradition has attributed to him. The writing style is so close to that of the Fourth Gospel that common

---

[17] Kruse, *The Letters of John*, 14.

[18] Hiebert (*The Epistles of John*, 14–15) provides a helpful analysis of "the elder John" question.

[19] Carson, Moo, and Morris, *Introduction*, 447.

[20] Kruse, *The Letters of John*, 36. R. Brown provides extensive chart documentation showing the significant similarities between 2, 3 John and the other Johannine writings and between 1 John and the Gospel of John (*Epistles of John*, 755–59).

authorship clearly is the best position to affirm.[21] The verdict of the early church was unanimous in its affirmation of John the apostle as author of the Fourth Gospel. The epistles of 2 and 3 John are obviously from the same pen as the author of 1 John. The author of that book claims to be an eyewitness (1 John 1:1–3). He writes with apostolic authority. Internal evidence suggests the author is now an aged man (cf. 1 John 2:1,28; 3:7; 2 John 1; 3 John 1), which is in harmony with the early church tradition that John was advanced in years when he wrote. This evidence is more than sufficient to withstand those who would seek authorship of these letters or elsewhere.[22]

2. Date and Place of Writing

Any determination for the date of these three letters is problematic. Usually, the relationship of 1 John and the Fourth Gospel is raised (which came first?), but again the evidence for making a judgment is at best inferential. Still, a reasonable reconstruction is at least plausible given certain textual clues, historical developments, and early church tradition.

Tradition is strong that John spent his latter years in the city of Ephesus ministering to the churches of Asia Minor. Irenaeus wrote, "John, the disciple of the Lord, who also leaned upon His breast, did himself publish a Gospel during his residence at Ephesus in Asia" (*Against Heresies, 3.1.1*). Therefore, it would seem reasonable to see the place of writing for the three epistles also as Ephesus.[23] We have already offered internal evidence that would indicate that John was an aged man when he wrote the epistles. It is also the case that church tradition says John was at Ephesus "remaining among them permanently until the time of Trajan" (*Against Heresies, 3.3.4*). Trajan reigned as Roman emperor A.D. 98–117. This fact would indicate John died toward the end of the first century, which sets a terminus for his writings. A date of somewhere between A.D. 85 and 100 is reason-

---

[21] B. F. Westcott states: "The writing [of 1 John] is so closely connected with the Fourth Gospel in vocabulary, style, thought, scope, that these two books cannot but be regarded as works of the same author" (*The Epistles of John* [New York: Macmillan, 1905], xxx).

[22] Counting votes is never a wise method of determining the correctness of a scholarly position. Still, it helps one to survey the field and note where particular individuals choose to stand. Those who affirm John the apostle as the author of the epistles include Alford, Barker, Bruce, Burdick, Hiebert, Lenski, Jackman, Kruse, Marshall, Kistemaker, Stott, and Westcott. Those who reject the apostle John as author, usually opting for a disciple or disciples of John within a Johannine community, include Brooke, Brown, Bultmann, Culpepper, Dodd, Grayston, Johnson, Strecker, and Smalley. D. M. Smith evaluates all the data and concludes, "The authorship of the Johannine Gospel and letters remains an enigma shrouded in mystery" (*First, Second, and Third John*, IBC [Louisville: John Knox, 1991], 18). The classic defender of the Johannine Community hypothesis is R. Brown [in addition to his commentary, see *Community of the Beloved Disciple*]. His thesis has exercised significant influence on Johannine studies at the end of the twentieth century. One must not forget, however, the speculative and inferential nature of his hypothesis.

[23] Hiebert, *The Epistles of John*, 18.

able. To be more precise than this is not possible, though numerous scholars tend to push the date of writing for the three letters into the nineties. Marshall points out that whatever date one affirms "must allow adequate time for the growth of the false teaching reflected in 1 John."[24] This is perhaps why many scholars believe a date in the late first century is the wisest judgment concerning the date of writing.

The priority of the Gospel of John or 1 John has been argued both ways.[25] Historical reconstructions such as those proposed by Burge and Kruse accept a modified form of the Gospel priority position.[26] Eighty percent of the verses in 1 John reflect ideas and themes found in the Gospel. Burdick argues: "This finding confirms the assertion that the readers were previously familiar, at the least, with Johannine teaching, but it also strengthens the probability that they possessed that teaching in the written form of the Fourth Gospel."[27] Burdick's position is plausible, and given the possibility that the epistles, especially 1 and 2 John, address Christological errors that resulted from a misinterpretation of the Gospel of John, the priority of the Gospel is tentatively affirmed.

What of the relationship of the three letters themselves? Again we have no way to be certain, and internal clues and church tradition provide virtually no help at all. Brown provides the most detailed study and rightly concludes that the most we can say is, "It is perfectly possible, then, that the three Johannine Epistles were composed about the same time."[28] The overwhelming similarities between the three letters certainly make this conclusion likely.

3. The Occasion of 1 John

What moved John to write his first epistle?[29] An internal investigation of the letter provides the following clues.

---

[24] Marshall, *The Epistles of John,* 47; see also D. Burdick, who provides an excellent treatment in a concise manner of "the testimony of tradition" for the time and place of writing for 1 John (*The Letters of John the Apostle* [Chicago: Moody, 1985], 40–42). He also dates 2 John (417) and 3 John (418) during the same period.

[25] Brooke has argued forcefully for the priority of 1 John (*Johannine Epistles,* xix–xxii). He is joined by K. Grayston, *The Johannine Epistles,* NCBC (Grand Rapids: Eerdmans, 1984), 12–14. Talbert notes, however, "The dominant construct in current research regards the Fourth Gospel as written before the epistles" (*Reading John,* 3). Talbert himself goes on to argue (p. 4), "The Gospel of John was written either after 1, 2, 3 John or at about the same time as they and is dealing with some of the same problems."

[26] G. M. Burge, *The Letters of John,* The NIV Application Commentary (Grand Rapids: Zondervan, 1996), 39; Kruse, *The Letters of John,* 2–3. S. S. Smalley also argues for the priority of the Gospel (*1, 2, 3 John,* WBC [Waco: Word, 1984], xxii).

[27] Burdick, *Letters of John the Apostle,* 40.

[28] R. Brown, *Epistles of John,* 30–32.

[29] The occasion of 2 and 3 John will be addressed in the commentary section of both books because of their particular focus, peculiarities, and brevity.

First John was written to a church or group of churches in crisis—churches who were being attacked by false teaching (cf. 2:18–28; 4:1–6; 5:6–7). Some individuals who had once been associated with the Christian community had adopted heretical doctrine, particularly as it related to Christology, and had left the church (2:19). Evidently, after their departure they continued to spread their teachings to those who remained within the Johannine churches. They went so far as to organize and send out itinerant teachers/missionaries who moved among the churches with the goal of converting those in the churches to their beliefs (cf. 2:26; 4:1–3; 2 John 7). Undoubtedly, this theological assault created confusion and crisis within the believing community. In response to this situation, the author penned 1 John, which has two primary objectives:

1. *To combat the propaganda of the false teachers.*—As the author addresses the beliefs of these heretics, he argues that these individuals are not genuine believers; they lack the marks of authentic Christianity in at least three areas.

    (1) *Doctrinally,* they have compromised the person and work of Jesus Christ. John criticized in the strongest terms those who did not confess Jesus of Nazareth as the Christ (2:22) and denied that Jesus had come in the flesh (4:2–3). Most likely (as we will argue more fully in the commentary), these false teachers were influenced by early Gnostic ideas. Gnosticism was a heretical movement that became prominent in the second century A.D. Although Gnosticism took many forms, it usually emphasized the essential goodness of spirit and the inherent evil or inferiority of all matter. Influenced by this type of understanding, these false teachers may have viewed Christ as some type of spirit, perhaps a spirit who had come upon the man Jesus during part of his ministry (from his baptism until his crucifixion; cf. 5:6–8). They refused, however, to directly associate "the Christ" with the human Jesus; this refusal led to a rejection of Jesus of Nazareth as the Christ, the unique God-man. Combined with this faulty view of the person of Christ was a deficient view of his death. First John contains specific statements that emphasize the atoning results of Christ's death (2:2; 4:10). Thus, as John highlights the importance of the incarnation, he also stresses the distinctive nature of Christ's work of atonement.

    (2) *Morally,* the false teachers minimized the seriousness of sin (1:6–10). They claimed that it was possible to have fellowship with God regardless of one's behavior (1:6). In contrast, John insists that one's relationship to God has serious ethical implications (cf. 2:3–4). A genuine knowledge of and love for God demands obedience (2:3–6; 5:3).

(3) *Socially,* these heretics failed because their spiritual pride resulted in a lack of brotherly love (2:9,11). John argues that love for other believers is a manifestation of genuine Christianity (3:14; 4:7–21).

2. *To reassure believers.*—First John was also written to fortify the assurance of salvation believers are rightly to possess. It provides not so much "test of life" (so R. Law) as "test for assurance." With the onslaught of these false teachings, doubt and confusion developed among believers. What (who) were they to believe—"the traditional teachings of the apostle" or the doctrines of these false leaders? To clear up this uncertainty, John reminds his churches of the truthfulness of Christianity which they had received in the beginning. He wants them to understand the reality of their faith so that they might know that they have eternal life (5:13). John provides his readers with tests or criteria by which they can evaluate the claims of those who have left the fellowship and "with which they could reassure themselves that they were in the truth (1 John 1:5–2:2; 2:3–11; 3:7–10,14–15; 4:4–6,7–8,13–15; 5:13,18–20)."[30]

John depicts Christian assurance from both an objective and a subjective perspective. Objectively, believers know the historicity and reality of Jesus Christ's life and work. The events of his life were observed by eyewitnesses and passed on to them (1:1–3). Similarly, those who have trusted God's Son possess eternal life (5:12). Subjectively, Christians know that their lives have been transformed through faith in Christ. John summarizes the characteristics of true Christianity as right belief, righteousness, and love; he wants these believers to observe the manifestations of their faith, which are evident in their lives and evidence of life.[31]

The contrast between the condemnation of the false teachers and the reas-

---

[30] Kruse, *The Letters of John,* 3.

[31] Burge provides a fine summary of John's opponents, focusing in particular on their Christology and ethics (*Letters of John,* 27–32). For more detailed treatments and theories concerning the seccessionists see J. Painter, "The 'Opponents' in 1 John," *NTS* 32 (1986): 48–71; H.-J. Klauck, "Internal Opponents: The Treatment of the Secessionists in the First Epistle of John," *Concilium* 200 (1988): 55–65; M. Hengel, *The Johannine Question* (Philadelphia: Trinity, 1989), 51–56; R. Brown, *Epistles of John,* 47–68; Smalley, *1, 2, 3, John,* xxxiii–xxv; Kruse, *The Letters of John,* 15–20. Kruse's treatment of this issue is also clear and concise, and his conclusion is worth considering: "The exact influence which led the secessionists to formulate their understanding of Christianity, whether it was the influence of their background in mystery religions (Painter), their particular interpretation of the Fourth Gospel (Brown), a pagan Hellenistic background involving dualistic ideas, or their experience of the Spirit (Klauck), will continue to be debated. But it does seem clear that whatever the influences that affected them were, they all led to a de-emphasizing of the incarnation and vicarious death of Christ and a concomitant de-emphasizing of the commands of Christ, especially the command to love one another" (*The Letters of John,* 19–20).

surance of believers is apparent throughout the book. First John shows that humanity can be divided into two groups—the children of God and the children of the devil (3:10). No other classification is possible.

The following chart helps to highlight the distinctive differences between the secessionists, who have left but continue to harass the Johannine churches, and the teachings John had put before them:

	Explanation	**Response of 1 John**
A New Theology	They compromised the uniqueness of the person and work of Jesus Christ.	Jesus Christ is the incarnate Son of God whose death provides forgiveness of sin.
A New Morality	They minimized the importance of sin; they claimed to have fellowship with God despite their unrighteous behavior.	Christianity has ethical implications; fellowship with God requires righteousness.
A New Spirituality	Their teachings resulted in spiritual arrogance; consequently, they did not show love to others.	God is love; thus, love for fellow Christians is a mark of true Christianity.

Though 1 John deals with specific problems caused by the secessionists who now evangelize for their cause, it does not indicate a specific destination (unlike 2 and 3 John). It is very probable that it was intended as a circular letter for the churches in the vicinity of Ephesus, the province of Asia Minor. When one thinks about the seven churches addressed in Revelation 2–3, these would be the likely recipients of John's first letter.[32]

4. The Purpose of 1 John

First John provides several keys that allow us to unlock the specific purpose(s) of this epistle. Four times in the letter John tells us why he writes:
1.   "We write this to make our joy complete" (1:4).

---

[32] Hiebert comments, "1 John is not a general epistle addressed to the Church as a whole but was directed to a group of churches within John's acquaintance" (*The Epistles of John*, 17). Brown adds, "It should be realized that the Johannine Epistles suggest a number of Johannine churches scattered over an area" (*Epistles of John*, 101). Brown also affirms Ephesus as the place of writing and churches scattered through Asia Minor as the most likely recipients.

    (To promote true joy in the child of God)
2. "I write this to you so that you will not sin" (2:1).
    (To prevent the child of God from committing sin)
3. "I am writing these things to you about those who are trying to lead you astray" (2:26)
    (To protect the child of God from false teachers)
4. "I write these things to you who believe in the name of the Son of God so that you may know you have eternal life" (5:13).
    (To provide assurance of salvation for the child of God)

It is popular and appropriate to see 1 John 5:13 as the governing purpose statement, but not the exclusive purpose statement. The parallel of 5:13 with the purpose statement of John's Gospel (20:31) is too apparent to be merely coincidental.[33] First John 5:13 brings together the other purpose statements in a unified theme. Whereas the Gospel of John is written with an evangelistic purpose, 1 John is penned to provide avenues of assurance whereby a believer can know he has eternal life through the Son.[34] Hiebert comments, "The contents of the epistle, we believe, are most advantageously studied in the light of the writer's purpose as stated in 5:13."[35]

5. Theology of the Epistles

The epistles of John contain a wealth of theological truth that demands careful attention. This fact is not always emphasized as clearly as it ought to be. The issues to which John gives attention and his manner of treatment are often distinct, allowing him to make his own unique contribution to the theology of the New Testament. Just as it is appropriate to talk of Pauline theology, it also is correct to speak of a Johannine theology, even when we restrict our analysis to his epistles.

We have already mentioned some of the theological and ethical emphases in the epistles, and we will address these and others again as they arise in the course of the commentary. Because of its importance, 1 John 1:1–2:2 will receive extensive examination grammatically and theologically in the

---

[33] A. Plummer writes: "The Gospel is written to shew the way to eternal life through belief in the incarnate Son. The Epistle is written to confirm and enforce the Gospel; to assure those who believe in the incarnate Son that they have eternal life" (*The Epistles of S. John* [1886; reprint, Grand Rapids: Baker, 1980], xlv).

[34] G. W. Dericksen provides an excellent analysis of the overarching purpose of 1 John. He gives special attention to the debate concerning whether 1 John was written to provide "Tests of Life" (the traditional view) or "Tests of Fellowship" ("What Is the Message of 1 John?" *BSac* 150 [1993]: 89–105), (a more recent view popularized by Z. Hodges). Following Smalley, he argues that we should give equal weight to the purpose statements of 1:4 and 5:13. His conclusion is not ours, but his treatment of the issue is worth consulting.

[35] Hiebert, *The Epistles of John*, 20.

body of the commentary. Following is a brief summary of several of the crucial doctrines John emphasizes in his letters.[36]

(1) The Doctrine of God

John highlights two characteristics of God. First, God is light (1 John 1:5). Second, God is love (1 John 4:8). Both of these qualities are essential attributes of God. To walk in the light is to walk in the life of God. To practice love is to demonstrate the character of God. Marshall points out, "The nature of God stands in the sharpest contrast to the devil and the world which are characterized by lies, hatred, and evil."[37] John also focuses on the fact that "God is revealed as the Father of Jesus Christ (1:2,3; 2:22,23,24; 4:14 [2 John 9]). To love the Son is to love the Father (5:1)."[38]

(2) The Doctrine of Sin

First John 3:8 states that the devil is the source of sin, for he has "sinned from the beginning." This probably is a reference to the beginning of creation (Gen 1–3) and the devil's activity in the garden and thereafter (cf. John 8:44; 1 John 3:12). Burdick claims: "It is apparent that sin in the individual is the result of the devil's hold upon a person, and victory over sin is in reality victory over the devil himself. The declaration that, 'the whole world is lying in the evil one' (5:19, author's translation) makes it clear that the same evil influence extends to the whole world."[39] John affirms that it is for the sins of this "whole world" that Christ was a propitiation (1 John 2:2). John describes sin as darkness (1 John 1:5–7), lawlessness or rebellion (1 John 3:4), and unrighteousness (1 John 5:17). Sin is universal and comprehensive. Therefore every person is a sinner and sins (1 John 1:8,10).

(3) The Doctrine of Christ

John provides a marvelous balance in addressing the person and work of Christ and the deity and humanity of Christ. "Jesus is presented as the Christ, the Son of God, and the reality of the incarnation of the preexistent Word of God is stressed."[40] Law referred to this as "the great Christological

---

[36] It is obvious that Paul and John have their own specific and particular theological interests and vocabulary. This is not to say, however, that the two are somehow in opposition or conflict with each other. As Burdick rightly notes: "It is not an exaggeration to say that the differences between Johannine and Pauline theology is as clear as the difference between summer and winter. This is not to suggest any disharmony between the two, for there is none. It is only to assert that each has its own distinctive characteristics that make it stand out in sharp relief against the other" (*Letters of John the Apostle*, 70).

[37] Marshall, *The Epistles of John*, 53.

[38] Kruse, *The Letters of John*, 34.

[39] Burdick, *Letters of John the Apostle*, 75.

[40] Marshall, *The Epistles of John*, 53.

thesis of the Epistle" and wrote, "That thesis is the complete, permanent, and personal identification of the historical Jesus with the Divine Being who is the Word of Life (1:1), the "Christ" (4:2) and the Son of God (5:5)."[41] Twenty-one times he is called the Son in 1 John and twice in 2 John. He is called "the 'Word of Life'" (1:1), which echoes John 1:1 and the *Logos* teaching. Further, John states that the Son "was with the Father" (1 John 1:2; cf. John 1:1–2) and is himself the "life" of God (1 John 1:1–2; cf. John 1:1–2). Jesus is the "true God and eternal life" (1 John 5:20), a direct affirmation of the Son's deity. He was sinless (1 John 3:5), he made atonement for the sins of the whole world (1 John 2:2; 4:10), and he destroyed the devil's work (1 John 3:8), accomplishing all of this by his bloody death (1 John 5:6). His death was a demonstration of the Father's love (1 John 4:9–11) for sinful humanity. He could do all of this because he took on tangible, real human flesh (1 John 1:1–3). As Burdick asserts, "So important is the doctrine of the Savior's humanity that it is employed as a criterion for discerning the false prophet from the true (4:1–3)."[42] He was no phantom. The incarnation was a true and genuine wedding of perfect deity and sinless humanity. The Son took to himself a complete human nature like that of Adam and Eve prior to their fall into sin. He was a real man and a sinless man.

(4) The Doctrine of the Holy Spirit

First John does not include an extensive body of material on the Holy Spirit, but what is present is significant. The Spirit primarily witnesses to the believer concerning the true teaching about Jesus the Christ (1 John 2:27; 5:7). The Spirit himself is a gift of anointing "that enables the Christian to enter into true knowledge."[43] He is a person who is distinct from the Father and Son and yet clearly has equal status with them (1 John 2:27; 4:2,13; 5:7). He has been given to the believer (3:24) and enables him to overcome the world (4:4). As the Spirit of truth (4:6), he helps the believer to recognize the false prophets who speak and teach wrongly concerning Jesus.

(5) The Doctrine of Salvation

The redemptive work of Jesus Christ has made possible our salvation (1 John 2:2; 3:16; 4:10). By believing and receiving the Son (1 John 5:10–

---

[41] Law, *Tests of Life*, 91. Burge adds: "What was revealed in the Incarnation must be the litmus test for all new theological insights. ... Historic Christology must be the touchstone for all Christian belief" (*Letters of John*, 35).

[42] Burdick, *Letters of John the Apostle*, 73.

[43] G. E. Ladd, *A Theology of the New Testament* (Grand Rapids: Eerdmans, 1974), 610.

13) one is born again (1 John 5:1), becomes a child of God (1 John 3:1–2), and receives the gift of eternal life. John's concept of eternal life (1 John 2:25; 5:11) is dualistic but in a Judeo-Christian sense. Ladd explains:

> His theology is structured in the dualism of the past and the future—the already and not yet. ... Like the Gospel, the epistle concentrates on the present experience of eternal life. It mentions eternal life at least ten times, always with emphasis upon the present. ... However, this experience of eternal life has a future cast. He who does the will of God abides forever (2:17). John looks forward to the realization of all that Christ means at his eschatological parousia (2:28). Although we have received life, although we have been born again (2:29), we are not yet like Christ. We await his parousia, when we shall experience an unimaginable change.[44]

In our current experience we are able through the new birth to do "what is right" (2:29). We may commit individual acts of sin (1:8,10; 2:1), but we will not habitually live in sin (3:6,7–9). We are enabled to "love one another," which provides assurance that we have been "born of God and know God" (4:7). In salvation God has come to live (abide) in us and we in God (4:15–16). This is a genuinely experiential reality and the basis for transformed living.

(6) The Doctrine of Eschatology

It was noted in the brief survey of salvation personal aspects of Johannine eschatology. To this must be added cosmic insights. John obviously lived in the expectancy that the parousia was imminent, for he said, "This is the last hour" (2:18). John was convinced that the "Christ event" had inaugurated the Messianic Age, and he clearly embraced the tension of the "already-not yet" reality of the reign of Jesus the Messiah. Certain events taking place in the churches gave further support of this perspective. The evidence included the presence of "many antichrists." Yet John looked to the eschatological coming of Antichrist as well (2:18; 4:3). Again we see a tension in John's soteriology and eschatology. Nothing he writes would indicate that he did not expect "a future consummation of the age, which would include the coming of antichrist, the second advent of Christ, resurrection, judgment, and eternal life. The advocates of realized eschatology have not succeeded in reducing such literal future events to mere present spiritual experiences."[45] John does see the world as already passing away (2:17), indicating that the victory of Christ won at the cross is already underway; and yet he awaits a final and climactic resolution. The day of judgment is coming (4:17). Those who live in God and he in them will have confidence in that day and will not have fear (4:18). On that day, when he

---

[44] Ibid., 612–13.
[45] Burdick, *Letters of John the Apostle,* 82.

comes, our transformation will be made complete, for "we know that when he appears, we shall be like him, for we shall see him as he is" (3:2).

John believes our faith in the Son of God must be orthodox. He believes faith cannot be separated from obedience and love. He sees faith expressing itself in righteous living. He is convinced that faith and assurance go together.[46] Assured of a right standing before God through faith in his Son who provided atonement for sin, we love God and others; and with this hope in us we purify ourselves, just as he is pure (3:3).[47]

6. Canonicity

The canonicity of 1 John was never questioned in early church history. The book was accepted into the canon immediately and without dissent. Origen affirmed it, and Eusebius classified 1 John with the *homologoumena* or undisputed books.[48] On the other hand, both 2 and 3 John were viewed as *antilogomena,* or disputed.[49] Eusebius did note that "they are well known and approved by many" (*H.E.* 3.2.5). It is likely the books were not widely circulated due to their private nature and brevity, and as a result they were not well known among the churches. Clear testimony for the two letters comes from the time of Clement of Alexandria.[50] Athanasius included them in his thirty-ninth Paschal Letter (A.D. 367), and the Council of Carthage (A.D. 397) accepted them as canonical.

Their eventual acceptance probably was due to the fact that they came to

---

[46] Marshall, *The Epistles of John,* 54–55.

[47] In addition to sections on theology in various commentaries, note also C. C. Black II, "The Johannine Epistles and the Question of Early Catholicism," *NovT* xxviii, 2 (1986): 131–58; J. Breck, *Spirit of Truth: The Origins of Johannine Pneumatology* (Crestwood, N.Y.: St. Vladimir's Seminary Press, 1991); K. J. Carl, "The Idea of 'Knowing' in the Johannine Literature," *Bangalore Theological Forum* 25 (1993): 53–75; W. R. Cook, "Hamartiological Problems in First John," *BSac* (1996): 249–60; M. J. Edwards, "Martyrdom and the First Epistle of John," *NovT* xxxi, 2 (1989): 164–71; J. M. Lieu, "What Was from the Beginning: Scripture and Tradition in the Johannine Epistles," *NTS* 39 (1993): 458–77; *New Testament Theology* [The Theology of the Johannine Epistles] (New York: Cambridge University Press, 1991); F. Martin, "The Integrity of Christian Moral Activity: The First Letter of John and *Veritas Splendor,*" *Cummunio* 21 (1994): 265–85; P. S. Minear, "The Idea of Incarnation in First John," *Int* xxiv (1970): 291–302; P. R. Raabe, "A Dynamic Tension: God and World in John," *Concordia Journal* 21 (1995): 132–47; G. S. Sloyan, *What Are They Saying about John?* (New York: Paulist Press, 1991), 69–98; G. B. Stevens, *The Johannine Theology* (London: Richard D. Dickinson, 1894); R. A. Whitacre, *Johannine Polemic: The Role of Tradition and Theology* (Chico, Cal.: Scholar's Press, 1982), 121–86.

[48] Schnackenburg provides a fine summary of the evidence (*The Johannine Epistles,* 46–47).

[49] There are seven *antilogomena* books in the NT: Hebrews, James, 2 Peter, 2 and 3 John, Jude, and Revelation.

[50] Schnackenburg, *The Johannine Epistles,* 274.

be seen as the work of the apostle John.[51] Given the difficult process and various obstacles these letters encountered, their inclusion in the canon of Holy Scripture is a testimony to the preserving work of the Holy Spirit and the sound judgments of the ancient church.

7. Structure and Form of 1 John[52]

Few issues are more difficult in Johannine studies than the structure of 1 John. There are almost as many opinions as there are commentaries on the book. The problem lies, in part, in the fact that the genre of 1 John is something of an enigma.[53] Sloyan points out that "1 John seems the least letter-like in its lack of the identification of a sender or an address to any recipients except the nonspecific 'little children.' It appears to be more a treatise sent broadcast to some in the John tradition."[54] Approaches to determining a structure or outline to the book can be divided into three groups: (1) traditional scholars who seek to discern basic topic or subject divisions (even sources) and an overarching outline through inductive analysis; (2) discourse analysis—linguist scholars who apply principles of semantic structural studies or "discourse linguistics" to discover the semantic relations that weave the epistle together as a unified whole; (3) rhetorical criticism—students of ancient rhetoric who seek to discover what, if any, rhetorical strategies common to the author's world were used to set forth and further his argument.[55]

(1) Traditional Approaches

R. Brown provides an extensive survey of other scholars who have divided 1 John into two, three, and seven parts. His own approach will be explained later.

Sample Proposed Divisions of 1 John

Division into Two Parts

1:5–2:28	2:29–5:13	Chaine, Verde, Tomoi

---

[51] Ibid., 275.

[52] The form and structure of 2 and 3 John are examined as part of the commentary on those letters.

[53] Talbert, *Reading John*, 6.

[54] G. S. Sloyan, *Walking in the Truth* (Valley Forge: Trinity Press, 1995), 1.

[55] Grayston notes: "Despite the common agreement that the Epistle lacks a discernible structure or logical progression of thought, even the most pessimistic critics attempt an analysis" (*The Johannine Epistles*, 4). He proposes a sixfold division dependent on emphasis rather than subject matter. J. Hill argues that 1 John is an example of the "community rule" or "church order" ("A Genre for 1 John," in *The Future of Early Christianity*, ed. B. A. Pearson [Minneapolis: Fortress, 1991], 367–77). His argument, though interesting, is not adequate.

1:5–2:29	3:1–5:12		Feuillet, Francis

Division into Three Parts

1:1–2:17	2:18–3:24	4:1–5:21	Thüsing
1:1–2:17	2:18–4:6	4:7–5:21	Ewald
1:1–2:26	2:27–4:6	4:7–5:21	Smit Sibinga
1:5–2:14	2:15–3:18	3:19–5:12	Erdmann
1:5–2:17	2:18–3:24	4:1–5:12	Hort, Hauck, Nestle, Pratt, Schnackenburg, Schneider, THLJ, Vogel, NEB
1:5–2:17	2:18–3:24	4:1–5:21	Gaugler
1:5–2:17	2:18–4:6	4:7–5:21	Westcott
1:5–2:27	2:28–3:24b	3:24c–5:21	Lutthart
1:5–2:27	2:28–3:24	4:1–5:12	Balz
1:5–2:27	2:28–4:6	4:7–5:12	Häring, Brooke, Jones
1:5–2:27	3:1–24	4:1–5:20	de Ambroggi
1:5–2:28	2:29–3:22	3:23–5:17	Huther
1:5–2:28	2:29–4:6	4:7–5:12	F.-M. Braun, de la Potterie, Skrinjar, SBJ
1:5–2:28	2:29–4:6	4:7–5:13	Malatesta
1:5–2:28	2:29–4:6	4:7–5:19	Nagl
1:5–2:28	2:29–4:6	4:7–5:21	Law
1:5–2:28	2:29–4:12	4:13–5:13	Dodd
1:5–2:29	3:1–4:6	4:7–5:13	JB
1:5–2:29	3:1–5:4a	5:4b–21	Bonsirven
2:3–28	2:29–4:6	4:7–5:21	Oke

Division into Seven Parts

Lohmeyer
1:1–4; 1:5–2:6; 2:7–17; 2:18–3:24; 4:1–21; 5:1–12; 5:13–21

Wilder
1:1–4; 1:5–2:17; 2:18–27; 2:28–3:24; 4:1–6; 4:7–5:12; 5:13–21

Giurisato
1:5–2:6; 2:7–17; 2:18–28; 2:29–3:10; 3:11–22; 3:23–5:4; 5:5–17

Houlden
1:5–2:11; 2:12–17; 2:18–27; 2:28–3:24; 4:1–6; 4:7–21; 5:1–12[56]

Each of these proposals has some measure of merit, and each has gained

---

[56] Brown, *Epistles of John,* 764. Law, *Tests of Life,* 1–24; R. C. H. Lenski, *The Interpretation of the Epistles of St. Peter, St. John and St. Jude* (Minneapolis: Augsburg, 1966), 366–67; and D. Jackman, *The Message of John's Letters* (Downers Grove: InterVarsity Press, 1988), 18, are representative of those who see the letter structured in the form of a spiral, inverted pyramid or cone whereby John again and again returns to address certain themes. There is certainly some truth to this perspective. Marshall (*The Epistles of John,* 22–30) gives a more detailed analysis of the outlines of Law, Brooke, Dodd, Malatesta, P. R. Jones, Schnackenburg, and Feuillet. He does not find any of these approaches adequate overall. He goes on to examine the redactional theories of K. Tomoi, E. von Dobschütz, Bultmann, Windisch, Preisker, Braun, Nauck, and O'Neill. He concludes that these theories also fail to account for the structure of the letter.

at least a small following. Each has also been subject to criticism, usually because they, at some point, fail to account for the "flow of argument" in the epistle.

(2) Discourse Analysis

This approach is usually applied by linguists and Bible translators. Rooted in the structuralist theories of Ferdinand de Saussure, this method looks at how grammar works on both the paragraph and discourse level. Surface structure and deep structure issues are examined. Speech-act theory and rhetorical strategies are also studied, and the text, as it is, is carefully examined. K. Pike and R. Longacre are well-known representatives of this approach to the study of texts. The following are several proposals set forth by this school.

1 John (R. Longacre)

INTRODUCTION — 1:1–2:29 — Embedded discourse of seven paragraphs
  1:1–4
  1:5–10—Covert exhortation not to profess to be sinless but to "walk in the light," confess our sins, and enjoy forgiveness.
  2:1–6—Covert exhortation not to sin.
  2:7–11—A new/old command is announced and inferentially connected with a covert command to love.
  2:12–17—Ethical peak of this embedded discourse. Here the writer develops his reasons for writing the epistle and warns against loving the world.
  2:18–27—Doctrinal peak. Remain in Christ and in his teaching in spite of adverse teaching and practice.
  2:28–29—Closure. Echoes previous paragraph: "Hold steady; don't get sidetracked."

BODY — 3:1–5:12 — Embedded discourse containing seven paragraphs
  3:1–6—Mitigated covert command to purify ourselves in v. 3.
  3:7–12—Mitigated covert command not to practice sin (v. 9).
  3:13–18—Mitigated command (not covert) to love by laying down our lives for the brethren (v. 16b; note use of "ought").
  3:19–24—"Hortatory essence" of book given in v. 23: "We should believe on Jesus and love one another."
  4:1–6—"Doctrinal peak" of the book; believe correctly regarding Jesus Christ.
  4:7–21—"Ethical peak" of the book; composed of two paragraphs (7–10 and 11–21). No mitigation now but covert exhortation: "Let us love one another."
  5:1–12—Conclusion of this embedded discourse (body) in that v. 1 refers to those who believe and love, harking back to the two previous paragraphs.

CONCLUSION—5:13–21. Theme of book clearly stated in v. 13, "that you may know." Purpose in writing is Assurance.[57]

A second discourse approach comes from a student of Longacre, Helen Miehle. She builds on his treatment but reaches different conclusions at certain points.

1 John (H. Miehle)

INTRODUCTION 1:1–10
  A 1:1–4
  B 1:5–10
BODY 2:1–5:12
  I. 2:1–3:6
    2:1–27
      2:1–17
        2:1–11
          2:1–6
            2:7–11
        2:12–14
        2:15–17
      2:18–25
      2:26–27
    2:28–3:6
  II. 3:7–5:5
    3:7–24
      3:7–18
        3:7–10
        3:11–18
        3:19–24
      4:1–6
      4:7–5:5
        4:7–10
        4:11–21
        5:1–5
        5:6–12
CLOSURE 5:13–21[58]

D. T.-C. Wu attempts something of an intersection between rhetorical

---

[57] R. E. Longacre, "Exhortation and Mitigation in First John," in *Selected Technical Articles Related to Translation* 9 (1983): 3–44.

[58] H. Miehle, "Theme in Greek Hortatory Discourse: Van Dijk and Beekman—Callow Approaches Applied to 1 John," Ph.D. diss., University of Texas at Arlington, 1988. Miehle obviously sees chiastic patterns in various sections. For our purposes we are more interested in simply showing her paragraph/section divisions. See G. H. Guthrie, *The Structure of Hebrews: A Text-Linguistic Analysis* (Leiden: Brill, 1994). Guthrie's work is warmly commended by W. L. Lane in his commentary on Hebrews in WBC (xc).

and linguistic (discourse) approaches. Drawing upon the work of G. Guthrie and his work on Hebrews (Guthrie speaks of "rhetorico-discourse analysis"), he offers a more eclectic study.[59] One will observe that his analysis is quite similar to more traditional approaches, but his method for arriving at his conclusions is not.

1 John (D. T.-C. Wu)

I. PROLOGUE: THE WORD OF LIFE (1:1–4)
II. LIGHT AND DARKNESS (1:5–2:27)
   A. Walking in the Light (1:5–2:2)
      a. God is Light (1:5–1:7)
      b. Renouncing Sin (1:8–2:2)
   B. The Command to Love (2:3–2:11)
      a. Knowledge of God and Keeping His Commandments (2:3–2:6)
      b. New Commandment (2:7–2:11)
   C. A Digression about the Church (2:12–14)
   D. Three Warnings (2:15–2:27)
      a. Warning against the World (2:15–2:17)
      b. Warning against the Antichrist (2:18–2:23)
      c. Warning against the Lie (2:24–2:27)
III. The Privileges and Responsibilities of God's Children (2:28–4:6)
   A. The Revelation of God's Children (2:28–3:10)
      a. The Confidence of God's Children (2:28–2:29)
      b. The Identity of God's Children (3:1–2)
      c. God's Children and the Children of the Devil (3:3–3:10)
   B. The Community's Message (3:11–3:12)
   C. The Marks of God's Children (3:13–3:24)
      a. Love in Community Life (3:13–3:18)
      b. Shoring up Christian Confidence (3:19–3:24)
   D. Test the Spirits (4:1–6)
IV. FAITH IN GOD AND LOVE ONE ANOTHER (4:7–5:12)
   A. God's Love Evokes Human Love (4:7–4:11)
   B. Confidence in God's Love (4:12–4:18)
   C. Appealing to Love Each Other (4:19–4:21)
   D. The Victory of Faith (5:1–5:5)
   E. Testimony to the Son (5:6–5:12)
V. EPILOGUE: FINAL REMARKS (5:13–5:21)
   A. The Confidence and Certainties of Believers (5:13–5:20)
   B. The Final Exhortation (5:21)

In a work prepared, in part, to assist missionaries in Bible translation, G. Sherman and J. Tuggy argue persuasively, in concert with Longacre, that 1 John "is a hortatory discourse, based on the occurrence of imperative verbs and other

---

[59] D. T.-C. Wu, "An Analysis of the Structure of 1 John Using Discourse Analysis," Ph.D. diss., The Southern Baptist Theological Seminary, 1997.

command forms."[60] They also point out that the surface form of 1 John is somewhat similar to modern English free poetry, making it difficult to always discern the relationship between various parts of the discourse.[61] Concerning this latter observation, we would imagine all students of 1 John would heartily agree. Building on the insights of several discourse approaches to 1 John, they structure and organize the epistle as shown in the chart on p. 43.

(3) Rhetorical Criticism

The application of rhetorical criticism and strategies to the biblical material became quite popular in the latter half of the twentieth century. Although the results have been somewhat uneven, a better understanding of how biblical authors sought to persuade their audiences to see their perspective and hear their argument has certainly been enhanced.

First John has received significant attention because of both its brevity and the difficulty in deciphering its structure. As we have seen, previous approaches have failed to produce a consensus, and it is the case that this approach also fails to bring a definitive solution. A number of scholars have argued for a chiastic structure for 1 John. Note the following examples:

1 John (P. Berge)

A The word of life 1:1–4
  B God is light 1:5–4:6
  B' God is love 4:7–5:5
A' The witness of faith 5:6–21[62]

J. C. Thomas[63] acknowledges the insights of Brown[64] and wisely builds his proposal around "the use of similar catch words/phrases and sections which parallel one another in terms of content." He goes on to argue that the structure of 1 John was intended to aid in its memorization.

1 John (J. C. Thomas)

A 1:1–4 — Prologue — Eternal Life
  B 1:5–2:2 — Making Him a Liar (Walking)
    C 2:3–17 — New Commandment

---

[60] G. Sherman and J. C. Tuggy, *A Semantic and Structural Analysis of the Johannine Epistles* (Dallas: Summer Institute of Linguistics, 1994), 6.

[61] Ibid., 7.

[62] P. S. Berge, "The Word and Its Witness in John and 1 John: A Literary and Rhetorical Study," in *Word and World,* Supplement Series 3 (1997): 143–62. As the title suggests, Berge sees a parallel literary relationship between the Gospel of John and 1 John. He also presents internal chiasms within his four major divisions (p. 151). The argument at this latter point is not very compelling.

[63] J. C. Thomas, "The Literary Structure of 1 John," *NovT* XL 4 (1998): 369–81.

[64] Brown, *Epistles of John,* 371–72.

The Constituent Organization of 1 John (G. Sherman and J. Tuggy) [a]

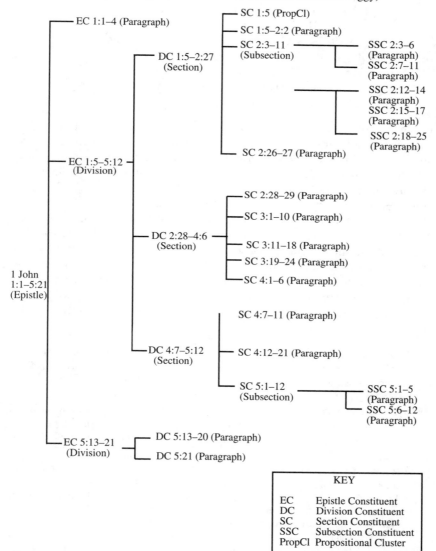

[a]Sherman and Tuggy, *Semantic and Structural Analysis,* 9. Again, one need not be familiar with the particulars of Discourse Theory to discern the major section and subsection analysis Sherman and Tuggy provide.

    D 2:18–27 — Antichrists
      E 2:18–3:10 — Confidence — Do Not Sin
        F 3:11–18 — Love One Another
      E′ 3:19–24 — Confidence — Keep the Commands
    D′ 4:1–6 — Antichrists
  C′ 4:7–5:5 — God's Love and Ours
  B′ 5:6–12 — Making Him a Liar (Testimony)
  A′ 5:13–21 — Conclusion — Eternal Life

In an excellent article that surveys various approaches to 1 John, P. J. Van Staden also argues "that the observance of the so-called chiastic styles presents an important key to a better understanding of the structure of 1 John." He does not argue for an overall chiasm but believes the letter can be divided into three main sections (1:5–2:17; 2:18–3:17; 4:1–5:12), which themselves contain numerous chiastic or parallel units.[65] K. Hansford argues in somewhat the same vein, stating that "the form of 1 John is a highly structural text, probably a homily or sermon, with poetic parallelisms and chiastic structures that the writer deliberately created to make his message more pleasurable and memorable for all time."[66] E. Wendland and K. Tollefson have recognized the contrastive or antithetical or dialectical strategies John employs in making his argument.[67]

D. Watson has attempted consistently to apply classic Greco-Roman rhetorical style and invention to 1 John. He argues:

> Repetition and emphasis, so common in 1 John, is integral to the rhetor's use of amplification techniques of Greceo-Roman rhetoric. These techniques include strong words, argumentation, comparison, accumulation, *expolitio, reflexio, regressio, conduplicatio, distributio,* synonymy … antithesis, personification, hyperbole, emphasis and development of commonplaces. Amplification is correctly found throughout the epistle. It must be pointed out that virtually every known rhetorical technique for amplification is utilized in the epistle.[68]

---

[65] P. J. Van Staden, "The Debate on the Structure of 1 John," *Hervormde Teologiese Studies* 47/ 2 (1991): 494. M. Sweazey makes a similar argument, though she divides the epistle at 1:5–2:28; 2:29–4:6; 4:7–5:13. See her "Chiastic Study of the First Epistle of John," Master's Thesis, St. Vladimir's Orthodox Theological Seminary, 1986.

[66] K. L. Hansford, "The Underlying Poetic Structure of 1 John," *JTT* 5 (1992): 125–74.

[67] E. R. Wendland, " 'Dear Children' Versus the 'Antichrists': The Rhetoric of Reassurance in First John," *JTT* 11 (1998): 40–84; K. D. Tollefson, "Certainty within the Fellowship: Dialectical Discourse in 1 John," *BTB* 29, no. 2 (1999): 79–89. His outline of 1 John (p. 84) is helpful and interesting. D. Neufeld draws somewhat similar conclusions through the use of speech act theory (*Reconceiving Texts as Speech Acts: An Analysis of 1 John* (Leiden: Brill, 1994). His analysis is helpful at points, but many of the positions he takes on historical issues are unnecessarily skeptical and unduly suspicious.

[68] D. F. Watson, "Amplification Techniques in 1 John: The Interaction of Rhetorical Style and Invention," *JSNT* 51 (1993): 117–18.

He identifies 1 John as primarily epideictic rhetoric (as opposed to judicial or deliberative) because its goal is to increase the readers' commitment to values they already hold. First John was written to the faithful community as an appeal to strengthen their devotion to stay true to the gospel of Jesus Christ, a value held by both the speaker and his audience.[69]

Talbert believes 1 John (like 1 Peter) alternates between the twin concerns of ethics and Christology.[70] Strecker focuses on the polemical nature of 1 John and outlines the book alternating *Parenesis* and *Dogmatic Exposition*.[71]

H. York argues that when a comparison is made between discourse analysis and rhetorical criticism, significant similarities exist and common results are gleaned. The methods can be complementary. He provides as an example a side-by-side comparison of the discourse model of Longacre and the rhetorical analysis of Klauck.

Comparative Structural Analysis of 1 John

Longacre (Mitigated Hortatory)	Klauck (Deliberativum)	
I. Introduction (1:1–2:29)	1:5–2:17	Capitatio Benvolentiae
1:1–10		
1–4		
5–10		
2:1–6		
2:7–11		
2:12–17 (ethical peak)		
2:18–27 (doctrinal peak)	2:18–27	Narratio
2:28–29 Closure	2:28–29	Propositio
II. Body of the Book (3:1–5:12)		
3:1–6	3:1–24	Probatio
3:7–12		
3:13–18		
3:19–24		
4:1–6 (doctrinal peak)	4:1–21	Exhortatio

---

[69] Ibid., 119. See also Watson, "An Epideictic Strategy for Increasing Adherence to Community Values: 1 John 1:1–2:29," in *Proceedings: Eastern Great Lakes and Midwest Biblical Societies* 11 (1991), 144–52.

[70] Talbert, *Reading John,* 7.

[71] Strecker, *The Johannine Letters,* xliv.

4:7–21 (ethical peak)

5:1–12   5:1–12   <u>Peroratio</u>

III. Closure of Epistle (5:13–21)[72]

York's conclusion is basically correct. There are genuine areas of compatibility, synthesis of methodology, and agreement between the two approaches. Neither method alone or together, however, has decisively settled the issue of the structure of 1 John. Significant disagreement still exists within both disciplines, though it is clear major strides have been made in better understanding the structure, strategies, and argument of 1 John.

A Proposal: The outline we propose attempts to utilize the best insights from traditional studies, discourse analysis, and rhetorical criticism. First John does exhibit a hortatory and epideictic rhetorical strategy. We also find Brown's proposal persuasive, which states that 1 John is modeled on the same general structure as the Fourth Gospel. Both have a fourfold division overall, with the themes of light and love developed variously in sections II and III. Note his comparison:

The Gospel of John

I.   The Prologue (1:1–18)

II.   The Book of Signs (1:19–12:50): "To his own he came; yet his own people did not accept him." The public revelation of the light brought a judgment, which separated believers who came to the light from the world and "the Jews" who preferred darkness to light.

III. The Book of Glory (13:1–20:29): "But all those who did accept him he empowered to become God's children." The "hour" of Jesus' glorification where he speaks and acts on behalf of a new "his own"— the believers.

CONCLUSION (20:30–31): A statement of the author's purpose.

IV.   The Epilogue (chap. 21)

I John

I.   The Prologue (1:1–4)

II.   Part One (1:5–3:10): The Gospel that God is light, and we must walk in the light as Jesus walked.

---

[72] H. W. York, "An Analysis and Synthesis of the Exegetical Methods of Rhetorical Criticism and Discourse Analysis as Applied to the Structure of 1 John," Ph.D. diss., Mid-America Baptist Theological Seminary, 1993. The two outlines come from Longacre, "Exhortation and Mitigation in First John," in *Selected Technical Articles Related to Translation* 9 (1983): 3–44 (previously noted); and H.-J. Klauck, "Zur rhetorischen Analyse der Johannesbriefe," *ZNW* 81 (1990): 204–24.

III.   Part Two (3:11–5:12): The Gospel that we must love one another as God has loved us in Jesus Christ.

CONCLUSION (5:13–21): A statement of the author's purpose.[73]

This commentary's outline does the following:

1.   It recognizes the two dominant themes of the epistle as being *Light* (1:5–3:10) and *Love* (3:11–5:12)

2.   It seeks to utilize rhetorical devices such as "hinge verses" (e.g., 2:28; 5:20) and other structural markers that most scholars use to separate one subject from another.

3.   The outline is itself hortatory, admonishing the reader to heed John's expected response to his word of instruction. R. R. Reno summarizes the situation well when he writes:

> The text of 1 John shimmers with what has been seen, heard and touched. The text speaks plainly, directly and clearly, and what is said is a proclamation that has the power of fellowship: our fellowship with each other, our fellowship with God and the fellowship of the Father with his Son. Like the name of God which the Psalmist invokes as the very power of salvation, a power of invocation which the author of 1 John echoes when he explains, "I write this to you who believe in the name of the Son of God, that you may know that you have eternal life" (5:13), so does the particular linguistic structure of 1 John contain the power to draw us into the fullest possible destiny in God's love.[74]

───────────── *OUTLINE OF 1 JOHN* ─────────────

Prologue: The Word of Life (1:1–4)
  I. God Is Light (1:5–3:10)
      1. Walk in the Light (1:5–2:2)
         (1) God Is Light (1:5–1:7)
         (2) Resist Sin (1:8–2:2)
      2. Obey the Command to Love (2:3–11)
         (1) Know God and Keep His Commands (2:3–6)
         (2) Learn the New Command and Love Others (2:7–11)
      3. Know Your Spiritual Status (2:12–14)
      4. Be Warned of Enemies of the Faith (2:15–28)

---

[73] Brown, *Epistles of John,* 124. A. Feuillet concurs with Brown's assessment that 1 John is patterned after the Gospel of John, though he outlines the letter differently. See his "Structure of 1 John," *BTB,* vol. III, No. 2 (1973): 194–216. Van Staden's criticism of Brown's proposal, in our judgment, is unconvincing ("The Debate on the Structure of 1 John," 489–90).

[74] R. R. Reno, "The Marks of the Nails: Theological Exegesis of the First Letter of John for Easter," *Pro Ecclesia,* Vol. VI, No. 1 (1997): 53.

PROLOGUE: THE WORD OF LIFE (1:1–4)
1. The Object of Proclamation Highlighted (1:1)
2. The Object of Proclamation Clarified (1:2)
3. The Purpose of Proclamation Announced (1:3a)
4. The Nature of This Common Fellowship Clarified (1:3b)
5. The Purpose of Writing Announced (1:4)
I. GOD IS LIGHT (1:5–3:10)
1. Walk in the Light (1:5–2:2)
(1) God Is Light (1:5–1:7)
(2) Resist Sin (1:8–2:2)
2. Obey the Command to Love (2:3–11)
(1) Know God and Keep His commands (2:3–6)
(2) Learn the New Command and Love Others (2:7–11)
3. Know Your Spiritual Status (2:12–14)
4. Be Warned of Enemies of the Faith (2:15–28)
(1) Beware of the World (2:15–17)
(2) Beware of the Antichrists (2:18–28)
5. Live Like Children of God (2:28–3:10)
(1) Be Confident and Ready for His Coming (2:28–3:3)
(2) Be Righteous and Do Not Sin (3:4–10)

PROLOGUE: THE WORD OF LIFE (1:1–4)

This initial segment of the epistle is similar to other significant opening passages (cf. Gen 1:1; Mark 1:1; John 1:1), but the text is unusual and presents several challenges for interpretation. The basic message is clear: the author proclaims to his readers a message regarding eternal life revealed to him and other eyewitnesses,[1] so that his readers might share (have the same fellowship) in that life. At the same time, these verses' unusual construction makes precise identification of the nature of that message difficult to ascertain.[2]

---

[1] Various theories denying that the author was an eyewitness are not convincing. For a survey of these proposals, see R. Schnackenburg, *The Johannine Epistles* (New York: Crossroad, 1992), 51–56; R. E. Brown, *The Epistles of John*, AB (New York: Doubleday, 1982), 158–61. For an indirect refutation through positive exposition, see commentary below. See also I. H. Marshall, *The Epistles of John*, NICOT (Grand Rapids: Eerdmans, 1978), 106.

[2] The fact that it is difficult for us does not mean that it was similarly difficult for John's original audience. They had the advantage of knowing the situation they were facing (and which John addresses), including firsthand knowledge of the nature of the Christological heresy. Moreover, they probably had been taught previously with similar words and metaphors that John uses in this epistle. Without this privileged knowledge, we have to discern the meaning of these words and metaphors from the epistle itself (and through cautious comparison with John's other writings).

First, these words take the place of a conventional salutation (e.g., "The elder [the sender] to the chosen lady and her children [the recipients]," 2 John 1)[3] that typically begins Hellenistic letters. The absence of a salutation raises questions over the genre of this text, that is, whether 1 John should be interpreted as an epistle or as another literary form with different rules and expectations. Scholarly debate on the genre of 1 John has thus far not reached any consensus concerning an understanding of the text as a literary whole.[4] Consequently, it is best to read 1 John as a pastoral work in which John applies his theology to the specific problem at hand, since the explicit content and exhortation of the text is addressed to a particular congregation(s) faced with a specific Christological heresy.[5] In other words, it is best to read 1 John as an epistle, though sermonic aspects also characterize it.

Second, the apparent similarity between this prologue and the prologue to the Gospel of John[6] raises questions about the extent and significance of the parallel. On the one hand, one could emphasize that a careful comparison with the prologue of the Gospel of John is necessary for a proper understanding of 1 John 1:1–4.[7] On the other hand, one could hear merely an echo of John 1:1 (and Gen 1:1) with, moreover, a different referent (the beginning of Jesus' earthly ministry in 1 John 1:1 instead of the absolute beginning of creation or eternity in John 1:1).[8] Ultimately, the issue is whether we can appeal to John's Gospel to throw light on interpretive difficulties in 1 John. After careful consideration of both 1 John and the Gospel of John as individual literary wholes, and after a careful comparison of their respective themes, we are convinced that such appeals are sound, provided that distinctive nuances arising from specific contexts are recognized.

Third, both the grammatical structure of 1 John 1:1–4 and the content

---

[3] See also 3 John and the letters of Paul. Note that 1 John also lacks a formal ending. But F. Francis has pointed out that many Hellenistic letters simply stop, without a formal closing formula ("The Form and Function of the Opening and Closing Paragraphs of James and 1 John," *ZNW* 61 [1970]: 125).

[4] For a survey of various views on the literary genre of 1 John, see Brown, *Epistles of John*, 86–92. Note also the introduction on structure and form (p. 37f.).

[5] Cf. Marshall, who, despite concluding that 1 John is "not so much a letter as a written sermon or address," judges that "[t]he close relationship ... evident between the writer and his readers, ... and the occasional reference to a specific situation (2:19) shows that the author was writing for the benefit of a particular group or groups of readers, so that the writing is in effect a letter" (*Epistles of John*, 99).

[6] See e.g., Brown, *Epistles of John*, 178–80; Schnackenburg, 50; S. S. Smalley, *1, 2, 3 John*, WBC (Waco: Word, 1984), 4; B. F. Westcott, *The Epistles of St. John*, rev. ed (Grand Rapids: Eerdmans, 1966), 3.

[7] E.g., Schnackenburg, *The Johannine Epistles*, 50.

[8] E.g., M. M. Thompson, *1–3 John* (Downers Grove: InterVarsity Press, 1992), 36–37.

conveyed by it are not readily apparent.[9] We will attempt to clear up these perplexities in the comments below.

1. The Object of Proclamation Highlighted (1:1)

[1]That which was from the beginning, which we have heard, which we have seen with our eyes, which we have looked at and our hands have touched—this we proclaim concerning the Word of life.

1:1 The NIV rendering focuses on the object of proclamation[10] and the text's ultimately personal referent (the "Word of life," i.e., the preincarnate Christ, instead of "the word of life," i.e., the gospel message). Although it is possible to take the object of proclamation as the gospel,[11] the balance of the evidence favors a reference to the preincarnate Christ. The most important evidence for this view is that the writer vividly describes perceiving this object with his senses in a way that goes beyond the mere reception of a message, that is, "we have seen with our eyes," "we looked at," and "our hands have touched."[12] Why, then, did John use the neuter pronoun "that which" to begin v. 1? It is because he wishes to draw attention equally to the "Word proclaimed" and the "Word as person." The message and the person ultimately cannot be separated. Each explains the other. The message about Jesus is intimately related to who Jesus is.[13]

---

[9] Brown observes that 1 John 1:1–4 has a good claim to having the most complicated Gk. in the corpus of writings attributed to the apostle John (*Epistles of John*, 152). Though our modern Eng. versions give short, easily readable sentences, the first three and a half verses are one long, complicated sentence in Gk. Moreover, the author switches word order (object first, instead of subject-verb-object) and delays giving the main verb, "we proclaim," until v. 3. Furthermore, between the object (which is itself a string of parallel relative clauses) and the main verb is a parenthesis that explains one of the elements of the object ("life") more fully. Cf. Marshall, *Epistles of John*, 99–100. In addition, the antecedent of the relative pronouns and their referents (what external reality that is referred to) are open to dispute.

[10] The NIV preserves the word order (and emphasis) of the Gk. by putting the object, "that which was from the beginning," before the subject and verb, "we proclaim."

[11] See, e.g., Westcott, *Epistles of St. John*, 6–7; C. H. Dodd, *The Johannine Epistles* (New York: Harper & Brothers, 1946), 3–5.

[12] This argument was decisive in Marshall's mind as well (see *Epistles of John*, 101). See also J. E. Weir, "The Identity of the Logos in the First Epistle of John," *ExpTim* 86 (1974–75): 118–20; K. Grayston, "'Logos' in 1 John 1," *ExpTim* 86 (1974–75): 279.

[13] See J. L. Boyer, "Relative Clauses in the Greek New Testament: A Statistical Study," *GTJ* 9 (1988): 247. A possible solution is that it is used as a neuter of abstraction, conceiving of the preincarnate Christ as "abstract Deity." This is supported by other occurrences of the neuter of abstraction in John's writings when a person is "being thought of in an abstract way." The neuter pronoun occurs in John 4:22 (referring to God) and 17:24. In John 6:37,39; and 17:2, the neuter pronoun has a neuter antecedent, "everything." But in these verses John was clearly referring to persons ("everyone"). In addition, 1 John 5:4 uses the neuter participle when clearly referring to persons begotten by God (cf. the masculine participle in referring to the same persons in 1 John 5:1).

In addition, the first relative clause, "that which was from the beginning," is actually structured differently from the following four (one in 1:3a) relative clauses. While all five relative clauses are the object of the main verb "proclaim" in v. 3b, the relative pronoun in the first relative clause is the subject of the verb "to be" ("was" in v. 1), whereas the relative pronouns in the other four clauses are the objects of various verbs of sense perception.[14] Besides this switch from subject to object within the relative clauses, the verb in the first relative clause ascribes what the Word of life is inherently (i.e., *it is* something), whereas the verbs in the remaining four relative clauses describe the sense perception of others concerning the Word of life (i.e., *we saw, heard, touched it*).[15] Most likely, the first relative clause is itself the antecedent of the following four relative pronouns, that is, deity, who is from eternity, the one John and his fellow apostolic eyewitnesses had seen and touched and proclaimed. The contrast in time frame between "that which was from the beginning" and what "we have seen with our eyes ... and our hands have touched" is then a contrast between eternity[16] and a

---

[14] Cf. Brown, *Epistles of John*, 154; R. Bultmann, *The Johannine Epistles*, Her (Philadelphia: Fortress, 1973), 7–8, n. 3.

[15] Contra Thompson, *1–3 John*, 36.

[16] Given the absence of any contextual indicators restricting ἀπ ἀρχῆς to a certain temporal point, it seems most likely to refer to eternity (cf. G. Delling, "ἄρχω, κτλ," *TDNT*, 1:481–82). Analysis of the relation between the imperfect, perfect, present, and aorist usage in 1 John 1:1–4 adds support to this reading. The main verb is the present tense, "proclaim," with its imperfective verbal aspect, which leaves the imperfect tense, "was," as the more remote tense. Given the likely judgment that John is portraying his proclamation as ongoing (he uses the present tense also for "write" in 1:4, portraying himself as in the activity of proclamation through writing), this contextual factor tells us that John is portraying the object of his proclamation as being in existence "from the beginning" and continuing to exist (imperfective aspect) at the time of his proclamation. The perfect tense verbs, "we have seen" and "we have heard" in v. 3, denote a given state of affairs (with stative verbal aspect) upon which the proclamation is dependent. Consequently, we may assert that John portrayed these events as having happened in the past and as having ongoing effects. The aorist tense verbs, "we have looked at," "we have touched," and "it was revealed" ("appeared," v. 2), probably convey their simple perfective verbal aspect, i.e., these events have happened. Since these past events of sense perception clearly refer to the incarnation of Jesus Christ and since we have argued that "what was from the beginning" is a personal reference to the preincarnate Christ (and, indeed, an ascription of his inherent being), the more remote imperfect tense and the unrestricted use of "from the beginning" point to the eternal being of the Son. For helpful introductions to the modern state of research into verbal aspect, see D. A. Carson, "An Introduction to the Porter/Fanning Debate," in *Biblical Greek Language and Linguistics: Open Questions in Current Research*, ed. S. E. Porter and D. A. Carson, JSNTSup 80 (Sheffield: JSOT Press, 1993), 18–25 and M. Silva, "A Response to Fanning and Porter on Verbal Aspect," ibid., 74–82. This analysis basically agrees with Porter that verb tense does not convey absolute time (even in the indicative mood) but primarily aspect. Other contextual factors convey the datum of time or timelessness. Through these contextual factors, different verb tenses take on the freight of conveying relative time in relation to one another by virtue of the interaction of their respective verbal aspects. See further S. E. Porter, *Idioms of the Greek New Testament*, 2nd ed. (Sheffield: Academic Press, 1994), 20–26. We have relegated this discussion to a footnote because of the potential difficulty of this subject to most readers of this commentary and because of the unresolved nature of the current debate over verbal aspect. R. Tan, a Ph.D. student at Southern Seminary, should be credited for this helpful analysis.

definite past event. In other words, John and other eyewitnesses saw this deity, who has life in himself from eternity, incarnated in time/space/history.

The interpretation above is strengthened by reading "concerning the Word of life" with the four verbs of perception in the relative clauses, that is, that which we have heard, seen with our eyes, looked at, and our hands have touched is concerning the Word of life.[17] "Concerning the Word[18] of life" designates the object around which these verbs of perception orbit.[19] In short, the eyewitnesses heard, saw, and touched the Word of life. The eternal Son of God, Jesus the Christ, had come in the flesh (cf. John 1:14).

2. The Object of Proclamation Clarified (1:2)

[2]The life appeared; we have seen it and testify to it, and we proclaim to you the eternal life, which was with the Father and has appeared to us.

1:2 This verse actually opens with an initial "and" *(kai)*[20] that introduces another thought in John's contemplation.[21] In effect, this new thought is a parenthetical explanation of "life" mentioned in the phrase, "the Word of life."[22]

---

[17] Similarly, Dodd, *Johannine Epistle*, 3. As Marshall notes, most commentators regard this phrase as "summing up the relative clauses and providing a second object to the verb 'we proclaim'" (*Epistles of John*, 102, n. 11). This view fails to account for the resumption of v. 3 with "what we have seen and heard." If "the word of life" were the only summary of these relative clauses, John would more naturally have resumed with something like "this life that we have seen and heard."

[18] Besides the unsuitability of attributing a message as the object around which these perceptions revolved, other reasons for taking a personal referent will be given below. For a clear summary of arguments *against* a personal interpretation of "Word" *(logos)* and for an impersonal meaning, see Brown, *Epistles of John*, 164–65.

[19] For the use of the preposition περί, "concerning," see M. J. Harris, "Appendix," *NIDNTT* (Grand Rapids: Zondervan, 1978), 3:1203. Most probably, the switch to an aorist, "we looked at," which does not differ in meaning from "we have seen," is a reiteration that prepares for a transition (cf. S. E. Porter, *Verbal Aspect in the Greek of the New Testament, with Reference to Tense and Mood* [New York: Peter Lang, 1989], 264). It seems likely, then, that one neuter pronoun governs both "we looked at" and "have touched" (also an aorist verb). The addition of "our hands have touched" and the specification of the object of perception through the prepositional phrase "concerning the Word of life" complete the emphasis on the concrete reality of the incarnation and identify the object as the incarnate Son of God.

[20] The NIV apparently judged the "and" insignificant and chose to omit it in translation.

[21] Cf. Westcott, *Epistles of St. John*, 8, on this characteristic use of the simple conjunction καί by John; see also D. E. Hiebert, "An Exposition of 1 John 1:1–4," *BSac* 145 (1988): 205.

[22] Cf. Brown, *Epistles of John*, 166. On the other hand, Brown is probably overinterpreting in taking the article "the" in "the life" as grammatical referring back to "of life" in v. 1. The previously mentioned noun is "the Word of life," not "the life," so that the grammatical phenomenon to which Brown appeals does not apply here. More likely, the article is used with "life" (an abstract noun) to focus on the quality of this life mentioned: it is the life, i.e., genuine life. (See D. B. Wallace, *Greek Grammar Beyond the Basics* [Grand Rapids: Zondervan, 1996], 226.) This interpretation is confirmed by John's clarification on the quality of this life, i.e., it is the eternal life which was with the Father. "The Word of life" is an objective genitive: The Word who gives life.

John makes clear that life has been revealed[23] and clarifies that this life is nothing other than "the eternal life, which was with the Father." The phrase, "the eternal life which was with the Father," points to a personal reference to the eternal Son of God as in v. 1.[24] John focuses on the quality of life here to emphasize that the revelation (incarnation) of this Word (who reveals life and is the Source of eternal life) is the revelation of eternal life itself.[25]

Notice that "the eternal life, which was with[26] the Father" (which "... we have seen, and borne witness, ... and was revealed to us") parallels "that which was from the beginning" ("which we have heard, ... seen with our eyes, ... and our hands touched ...") as the object of the sense perception of eyewitnesses. The object of eyewitness proclamation is one and the same: "That which was from the beginning," who is "the Word of life," is also "the eternal life, which was with the Father." The first phrase emphasizes Jesus' deity, while the second phrase focuses on Jesus' revelation of eternal life. Thus, the beginning and the conclusion of 1 John (see 5:20)[27] assert the same fact: the eternal Son of God, who is the true God and eternal life, has been revealed in history.

This truth is the key to the purpose of the epistle: John is fighting a Christological heresy that involved the denial of the incarnation of deity, that is, the denial that the Christ was the historical Jesus. Apparently, the heresy involved the separation of "Christ" and "Son of God" from "Jesus." The issue this epistle addresses is not that the heretics believed Jesus to be someone other than the Christ (and believed in Jesus anyway), but rather

---

[23] The NIV's rendering of the passive ἐφανερώθη as "appeared" obscures the sense of God's sending (and thus revealing) of Christ: the eternal life that was with the Father and was revealed to us (implied by the Father; cf. 1 John 4:9–10,14; 5:11; see also John 1:1–2; 3:13,16–17,31,34; 4:10; 5:28–29,37–40; 6:32–33,37–40,56–58; 7:28–29; 8:12 with 21,26, and 29; 9:4; 10:36,42; 12:44–50; 13:3,20; 14:24; 16:6,27–28; 17:3,8,18,23,25; 20:21).

[24] Cf. the excursus on ζωή, "life," in G. Strecker, *The Johannine Letters* (Minneapolis: Fortress, 1996), 16–17.

[25] Cf. Brown, *Epistles of John*, 166. Brown also notes that Jesus says "I am the life" in John 11:25; 14:6. As Marshall observes, what was of crucial importance to John and his readers was "the personal manifestation of eternal life in the historical person of Jesus" (*Epistles of John*, 104).

[26] The sense of πρὸς τὸν πατέρα, "with (i.e., in the presence of) the Father" probably goes beyond simple spatial proximity. "[W]hen *pros* describes a relationship between persons it must connote personal intercourse rather than simply spatial juxtaposition or personal accompaniment" (Harris, "Appendix," 3:1205). Cf. Brown, *Epistles of John*, 168–69, who also argues that the "added connotation of relationship toward the Father" is present.

[27] See comment on that verse. Cf. Wallace, *Greek Grammar*, 326–27, for a good defense of Christ as the referent in 1 John 5:20.

that they believed the Christ to be someone other than Jesus.[28] This was a direct assault on the person of Jesus (a denial of his deity) and one that would call into question his work of atonement as well. John writes to assure his readers that they and only they, who believe in Jesus, the incarnate Son of God, deity enfleshed, have eternal life (cf. 1 John 5:11–13). By so doing, John equips his readers to heed his concluding command to guard themselves from idols, that is, false christs and false religion. In short, John's central purpose is to encourage his readers to persevere in their belief in the apostolic proclamation of the Christ as Jesus, the incarnate Son of God.

3. The Purpose of Proclamation Announced (1:3a)

³We proclaim to you what we have seen and heard, so that you also may have fellowship with us.

1:3a In the Greek this verse opens with a repetition of the phrase "what we have seen and heard" to signal the resumption of the grammatically incomplete sentence begun in v. 1 (again the main verb, "we proclaim," does not occur until here in v. 3, even though the NIV added this verb in v. 1 to clarify the thought).[29] One might notice that "seeing" is emphasized in each of the first three verses, and the order of hearing and

---

[28] Cf. D. A. Carson, "The Purpose of the Fourth Gospel: John 20:30–31 Reconsidered," *JBL* 108 (1987): 643. Carson's study corrects L. C. McGaughy's conclusion (see *A Descriptive Analysis of Εἶναι as a Linking Verb in New Testament Greek* (SBLDSup 6 [Missoula, Mont.: SBL, 1972], 51–52) that John 20:31; 1 John 2:22; 4:15; 5:1; and 5:5 are the only five exceptions to the rule that the noun with the article (where there is no expressed or implicit pronoun or a competing articular noun [see further Wallace, *Greek Grammar*, 43–44]) is the subject of the sentence with the equative verb, ἔστίν ("is"), regardless of word order. Wallace's objection (p. 46, n. 34) to Carson's grammatical argument fails because the example of Acts 11:20 should be read "the Lord Jesus," not "Jesus as the Lord" (cf. Acts 16:31 and Wallace's own identification of this same construction there as accusative in simple apposition, i.e., "the Lord, *that is*, Jesus" [p. 198]). First John 2:22 should be read, "Who is the liar if not the one who denies that *the Christ is Jesus* (Ἰησοῦς ... ἔστιν ὁ χριστός)." The question is not "Who is Jesus?" Rather, it is "Who is the Christ?" Likewise, 1 John 4:15 and 5:5 should be read, "The Son of God is Jesus," while 1 John 5:1 should be read, "The Christ is Jesus." For a strong argument that John 20:31 should be read, "These things have been written that you might believe that *the Christ is Jesus*," see Carson, "Purpose," 639–51. As additional support for this reading, we should notice John 5:15 (the only other instance in John's writings where a proper name precedes an articular noun in a subject-predicate nominative construction). There the proper name "Jesus" is in a sentence with an equative verb, "is," together with an articular substantival participial clause. The context of the story surrounding John 5:15 makes clear that this articular noun is the subject: Since the subject is the known entity (cf. Wallace, *Greek Grammar*, 42) and the man originally did not know who had healed him, John 5:15 is telling us that the man learned that the one who had made him well (the subject) was Jesus (the predicate nominative).

[29] Cf. Marshall, *Epistles of John*, 104.

seeing in v. 1 has been reversed to seeing and hearing here in v. 3. Although commentators have given various suggestions, including mutually exclusive ones,[30] it seems that the sequence of verbs leading up to v. 3 places emphasis on concrete seeing: "What we have *seen with our eyes,* what we have *beheld,* ... the life was *revealed,* and we have *seen,* and *borne* witness, ... the eternal life which was with the Father and was *revealed* to us."[31] In effect, John highlights the reality of the incarnation of the Word of life by giving first place to seeing. John (and the other apostolic witnesses) heard an incarnate Person, whom he saw also with his own eyes. This incarnate Person, whom he saw and heard,[32] is the One that he proclaims, in turn,[33] to his readers.

John proclaims the incarnate Jesus Christ to his readers in order that they also should have fellowship with him. The precise nuance of the noun *koinōnia,* "fellowship," is not easy to determine. It occurs in John's writings only four times (all within 1 John 1:3–7) and a total of fifteen times elsewhere in the New Testament (thirteen times in Paul's writings).[34] It could convey, among other things,[35] the idea of "oneness in community,"[36] "having (something) in common,"[37] or "common participation or sharing in something."[38] Several observations are worth noting.

First, it is through the proclamation of the incarnate Word of life that

---

[30] Compare, e.g., A. E. Brooke, *The Johannine Epistles,* ICC (Edinburgh: T & T Clark, 1948), 7, with Bultmann, *The Johannine Epistles,* 8. See also Westcott, *Epistles of John,* 11. For the opinion that the different order is immaterial, see Brown, *Epistles of John,* 169–70.

[31] Both the translation and emphasis are mine.

[32] Perhaps the desire to underscore "seeing" and "hearing" (perfect tense) also accounts for the switch to the aorist tense form for "beholding," "touching," and "was revealed."

[33] The NIV omits καί, "also," in its translation. Note that many manuscripts and witnesses omit this καί. However, the better textual witnesses preserve it (see Brown, *Epistles of John,* 170, and the textual apparatus of the Nestle-Aland 27th ed. Gk. text). The inclusion of "also" or "in turn" in translation would better convey the logical sequence of eyewitness to subsequent hearers present in the Gk. Cf. Strecker, *The Johannine Letters,* 19.

[34] Acts 2:42 and Heb 13:16; Rom 15:26; 1 Cor 1:9; 10:16 (twice); 2 Cor 6:14; 8:4; 9:13; 13:13; Gal 2:9; Phil 1:5; 2:1; 3:10; and Phlm 1:6.

[35] For a helpful, brief survey, see J. Schattenmann, "κοινωνία," *NIDNTT,* 1:639–44.

[36] See Brown, *Epistles of John,* 170, who appeals to references to being "one" in John 17:11,21,22,23 and ostensible parallels in the Qumran community.

[37] Cf. Marshall, *Epistles of John,* 104.

[38] See F. Hauck, "κοινός, κτλ," III:798. It is doubtful, however, whether κοινωνία "always has the root meaning of participation in something with others" (as is claimed in a master's thesis, Dallas Theological Seminary, 1975, by G. B. Christie, "An Interpretive Study of 1 John 1:9"). For a similar position see P. Perkins, "Koinonia in 1 John 1:3–7: The Social Context in the Johannine Letters," *CBQ* 45 (1983): 631–41. Excursuses on *koinonia* can be found in C. Kruse, *The Letters of John,* The Pillar New Testament Commentary (Grand Rapids: Eerdmans, 2000), 59–61; R. Schnackenburg, *The Johannine Epistles* (New York: Crossroad, 1992), 63–69; Strecker, *The Johannine Letters,* 20.

John envisions the accomplishment of his purpose of bringing his readers to fellowship with him and other eyewitnesses. As Eichler observes, "[To] 'have fellowship' with one another and with Christ (1 Jn. 1:6f.) is to 'know' him (1 Jn. 2:3) and to 'abide' in him (v. 6)."[39] This fellowship's basis, then, is in the apostolic preaching of the historical Jesus as well as the readers' response of faith in the subject of that proclamation.

Second, the reality of this fellowship is shown in the readers' walking in the light as God is in the light (cf. 1 John 1:6–7). Loving one's brothers and sisters in Christ is, in turn, evidence of being in the light (cf. 1 John 2:9–11; it is the equivalent of knowing God [cf. 1 John 4:8; also 4:16]) because God is love, and Christian love originates from God (1 John 4:7–8). This fellowship, then, is nothing less than a fellowship in the light and in love.

Third, the presence of Christian love is an evidence of having eternal life (1 John 3:14–15). Walking in the light and loving one another demonstrates the possession of eternal life. The possession of eternal life is, in turn, predicated on confessing that the Son of God is Jesus and continued abiding in that apostolic confession (1 John 2:22–25). By this believing confession of Jesus as the Christ, one has the Son and therefore has eternal life (1 John 5:12–13). In summary, faith in the incarnate Son of God, Jesus the Christ, transfers one from the realm of death to life, from darkness to light, and this life that one now possesses through faith makes its presence known by means of the love that a Christian has for his fellow Christians. Fellowship with the Father and his Son, then, is essentially the same thing as having eternal life. Still, what is the precise nature of this "fellowship"?

4. The Nature of This Common Fellowship Clarified (1:3b)

And our fellowship is with the Father and with his Son, Jesus Christ.

1:3b While it is faith in the apostolic proclamation concerning Jesus that brings one into Christian fellowship, if the sense of "fellowship" is common participation in something, then that something in this context would appear to be eternal life. "Our fellowship is with the Father and with his Son" (v. 3b), and that which is shared is "the eternal life which was with the Father and has appeared to us" (v. 2) in the person of the Son. The immediate context is eternal life.[40]

This fellowship is dependent on one's reception of life, which is, in turn, dependent on one's believing reception of the Word of life, Jesus as the incarnate Son of God. "Fellowship" further denotes the "oneness in com-

---

[39] J. Eichler, "ἔχω," in *NIDNTT,* 1:638.

[40] John could easily have just said "we have eternal life." His use of the word "fellowship" probably adds some level of richness to his theological understanding of the nature of this life.

munity" with other believers, with the Father, and with his Son that results from faith in this Son. Such fellowship for John is, in fact, inseparable from having eternal life: to have eternal life is to have fellowship with the apostolic witnesses who have testified concerning the Word of life. Fellowship with these witnesses is, in turn, nothing less than[41] fellowship "with the Father and with his Son, Jesus the Christ."[42] John's purpose statements in 1 John 1:3 and in 1 John 5:13[43] are, thus, practical equivalents: John proclaims Jesus as the Christ, the incarnate Son of God, to assure them in their faith and encourage them to persevere (cf. 1 John 5:21). Failure to persevere in this faith is, by implication, to exclude oneself from the apostolic fellowship, fellowship with God the Father and with his Son, and eternal life.[44]

5. The Purpose of Writing Announced (1:4)

4We write this to make our joy complete.

1:4   Though some uncertainty exists about the precise reading of this verse, "our[45] joy" would seem to be the correct reading. One could have expected John to say that his purpose in writing was to achieve his readers' joy rather than his own joy. It is granted that he is writing for himself and the rest of the apostolic witnesses. Still, does his statement not smack of selfishness? Such a conclusion is overly hasty and unwarranted. Even if "our joy" referred exclusively to John's and the apostolic witnesses' joy,

---

[41] The Gk. has a καί ... δέ construction where the first "and" connects the clause to the preceding verses while the second "indeed" emphasizes the noun clause, "our fellowship" (cf. Brown, *Epistles of John,* 171). Use of the rare possessive adjective form ἡμετερα ("our") instead of the expected possessive pronoun ἡμῶν also confirms this emphasis on "our fellowship." John is categorically identifying the apostolic fellowship as the fellowship with the Father and with his Son.

[42] Some argue that the coordination of "with the Father and with the Son" "implies sameness of essence" (see Westcott, *Epistles of St. John,* 12) or that "Jesus is regarded as one (in being and function) with the Father" (see Smalley, *1, 2, 3 John,* 13). While we would certainly affirm the truth of these assertions, it may also be the case that the implication we should draw from the coordination and repetition of μετά ("with") (instead of uniting both nouns under one preposition and one article) is that John is distinguishing the Father and the Son as distinct Persons (cf. Brown, *Epistles of John,* 171). While the Son is one in essence with the Father (being God, cf. John 1:1 and 1 John 5:20), he is not identical in every respect with the Father. This verse provides one of the bases for the doctrine of the Trinity.

[43] Note also 2:1,26.

[44] For a similar conclusion, see Marshall, *Epistles of John,* 105.

[45] The majority of witnesses actually read "your" (ὑμῶν) instead of "our" (ἡμῶν) joy (see the textual apparatus of the UBS 4th ed. Gk. text and *TCGNT,* 639). But the earliest and best witnesses read "our." Moreover, since copyists probably expected "your" as well (and perhaps recalling "that your joy may be fulfilled" in John 16:24), it is likely that they either intentionally or unintentionally "corrected" the text from "our" to "your" joy.

their joy would be akin to that of a loving pastor who longs for the perseverance (in faith) and continuing fellowship of the people for whom he is responsible.[46] This understanding is supported by John's expression in 3 John 4: "I have no greater joy than to hear that my children are walking in the truth" (also 2 John 4 and 3 John 3). The context in 1 John 1:1–4, however, points beyond this exclusive joy.

The message rather than the messenger is highlighted in the main clause: "these things[47] ["this," NIV] we write."[48] This emphasis is one clue that we should not take the purpose of John's writing to be his joy alone. Moreover, the parallel structure of 1:3a and 1:4, both with a purpose clause introduced by "that" *(hina),* suggests that what is being proclaimed (v. 3a) and written (v. 4) is the same message.[49] Both what John and the apostolic witness had proclaimed to his original readers in the past and his continuing proclamation to them[50] are the same message ("these things")[51] that he was pro-

---

[46] Cf. Marshall, *Epistles of John,* 105; Schnackenburg, *The Johannine Epistles,* 62–63; Hiebert, "1 John 1:1–4," 210.

[47] It is disputed whether "these things" (ταῦτα) refers to what precedes (1 John 1:1–3; Hiebert, "1 John 1:1–4," 209), what follows (1 John 1:4–5:21; e.g., Schnackenburg, *The Johannine Epistles,* 62, n. 43), the entire letter (as a complete concept in the writer's mind, e.g., Brooke, *The Johannine Epistles,* 9; Westcott, *Epistles of St. John,* 13), or 1:4–5:13 (with two purpose statements bracketing one another, one pointing ahead, the other pointing back; e.g., Brown, *Epistles of John,* 173).

[48] Instead of ἡμεῖς, "we," the majority of witnesses have ὑμῖν, "to you" (see the textual apparatus of the UBS 4th ed. Gk. text and *TCGNT,* 639). "We," however, is supported by the earliest and best witnesses. The NIV follows this evidence. The "we" could be seen as redundant because the Gk. verb includes it implicitly (i.e., the text reads "we write" with or without the pronoun "we"), whereas "to you" is what the reader would have expected (indeed, the idea is implicit: the proclamation "to you" in v. 3 is done through John's writing). Most likely, scribes intentionally or unintentionally "corrected" the original reading of "we." While the redundant pronoun "we" could be emphatic (e.g., Brown, *Epistles of John,* 172; Smalley, *1, 2, 3 John,* 14), its position at the end of the main clause (ταῦτα γράφομεν ἡμεῖς) more probably draws attention away from "we" (on word order and clause structure, see Porter, *Idioms,* 286–97, esp. 295–97). The message rather than the messenger is underscored.

[49] Cf. J. R. W. Stott, *The Epistles of John,* TNTC (Leiscester: InterVarsity Press, 1964), 65. This interpretation is strengthened by "to you" present in v. 3a but implied in v. 4. The same audience is in view in both the proclamation and the writing.

[50] This judgment on the force of the imperfective aspect of the present tense, "proclaim," is derived from the context of the epistle: The original readers were believers (e.g., 5:13) and had presumably been converted from hearing John or another apostolic witness or had received the apostolic witness through others (1:5 suggests that the apostolic witness has not changed—which we heard from him [Jesus] and declare to you).

[51] Note also that while the singular demonstrative pronoun is used regularly to refer to either an antecedent or a postcedent, "the plural is almost exclusively shut up to retrospective uses" (Wallace, *Greek Grammar,* 333). Wallace produces the lone exception of 3 John 4, which has a "that" [ἵνα] signaling the postcedent). John's usage in 1 John adds even greater weight to seeing "these things" as referring to what precedes (cf. 1 John 2:1; 2:26; 5:13).

claiming to them in the process of writing[52] this epistle. Since the purpose of the proclamation was that his readers may have fellowship with him and the apostolic witnesses, and since this oneness in community is presumably mutual, the joy is likely mutual as well: your joy as well as ours.[53]

Moreover, the next occurrence of a "we" subject in a main clause (1:6)[54] and almost every "we" in the rest of the epistle are inclusive.[55] After marking out the unique role of the apostolic eyewitnesses through the exclusive "we" in 1:1–4a and naming their purpose as mutual fellowship and joy between them and subsequent believers, the focus on the message over the messenger in 1:4b facilitates a transition to an emphasis on the message in the remainder of the letter (1:5–5:21). The exclusive "we" disappears, except as a bridge establishing that the message in 1:5–5:21 comes from these eyewitnesses (1:5; 4:6). Since these eyewitnesses and subsequent believers are one in unity by virtue of faith in the same incarnate Christ, John can include himself with his readers in expounding the implication of the message concerning the person and teaching of Jesus. This common fellowship accounts for the inclusive "we's" in the rest of the epistle.[56]

What, then, is the nature of this "joy" *(chara)* to which John refers? Remarkable parallels in wording almost certainly point to Jesus' words in John 15:11[57] and 16:24.[58] In those contexts joy is the result of abiding in

---

[52] Repeat of the verb "write" (1 John 2:1,7,8,12,13,14,21,26; 5:13) seems to be a clear signal that he was in the process of writing and proclaiming this message. Since the rest of the epistle expands upon the content of this message introduced in 1:1–3, the message to which "these things" refers actually encompasses the message of the entire epistle. But to say that "these things" refers to the message of the entire epistle confuses the distinction between grammatical referent and the external, objective state of the referent. In other words, "these things" refers only to the eyewitness testimony to the incarnate Son of God mentioned in 1:1–3, even though we do learn more about the content of this testimony in the rest of the epistle.

[53] Cf. 2 John 12, which has the exact wording, except that the order of the two components (ἡ πεπληρωμένη) is reversed in 2 John 12.

[54] The "we" in "which we heard ... and announce" in 1:5 is exclusive but is in a relative clause that picks up the exclusive eyewitness sense from 1:1–4.

[55] Besides the one in the relative clause in 1:5, there are only four other exceptions. Three are found in 4:6, where the apostolic eyewitnesses are placed in direct contrast with false prophets (4:1ff.). The other one is in 4:14.

[56] Though he wrongly reads the inclusive "we" back into 1:1–4, Dodd rightly sees John's use of the inclusive "we" in 1:5–5:21 as founded upon the nature of the church as a fellowship in a common faith and bond of love (*Johannine Epistles,* 9–10).

[57] Ταῦτα λελάληκα ὑμῖν ἵνα ἡ χαρὰ ἡ ἐμὴ ἐν ὑμῖν ᾖ καὶ ἡ χαρὰ ὑμῶν πληρωθῇ ("these things I have spoken to you in order that my joy may be in you and that your joy may be fulfilled").

[58] ἕως ἄρτι οὐκ ᾐτήσατε οὐδὲν ἐν τῷ ὀνόματί μου αἰτεῖτε καὶ λήμψεσθε, ἵνα ἡ χαρὰ ὑμῶν ᾖ πεπληρωμένη ("until now you have asked nothing in my name; ask and you will receive in order that your joy may be fulfilled"). Cp. 1 John 1:4: καὶ ταῦτα γράφομεν ἡμεῖς, ἵνα ἡ χαρὰ ἡμῶν ᾖ πεπληρωμένη ("And these things I write to you in order that our joy may be fulfilled"). Cf. Dodd, *Johannine Epistles,* 9; Smalley, *1, 2, 3 John,* 14. The difference in pronouns reflects the different addressees: Jesus spoke directly to the apostles in the Gospel of John (hence "your joy"), and the apostolic witnesses addressed subsequent hearers and readers in 1 John (hence "our [i.e., your and our] joy" in fellowship through faith in Jesus).

Christ (John 15:4), asking and receiving in prayer (John 15:7b; 16:24), and resultant fruit bearing (John 15:8).[59] This fruit bearing is defined in terms of keeping Christ's commandments, defined as loving one another just as Christ loved them (climaxing in laying down his life for them; John 15:10,12–13). This joy is nothing less than the joy that comes from abiding in Christ's love, just as Christ's joy came from abiding in the Father's love (John 15:9–11). Returning to the context of 1 John 1:1–4, it is the joy that results from fellowship with the apostolic witnesses and with the Father and with the Son.[60] Consequently, this fulfillment[61] of joy is enjoyed during our earthly sojourn through faith in Christ, even though the full experience of it must await Christ's return and the consummation of all things.[62] In effect, John's purpose to achieve the fulfillment of his and his readers' joy (v. 4) is one and the same as his purpose to keep his readers' in fellowship with him and the other apostolic eyewitnesses (v. 3).

In John's theology it is impossible to take away this joy from the true believer (cf. John 16:22; also 17:12–13). Those who depart from the visible fellowship of the church never were part of the fellowship, that is, they never believed in Christ Jesus and never had eternal life (1 John 2:19; cf. John 6:60–71[63]). Yet John's theology of perseverance is precisely a theology of perseverance in faith in Christ Jesus[64] and persevering by Christ Jesus (John 10:27–30). Believers are sustained in their faith by a fresh proclamation of Christ Jesus and his teachings, applied [in this context] in specific ways to combat the Christological heresy that threatened the health and life of the church by denying that the Christ is Jesus, the incarnate Son of God.

---

[59] Cf. D. A. Carson, *The Gospel According to John* (Leicester: InterVarsity Press, 1991), 546.

[60] Smalley notes that "fullness of joy" is "a familiar idea in the Johannine literature (cf. John 3:29; 4:36; 15:11; 16:24; 17:13; see also 2 John 12), where it is regularly associated with the notion of fellowship with God or with other believers" (*1, 2, 3 John,* 15). This fellowship is maintained by keeping God's commandments (cf. "abides in him" in 1 John 3:24), which is defined in 1 John 3:23: "And this is his commandment, that we believe in the name of his Son Jesus Christ, and love one another, just as he commanded us."

[61] The passive verb, "fulfilled" or "be filled," underlies "the fact that it is God who completes this joy" (R. Schippers, "πληρόω," *NIDNTT,* 1:741).

[62] Though it is tempting to read v. 4 as referring to perfected joy in eternity, thus bringing us from eternity (v. 1) to eternity (v. 4) (see Smalley, *1, 2, 3 John,* 15), it is best to see this joy as fulfilled in the present reality of fellowship with the Father, his Son, and other believers (cf. John 16:22ff.; so Schnackenburg, *The Johannine Epistles,* 63; see also E. Beyreuther and G. Finkenrath, "χαίρω," in *NIDNTT,* 1:359).

[63] See Carson, *John,* 300–304.

[64] John's prophetic messages in Rev 2:1–3:22 give a broader glimpse of this theology of perseverance from different angles. For a concise explanation of the logical flow of these prophetic messages, see G. K. Beale, *The Book of Revelation,* NIGTC (Grand Rapids: Eerdmans, 1999), 224–27. Also note the excellent treatment on perseverance by T. R. Schreiner, "Perseverance and Assurance: A Survey and a Proposal," *SBJT,* vol. 2, no. 1 (1998): 32–62.

─────────── **I. GOD IS LIGHT (1:5–3:10)** ───────────

First John 1:5 is the immediate basis for 1:6–2:2, though it is the foundational basis for 1:6–3:10. Six conditional clauses weave 1:6–2:2 into a unit. The three "if we say" statements (1:6,8,10) are prominent. The word "sin" occurs five times explicitly, and two times the idea is implicitly conveyed by the word "darkness." The believing community must have a correct view of sin. This correct understanding comes by rightly grasping the truth concerning God's nature and the work of Christ. We should live in fellowship with God who has fullness of life in himself and is moved to forgive us of our sins on the basis of the advocacy and atonement of Jesus Christ the righteous one.

1. Walk in the Light (1:5–2:2)

(1) God Is Light (1:5–7)

⁵This is the message we have heard from him and declare to you: God is light; in him there is no darkness at all. ⁶If we claim to have fellowship with him yet walk in the darkness, we lie and do not live by the truth. ⁷But if we walk in the light, as he is in the light, we have fellowship with one another, and the blood of Jesus, his Son, purifies us from all sin.

1:5–7 This striking affirmation of God's nature catches one by surprise. John switches his attention to God after having announced that he is writing to his audience concerning the incarnate Son of God, the Word of life, so that they may persevere in their fellowship and joy with the apostolic eyewitnesses.[65] What precisely does John mean by the metaphors "light" and "darkness"?

Verse 6 would seem to provide the key that reveals the connection between the prologue (1:1–4) and these verses. John affirms that God is light and has no darkness in him at all in order to rule out claims to fellowship with him by those walking in the darkness. In short, John introduces a statement concerning God's nature[66] to define the qualifications necessary

---

[65] Cf. the question asked by Westcott, *Epistles of St. John,* 14.

[66] In Gk. the normal word order of demonstrative pronoun and verb is reversed, e.g., ἔστιν αὕτη instead of αὕτη ἐστιν. It could be a meaningless variation (so Brown, *Epistles of John,* 193). Since this is the only occurrence, it seems likely Westcott is right in saying that it signals "unusual emphasis" on "the absoluteness, the permanence, of the message" (*Epistles of St. John,* 15). The fact that this predication of this message (ἐστίν, "is") comes fresh on the heels of the predication of eternal existence to the One who brought the message (ἦν, "was" from the beginning, 1:1; and the eternal life which ἦν, "was," with the Father, 1:2) adds plausibility to this suggestion.

for fellowship with God (see the definition of fellowship in 1:3b). The fact that the ultimate purpose of John's proclamation and writing is that his audience may participate in the Christian (apostolic) fellowship (and joy) with the Father and with his Son (1:1–4) obliged him to set forth the conditions of this fellowship.[67] This functional purpose did not compel John to fabricate an affirmation about God, however. John explicitly states that he received this message from Jesus himself[68] and announces it to his readers as an authorized messenger.[69]

What, then, do the metaphors "light" and (absence of) "darkness" tell us about God's nature? Many scholars hold that the primary, if not exclusive sense, is ethical.[70] God is morally good is the idea. Marshall's paraphrase of this verse is representative of this view: "God is good, and evil can have no place beside [in] him."[71] Others maintain that both notions of absolute truth (linked with illumination/revelation) and absolute righteousness (linked with God's holiness) are present.[72] Since John states that he heard this message *(angelia)*[73] from Jesus, a helpful place for us to search for more details on this message is in the Gospel written by him.[74] Thus it is necessary to discern how John uses "light" in his Gospel as well as how "light" is used in the context of 1 John.

---

[67] Cf. Westcott, *Epistles of St. John,* 14; Marshall, *Epistles of John,* 108.

[68] ἀπ᾽ αὐτοῦ, lit. "from him," but undoubtedly a reference to Jesus Christ. As Marshall notes, "the reference to hearing and the fact that the content of the message is about God both suggest that Jesus is the author of the message (cf. Jn. 1:18; 3:32)" (*Epistles of John,* 108, n. 1). Furthermore, Jesus Christ is the nearest third-person antecedent (v. 3b). Brown observes that Brooke is "virtually alone among modern commentators in defending a reference to God" (*Epistles of John,* 11).

[69] The word "declare" (ἀναγγέλλω) could simply mean "to tell," but since 1:5 follows 1:1–4 (where eyewitness testimony to the proclamation of Jesus is emphasized), John's announcement is that of an authorized messenger. The fact that John traces this message back to Jesus, whom he had heard in person, strengthens and supports this interpretation.

[70] E.g., Marshall, *Epistles of John,* 109; Schnackenburg, *The Johannine Epistles,* 74; Dodd, *Johannine Epistles,* 19–20; E. R. Achtemeier, "Jesus Christ, the Light of the World: The Biblical Understanding of Light and Darkness," *Int* 17 (1963): 448.

[71] Marshall, *Epistles of John,* 109.

[72] E.g., Christie, "An Interpretive Study of 1 John 1:9," 29, who follows Stott, *Epistles of John,* 70–72; Smalley, *1, 2, 3 John,* 20; Hiebert, "1 John 1:1–4," 331.

[73] ἀγγελία occurs only twice in the NT (here in 1:5 and in 3:11). We should interpret this word to mean simply "message," even though this "news" or "message" may be good news in certain contexts. E.g., Brown points to Prov 12:25 and 25:5 as proof that ἀγγελία can mean "good news" (*Epistles of John,* 193). But in those contexts "news" is modified by the adjective "good" (ἀγγελία ἀγαθή), whereas we have no parallel contextual modifiers in 1 John 1:5. Isa 28:9 is also very doubtful in context (see J. N. Oswalt, *The Book of Isaiah Chapters 1–39,* NICOT [Grand Rapids: Eerdmans, 1986], 511). Kruse (*Letters of John,* 62, n. 13) notes that the author never uses the word *evangelion,* "which is commonly used elsewhere in the NT for the gospel message."

[74] In my opinion the defense of John's common authorship of the Gospel and epistle in Westcott (*Epistles of St. John,* xxx–xxxii) has yet to be refuted.

Excursus: "Light" in the Gospel of John

The first occurrence of the metaphor "light" in John appears in 1:4: "In him [the Word] was life and that life was the light of men."[75] "Light" and "life" in this verse relate to the self-existing life of the Word [Logos] dispensed at creation, whereas the rest of the occurrences in John relate to salvation.[76] Another consideration is that "the life" here is equated with[77] "the light of human beings." The question that naturally surfaces is why John introduces the metaphor "light" at this point. It would be easy to understand John to say that the Word's life was the life of human beings. Why did he not simply say, "That life was the life[78] of human beings?" This is no mere academic question. Besides the need to understand John 1:4 itself, we need to understand how John uses "light" because his Gospel develops an elaborate theology around the metaphor of light. This usage in the Gospel, in turn, will likely shed light on John's usage in 1 John.

That light represents the source of life would seem to fit best with the biblical data.[79] John identifies the self-existing life of the Word as the light of human beings (i.e., the Word's life = human beings' light). Light, in turn, represents the source of human beings' life: "In the Word was life, and that life [which is in the Word] is the light [i.e., the source of life][80] of human beings." John 1:3 would

---

[75] There is debate over division of clauses in John 1:3–4, but the NIV rendering, "Through him all things were made; without him nothing was made that has been made. In him was life, and that life was the light of men," is preferable over the NEB: "No single thing was created without him. All that came to be was alive with his life, and that life was the light of men" (see Carson, *John*, 137–38).

[76] Carson, *John*, 119. The context of creation in 1:1–5 makes it unlikely that "that life" is eternal life here (contra G. F. Shirbroun, "Life," in *Dictionary of Jesus and the Gospels* [Downers Grove: InterVarsity Press, 1992], 469; and Brown, *John I–XII*, 7).

[77] The Gk. construction is ἡ ζωὴ ἦν τὸ φῶς τῶν ἀνθρώπων. Since both nouns are definite (as seen from the article), it is a convertible proposition (i.e., interchangeable). The light is the light of human beings, and the light of human beings is the light. On the convertible proposition, see Wallace, *Greek Grammar*, 41–42, 45.

[78] If John had said "that life was the life of human beings," we could have, at least theoretically, an interchangeable proposition: The Word's *(Logos)* self-existing life is the life of human beings; the life of human beings is the Word's *(Logos)* self-existing life. The resulting theological proposition could be understood to affirm the self-existence and, hence, the divinity of human beings. John obviously would not express such a notion.

[79] C. Baylis's thesis is that light = life ("The Meaning of Walking 'in the Darkness' (1 John 1:6)," *BSac* 149 [1992]: 214–22). Although Baylis's conclusion is unsatisfactory, his work is important and worthy of careful consideration.

[80] This interpretation fits one of the ways "light" imagery is used: "Light in the Bible is first of all physical, the very basis of life on the earth. This primacy of light to life itself is signaled in the Bible by the fact that God's creation of light is the first recorded event: And God said, 'Let there be light'; and there was light. And God saw that the light was good' (Gen 1:3–4, RSV)" ("Light" in *Dictionary of Biblical Imagery* [Downers Grove: InterVarsity Press, 1998], 509). In Job light is associated with life, and darkness is associated with nonbeing or death (ibid., 510–11). Cf. Achtemeier: God's word in the Old Testament does "more than impart understanding. It gives life and salvation … (Mic. 7:8; Isa. 9:2; 42:16; 51:4; 58:8; 60:1; Ezra 9:8)" ("Jesus Christ, the Light of the World," 441). Moreover, God's giving of this light is "synonymous with the gift of life (Ps. 36:9; 56:13; Job 33:28–30)." In addition, the psalmist portrays God's deliverance thus, "'Yea, thou dost light my lamp; the LORD my God lightens my darkness' (Ps. 18:28)." It would seem that other passages in both the OT and NT need to be read similarly. The most important is perhaps Ps 36:9, "For with you is the fountain of life; in your light we see light." This verse comes in the context of a psalm praising God's lovingkindness in creating and sustaining both human beings and animals. If the two parts of this verse are synonymous (which is likely), it would mean that in God's revealing of life (God being the Source [=fountain] of life), human beings have derived life.

essentially be emphasizing the agency of the Word in the creation of all that exists, and 1:4 would be insisting that the Word, who is life in himself, is the Source of all derived human life (cf. Col 1:16–17). Understood in the context of creation, "the light shines in the darkness and the darkness did not overcome[81] it" (John 1:5) would refer to light (the source of life from the Source of life) giving derived life in creation: "And God *said,* 'Let there be light'" (Gen 1:3, NIV, emphasis author's). Since the Word was with God in the beginning (John 1:1)[82] and shares the same essence with God (John 1:2),[83] he shares the same self-existing life as the Father. The Word's self-existing life is, in turn, the light (i.e., the source of life) of human beings.[84] In effect, God's command in Gen 1:3 to reveal light was a command, given power by the self-existing life of his Word, to create derived creaturely life (with the self-existing life of his Word as the source of this creaturely life). Note the care with which John frames his theological proposition: Human beings derive their life from the self-existing life of the Word, yet the life of human beings is derived and not identical to the self-existing life of the Godhead.

If the above interpretation is correct, the question now is whether John uses this metaphor in the exactly same way throughout the rest of his writings. The answer is apparently yes and no. In John 1:7–8 "the light" now appears to refer to Jesus, the incarnate Word, concerning whom John the Baptist bears witness. Likewise, Jesus is clearly the referent of 1:9: "The true light, which gives light to every human being was coming into the world."[85] In other words, the external referent of the metaphor (the person or thing of which the metaphor says something) has changed. Yet the essential content of the metaphor, that is, what the metaphor is supposed to tell us about its referent, remains the same: Jesus is the light, that is, *the Source of life.*

Another issue is introduced by the adjective "true" *(aléthinos),* which is added to "the light." John 1:9 is one passage in John where "the notion of 'true' or 'genuine' shades off into 'ultimate,' because the contrast is not simply with what is false but with what is earlier and provisional or anticipatory in the history of God's gracious self-disclosure."[86] John's point is that the incarnate Word was *the* light, the *true* light, the Source of genuine and ultimate life, that is, *the Source of eternal life.*[87] In other words, even the content of the metaphor "light" is

---

[81] For four alternative interpretations of this verb, see Brown, *John I–XII,* 8. John is describing the victory of the light over darkness (darkness did not overcome light [see Gen 1:3–4], even though "darkness was over the surface of the deep" [Gen 1:2] prior to God's Word commanding the revelation of light). Cf. Carson, 119, 138.

[82] ἐν ἀρχῇ, "in the beginning," probably alludes to the origin of creation in Gen 1:1 (which also begins with ἐν ἀρχῇ in the Gk. translation of the OT, the LXX). Cf. Carson, *John,* 113–14.

[83] For a fine discussion of the grammar and theology in John 1:1, see Wallace, *Greek Grammar,* 266–69.

[84] Gen 1:3–4, and then 1:26–28 and 2:7 probably form the background to John's thinking in this relation.

[85] Adopting essentially the NIV rendering. See Carson, *John,* 121–22 for a defense of this rendering. See also Brown, *John I–XII,* 9.

[86] Carson, *John,* 122.

[87] Carson rightly says that the incarnation of the Word is "the genuine and ultimate self-disclosure of God to man" (ibid.). Further, it could be added that the content of that self-disclosure is nothing other than eternal life in him.

changed because we are now dealing with "the true light," that is, the true light is the source of the true life. Therefore John 1:9–11 refers to the incarnation (revelation)[88] of this Source of life ("who gives light" [*photiei;* in the sense of reveals eternal life] to all human beings," 1:9) and his rejection by the fallen[89] world of human beings (despite the fact that they have their existence through him, 1:10).[90] Yet as many as received[91] him (the true light, i.e., the Source of eternal life), he gave to them the power[92] to become children of God (1:12).

John 2:23–3:21 must also be examined in this development of John's theology of light. John's point here is that human beings are incapable of true faith in Jesus unless they are begotten from above[93] by the Father through the Spirit.[94] These human beings are [spiritually] dead to God, even though they are [physically] alive, and they are in need of new life, eternal life (hence the necessity of regeneration). In John 3:3 and 5, Jesus makes clear that regeneration from above is the prerequisite for seeing or entering the kingdom of God[95] (seeing "the kingdom of God" [*basileian tou theou*] is equivalent to having "eternal life"[96]). Jesus explains further in John 3:14–16 that his death and exaltation on the cross[97]

---

[88] The sense of revelation comes from ἦν ... ἐρχόμενον εἰς τὸν κόσμον, "was coming into the world."

[89] See Carson, *John,* 122–23 on this negative connotation of the term "the world" (ὁ κόσμος).

[90] John 1:11, "He came to his own," probably narrows down the specific revelational activity of Jesus to Israel (perhaps "his own home," as in 16:32; 19:27, "and his own people did not receive him"; cf. Carson, *John,* 124–25). See also Brown, *John I–XII,* 30. The implication of the conjunction of v. 10 with v. 11 is that Israel is part of the fallen world (as is clear from the rest of the Gospel, e.g., 1:29; 2:23–3:36; 8:21–47).

[91] John adds in 1:13 that "those who received him" are those who had been begotten by God (the relative pronoun οἵ that begins v. 13 is nominative plural and refers back to "as many as received him" in v. 12). This theme of the Father being the One who gives a people to Christ is found elsewhere in John 6:36,39,44,65; 10:26–29; 17:2–3,6,9,24; 18:9. Cf. Carson's commentary on these verses. For a fine exposition of the meaning of John 6:22–65, see B. A. Ware, "The Place of Effectual Calling and Grace in a Calvinist Soteriology," in *The Grace of God, the Bondage of the Will,* ed. T. R. Schreiner and B. A. Ware (Grand Rapids: Baker, 1995), 2:348–56.

[92] The word ἐξουσία could have the sense of "authority" or "power." Since sonship is by means of divine begetting, the notion of "power" rather than a legal sense of "authority" seems more likely (cf. Brown, *Epistles of John,* 10–11).

[93] While the verb γεννάω can mean either "to be born" (by a mother) or "to be begotten" (by a father), passages in John like John 1:12 and 1 John 3:9 indicate that John uses this verb to mean "beget" in relation to regeneration (cf. Brown, *John I–XII,* 130). At the same time, the adverb ἄνωθεν could mean "again" or "from above." The context of regeneration by the Father (1:13) and the Spirit (3:5) as well as John's other uses of ἄνωθεν to mean "from above" (3:31; 19:11,23) indicate that "from above" is more likely the meaning here (cf. Carson, *John,* 189).

[94] For a fine exposition of John 3:3–8, see J. Murray, "Regeneration," in *Collected Writings of John Murray* (Carlisle, Penn.: The Banner of Truth Trust, 1977), 2:174–88.

[95] See ibid., 2:174–79.

[96] The occasional interchange of "the kingdom of God" and "eternal life" in the Synoptic Gospels (e.g., Mark 9:43–47 par.; 10:17–30 par.; Matt 25:31–46) demonstrates that these two terms refer to the same reality. See C. C. Caragounis, "Kingdom of God/Heaven," in *Dictionary of Jesus and the Gospels,* 429. Cf. Carson, *John,* 188.

[97] See Carson, *John,* 201 on "lifted up" in 3:15.

(which is the ultimate expression of the amazing quality of God's love for the fallen world of human beings) was necessary in order that everyone who believes in him should have eternal life. Those who believe in Jesus are saved (i.e., have eternal life), and those who do not believe in Jesus are already judged (3:17–18). The nature of this judgment is made clear by 3:19: "This is the judgment: the light has come into the world and yet human beings loved the darkness rather than the light because their works were evil" (author's translation). In other words, Jesus, the Light, the Source of eternal life, has been revealed to fallen human beings, and yet they preferred death to the eternal life Jesus revealed[98] because they loved darkness and, as a result, were evildoers.[99] These evildoers hate the Source of life and will not go to him for life lest they are exposed and convicted[100] as evildoers (3:20). Those who practice the truth, however, go to the Source of eternal life, in order that God's work in them (cf. John 6:28–29) should be revealed (3:21). Those who do not believe in Jesus are already judged, not only because they sin, but because they are sinners, that is, they are dead to God.[101] In short, the imagery of death and the necessity of new life in the Nicodemus story of 3:1–15 and the contrast of "the light" and "the darkness" in the extended comment in 3:16–21 have the same reference points: lack of eternal

---

[98] I extend the sense of "the light" here to the eternal life revealed by Jesus, rather than simply the Source of life, for two reasons. First, the sense of revelation is implicit in "the light [the Source of eternal life] had come into the world." The coming of the Source of life reveals life. Second, "the light" is contrasted with "the darkness," yielding a contrast of the presence or absence of light. The presence of light (which is the Source of life) means the presence of life, while the absence of light means the absence of life (i.e., death).

[99] "The works" (τὰ ἔργά) of a person reveal the nature and origin of a person. See e.g., John 8:34; 37–47. Cf. the theme that Jesus' works reveal his identity and origin from God (see A. J. Köstenberger, *The Missions of Jesus and the Disciples according to the Fourth Gospel* [Grand Rapids: Eerdmans, 1998], 72–73). Contrary to Baylis's contention, the view that darkness = sin would not have a difficulty with 3:19 because the meaning would then be "human beings loved sin ... for they were sinners" ("The Meaning of Walking 'in the Darkness' [1 John 1:6]," 216). My contention, instead, is that spiritual death, i.e., lack of eternal life due to rejection of the revelation of eternal life in Jesus, is the actual referent of darkness. This rejection of Jesus is sin. Moreover, sinners carry out all kinds of sin because they are in this state of death. In other words, sin is inseparably related to darkness, but darkness itself refers to the state of spiritual death.

[100] Taking ἐλέγχω as meaning "to reveal and convict of sin" (see H. G. Link, " ἐλέγχω," *NIDNTT,* 2:141).

[101] If the above understanding is correct, the conception in John 3:19–21 is similar to Paul's conception in Eph 2:1–10: The Ephesian Christians are described as "dead in [the sphere of] their trespasses and sins" while they were still part of the world, prior to their conversion; but God showed mercy to them, giving them the gift of salvation (including faith), in order that they may walk in the good works prepared beforehand by God. For this imagery of "death" in the realm of sins, see also Col 2:13; Rev 3:1; and esp. John 5:24–25. As A. T. Lincoln observes, "[Outside] the Pauline corpus the greatest similarity to the usage in Eph 2:1,5 is found in the Johannine literature where there is a strong realized eschatology of life and death (cf. John 5:24,25; 1 John 3:14)" (*Ephesians,* WBC [Dallas: Word, 1990], 93). This usage probably goes back to Gen 2:17; 3:3–4,22–24. As G. J. Wenham points out in his comment on Gen 3:4–5, Adam and Eve were dead already when they were expelled from the Garden of Eden, away from the presence of God. Likewise, lepers expelled from the camp of the Israelites entered into the realm of death and were, thus, instructed to behave like mourners (Lev 13:45) (see further *Genesis 1–15,* WBC [Waco: Word, 1987], 74–75, also 85–86).

life, the necessity of receiving eternal life, that faith in Jesus, the Source of eternal life, is the way to receive eternal life, and that both the revealing of this eternal life (in Jesus) and the actual reception of this eternal life are a gift from God.[102]

John 8:12 grants further confirmation for the above analysis of the import of "light." This verse comes on the heels of 7:37–39,[103] where Jesus had promised that those who believe in him would receive the Holy Spirit. The Spirit is likened to "streams of living water [that] will flow from within him (the one who believes in Jesus)."[104] Since Jesus is the Source of eternal life and the Source of the Holy Spirit (cf. 1:32–34; also chaps. 14–16), it is Jesus who gives the Spirit (who will be given on the basis of Jesus' death and exaltation, 7:40), who will be an internal Source of eternal life[105] to the believer, keeping the believer nourished by the ultimate Source of life, Jesus Christ (cf. the vine imagery [the vine = the source of the branches' life] in chap. 15). In response to division over his words and unbelief, Jesus reiterates and develops his point from 7:37–39 using different imagery in 8:12ff. His point is the following: "Since I am the light of the world, whoever follows me will never walk in darkness, but will have the light of life." When we explain the imagery, the result is thus: "Since Jesus is the Source of eternal life to human beings, whoever believes in him will not live in spiritual death but will live in the eternal life he reveals."[106] Other passages using the metaphor "light" should be interpreted similarly.[107]

---

[102] John 3:22–36 makes the same basic points, with John the Baptist adding his testimony. This section (the climax to chap. 3) ends with, "Whoever believes in the Son has eternal life, but whoever disobeys [rejects] the Son will not see life (cf. 'seeing' the kingdom, 3:3)." Cf. Carson, *John*, 214.

[103] 7:40–52 indicates the reaction to Jesus' claim. Then 8:12ff. is Jesus' response (note the πάλιν, "again"; so also Carson, *John*, 337). The story of the woman caught in adultery in 7:51–8:11 most likely was not originally part of the Gospel of John. For a good explanation of why this narrative is a later insertion, see Carson, John, 333.

[104] Ibid., 328. Cf. 4:14. For the debate over the translation of this verse and a decisive demonstration of the correctness of this translation, see Carson, *John*, 323–28.

[105] The imagery here actually suggests continued nourishment of life toward a culmination in the final resurrection.

[106] "Walking" (περιπατέω) is a metaphorical way of saying "living." The contrast between darkness and light again requires an extension of the second occurrence of "the light" in this verse to the life that Jesus reveals, and not just Jesus as the Source of life (as in the first occurrence). The "light of life" is an objective (verbal) genitive, i.e., the light that brings life (cf. Carson, *John*, 338), which fits with taking light as signifying the source of life. The parallel expression "the bread of life" does not cast doubt on the objective (verbal) genitive interpretation, even though a verbal genitive requires the head noun ("the bread" here) to have an implicit verbal idea. Even though bread does not contain a verbal idea, when we remember that bread is merely a metaphor (i.e., that which is a source of life) the problem disappears.

[107] John 9:5; 11:9,10 use the analogy of physical light from the sun, which is the source of the ability to carry on the activities of life. Jesus' point in John 12:35–36,46 is that his hearers should live in the life he has revealed (i.e., believe in him as the Source of eternal life) while he is still with them, revealing eternal life. John 5:35 is slightly different because John's "light" is the light of "a burning and shining lamp" (ὁ λύχνος ὁ καιόμενος καὶ φαίνων). His light was a derivative source, testifying to Jesus, the true Light (in much the same way that a lamp pales in comparison with the sun but shares in and points to the infinitely greater light-giving qualities of the sun). The point here is that John the Baptist was a source of bright witness to Jesus (the life).

Excursus: "Light" in 1 John

In 1 John 1:5 we immediately notice two strange features in the usage of "light" in comparison to John's Gospel. First, the subject of the sentence is God, rather than Jesus. Second, the predicate noun is "light," rather than "the light." On the other hand, the familiar contrast between "light" and "darkness" occurs.

"God is light" means that God has the quality of being a Source of life. [108] Further, in emphasizing that in him "there is no darkness at all" (i.e., no lack of life),[109] John asserts that God is fullness of life itself (the ultimate Source of life).

John draws two sets of implications from this affirmation that God (as Jesus revealed him)[110] is fullness of life itself without even a trace of deficiency (of life). The next two uses of "light" appear in the first set, which consists of a contrasting pair of declarative statements. Since "light" occurs in contrast with "darkness" in terms of "walking," the nuance of "light" becomes walking in[111] "the fullness of life (revealed by Jesus, the Source of life)," and the nuance of "death" becomes walking in "the realm/state of death (without Jesus' revelation of life)." The negative declaration maintains that claims to fellowship with God are inconsistent with living in the state of death. The positive declaration asserts that only by living in the fullness of life (revealed in Christ), as God is fullness of life himself, will one have fellowship with God and the forgiveness of sins through the atoning death of Jesus his Son.

The three other occurrences of "light" in 1 John (2:8,9,11) all relate to Jesus. The message of 2:8 is that the fulfillment of the love commandment ("a new commandment," *entolēn kainēn*)[112] is now a reality[113] not only in Jesus but in John's Christian readers (cf. John 15:12–14). John writes to his readers this new commandment, which is now a reality in them because[114] "the darkness is passing and the true light is already shining" (1 John 2:8b, NIV).

---

[108] Light is a qualitative noun. John does not confuse God's and Jesus' roles, though both Persons of the Trinity have life in themselves (cf. John 5:26). Only Jesus is "the light," the Source of life that reveals life to human beings.

[109] Brown notes that the double negative "no darkness, none at all," highlights this negation (*Epistles of John,* 195). John's primary purpose is to rule out any darkness in God. His positive statement is subordinate to that purpose. Luther (*John,* 227) simply comments, " There is no darkness in him, not even the slightest."

[110] Perhaps with John 1:18; 14:6–7,9–11 in mind.

[111] I interpret the preposition ἐν as indicating the sphere or realm of light.

[112] The switch from the plural "commandments" in 2:3–4 to the singular "a new commandment" in 2:7–8 probably reflects John's viewpoint that all the commandments are "summed up in one" (Marshall, *Epistles of John,* 129). This usage parallels his use in his Gospel. The only other command in both the Epistle and the Gospel is to believe in Jesus and his words.

[113] See Brown, *Epistles of John,* 267 on the meaning of ἀληθὲς in this verse.

[114] While it is grammatically possible that the causal ὅτι clause offers the reason for the realization of the new commandment in his readers, the context favors taking it as offering the reason for John's writing. In other words, the theological truth stated in 2:9 grounds his assertions following in 2:9–11. Moreover, John usually gives either a purpose or reason for his writing (see esp. 1 John 2:12,13,14 [three times],21; cf. John 20:31; 1 John 1:4; 2:1; 5:13; 2 John 12). For the other options see Smalley, *1, 2, 3 John,* 57 and Brown, *Epistles of John,* 268.

Although Jesus is clearly involved, does "the true light"[115] refer to Jesus him-self or to "the light brought by Jesus"?[116] Since the only other occurrence of the exact term in John 1:9 refers to Jesus, it may do so in 1 John 2:8b as well. Yet one could argue that since "the true light" is said to be "already shining," that is, shin-ing from the past to the present,[117] the reference cannot be to Jesus directly but must be to the eternal life Jesus had revealed. In addition, "the true light" is con-trasted with "the darkness" so that the contrast is likely between the realm of death (cf. 2:16–17) and the self-manifesting activity of eternal life that Jesus has revealed. Furthermore, this reality grounds the realization of the love command-ment in John's readers (lit., "in you," *en humin*). The love commandment is being realized in his readers precisely because the eternal life that Jesus has revealed is operative in them.

The explication of 2:8 in 2:9–14 supports the understanding that "the true light" is the eternal life revealed by Jesus. In 2:9 John is asserting that those who claim to have eternal life while yet hating Christians[118] are really still in the state of spiritual death. On the other hand, those who love other Christians are living in the eternal life that Jesus has revealed, and there is nothing in them to make them stumble (2:10).[119] John underscores the state of the one who hates Chris-tians in 2:11: he is in a state of death, he lives in the state of death, and he does not even realize his own spiritual deadness because the state of death has taken away his ability to see his real condition. On the other hand, John declares that the reason he writes to his original readers is that the eternal life revealed in Jesus is truly operative in them (2:12–14).

In summary, John uses "light" and even "the true light" to refer to a different referent in 1 John than in his Gospel. Yet the essential content conveyed by "light" remains the same: inherently, light is a source of life; when light is revealed, it reveals life. God is fullness of life himself (1:5), and therefore those who would have fellowship with him must have the fullness of life themselves.

---

[115] τὸ φῶς τὸ ἀληθινὸν. Note again the relevant discussion on John 1:9 in the Excursus on "Light" in John for the significance of the addition of the adjective "true." See also in Kruse the note on "Light and Darkness" (*Letters of John*, 65–66) and the note on "Truth" (pp. 67–68).

[116] E.g., Schnackenburg, *The Johannine Epistles,* 106; Marshall, *Epistles of John,* 130; Smal-ley, *1, 2, 3 John*, 58.

[117] E.g., Schnackenburg, *The Johannine Epistles,* 106, followed by Marshall, *Epistles of John,* 130, n. 34. Since this causal clause is related to 2:8a, which is referring to the present time ("which is true in him and in you"), John is, indeed, grounding his writing in the present, ongoing reality that the darkness is passing away and the true light is already shining. Therefore there can be no dispute as to the time frame involved.

[118] The Gk. reads ὁ λέγων ἐν τῷ φωτὶ εἶναὶ καὶ τὸν ἀδελφὸν αὐτοῦ μισῶν, "the one who says he is in the light and yet hates his brother." "His brother" refers to brothers and sisters in Christ, i.e., other Christians. The use of this term, however, does not imply that the one making this false claim is himself a Christian. John is using this terminology to show the incongruity of the claim (cf. 1 John 5:1). For a unique counterposition advanced throughout his commentary see Z. Hodges, *The Epistles of John* (Irving, Tex.: Grace Evangelical Society, 1999).

[119] See Marshall, *Epistles of John,* 132 for a good explanation of the phrase "and there is noth-ing in him to make him stumble."

Since human beings are in a state of death, they may have fellowship with God only by faith in Jesus, who reveals himself as the Source of eternal life and gives that life to them. This eternal life revealed by Jesus has been revealed from the time of his incarnation even until the time of John's writing of this epistle (2:8b). Because of the reality and self-manifesting activity of this eternal life, John can declare that those who do not love other Christians do not have this eternal life, whereas those who love other Christians are living in this eternal life.

The apostolic witnesses declare (a message that they heard from Jesus himself) that God is light, fullness of life itself, and has no lack of life in him at all. While light could mean, and does in other contexts, what is good, true, holy, or pure, here it is the idea of life, eternal life, the life of God, that grows out of this metaphor. This message is the enduring apostolic message. John grounds the qualifications necessary for fellowship with God in the very nature of God as light having fullness of life in himself.

Having stated that God is light by his very nature and as a result has fullness of life in himself, John is able to deny the claims of fellowship with God to those who live in the darkness of death. In the context of this epistle, John must be aiming these statements against those who reject Jesus as the incarnate Son of God. These persons are, in reality, living in the state of death because eternal life is found only in this Jesus, the Jesus whose identity is the Son of God. John's purpose was to ensure that his readers not fall into the same sin as these heretics (see comment on 2:1). Therefore he uses the inclusive "we" to apply his statements to them.[120] It is a wise and effective rhetorical device at this early stage of the epistle.

At the same time, John's statements apply to all subsequent claims to knowing God apart from faith in the Jesus who is the subject of apostolic witness. The universal applicability of John's statements stems from his use of the "if ... then" formula to make universal statements that are true anytime and anywhere in 1:6–10.[121] We know that these "if ... then" clauses

---

[120] Why did John say "if we" when he could easily have said "whoever" (as in 2:5) or "if anyone" (as in 2:1b) or "the one who" (using a substantival participle; as in 2:4,6)? In light of 2:1a, John probably uses the inclusive "we" because his purpose was to apply these theological statements to his readers and himself. If John or any of his Christian readers were to fulfill these negative conditions in vv. 6,8,10, which for them would mean to deny Jesus Christ, they would suffer the inevitable effects described. The conditions are not stated as fulfilled, however, and John actually believes that genuine believers could never fulfill those conditions (e.g., 1 John 2:12–14,21,26–27; 5:4–5,12–13,18). These statements perform the function of prospective warnings. On such warnings see Schreiner, "Perseverance and Assurance," 52–58.

[121] First John 1:6,7,8,9, and 10 represent five third class conditional sentences in the Gk. The common denominator in all such sentences is futurity, i.e., the condition expressed in the protasis (the "if" clause), is contingent on any number of unfulfilled factors. John is neither saying that he or his readers have or have not, are likely to or are unlikely to say or do the things expressed in the "if" clauses. For the correction of the views expressed in older grammars (and followed by many commentaries) on the third class conditional sentence and the subjunctive mood, see J. L. Boyer, "Third and (Fourth) Class Conditions," *GTJ* 3 (1982): 163–75.

are universal theological maxims because they are founded upon the very nature of God (1:5). Since God's nature never changes, these theological maxims remain true for all time.

These "if ... then" clauses reason from the cause to the effect.[122] In v. 6 two suppositions are conjoined in the "if" clause as one cause, with two corresponding effects. The force of the entire construction is as follows: If we claim that we have fellowship with God and yet do not live in the eternal life revealed by Jesus (implicitly by faith in this Jesus), we are lying and not doing the truth (i.e., we are not obeying God's word).[123] The truth, in light of this context, is nothing other than the truth God has revealed in Jesus (1:8,10; cf. John 14:6).

After stating a negative theological maxim (aimed specifically against those who held to the Christological heresy John was addressing), John states its positive corollary in v. 7: It is those who live in the eternal life revealed in Jesus that have fellowship with God (and God with them) and are sinless in God's sight. The evidence of true mutual[124] fellowship with God is one's living in the fullness of life revealed by Jesus. While those

---

[122] There are basically three kinds of relationships between the "if" part (protasis) and the "then" part (apodosis) of all conditional sentences. The relationship can be cause and effect, evidence and inference, or equivalence. See further Wallace, *Greek Grammar*, 682–84. In 1 John 1:6 the effects of "lying" and "not doing the truth" are caused by the claim of fellowship with God and yet living in death.

[123] This interpretation of 1:5–10 differs in its primary focus from the view commonly found among other commentators. I am not convinced, however, that the views are mutually exclusive, and they may actually complement each other (e.g., with the ethical emphasis naturally flowing out of the Christological). For a concise statement of the conventional ethical view on these verses, see Marshall, *Epistles of John*, 110–12.

[124] Almost all the commentators consulted think that μετ ἀλλήλων, "with one another," refers to the fellowship among believers (e.g., Marshall, *Epistles of John*, 111; Schnackenburg, *The Johannine Epistles*, 78; Strecker, *The Johannine Letters*, 30; Smalley, *1, 2, 3 John*, 23–24; Brooke, *The Johannine Epistles*, 15; Westcott, *Epistles of St. John*, 21; Brown, *Epistles of John*, 239; Thompson, *1–3 John*, 45; Bultmann, *The Johannine Epistles*, 19–20; Stott, *Epistles of John*, 75; also D. E. Hiebert, "An Exposition of 1 John 1:5–2:6," *BSac* 145 [1988]: 333). The only exception located is Z. C. Hodges, "Fellowship and Confession in 1 John 1:5–10," *BSac* 129 (1972): 53. A slight complication is added by the presence of the variant αὐτοῦ, "him," i.e., fellowship with God rather than fellowship with one another. This variant is clearly a late correction of the text. While disagreeing with Hodges on most other points, his contention that the context favors understanding this fellowship as mutual fellowship between God and Christians is worthy of careful consideration. The following are refinements and additions to Hodges' arguments: First, while v. 7 need not be the converse of v. 6, it likely makes a strong counterclaim to the false claim in v. 6. Since the false claim is a claim about fellowship with God, we expect that the counterclaim should be about fellowship with God as well. Moreover, even though John spoke of fellowship with his readers in v. 3, he also clarified that the apostolic fellowship is a fellowship with the Father and with his Son (v. 4). Furthermore, the comparative clause "as he is in the light" places those who walk in the light in the same realm as the Father, so that it is most natural to understand that the Father and these believers enjoy mutual fellowship as a result of being in the same realm.

without Christ can only make false claims about having fellowship with God (1:6), Christians actually have fellowship with God and God with them through Jesus, who is the only Mediator between God and human beings (cf. John 14:9–21,23; 17:22–23; also 1 Tim 2:5).

The second effect in John's reasoning indicates that the conditions necessary for fellowship with God are fulfilled by Jesus' death. His logic is thus: Those who live in the eternal life revealed in Jesus have every[125] single one of their sins, which defile and make one unfit for fellowship with God,[126] cleansed[127] through Jesus' atoning death.[128] Since 1:5–2:2 should be interpreted as a unit, the nature of this cleansing will be explored further below. In addition, the implications of the whole will be summarized at 2:2.

(2) Resist Sin (1:8–2:2)

⁸If we claim to be without sin, we deceive ourselves and the truth is not in us. ⁹If we confess our sins, he is faithful and just and will forgive us our sins and purify us from all unrighteousness. ¹⁰If we claim we have not sinned, we make him out to be a liar and his word has no place in our lives.

¹My dear children, I write this to you so that you will not sin. But if anybody does sin, we have one who speaks to the Father in our defense—Jesus Christ, the

---

[125] Since πᾶς ἁμαρτίας is without the article, it may be focusing either on the class of sin distributively ("every," i.e., focusing more on each individual member) or as a whole ("all") (see C. F. D. Moule, *An Idiom-Book of New Testament Greek,* 2nd ed. [Cambridge: University Press, 1959], 94–95; Wallace, *Greek Grammar,* 253). The former is more frequent in the πᾶς + noun without article construction. Since the πᾶς + noun construction does not need the article to be definite (see Wallace, *Greek Grammar,* 253), we need not translate this noun clause as "every kind of guilt."

[126] Καθαρίζω, "cleanse, purify," is being used in a cultic sense. The verb appears only here and in 1:9 in John's writing. The image that John expects his readers to see is that of sin as impurity that is unacceptable to Yahweh and separates one from the worship of God and from presence in the camp with God's people (cf. Westcott, *Epistles of St. John,* 22). See H. G. Link and J. Schattenmann, "καθαρός," in *NIDNTT,* 3:104 on this link between purity and the worship of Yahweh in the OT. Much of the OT teaching on cultic purity and impurity is found in Lev 14–16 and Num 8; 8.

[127] Some commentators (e.g., Westcott, *Epistles of St. John,* 21; Brown, *Epistles of John,* 203; Smalley, *1, 2, 3 John,* 26) suggest that cleansing includes both the forgiveness of sin's guilt and the removal of sin's power in the human heart. Since the discussion in 1:5–10 pertains to fellowship with God, the condition necessary for fellowship must be in view. This condition is nothing less than sinlessness (cf. this discussion on 1:8,10 above), which is achieved by the forgiveness of sins in those who believe in Jesus, the propitiation of sin (cf. 1:9; 2:2; 4:10).

[128] The blood (τὸ αἷμα) is "a symbol for the crucifixion of Christ, and its background is to be located in Jewish sacrifice" (Smalley, *1, 2, 3 John,* 24). Westcott's theory that "[t]he Blood always includes the thought of the life preserved and active beyond death" is not compelling (*Epistles of St. John,* 36; see 34–37). The atoning quality of the blood comes from the death, not the life, of the sacrificial victim (see L. Morris, *The Apostolic Preaching of the Cross,* 3rd ed. [Grand Rapids: Eerdmans, 1965] 112–28).

Righteous One. ²He is the atoning sacrifice for our sins, and not only for ours but also for the sins of the whole world.

1:8–10 Following the phrase "the blood of Jesus his Son cleanses us from every sin," 1:8–10 offers additional universal maxims (framed with John's particular opponents in mind) that rule out false ideas of the condition necessary for fellowship with God. The claim to be "without sin"[129] probably arose from John's opponents' understanding that fellowship with a holy God required one to be sinless. Verses 8 and 10 are essentially parallel: the heretics argued that the condition for fellowship with the Father is sinlessness. Therefore they claimed to be sinless. Yet in this very claim they rejected God's word (1:10; i.e., the truth God has revealed in Jesus, 1:8),[130] deceived themselves, and made God out to be a liar.[131] Sinlessness is theirs by virtue of life in Christ alone. It cannot be located merely within themselves.

In contrast to these fatal errors of rejecting Jesus and claiming personal sinlessness, John makes clear in 1:9 that it is those who confess their sins by believing in Jesus who have fellowship with the Father and fulfill the condition for fellowship. If our identification of vv. 8–10 as dealing with the condition necessary for fellowship with God is correct, John's point is that the true condition for fellowship is the confession[132] of our sins. Yet John does not dispute their premise of the need for sinlessness. "When someone acknowledges and avows his fault ... honestly [neither hiding nor denying his sins], he experiences God's faithfulness and righteousness in

---

[129] Westcott, *Epistles of St. John,* 23 wrongly reads the idea of the denial of having a sinful nature into the phrase ἁμαρτίαν οὐκ ἔχομεν. Christie rightly observes that John's usage (John 9:41; 15:22,24; 19:11) points toward the idea of the guilt associated with sin ("An Interpretive Study of 1 John 1:9," 45). Most likely, it is the existing state of having sinned and thus having guilt from the sin (cf. Brown, *Epistles of John,* 205–6). It seems that we need not radically disassociate the practice of sin from the guilt contracted from the act: "We have no sin" (ἁμαρτίαν οὐκ ἔχομεν, 1:8) and "we have not sinned" (οὐχ ἡμαρτήκαμεν, 1:10) are thus practical equivalents. Cf. Schnackenburg, *The Johannine Epistles,* 84, n. 56; Marshall, *Epistles of John,* 115.

[130] Since 1:8 and 1:10 are parallel, "the truth is not in us" (1:8) and "his word is not in us" (1:10) are synonymous. For the significance of "the truth" as the truth God has revealed in Jesus, see comment on 1:6.

[131] 1 John 1:6–10 is actually conceptually parallel to 1 John 5:9–12: "Anyone who does not believe in the Son of God has made him out to be a liar, because he has not believed the testimony God has given about his Son. And this is the testimony: God has given us eternal life, and this life is in his Son. He who has the Son has life; he who does not have the Son of God does not have life" (NIV). Again we find that John frames both the beginning and the end of his epistle with the same themes. Cf. the comments on those verses.

[132] While confession of sin could be made either publicly or privately, the context of 1:7 and 1:9, with God being the One to whom one confesses, makes it unlikely that John is referring to a public confession. See Schnackenburg, *The Johannine Epistles,* 82. For the opposing view see Brown, *Epistles of John,* 208.

the forgiveness of sins."[133] By virtue of the cleansing effect of Jesus' atoning death, believers' sins are forgiven.[134] In effect, they are sinless in God's
sight (though not in themselves) and fit for fellowship with him.

In the context, God's faithfulness and righteousness *(pistos kai dikaios)*
must relate to "the truth" (vv. 6,8) and "his word" (v. 10). Furthermore,
Marshall rightly observes that "[t]he faithfulness lies in [God's] adherence
to his promises that he will forgive his people. ... The [righteousness] lies
in the inherent rightness of the act; if the conditions are fulfilled, God
would be wrong to withhold forgiveness."[135] If our interpretation of 1:7 is
correct, God's promise here is specifically his testimony to having given his
Son that those who believe in Jesus should have eternal life (cf. 5:11–12).
Because God has sent his Son as Savior of the world (cf. 4:14), to those
who confess their sins by trusting in this Jesus whom God has revealed
(taking 1:7 and 1:9 together), God is faithful and righteous to forgive[136]
them their sins and cleanse them from all unrighteousness.[137] God is able
and righteous in forgiving because these sinners will have confessed their
sins and trusted in God's revelation of eternal life in Jesus his Son, whose
death is the basis for forgiveness.

2:1–2   With the direct but affectionate address "my dear children"[138]

---

[133] D. Fürst, "ὁμολογέω," *NIDNTT,* 1:346.

[134] ἀφιήμι reflects a legal background, lit. meaning "to let go, release" something. Here the
guilt and liability to punishment for sin is let go, i.e., forgiven (cf. Brown, *Epistles of John,* 211).

[135] Marshall, *Epistles of John,* 114. Marshall quotes Mic 7:18–20, "Who is a God like thee, par-
doning iniquity and passing over transgression for the remnant of his inheritance? He does not
retain his anger forever because he delights in steadfast love. ... Thou wilt show faithfulness to
Jacob and steadfast love to Abraham, as thou hast sworn to our fathers from the days of old." He
also cites Deut 32:4; Rom 3:25; and Heb 10:23. Brown adds that the descriptions "faithful and righteous" reflect "a covenant attitude toward God" (*Epistles of John,* 210). J. M. Lieu believes Exod
34:6 may be in the background of 1 John 1:9 ("What Was from the Beginning: Scripture and Tradition in the Johannine Epistles," *NTS* 39 [1993]: 458–77).

[136] J. Boyer is probably right in suggesting the ἵνα clause is epexegetic to the two adjectives
("The Classification of Subjunctives: A Statistical Study," *GTJ* 7 [1986]: 16). It is possible that the
ἵνα clause is a substitute for the infinitive of result here (see BDF, 3915 and most commentators).

[137] 1 John 5:17 shows that "unrighteousness" (ἀδικία) is synonymous with "sin" (ἁμαρτία)
(Marshall, *Epistles of John,* 114).

[138] τεκνίον is a diminutive of τέκνον, lit., "small child." The NIV's rendering as "dear children" reflects the endearment expressed through the term. Cf. Marshall, *Epistles of John,* 115.
Thompson gives the following summary of the significance of three words for children used in
John: "*Teknia,* the plural of *teknion,* ... underscores the author's pastoral concern and special relationship to the readers (2:1,12,28; 3:7,18; 4:4; 5:21); *paidia* (2:14,18), a diminutive of *pais,* is used
in direct address to the readers for the sake of variety. ... [Cf.] Proverbs 4:1; 5:1; 7:24; 8:32. *Tekna*
is used of Christians as children of God (1 Jn 3:1–2,10; 5:2) or church members (2 Jn. 1,4,13; 3 Jn.
4) and of unbelievers as 'children of the devil' (3:10)" (*1–3 John* 48, note on 2:1). See also Brown,
Epistles of John, 213–15. The use of these phrases also serves a rhetorical purpose, providing for
a transition from one topic to another.

and the switch to the first person singular, "I write,"[139] John draws his readers' attention to his direct exhortation to them. This direct address and the statement of the purpose of his writing as "in order that you may not sin" indicate John's primary purpose in writing 1:5–10. Even though John was responding to the heretics in ruling out false conceptions of fellowship with God (in teaching correct theology), his primary purpose was to instruct and warn his readers against sinning in the same manner as the heretics. Specifically, he has in mind the claim to sinlessness (1:10), which makes God out to be a liar and does away with the need for God's word concerning Jesus (cf. 1:6,8).[140] If one could truly be sinless on one's own, God would be lying in revealing Jesus as the only way to receive eternal life and to have fellowship with God (cf. John 14:6). God's testimony to the eternal life revealed in Jesus has no place in such a person's heart. Read in light of 1:5–10, John's purpose is that his readers should not sin particularly by denying God's revelation of eternal life in Jesus (cf. 5:9–10).[141]

---

[139] Smalley makes the following good observation on John's use of "I write" here: "John appears to use the first person *singular* for direct address or exhortation; as here, when he abandons the first personal (sic) plural which he has employed throughout the first chapter, and distinguishes his audience as 'you.' He tends to use the first person plural ('we') either when he is associating himself with those who are the guardians of the apostolic faith in the transmission of the kerygmatic message (so 1:1–3), or when he is identifying himself with his readers in terms of basic Christian experience" (*1, 2, 3 John*, 35). Note that Smalley does not hold to the eyewitness view of 1:1–3 (*1, 2, 3 John*, 8). With a correction on that respect, his observation stands.

[140] Abstractly considered, ταῦτα, "these things," could refer to 1:6–10, 1:1–10, or the entire letter (see Smalley, *1, 2, 3 John*, 35). But "these things" most naturally refers to 1:5–10 (the ταῦτα γράφομεν in 1:4 marks the previous section; see comment on 1:4). In fact, ταῦτα + the verb γραφω (1:4; 2:1; 2:26; 5:13) is a helpful discourse marker of John's division of thought.

[141] Instead of a pause in thought (contra Marshall, *Epistles of John*, 115), 2:1 states the purpose of 1:5–10 and should be read in full continuity with it. The typical interpretation of John's statement in 2:1 is well represented by Marshall: "It was possible that the readers might interpret what John had just written with its emphasis on the fact that Christians were not free from sin as a license to sin … John, therefore, had to make it quite clear that his purpose was that Christians should not sin" (*Epistles of John*, 116; cf. Smalley, *1, 2, 3 John*, 35; Westcott, *Epistles of St. John*, 41; Dodd, *Johannine Epistles*, 23–24; Bultmann, *The Johannine Epistles*, 22; Schnackenburg, *The Johannine Epistles*, 85; Brooke, *The Johannine Epistles*, 22). This view, however, actually makes little sense of John's statement. John says, "I wrote 1:5–10 in order that you may not sin." If taken in the sense this view requires, John would be saying, "I wrote 1:5–10 to tell you that Christians do sin and should confess their sins, but do not misunderstand me by then thinking that Christians are free to sin all they want: I really wrote 1:5–10 in order to tell you not to sin." Whatever view one takes on the referent of "these things," these thoughts are not found in the text. They are, at best, a possible response to a possible misinterpretation by John's readers. Furthermore, this misinterpretation is itself quite unlikely given the presence of 1:5–7. On the other hand, John is better seen as saying, "I write about the implications of these heretics' teachings in 1:5–10 (which heretics are sinning by denying their sin and therefore denying God's testimony about Jesus) in order that you may not sin (by following them)." Still, John is a realist and as a pastor is very much aware of the weaknesses of his children. It is recognition of the possibility of sin in general by believers that its remedy is addressed in 2:16: "But if anyone does sin …"

The conjunction at 2:1a *(kai)* should be translated "and" rather than the NIV's "but."[142] After warning his readers against denying sin (and thus denying God and Jesus) like the heretics, John adds the thought about the abiding effects of dealing with sin in the proper way (i.e., through Jesus) for himself and his readers.[143] Moving to address the work of Jesus Christ, John adds another related thought using "and" in 2:2, that is, Jesus' propitiation is the basis for these abiding effects not only for them but for all alike.

John has already indicated in 1:7 that those who have fellowship with God are those who live in the eternal life God has revealed in Jesus. To have this eternal life they must believe in God's testimony concerning Jesus, which implicitly indicts the spiritual deadness of every human being (see comment on 1:6–7). Moreover, this faith in God's testimony of Jesus involves a confession of their sins. As a result of their confession of sin through faith in Jesus, they justify God's word against themselves as spiritually dead sinners and believe in God's provision of Jesus as the only Source of eternal life (cf. John 14:6). Consequently, God is faithful (to his Word promising forgiveness and life in Jesus) and righteous (in granting forgiveness and life) (1 John 1:9). For this reason John can say that if any of his readers sin, they have "one who speaks to the Father in [their] defense" (2:1b). This Jesus can speak in their defense because he himself is the One who reconciles those who believe in him to the Father (2:2).

Having seen the general flow of thought above, we must still examine the details in 2:1b–2:2. There are at least six questions that we need to answer. First, what is the logical relationship between the "if" and "then" clause? Second, why does John switch to "if anyone" *(tis)* rather than "if you" (continuing his direct address from 2:1a) or "if we" (as in 1:6–10)? Third, what is the precise meaning of the word "paraclete" *(paraklētos,* translated by the NIV as "one who speaks ... in our defense")? Fourth, what is the significance of the title "the Christ" and the term "righteous" in this passage? Fifth, does "atoning sacrifice" (the NIV's translation of *hilasmos*) mean propitiation or expiation? Sixth, what is the nature and scope of Jesus' "atoning sacrifice" in light of the expression "for the whole world"? Each of the last four questions is pregnant with theological importance.

Since 2:1b comes in the form of a conditional sentence, the most important question for determining its meaning is the logical relation between the

---

[142] John never uses καί to connect opposing thoughts in 1 John. He uses either δέ or ἀλλά. See δέ as "but" in 1:7; 2:5,11,17; 3:17; 4:18 (the δέ in 5:5 and 5:20 are probably just "and"). See ἀλλά as "but" in 2:2,7,16,19 (twice), 21,27; 3:18; 4:1,10,18; 5:6,18. Cf. the literal translation of the NASB on these verses. (The NASB does inexplicably translate καί in 2:20 as "but"; it also translates ἐὶ μὴ, "except," as "but" in 2:22 and 5:5).

[143] On this characteristic of John's use of καί, see Westcott, *Epistles of St. John*, 8, 42.

"if" and "then" clauses.[144] The first possible category is equivalence: A ("if" clause) = B ("then" clause). Whatever the precise meaning we give to the individual elements in this conditional statement, however, it is inconceivable to see A ("And if anyone does sin") as = B ("we have a Paraclete, Jesus Christ the Righteous"). We are left with two other possible categories: (1) Cause-Effect, that is, "if" A happens, "then" B happens; and (2) Evidence-Inference, that is, "if" A (ground/evidence), "then" B (inference/implication). The difference between these two categories is this: In evidence-inference the "if" clause is not the cause of the "then" clause. Indeed, the "then" clause is often (though not always) the cause of the "if" clause.[145] If we opt for the evidence-inference interpretation, the result for 2:1b would be thus: If and when sin does happen, it enables us to infer that we have a Paraclete with the Father. This view makes little sense in the context.[146] The logical relationship, then, must be cause and effect: If sins happens (cause), then the Paraclete (Jesus) is there with the Father for us (effect). With this insight we will attempt to interpret the individual elements of this conditional sentence more precisely.

Abstractly speaking, "if anyone" could mean exactly that, "anyone," without restriction. If 2:1b is a cause-effect conditional sentence, however, "we have a Paraclete with the Father, Jesus Christ the Righteous" is dependent on the fulfillment of "if anyone sins." Yet just *anyone* sinning could hardly bring about the effect of John and his readers[147] having a Paraclete with the Father. In context, "anyone" has to be "anyone [of us]," that is, John or any of the believing community. "Anyone," then, most likely highlights the individual character of both sin and participation in the benefits of Christ's work. Yet the "we" shows that John is speaking of those who are in the apostolic fellowship (of apostolic eyewitnesses and subsequent believers in apostolic testimony as one community; cf. 1:3–4).[148] As such, the group that has Jesus as Paraclete with the Father cannot be extended beyond the

---

[144] See S. E. Porter, "What Does It Mean to Be 'Saved by Childbirth'?" in *Studies in the Greek New Testament: Theory and Practice* (New York: Peter Lang, 1996), 266. This essay by Porter, which is a model of careful and systematic exegesis of a difficult passage, is also found in *JSNT* 49 (1993): 87–102. See also Porter, *Verbal Aspect,* 319–20. For a simple explanation of the three categories of logical relations, see Wallace, *Greek Grammar,* 682–84.

[145] See further Wallace, *Greek Grammar,* 683.

[146] The best sense that could be made out of this interpretation would be: And if sin happens, (we know that God has allowed it to happen so that) we can infer that we have a Paraclete with him (who makes sure that our sins do us no harm).

[147] The "we" here cannot be interpreted to include the whole world because John explicitly expands the scope of Jesus' work to include not only "us," but also "the whole world." See comment on 2:2.

[148] Cf. Westcott, *Epistles of St. John,* 42; also Smalley, *1, 2, 3 John,* 36.

boundaries of those who are in the apostolic fellowship.

What, then, is the precise meaning of "Paraclete"? That is, what does this verse teach us about what Jesus' does for us with the Father? There are two difficulties in determining the precise meaning of "Paraclete." First, we are uncertain of the significance of the term "Paraclete" being ascribed to Jesus here, when it was ascribed to the Holy Spirit in John's Gospel. Second, we are uncertain whether this term was a technical term in early Christian usage. It may be a mistake to assume that it is a technical term and then associate the full range of functions associated with the Holy Spirit (of whom this term is used in John) as part of the meaning of the word itself.[149] This caution is warranted by the fact that this term occurs only five times (John 14:16,26; 15:26; 16:7; 1 John 2:1), and then only in John's writings.

In light of the lack of evidence for technical usage and the evidence of various meanings associated with the term in John's usage,[150] it is best to see the term as merely designating "one called in to help," "one who comes alongside in time of need." The way in which *this* "Helper" helps is, in turn, determined by the specific situation in which the word occurs.[151] In the context of 1 John 2:1b, *this* "Helper" must help Christians when they sin.

Elsewhere in John, we know that God has, as it were, a lawsuit against those who sin (e.g., John 3:18–21,36; 4:27–29; 16:8–11; 1 John 3:3,6,14). In the immediately preceding context (1:5–10), fellowship with God is described as requiring the confession of sins through the reception of God's

---

[149] As G. E. Ladd explains, the problem with John's use of the word "Paraclete" is that his use seems to go beyond the usual contexts in which the word is used elsewhere in Hellenistic writings (*A Theology of the New Testament* [Grand Rapids: Eerdmans, 1974], 293). But the problem is resolved if we recognize that "paraclete" is not a full technical term. There is a crucial difference between technical and nontechnical terms. Only if "Paraclete" is a technical term can the functions ascribed to its referent in specific contexts be fully ascribed to the meaning of the word itself. At the same time, external referents, like concepts and entities, are not fully described by specific terms, technical or otherwise. See the fine article by K. Grayston, "The Meaning of *Parakletos,*" *JSNT* 13 (1981): 67–82, who also argues for the general meaning. On the difference between technical and nontechnical terms, see further M. Silva, *Biblical Words and Their Meaning: An Introduction to Lexical Semantics,* rev. ed. (Grand Rapids: Zondervan, 1994) esp. 29–31, 107–8.

[150] On the functions associated with the Spirit's role as "Helper," see Carson, *John,* 399–400; Brown, *John XIII–XXI,* 1139–41.

[151] Similarly, Brooke, after examining the evidence of the wider Hellenistic and Jewish use of the term, writes: "The help it describes is generally assistance of some sort or other in connection with the courts of law; but it has a wider signification also, the help of anyone who 'lends his presence' to his friend. Any kind of help, advocacy, intercession, or mediation may be suggested by the context in which it is used" (*The Johannine Epistles,* 26). The term παράκλητος itself is probably a verbal adjective of παρακαλέω, "to call alongside," and is passive in force, "one who is called alongside" (Carson, *John,* 499; cf. G. Braumann, "παράκλητος," in *NIDNTT,* 1:88). Brown, *John XIII–XXI,* 1136–37, lists three other suggestions.

word revealing Jesus as the Source of eternal life. Moreover, the death of Jesus is said to cleanse every sin because God is faithful and righteous in forgiving because of his promise concerning Jesus. Jesus' death, the confession of sins through faith in Jesus, and forgiveness are thus vitally related to the concept of "Helper." Our determination previously that the "anyone" is restricted to those within the apostolic fellowship allows us to define the role of this "Helper" even more precisely. Jesus is the Helper of those who are in the apostolic fellowship, which persons are, by definition (1:7,9), those who have confessed their sins through faith in Jesus.

To help determine how Jesus' death and forgiveness are related to the term "Helper," it is necessary to answer the fourth question posed above: What is the significance of the title "the Christ" *(christos)* and the term "righteous" *(dikaion)* in this passage?[152] Any reading of John and 1 John will show that the issue of Jesus' messiahship (Christ = Messiah) is of vital importance in these writings. The formula "Jesus Christ" has "lost nothing of its predicative character,"[153] that is, one should read "Jesus the Christ" (a full title, which is a technical term), instead of "Jesus Christ" (as if "Christ" was Jesus' last name).

In John's Gospel "the Christ" is identified as "the Son of God" and "the King of Israel" (cf. 1:41,49). When Jesus was asked whether he was the King of the Jews (18:33), he replied that "his kingly authority did not come from this world and could not be promoted by worldly means of force of arms (18:36). Jesus was [then] mocked as King of the Jews (19:3) and executed with the title 'King of the Jews' on his cross (19:19)."[154] At the very least, the title "the Christ" in 1 John 2:1b involves the idea that Jesus is *the* unique anointed King from God. In the context of 1 John, the association of the term "Christ" with Jesus' death and forgiveness probably plays a role in determining the nature of the role of "the Christ." No other christ other than this Jesus, who is incarnate God (1:1), the One who reveals eternal life to a spiritually dead world of human beings (1:1–3), Son of God (1:3; also "the Christ"), whose death cleanses from every sin (1:7), is the very One who is the Helper of Christians.

In translating the adjective *dikaios* as "the Righteous One," the NIV is taking this adjective as a title of Jesus. The alternative is to see it as a predicate adjective, "being as He is righteous."[155] If one adopts this understanding, John's reason for using this adjective was to stress the efficacy of

---

[152] Determining John's conception of "Christ" *(christos)* is just as important.

[153] K. H. Rengstorf, "χριστός," in *NIDNTT,* 2:339.

[154] Ladd, *Theology of the New Testament,* 243.

[155] Westcott, *Epistles of St. John,* 43; also Smalley, *1, 2, 3 John,* 37. Alternatively, one could see the term as an epithet and still just see it meaning that Jesus is righteous (e.g., Schnackenburg, *The Johannine Epistles,* 87).

Jesus' help: "The righteous Christ is the Doer of the will of God (his obedience is both passive and active) in the fullest sense,"[156] and therefore he is able to help those less righteous than he. Jesus the Christ certainly is nothing less than the Righteous One *par excellence* (cf. 1 John 2:29; 3:7), so this view is at least what this term means. If the term is a title, "the Righteous One," the same stress on Jesus' righteousness, and therefore on the efficacy of his help, could be its extended meaning as well. Nevertheless, it is possible that "the Righteous One" is a title that recalls the Righteous Branch of Jer 23:5–6 and/or the Suffering Servant described in Isa 52:13–53:12 (cf. Isa 53:11). The contexts in the book of Acts, where this title is ascribed to Jesus, seem to indicate a link to the conception of Jesus as the Righteous Servant who suffered and died an atoning death (Acts 3:14; 7:52; 22:14).[157] The focus on the cleansing effect of Jesus' death (1:7), the forgiveness of sins (1:9), his role as Helper when anyone of his followers sins (2:1), and his role as "the atoning sacrifice" for the sins of the whole world (2:2) make this interpretation of the title quite possible.[158]

The picture gleaned from the above examinations is that of a Helper who helps his followers whenever they sin by his atoning death (1:7), his righteousness (2:1b), and his role as their King (2:1b). Moreover, it is an ongoing work, since his function as their Helper is "with the Father"[159] whenever any of his followers sins.[160] Schnackenburg's suggestion that Jesus' high-priestly role lies behind this verse commends itself best in light of the evidence gathered above:

> The whole picture is strikingly reminiscent of Heb. 7:25ff. The high priest, who is "holy, blameless, undefiled, separated from sinners," has offered himself once and for all and now lives forever to be the advocate of those who 'by him draw near to God.' ... In addition to the idea of God as faithful and merci-

---

[156] G. Schrenk, "δίκη κτλ," *TDNT*, 2:189.

[157] On the reasons for seeing Acts 3:13–15 as alluding to Isa 52:13–53:12, see J. B. Polhill, *Acts,* NAC (Nashville: Broadman, 1992), 26:131. A. Oepke states that Jesus' "mediatorial representation culminates in intercession ([John] 17, 1 John 2:1) and death (10:11; 12:32; 17:19 etc.). The atoning significance of this is particularly emphasized in 1 Jn. (1:7; 2:2). Allusion to Is. 53 is again patent" ("μεσίτης, κτλ," *TDNT*, 4:623). If one takes the book of Acts to be a historical representation of the preaching of the early church, an Isaianic link with this title in Acts may well indicate the same Isaianic link where this title is used elsewhere as a title for Jesus.

[158] Studies in biblical theology that do a thorough study of at least Isaiah and the influence and use of the book of Isaiah in Acts and the Gospel of John is required to give us more certainty on this issue. We hope such studies will be forthcoming in the future.

[159] Probably "with the Father" in the sense of being in the Father's presence. See Schnackenburg, *The Johannine Epistles,* 86. Kruse notes, "The way the author expresses himself here, saying, literally, 'we have an advocate with the Father' *(pros ton patera),* recalls both John 1:1 and 1 John 1:2," where *pros ton theon* and *pros ton patera* occur (*Letters of John,* 72, n. 32).

[160] Cf. Schnackenburg, *The Johannine Epistles,* 86.

ful (1:9), we now have Jesus Christ as the priestly advocate and mediator. He relieves the faithful of all their anxiety about their salvation, now once more endangered by sin, and he assures them that in spite of their weakness they can draw near to the throne of grace (cf. Heb 4:16; 10:19ff.).[161]

This interpretation not only fits the data in 1 John 1:5–2:1 but also is supported by the portrayal of Jesus in John 17 (as well as the cultic terminology in 1 John 2:2). The idea of intercession is probably involved as well (cf. 1 John 5:18). In short, Jesus is now in the Father's presence as the eternal High Priest, who, having atoned for the sins of his people, now stands as their effective Advocate to ensure that their sins do not disqualify them from fellowship with the Father. On the one hand, John's readers could follow the heretics in denying their sin and Jesus, and thus sinning (probably the somewhat cryptic "sin unto death" mentioned in 1 John 5:16), which is the path of death. On the other hand, John's readers could confess their sins by believing in God's word concerning Jesus, which takes care of their sins for all time and is the path of life (i.e., fellowship with the Father and with the Son).

Before answering the fifth and sixth questions, it is necessary to examine the connection between 2:2 and 2:1b more closely. Following on his discussion of the efficacy of Jesus' role as Advocate to deal with every sin of the believer, John adds that this Jesus,[162] who is "Advocate," "Christ," and "Righteous One," is "the atoning sacrifice *[hilasmos]* for our sins, and not only for ours but also for the sins of the whole world" (NIV). The connection is that John moves from Jesus' present Advocacy to its prior basis: His atoning sacrifice for John's sin, his readers' sin, and for the sins of the whole world.[163]

The meaning of the word *hilasmos,* which occurs only here and in 1 John 4:10 in the New Testament, is the subject of intense debate. On the "subjective" view, God is the subject of the action. He removes the defilement of sin by causing it to be covered. This is what is meant by "expiation." Often proponents of this view minimize or deny the presence of personal wrath on God's part toward the sinner.[164] On the objective view, God is the object of an offering of sin, that is, God's wrath is placated. This

---

[161] Ibid., 87. Cf. Westcott, *Epistles of St. John,* 43.

[162] καὶ, "and," marks the next step in John's contemplation. The pronoun αὐτὸς is emphatic and signals that 1 John 2:2 is primarily meant to state something about Jesus. Instead of leaving it untranslated like the NIV, it is preferable to signal the emphasis by translating "He himself" as in the NASB.

[163] Cf. Schnackenburg, *The Johannine Epistles,* 86; Westcott, *Epistles of St. John,* 44; Marshall, *Epistles of John,* 117.

[164] See, e.g., Westcott, *Epistles of St. John,* 87; Dodd, *Johannine Epistles,* 25–27; Brooke, *Epistles of John,* 28. Dodd's important essay challenging the propitiation view is *"Hilaskesthai: Its Cognates, Derivatives and Synonyms in the Septuagint,"* *JTS* 32 (1931): 352–60.

is what is meant by "propitiation." Proponents of this view often include both propitiation and expiation as two aspects of the same atoning sacrifice of Jesus. Marshall represents this view well: "In order that forgiveness may be granted, there is an action in respect of the sins which has the effect of rendering God favorable to the sinner."[165] The biblical evidence is heavily in favor of the propitiation view.[166] In addition, two questions with which Morris challenges proponents of the expiation view have never been satisfactorily answered:

> [First,] 'Why should sin be expiated?' 'What would be the consequences to man if there were no expiation? ... It seems evident on the scriptural view that if sin is not expiated, if men 'die in their sins,' then they have the divine displeasure to face, and this is but another way of saying that the wrath of God abides upon them. It seems that expiation is necessary in order to avert the wrath of God, so that nothing seems to be gained by abandoning the concept of propitiation... .
>
> [Second,] [What is] the meaning to be given to expiation[?] As commonly used the term seems to signify the removal of sin or guilt, but neither of these is a *thing* which can be objectively removed. Expiation can be given an intelligible meaning only when we move into the realm of personal relations. Sin has altered the relations between God and man, and expiation cannot be understood apart from the effects of an expiatory act on these relations. Unless we are prepared to say that in expiation all that happens is a subjective change in man, it would seem that we are committed to the view that expiation has a Godward aspect so that God now treats the sinner differently from before. Instead of God's severity the sinner experiences God's grace, which is only another way of saying that propitiation has taken place.[167]

Within 1 John the idea of God's coming judgment (which implies his wrath against sinners) through the revealing of Jesus a second time is clearly present (e.g., 2:28; 4:17–18). The Gospel of John likewise presupposes God's judgment and wrath (e.g., 3:16–21,36 [to which Morris alludes

---

[165] Marshall, *Epistles of John,* 118.

[166] See L. Morris, *The Apostolic Preaching of the Cross,* rev. ed. (Grand Rapids: Eerdmans, 1965), 144–213. Brown gives a good summary of the main lines of argument: (i) In "cultic passages it is often impossible to distinguish propitiation from expiation." (ii) There are clear biblical passages that refer to "propitiating God without any pagan or pejorative connotation," e.g., Ps 106:30; Zech 8:22. (iii) The wrath of God is frequently present in the context of the use of *hilasmos*-related words in the LXX. (iv) The "imagery that sacrifices have a pleasing smell to God cannot be separated from propitiation." (v) The Apostolic Fathers (second century church leaders) display their understanding as that of propitiation in contexts dealing with both OT and NT. (vi) God's wrath is not inconsistent with his providing the means of removing sin and turning away his own wrath (*Epistles of John,* 219). See also the wealth of information cited in the footnotes in Marshall, *Epistles of John,* 117–19, and the note on *Hilasmos* in Kruse, *Letters of John,* 75–76.

[167] Morris, *Apostolic Preaching of the Cross,* 211–12. See also the appendix: "Propitiation or Expiation: The Debate Over *Hiloskomai.*"

above]; 5:28–29; 8:21–24 [to which Morris alludes]; 15:6; 16:8–11; esp. 1:36; 11:49–52 with the crucifixion of Jesus in chap. 19). Most importantly, in the immediate context of 1:5–2:1, the concepts of the forgiveness of sins, the resulting fellowship with God, and the Advocacy of Jesus (whenever Christians sin) imply that sins are not only an impersonal barrier to fellowship but include the aspect of personal favor and disfavor. The considerations above require that at the very least, Jesus' "atoning sacrifice" involved the propitiation of God's wrath by taking on the punishment due for the sins that needed removal (expiation). Fellowship with God is possible because the sins that caused offense to God have been removed through Jesus' atoning sacrifice, so that God's wrath no longer abides on those who have fled for refuge in the Lamb of God, who takes away the sin of the world.

The last question is quite significant: What is the nature and scope of Jesus' "atoning sacrifice" in light of the expression "for the whole world" *(peri holou tou kosmou)?* Some insist, and with good reason, that this phrase means that "the scope of divine salvation is ultimately regarded as all-inclusive."[168] These kinds of statements, however, need some kind of qualification. Universal in *provision* is not to be equated with universal in *application.* Only universalists, that is, those who claim that every single human being will be saved, mean that divine salvation is all-inclusive in an absolute sense. Universalism is plainly ruled out, however, unless one believes that John contradicts himself directly in the same epistle (e.g., 1:5–10; 2:28; 3:14,15; 5:12,16).

The NIV includes at the end of v. 2 the words "the sins of" even though they do not appear in the Greek text. Because these words are not in the original, some scholars have argued that "for the whole world" should be taken as "covering not only sins but all the evil effects of sin in the

---

[168] Smalley, *1, 2, 3 John*, 40. See also Westcott, *Epistles of St. John*, 45. Luther (*John*, 237) certainly held to a view of universal atonement: "It is certain that you are a part of the world. Do not let your heart deceive you by saying: 'The Lord died for Peter and Paul; He rendered satisfaction for them, not for me.' Therefore let everyone who has sinned be summoned here, for He was made the expiation for the sins of the whole world and bore the sins of the whole world." Calvin's comments here (*The Gospel according to St. John, Part Two, 11–21* and *The First Epistle of John*, CNTC, [Grand Rapids: Eerdmans, 1988], 244) would seem to point in the direction of particular redemption. He stated, "Therefore under the word 'all' he does not include the reprobate, but refers to all who would believe, all those who were scattered through various regions of the earth." Calvin's view of the extent of the atonement is complex, and he is claimed by both universal and particular redemptionists. K. D. Kennedy in a recent dissertation makes, in my judgment, a compelling defense of universal atonement in Calvin. As to 1 John 2:2 he notes that Calvin is confronting what appears to be full-blown universalism taught by certain "fanatics" and that "he is arguing against those who wish to extend salvation to all the reprobate, even to Satan himself" ("Union with Christ as Key to John Calvin's Understanding of the Extent of the Atonement" [Ph.D. Diss., The Southern Baptist Theological Seminary, 1999], 58).

world."[169] The construction of the sentence, however, is against this interpretation. The point of the "not only for [*ou peri de monon*] ... but also for [*alla kai peri*]" is to extend the provision of Jesus' propitiation of sins to include not only the sins of John (and his fellow apostolic eyewitnesses) and his original readers but also the sins of the whole world.[170]

John affirms that Jesus is the propitiation for the sins of the whole world. Since universal salvation is not an option (as seen above), this propitiation does not itself guarantee the actual salvation for the whole world. The provision for all have been accomplished. The reception and application of that provision is appropriated by faith. The efficacy of Jesus' propitiation for salvation personally and individually is dependent on one believing in Jesus. Although it is possible to say that "the whole world" is John's way of saying all the nations (but not intending every single person), and that "the propitiation for the sins of the whole world" is meant to stress the exclusivity of Jesus' work (i.e., Jesus is *the only* propitiation for all alike), such a view does not provide a satisfactory answer to John's "not only for ours but also for ..."

To be sure, it is a mystery that Jesus' propitiation is for everyone and yet only some are saved. It is evident, however, that no one is saved unless he believes in Jesus and equally evident that many reject God's universal invitation and command to believe in this Jesus. Total depravity affirms that every part of our being is infected with the disease of sin. We are fallen creatures. Human beings are sinful in all aspects of their humanity and are unwilling and unable to receive God's salvation revealed in Jesus apart from the enabling work of the Holy Spirit (e.g., John 1:10–11; 2:23–3:8; 3:19–20; 5:39–47; 6:63–64; 8:42–47; 1 John 4:9–10; 5:19). Salvation is the work of God from beginning to end, and it is what he has done for those who believe that enables them to become Jesus' true disciples and God's children (e.g., John 3:8; 6:37,39,44–45,65; 10:26–29; 17:2,6,9). God is effectual in calling and drawing those he has chosen to Jesus for salvation (e.g., John 1:13; 3:8,21; 6:37,39–40,44–45; 6:63–64,65; 17:2,6). Furthermore, the perseverance of the saints involves the true disciples of Jesus abiding in faith in Jesus so that they all endure to the end and are saved (e.g., John 6:39–40; 10:27–29; 15:16; 17:11–12,15; 1 John 5:4–5,18). In a grand mystery of redemptive love, God's sovereign election and his effectual calling of his chosen ones works in beautiful concert with those who believe, persevere, and are saved. Jesus' propitiation does not produce regeneration. Actual salvation is accomplished by Jesus' propitiation and

---

[169] Brown, *Epistles of John*, 222; cf. Westcott, *Epistles of St. John*, 45.

[170] Smalley rightly points out that the repeat of περί ("for") in front of ὅλου τοῦ κόσμου, "the whole world," signals that it is the sins of the world rather than the world in general that is the concern of Jesus' atoning sacrifice (*1, 2, 3 John*, 40).

the believer's response of faith.[171]

First John 1:5–2:2 fits into John's purpose of underscoring both the universality and the exclusivity of salvation through Jesus. While the heretics claimed that they could have fellowship with God (= having eternal life) without believing in God's gift of eternal life in Jesus (see comment on 1:5–10), John strongly affirms that Jesus is the only way of salvation for all. Jesus is the propitiation for the sins not only of John (and his fellow apostolic eyewitnesses) and his original readers, but also for the rest of the world for all time (without intending to say that everyone inclusively is saved). Jesus, Jesus and no other, is the Savior for all humanity. To enjoy the benefits of his wonderful provision requires a response of faith. Without this faith, though the provision has been made, the enjoyment of its benefits are tragically missed.

Summary and Implications of 1:5–2:2

The two statements that begin and end this section of 1 John—"God is light; in him there is no darkness at all" (1:5), and "he is the atoning sacrifice for our sins, and not only for ours but also for the sins of the whole world" (2:2)—summarize many central themes of the biblical gospel. God is fullness of life himself, and those who would have fellowship with him must receive the eternal life God has revealed in Jesus. This Jesus is the only Savior for all, the only One who satisfies the wrath of God by taking on the guilt and punishment for sins. In between these statements, John rules out false conceptions of the condition necessary for fellowship with God (i.e., one must not claim personal sinlessness) and warns against for-

---

[171] Two common and important questions are often raised at this point: (1) How do sins get punished twice if Jesus actually died for all sins and yet unbelievers go to Hell for their sins? And (2) how about those who never hear about Jesus? To the first question we answer that the rejection of Jesus' propitiation brings one's sins back upon oneself. The provision made on one's behalf still requires appropriation to enjoy the application. Jesus made a saving deposit on behalf of every person. A personal withdrawal is the means whereby that deposit becomes one's own. On the second question the theological dictum that revelation brings responsibility is helpful. God judges on the basis of what we know and receive/reject, not on the basis of what we do not know. Those who perish apart from special revelation are condemned for their rejection of the light they received via natural revelation (creation/conscience; cf Rom 1:18–3:20). The standard of judgment is just and fair, but it does not begin to approach the severity of those who reject the special and final revelation of God as disclosed in Jesus the Son. Those who never hear perish apart from the salvation or aggravated guilt brought on by special revelation (in the same manner that Gentiles were judged when special revelation was restricted to the Jews). In effect, this view takes Jesus as the only propitiation for the whole world and the actual propitiation for the whole world that will hear about him and receive him. But let it be added that those who seek the Lord will find him (Jer 29:13). Those who do respond to what light they have will be granted further light. Both the story of the Ethiopian eunuch (Acts 8:26–40) and of Cornelius (Acts 10) would seem to support this.

saking Jesus. John also declares the only way to meet the condition necessary for fellowship with God: the confession of our sins through believing in Jesus. In addition, Christians who confess their sins need not fear disqualification from fellowship with God, for Jesus is now their Advocate who appears before the Father on their behalf, and the basis of his advocacy (his propitiation for sins) is all-sufficient.

Together with 1 John 1:1–4, 1:5–2:2 rules out any other way of having fellowship with the true God except through faith in Jesus the Christ (who is the true God and eternal life; cf. 5:20) as witnessed in the apostolic proclamation. By implication no other religion, good works, good intentions, or anything else will grant the eternal life found only in Jesus and received only by believing in the apostles' witness to him.

The fact that Jesus' propitiation is the only propitiation for all demands that the church proclaim this Jesus to the whole world. Like John, our joy is not complete until the full number of those whom God has given to Jesus believe in him and the whole apostolic fellowship enter into the new heaven and new earth (where God will dwell with his people forever as their God [Rev 21–22]).

The fact that faith in Jesus is the only way of fellowship with God (which is eternal life itself) demands and compels the church to take seriously the call to perseverance in faith. John wrote to warn and instruct his original readers against following the fatal errors of the heretics, even though he was convinced that his readers were indeed Christians.

At the same time, Christians are those who continually confess their sins as we continually believe in Jesus (walking in the light and confessing sins are most certainly portrayed as a continuous state).[172] Christians, by definition, believe in Christ and confess their sins. This truth rules out the teaching of perfectionism this side of heaven, that is, that Christians can get to a stage where they do not sin in this life.

Finally, what about the debate over whether this passage in 1 John gives tests of life (to distinguish true believers from unbelievers)[173] or tests of fellowship (in the sense of daily fellowship with God).[174] As the exegesis above shows, John's purpose was to provide assurance by warning and instructing his readers against following the sin of the heretics in rejecting Jesus and claiming personal sinlessness. First John 1:5–10 thus gives descriptive, universal maxims of the way of death and the way of life. In its original context these maxims are tests of true and false teaching in the first instance.

---

[172] Even though 1 John 1:5–10 contains omnitemporal, universal maxims, when applied in concrete situations (i.e., when one applies it to a specific person in time), the durative aspect of the present tense probably applies.

[173] See e.g., Stott, *Epistles of John*, 72–73.

[174] See e.g., Hodges, *Epistles of John*, 48–60.

The test of fellowship view is true in so much that Christians are those who continually live by faith in Jesus and confess their sins; yet John conceives of "fellowship" as more than just a temporal sort of fellowship (see comment on 1:3). Christians are, by definition, those who have fellowship with God, which fellowship is guaranteed by the propitiation of Christ and his advocacy whenever their sins might appear to threaten that fellowship. Proper applications of this passage to daily Christian living are as follows: daily and continually believe in Jesus, confess your sins, and trust in Christ's sufficient work for you. If you do these things, assurance is certain to be yours.

The test-of-life view is true in as much as Christians, by definition, meet the description of the positive maxims, whereas unbelievers, by definition, fit the negative ones. Moreover, John does give two tests of life in the rest of 1 John: loving one another and believing that the Christ (or the Son of God) is Jesus. The error of the test-of-life view is in misreading 1 John 1:5–10 as an ethical test when it gives the foundational maxims that distinguish between the way of life and the way of death. The rest of the epistle gives the two tests of life: the faith test and the love test (which includes the ethical aspect).

2. Obey the Command to Love (2:3–11)

This section of John's epistle focuses on the connection between obedience and the knowledge of God and builds upon the right understanding of sin, which is established in the preceding section of text. The central aspect of Christian obedience is found in the command of love that is both new and old and is given its greatest illustration in the way the historical Jesus walked during his time on earth.

The terminology used in this section also mirrors the preceding section. The author again focuses on the dichotomous relationship between "light" and "darkness" to describe the realm in which an individual lives and states that the realm one occupies is based on one's response to the command of obedience. The themes of "the truth" and "the lie" are also employed. These two always stand in stark contrast to each other.

Finally, this section is shaped by a proper understanding of the whole of the Christ event. While a proper understanding of sin comes through understanding that Jesus, in his death, was the propitiation for the sins of the world (1:5–2:2), a proper understanding of obedience comes through the imitation of the perfect obedience to God that was demonstrated in the life of the historical Jesus of Nazareth and delineated in his command of love.

(1) Know God and Keep His Commands (2:3–6)

³We know that we have come to know him if we obey his commands. ⁴The man who says, "I know him," but does not do what he commands is a liar, and the truth is not in him. ⁵But if anyone obeys his word, God's love is truly made complete in him. This is how we know we are in him: ⁶Whoever claims to live in him must walk as Jesus did.

2:3 The initial phrase, *kai en toutō,* "now by this," is transitional in the Greek text and thus indicates that John is addressing a different issue. Its omission from the NIV serves to remove the ambiguity that the transition introduces into the text. First, the *kai,* usually translated "and," should not be taken as a simple connective but should be translated as "now." This construction is similar to the one employed at the beginning of 1:5 and marks a new topic of discussion. After these three conditional sentences that explain the separation (walking in darkness) that sin causes between God and humanity, John "now" describes how the readers of this epistle can know that they know the God who is light.[175] Second, the omission of a translation of *en toutō* places the emphasis of the sentence on the condition that follows in the verse ("We know ... if") and removes the possibility that the basis for knowing that we know him is found in 2:1–2. The NIV relates in an explicit way the sense of what John was explaining to those who read this letter at the end of the first century.[176] An abruptness in the transition of the NIV, however, is not present in the Greek text.

The condition put forth by John is that we can have assurance that we know "him" if we obey (keep) his commandments. The importance of the

---

[175] Brown, *Epistles of John,* 248.

[176] There has been much debate among scholars as to whether the pronoun in the construction ἐν τούτῳ points to the preceding or the following thought. This idiom occurs five times in John's Gospel (4:37; 9:30; 13:35; 15:8; 16:30) and twelve times in the epistle (2:3,5c; 3:10,16,19,24; 4:2,9,10,13,17; 5:2), without counting 2:4b and 2:5b, where it refers to a person (Brown, *Epistles of John,* 248). Smalley notes that on ten occasions, with variations, this construction occurs with the verb γινώσκω, as in this verse (Smalley *1, 2, 3 John,* 44). Brown notes that there is no point in the study of this epistle more debated than whether the "this" in 1 John (always or normally) refers to what precedes or what follows. The construction in 2:3 falls into the category of ἐν τούτῳ followed by a subordinate clause or a prepositional phrase, and there are some passages where it is not altogether clear if the following prepositional phrase or subordinate clause is related to ἐν τού-τῳ (cf.1 John 2:19; 4:17). Brown goes on to note that it is clear in other constructions of this sort that the subordinate clause or the prepositional phrase is not related to the pronoun (cf. John 4:37; 16:30; 1 John 2:5c). He concludes, however, that in passages where ἐν τούτῳ is linked with a following prepositional phrase or a subordinate clause that the statement must have a "primary thrust forward" to the clause or the phrase because otherwise the phrase or the clause would have no grammatical function. When this principle is applied to our present passage, there is no doubt that the conditional clause explains the "this" (*Epistles of John,* 248–49). Cf. also R. L. Thomas, "Exegetical Digest of 1 John," 103 (© 1984 R. L. Thomas); Schnackenburg, *The Johannine Epistles,* 95; Strecker, *The Johannine Letters,* 40.

transition *(kai en toutō)* used by John in this passage becomes evident when one attempts to determine the antecedent for the pronoun *auton* (him). If "this" refers to what precedes immediately in the text, the pronoun would refer to Jesus Christ, the last mentioned person in the text (2:1). It seems, however, that the pronoun, like the *autos* forms in 1:6,7,10, refers to God, who is last referred to as God in 1:5.[177] "The problem that the author is dealing with is how to know the God who is light, not how to know Christ. All the secessionist-inspired claims in 1:5–2:11 concern God."[178]

Forty-two times in this epistle John uses a form of the word "know." Here the double use of *ginōskō* emphasizes the importance of knowing that one has a relationship with God. This verse contains two of twenty-five occurrences of this verb in 1 John. Interestingly, John does not use the cognate noun *gnōsis* in this letter or in the Gospel, while the use of the verb *(ginōskō)* and the concept of the "knowledge of God" are pervasive in both. This does not necessarily indicate that John was avoiding the use of a technical term used by his adversaries. It may reflect only the Semitic tendency to employ verbs wherever possible instead of the cognate noun. Still, it is possible that John avoided this term in order to state his message in a manner that could not be misused by his opponents and would not be misunderstood by his readers.[179] The focus on "knowing" God seems to imply that John's adversaries advocated a system of belief emphasizing that salvation in some sense was gained through *gnōsis* (knowledge). It would be a mistake to think that these systems were as fully developed as the detailed systems of Basilides and Valentinus in the second century, but it would be just as great a mistake to discount the (proto-) Gnostic tendencies that John seems to be combating.[180] In the prologue of 1 John, the apostle directs his argument against those who have either denied or downplayed the importance of the humanity of Jesus Christ, thus displaying an early form of what was later called the heresy of Docetism. In fact, John never uses "Christ" without associating it with and defining it by the use of the earthly, human name Jesus. This failure to see the importance of the life that is lived in the body could also lead to distorted views of sin, the issue John addresses in 1:6–2:2.

---

[177] Brown, *Epistles of John*, 249. He notes that there is often little distinction between God and Christ in the epistle but argues that this principle should not be employed in the given passage. Smalley argues that because of the description of Jesus as a lawgiver in the verses that follow that "God in Christ" need not be excluded (*1, 2, 3 John*, 45). Thomas ("Exegetical Digest of 1 John") argues that the referent of the pronoun is Jesus Christ because of the fact that Jesus Christ is the last person mentioned in the text and his belief that the arguments in favor of the pronoun referring to God are "circuitous." This view is also supported by A. T. Robertson in *WP* 6:210.

[178] Brown, *Epistles of John*, 249.

[179] Smalley, *1, 2, 3 John*, 44.

[180] Ibid.

It is clear from this verse that the knowledge of God cannot be defined as mere intellectual "knowledge" alone. This is precisely the view that John was combating. Real knowledge of God contains an intellectual, moral, and spiritual component that cannot be separated. The "knowledge" of God described throughout the text of Scripture is not only intellectual but also experiential and dynamic. This knowledge is not gained through abstract speculation but through living life in a spiritual relationship with the one true God. In fact, the promise of the restoration from exile, given to Jeremiah, was that the people of God would know the Lord.[181] The Israelites had a spiritual relationship with the Lord that was established through his election of the nation and the promise he made to Abraham, but their failure to live out the commands of God outlined in Deuteronomy 27–32 led to their ejection from the land and exile in Babylon. The history of Israel provides unmistakable evidence that communion and fellowship with God require obedience to his commands.[182]

The perfect tense form of the second use of "know" *(ginoskō)* in this verse, along with the conditional clause[183] that concludes the verse ("if the commandments of him we keep"), outlines the spiritual growth that is expected in the life of the believer. Because one has come to know God (an event occurring in the past with continuing effects) through belief in Jesus Christ, whose death was the atoning sacrifice for the sins of the world, he now must keep the commandments of God. This knowledge flows naturally from the promise of the new covenant in Jeremiah. When the new covenant is established (through the death and resurrection of Jesus Christ), God will write his law upon the hearts of those who are his. Their hearts will be changed so that now they will obey. Therefore keeping the commandments is "not a condition" of knowing

---

[181] Jer 31:31–34: "The time is coming," declares the Lord, "when I will make a new covenant with the house of Israel and with the house of Judah. It will not be like the covenant made with their forefathers when I took them by the hand to lead them out of the land of Egypt, because they broke my covenant, though I was a husband to them," declares the Lord. "This is the covenant I will make with the house of Israel after that time," declares the Lord. "I will put my law in their minds and write it on their hearts. I will be their God and they will be my people. No longer will a man teach his neighbor or a man his brother saying, 'Know the Lord,' because they will all know me, from the least to the greatest," declares the Lord. "For I will forgive their wickedness and will remember their sins no more."

[182] Smalley, *1, 2, 3 John*, 45. R. A. Culpepper, *1, 2, 3 John*, Knox Preaching Guides (Atlanta: John Knox, 1985), 23–24.

[183] This ἐάν clause with the subjunctive is a condition of the third class (undetermined but with the prospect of determination). The conclusion of the third class is not determined as is true of the first and second class clauses, but the subjunctive mood "brings the expectation within the horizon of a lively hope in spite of hovering doubt" (A. T. Robertson, *A Grammar of the Greek New Testament, In Light of Historical Research* [Nashville: Broadman, 1934], 1016). The fulfillment of this clause is held out in the future (i.e., the keeping of the commandments), but there is an expectation, maybe even an assurance, that these commands will be fulfilled by those who are believers.

God "but a sign" that one does know God.[184]

2:4 This verse introduces a triad of participial phrases, relating claims that could properly be made by believers but are being used incorrectly by John's adversaries because their behavior is not consistent with the proper knowledge (belief) of God. The clauses used in these verses could indicate a quotation of the words being used by the secessionists (indirect discourse; cf. 2:19).[185] The three versions of the heretical assertions about their understanding of sin, specified in 1:6,8,10, differ from these claims in that these statements could be adopted by the true believer who is obedient. These three statements in a sense repeat and amplify the truth about the knowledge of God that is introduced in v. 3, for all three statements explain how an individual can know God, that is, have a proper relationship with him. In addition, each claim about knowing God put forth in these verses is attached to a test related to Christlike obedience.[186]

Verse 4 is the converse of 2:3, and it explains that the one who claims to know God but is consistently disobedient is a liar. John implies that this individual will be exposed as a liar by his disobedience to God's commands. What is internal will eventually come to the surface. The condemnation of this person is quite similar to what John says in 1:6,8. Not only is the claim of this individual false, but the truth is altogether absent from his life.[187] As Schnackenburg writes: "He lacks the divine nature which alone makes possible the genuine knowledge of God. In this sense 'the truth' is synonymous with the 'Spirit of truth' (cf. 4:6; John 14:17). To enjoy genuine gnosis a person must be 'of the truth' (cf. John 18:37; 1 John 2:21; 3:19)."[188]

2:5 John restates the claim made in the previous verse in a manner that links the proclamation of knowing God with the practice of proper Christian behavior epitomized in love. John cites the love of God precisely because it makes known the command par excellence of Jesus in the Johannine literature, "to love each other as I have loved you" (John 15:12).[189] This emphasis on the connection between love and obedience is shown throughout John 13–16 and could very well be the basis for John's focus on the commandment to love given by Jesus in this part of the epistle.

The initial clause of v. 5, which the NIV translates, "But if anyone obeys his word," is set apart from the rest of the verse. It is a nominative absolute

---

[184] Strecker, *The Johannine Letters*, 40.

[185] Brown, *Epistles of John*, 253.

[186] Ibid., 46.

[187] Smalley, *1, 2, 3 John*, 46; F. F. Bruce, *The Epistle of John* (Grand Rapids: Eerdmans, 1970), 51; Brown, *Epistles of John*, 281; Schnackenburg, *The Johannine Epistles*, 97.

[188] Schnackenburg, *The Johannine Epistles*, 97.

[189] Brown, *Epistles of John*, 282.

in the Greek text and may be more literally translated, "But whoever keeps his word." In stark contrast to the one who claims to know God but does not keep his commands and is branded a liar, the person who keeps God's word is indwelt by the truth and the love of God has been completed in him.[190]

The proper sense of the genitive construction *agapē tou theou* must be addressed. Should it be translated as a subjective genitive: "God's love for man" (like the NIV), an objective genitive: man's love for God, a qualitative genitive: God's kind of love (so Marshall), or simply as "love of God," keeping the ambiguity of the statement? The subjective genitive describes the love that God has for human beings, and the obedience to keep God's word is motivated from having received the love that God has given through his Son. The objective genitive describes the love that a man or woman has for God, which is shown through obedience. The qualitative genitive relates the kind of love that is characteristic of God. The qualitative genitive thus has the strength of including both the objective and subjective meanings of the genitive in that the love can both be for God and come from God. This understanding acknowledges the difficulty of the interpretive decision. Although the arguments in favor of the subjective genitive view are strong, and theologically any love that we have for God must find its origin in him, it seems that the objective idea best fits the context of John's argument.[191] Our love for God reaches a "marked out in advance" goal when we keep his word.

The verb translated "made perfect" *(teleioō)* is in the perfect tense and is used four times in this epistle, always to describe the completion or perfection of love (4:12,17,18). Brown observes: "Since keeping the commandments (or God's word) certainly involves living out the commandment to love one another, the love of God revealed to us in Jesus Christ reaches its perfection when the same love is shown to 'one another' and to the God who abides in the Christian."[192] God's love achieves its purpose when we keep his word.

The final section of this verse also is marked off by an *en toutō* (cf. the beginning of 2:3). Previously it was argued that the *en toutō* looked forward to the conditional clause that was to come. In this instance the *en toutō* ("by this") phrase is not followed by a preposition or a dependent clause. As a

---

[190] Ibid., 254; Thomas, "Exegetical Digest of 1 John," 108. There is an antithesis between ὁ λέγων ("the one saying") in v. 4 and ὅς ἂν τηρῇ ("but whoever keeps") in v. 5 that should not be missed. Thomas notes that the position of the nominative absolute brings it into "emphatic contrast with ὁ λέγων."

[191] For a detailed discussion of each position see Thomas, "Exegetical Digest of 1 John," 110–13 and Brown, *Epistles of John*, 255–57. Brown chooses the noncommittal "love of God," "which has the dubious advantage of ruling out nothing" (p. 257).

[192] Brown, *Epistles of John*, 257.

result, the phrase can point to the independent clause that follows it and to what will be addressed in the next verse or conclude the discussion that precedes it. It seems that this is a classic Johannine "saddle text"[193] that ties together the material that has come before with the material that is to follow. This transition serves to sum up what precedes, in a sense framing the discussion, and lays the foundation for what comes next (the discussion of abiding in him).[194]

The statement "This is how we know we are in him" is an example of the Johannine theology of immanence (the Christian in God/Jesus; God/Jesus in the Christian; God and Jesus in each other). This concept can be found thirty-five times in the Gospel and the Epistles in formulas like *einai en* ("to be in") and *menein en* ("to abide or remain in"). When one is born of God, he has been begotten into an intimate relationship with each member of the Godhead—Father, Son, and Holy Spirit—and it is the keeping of the commandments that bears witness to this union. It seems that John's adversaries would like to describe this union as a mystical union meant only for a few. The Old Testament background to the indwelling presence of God points in a different direction. As one reads the prophets, he is struck by the fact that in the promised restoration, God will dwell in the New Jerusalem among his people (Ezek 48:35), and in the new covenant the one who believes will have an intimate knowledge of God brought about through the indwelling of the divine Spirit, having the law written upon his heart, which is a circumcising of the hearts of his people (Deut 30; Jer 24; 31; Ezek 36). In the Johannine description of the new covenant this indwelling takes on a mutuality not fully described in the Old Testament, for God not only dwells in the believer but the believer is also in God. This idea can be seen in Jesus' prayer in John 17, "that all of them may be one, Father, just as you are in me and I am in you" (17:21). This is not a mystical status meant for an elite few but a spiritual relationship for all who truly believe in Jesus, the mediator of the new covenant.[195]

2:6 Verse 6 is the second of the secessionists' claim to know God that when rightly understood can be made by a believer. This claim acts as an example that illustrates what is described in v. 5b. The accuracy of the claim is measured by the extent to which the individual walks as Jesus did during his earthly life and ministry.[196]

---

[193] Cf. G. Borchert, *John 1–11*, NAC (Nashville: Broadman & Holman, 1996).

[194] Brown, *Epistles of John*, 258.

[195] Ibid., 283–84. For a detailed analysis of Johannine Formulas of Immanence, see Schnackenburg, *The Johannine Epistles*, 99–103.

[196] The NIV interprets the original pronoun in the Gk. text by placing the antecedent (Jesus) in the translation. John uses this pronoun as a clear reference to Jesus in this epistle on five other occasions (3:3,5,7,16; 4:17). Cf. Thomas, "Exegetical Digest of 1 John," 117, Robertson, *WP* 6:211.

The first part of this verse might be translated more literally "the one who is claiming to abide in him." It seems that the NIV translation, while keeping the sense of the language, has failed to fully show the connection of v. 6 to v. 5b and the progression of thought present in these verses. The first reference to being in him (v. 5) clearly refers to God, even though the mutuality of the relationship does not exclude Jesus. In this use of immanence language, the antecedent of the pronoun is less explicit because of the condition that follows. Although the pronoun likely refers to God, it would be a mistake to miss the Christocentric focus of the verse. As Smalley states, "John makes it clear that the ultimate knowledge of God the Father is disclosed through Jesus, his Son."[197]

The one who claims to abide in God (Jesus) is faced with the obligation (debt) of conforming his life to the example that was set by the historical Jesus in his life. To live (abide) in God one must know God, and ultimate knowledge of God comes only through an intimate knowledge of and relationship with Jesus Christ, the Son of God. This intensely personal relationship with Jesus that is both permanent and continuous acts as the basis for and provides the power to live ethically.[198] In this verse the indicative and the imperative of the Christian life are joined together as a cause and effect. This union occurs only to the degree that the soteriological significance of the death and resurrection of Jesus the Christ precedes the ethical imperative, so that the indicative of the Christ-event becomes the foundation for and the content of the imperative.[199]

(2) Learn the New Command and Love Others (2:7–11)

[7]Dear friends, I am not writing you a new command but an old one, which you have had since the beginning. This old command is the message you have heard. [8]Yet I am writing you a new command; its truth is seen in him and you, because the darkness is passing and the true light is already shining.

[9]Anyone who claims to be in the light but hates his brother is still in the darkness. [10]Whoever loves his brother lives in the light, and there is nothing in him to make him stumble. [11]But whoever hates his brother is in the darkness and walks around in the darkness; he does not know where he is going, because the darkness has blinded him.

2:7–8 These verses, with the initial *agapētoi,* "Dear Friends" (lit., "beloved") appears to begin a new thought. Still, v. 7 continues and amplifies the thought that was begun in v. 6. There is a certain degree of semantic overlap to be sure with the continued discussion of God's commands. This

---

[197] Smalley, *1, 2, 3 John,* 52.
[198] Ibid.
[199] Strecker, *The Johannine Letters,* 43.

assertion is based on both the content of the verses and the literary structure of the passage as a whole. The focus of 2:6–8 is on knowing God as he has been revealed in his Son, Jesus Christ. Here John draws on the pattern of the life and ministry of Jesus and the content of the gospel message, which they had previously heard, to address the attacks his adversaries had made against the ethical standard the author taught his dear friends.[200]

The command John advocates is not some new, novel ethical ideal divorced from the heritage of the believing community. John's opponents had minimized the importance of ethical behavior. John uses these verses to illustrate that this command is not one more restriction that has been placed on those who have believed, and he shows that these commands are not contradictory to the apostolic message. This message is, in fact, embedded in the apostolic witness they had received from the beginning of their Christian experience. It is the good news that contains both the record of God's saving work in the life, death, and resurrection of Jesus Christ and the instruction about how those who have received God's grace are to live in this fallen world. These ethical commands had always been a part of the Christian community. The commandment cited in 2:7 is the summation of all of the precepts previously mentioned. It is the command of love. Smalley concludes: "The summation of the moral law of God is to be found in the command to love; and this love is exemplified supremely in the life and ministry of Jesus, whom believers are called to imitate (v. 6)."[201] This message can also be characterized as old or from the beginning because it has roots in the law (cf. Lev 19:18; also Rom 13:8–10) and because the love command was an integral part of the exhortation given to all believers at the start of the Christian life (Eph 5:2; Jas 2:8; 1 Pet 2:17).[202]

In what seems on the surface like a contradictory statement, John goes on to assert in v. 8 that this command is also new. How? The law of love is new in the sense that it is seen in Jesus and established by him through his death and resurrection. This command is also new in that Jesus by his obedience fulfilled the whole of the law and gave it "a depth of meaning that it had never known before" (John 13:34b,35).[203] Finally, this command is new because for those who believe it makes possible a new and eternal life in which they are motivated by the grace of God to fulfill the law of self-sacrificing, Christlike love.[204]

---

[200] Culpepper, *1, 2, 3 John*, 29; Smalley, *1, 2, 3 John*, 53.

[201] Smalley, *1, 2, 3 John*, 53; also Marshall, *Epistles of John*, 129.

[202] Smalley, *1, 2, 3 John*, 54–55; Bruce, *The Epistles of John*, 55, Culpepper, *1, 2, 3 John*, 29; Brown, *Epistles of John*, 264–65.

[203] Bruce, *The Epistles of John*, 54.

[204] Culpepper, *1, 2, 3 John*, 30, Smalley, *1, 2, 3 John*, 56; Schnackenburg, *The Johannine Epistles*, 105.

The final part of the verse provides the exegetical contextual basis for the claim because "its truth is seen in him and you, because the darkness is passing and the true light is already shining."[205] In this explanation John contrasts the darkness, where there is confusion and no understanding of God's revelation, and the light, where individuals can have fellowship with God and understand his revelation. John declares that with this new commandment a new age has been established in which the darkness will eventually be banished from the earth. Jesus Christ, the Light of the World (John 8:12), has come to destroy the darkness of sin and death and to inaugurate the Kingdom of God, which is characterized by light and love. In his earthly ministry Jesus initiated this kingdom through his submission and perfect obedience to the will of the Father. In his death and resurrection the power of sin and death was broken and the kingdom was inaugurated. The transformed lives of his followers provide infallible evidence for this victory. The battle, however, is not over. Despite the fact that the victory over darkness has been secured, the complete eradication of evil and the end of the old age will not occur until the consummation of all things. The final triumph is in the process of being worked out. This passage describes in gripping, symbolic language the inaugurated eschatology present throughout the New Testament. The eschaton is in one sense already realized, but not yet in its fullness.[206]

2:9 In v. 9 the final claim related to an individual's knowledge of God is put forth. Again it is a claim that could rightly be made by a believer if the test associated with the claim and elucidated in 2:10–11 is carried out. This final claim picks up the theme of light that John uses in the previous verses to describe the inauguration and consummation of the Kingdom of God. It also draws from the terminology of chap. 1, where God is described as light (1:5) and the believers are encouraged to walk in the light as God is in the light (1:7). This claim is something of a climax in that John has moved from knowing God to abiding in him and now to living in the light. The believer who walks in the light shares a special intimacy with God through the work of Jesus Christ. As previously seen, he shares the very life (eternal) of God. To walk in the light is to live out the life of God. He will give evidence of his abiding union in the light as he meets the challenge and opportunity to develop Christian character and conduct that is in step with confession and the command of love.[207]

---

[205] There has been much discussion concerning what is stressed about the command by the relative clause that follows, "because the darkness is passing …" Thomas has a careful discussion of the issues involved (see "Exegetical Digest of 1 John," 128–30).

[206] Bruce, *The Epistles of John,* 54; Smalley, *1, 2, 3 John,* 58; Schnackenburg, *The Johannine Epistles,* 106; Ladd, *A Theology of the New Testament,* 612–13; D. Guthrie, *New Testament Theology* (Downers Grove: InterVarsity, 1981), 798–801.

[207] Smalley, *1, 2, 3 John,* 59–60.

Verses 9–11 must be read against the backdrop of the secessionists and the contradiction of their confession and behavior. The term *adelphos,* translated "brother," could mean any neighbor, in line with the command of Lev 19:18. The LXX use of the term makes this possible. From the context it may be better to conclude that John is here referring only to those who have believed that Jesus is the Christ, the Son of God.[208] Vaughan's argument, however, seems more plausible. What we have here are persons with visible, though temporary, connection with the church. However, their behavior makes it evident they have never left the darkness. Those they call(ed) brothers they hate (pre. tense). The conclusion is clear: they are lost. They have never been regenerated.[209] Those who hate their brother differ from the children of God in that they are still in the darkness and may even love being in that state (John 3:19). The gravity of this situation is that the one who claims to be in the light but does not love his brother is deceived and in reality is a member of the kingdom of darkness.

There are no shades of gray when it comes to John's discussion of an individual's relationship with God. One is either in the light or in darkness. One either loves his brother or hates him. When someone is in the light, he is enabled to love. The one who is in darkness has no capacity to love, for, as we will see, his eyes have been blinded by the darkness.[210]

2:10 In 2:10–11 John presents two axioms that explain the example that is given in v. 9. The first is a positive description of the consistent love of the brother that takes place in the light. The second describes the negative state of confusion and blindness that results from living in darkness. If one loves his brothers, he abides in the light, and it is evidence that he knows God and has fellowship with Jesus Christ. The unwavering nature of this love is emphasized. There is a consistency that is part and parcel of their love.[211]

The second portion of this verse poses two exegetical difficulties for the interpreter. First, does the pronoun in the phrase *en auto* refer to the believer (NIV) or to the light where that believer remains (RSV)? Second,

---

[208] See Brown, *Epistles of John*, 270–73. Brown offers a detailed discussion of this issue, noting that much of the problem comes from the introduction of the commands in the Synoptics to love one's neighbor as oneself. He notes that in Johannine thought the "spiritual" term "brothers" must be confined to "those who believe in his [Jesus'] name—those who were begotten not by blood, nor carnal desire, nor by man's desire, but by God" (John 1:12–13). This spiritual relationship also entails an acceptance of Johannine Christology (1 John 5:1). Of course John never entertains the thought that one might love his brothers and hate unbelievers and find this pleasing before God.

[209] C. Vaughan, *1, 2, 3 John* (Grand Rapids: Zondervan, 1970), 47–49. Vaughan's treatment of these verses is superb.

[210] Brown, *Epistles of John*, 289–90; Bruce, *Epistles of John*, 56.

[211] Smalley, *1, 2, 3 John*, 61; Culpepper, *1, 2, 3 John*, 31.

does this part of the verse mean that in the light the believer cannot be tripped up or that he cannot cause others or himself to stumble?

Those who agree with the NIV argue that the pronoun *(auto)* should be taken as a masculine pronoun referring to the one who loves his brothers. In favor of this interpretation is the fact that John has a predilection toward the personal use of this construction in 2:4–5,8, resulting in the idea that there is nothing in the believer to cause stumbling. One might cite 1:8, "The truth is not in us"; 1:10, "His word is not in us"; and 2:4, "No truth in such a person" to support this position. Verse 11, however, is set in contrast to v. 10. It does not clarify the ambiguity because the first part of the verse relates that the one who hates his brother is in darkness, favoring an "in it" translation; but the final section of the verse describes the blinding action of the darkness and thereby favors an "in him" translation.[212]

The second option is that the pronoun is neuter and refers to the light just mentioned in the verse, resulting in the idea that within the sphere of light there is nothing to cause stumbling. This view is supported first by the fact that the nearest possible antecedent for the pronoun is the light *(to photi)*. Second, there seems to be a parallel in John 11:9–10 that states, "A man who walks by day will not stumble, for he sees by this world's light. It is when he walks by night that he stumbles, for he has no light." Third, as mentioned above, the description of the one who hates his brother being in the darkness (v. 11a) supports making light the antecedent. The best understanding of the passage makes light the antecedent of the pronoun, resulting in the following translation: "In it [light] there is no stumbling."[213]

This interpretation raises another question: does stumbling *(skandalon)* take place in the life of the believer, or does the believer cause others to stumble into the darkness? In its normal New Testament usage *skandalon* is used to describe actions that result in the stumbling of others. This is the meaning intended when John uses the verb *skandalizō* (John 6:61; 16:1; Rev 2:14). It is possible that a man might cause others to stumble due to a lack of love, but when this verse is taken with 2:11, it would be best to interpret the clause as referring to the person himself who is stumbling.[214] Brown notes that "it is simpler to think that love for one's brothers will prevent the person from leaving the Community or will save him from sins

---

[212] See Brown, *Epistles of John*, 274.

[213] Thomas, "Exegetical Digest of 1 John," 139–41; Brown, *Epistles of John*, 274; Smalley, *1, 2, 3 John*, 62; Schnackenburg, *The Johannine Epistles,* 108. Both Thomas and Brown provide detailed discussions of each position, noting the advocates of each.

[214] Westcott, *Epistles of St. John,* 56; Smalley, *1, 2, 3 John*, 62; Thomas, "Exegetical Digest of 1 John," 139–41. It is possible to see σκάνδαλον as having God as the person of offense. Hence the one in the light does not stumble and bring an offense against God. Although this understanding is certainly possible, the context would seem to lead our interpretation in a different direction.

against the *koinōnia,* the spirit of communion that binds one to God."[215] A believer lives in the light, the very life of God, and gives evidence of his position by loving his fellow believers. This life, lived in this manner, provides no occasion for offense. Christians can walk without stumbling because they see where they are going and the result is they do not cause others to fall.[216]

2:11   John concludes his argument in 2:11 by giving the negative axiom that contrasts v. 10 and explains v. 9. Those who hate their brothers live in a state of darkness where there is not just an absence of love, but an absence of God. In this darkness the individual is exiled from fellowship with the Father, his Son, Jesus Christ, and the believing community. Far from knowing God, those who hate their brothers walk around confused and lost, not knowing where they are going.[217] "In other words, unethical behavior not only contradicts the claim to be a Christian; it actually contributes to a spiritual downfall."[218]

Spiritual darkness is not a passive reality. It goes on the offensive. Darkness attacks those living in it so that they become increasingly trapped in this realm of confusion and blindness. In a real sense what we do is what we become. How we live is who we are. The longer one remains in this realm of darkness, the more difficult it becomes to see the sin that is in one's life, and the less likely one is to see his need to confess his sins so that fellowship with God can be restored. Habitual hatred leads to more hatred, and the possibility of loving becomes less and less likely.[219]

3. Know Your Spiritual Status (2:12–14)

[12]**I write to you, dear children,**
    because your sins have been forgiven on account of his name.
[13]**I write to you, fathers,**
    because you have known him who is from the beginning.
I write to you, young men,
    because you have overcome the evil one.
I write to you, dear children,

---

[215] Brown, *Epistles of John,* 275.

[216] Smalley, *1, 2, 3 John,* 62.

[217] Culpepper, *1, 2, 3 John,* 32.

[218] Smalley, *1, 2, 3 John,* 63.

[219] Ibid.; Schnackenburg, *The Johannine Epistles,* 108. The background to this metaphor of "blindness" can be found in Isa 6:10. It describes God's method of dealing with those who are intent on following their own plans. John also uses this metaphor in the Gospel (12:40) when he applies it to the people in the crowd who did not believe despite the fact that they had seen the signs that Jesus is the Christ. Seeing and not believing, they moved further into the realm of darkness, hardness of heart, confusion, and blindness.

because you have known the Father.
[14]I write to you, fathers,
    because you have known him who is from the beginning.
I write to you, young men,
    because you are strong,
    and the word of God lives in you,
    and you have overcome the evil one.

This section appears, at first glance, to be a self-contained unit that has little connection to the arguments that precede and follow it. This has caused some commentators to develop redactional histories for the text, proposing that these verses come from different sources and address different issues. A closer examination of the text, however, reveals that there is a connection between 2:12–14 and the context in both directions and that there is a progression in the ideas that are discussed. The connection, however, is semantic rather than structural. That many see a digression here is not without warrant given the change of style. Having just completed two triadic discussions of the boasts and claims of the secessionists (1:6,8,10; 2:4,6,9), John in 2:12–14 wants to encourage, as Culpepper notes, "the community of the faithful by assuring them that the benefits of the new covenant are theirs and warns them against the dangers that remain."[220] He shows that what is true of the members of the community is not true of the secessionists. In this he continues to develop a previous theme. The description of the believers in 2:12–14 serves further as an introduction to the exhortation to resist the temptation of living with a mind set on the transitory things of the world system that are opposed to God.

First John 2:12–14 has a highly structured repetitive format that is almost poetic. This is evident both in the Greek and English texts with its repetition and rhythmic flow.[221] John expresses great confidence in his readers as he reminds them of their vital relationship with God. Then 2:15–17 acts as a bridge to the verses that follow in its direct exhortation to the community.[222]

Four basic issues face the interpreter of this enigmatic text: (1) What is the reason for the tense change that occurs between v. 13 and v. 14 (the NIV unfortunately does not reflect the grammar at this point)? (2) How many

---

[220] Culpepper, *1, 2, 3 John*, 33; cf. Smalley, *1, 2, 3 John*, 67. The verses refer to things previously mentioned in the following manner: for v. 12 see 1:9 as well as 2:1; for v. 13 see 1:1 and 2:3; for v. 13c see 2:3; for v. 14a,b see 1:1 and 2:3; for v. 14c see 1:8,10.

[221] G. Sherman and J. C. Tuggy, *A Semantic Structural Analysis of the Johannine Epistles*, (Dallas: Summer Institute of Linguistics, 1994), 39–40. G. M. Burge refers to the "virtually perfect" symmetry of the text (*The Letters of John*, NIV Application Commentary [Grand Rapids: Zondervan, 1996], 112). *UBSGNT*, 3rd ed., also adopts a poetic structuring of these verses.

[222] Smalley, *1, 2, 3 John*, 66–68; Brown, *Epistles of John*, 316–17.

groups of people are included in those addressed in these verses (one, three, or two)? (3) How should one translate *hoti* in these verses? The NIV translates it as "because" all six times it appears. (4) Why does John employ so much repetition in 2:12–14?

Two basic presuppositions undergird the various solutions put forth to explain the tense change from the present in vv. 12 and 13 to the aorist in v. 14. The first is that the author in his use of the present tense refers to what is written in 1 John, while the aorist verbs refer to what he has written in another letter or in the Gospel. The second school of thought asserts that the aorist and the present tense verbs both refer to what is being written in this epistle. Some in this latter group argue that the aorist verbs refer to what John has already written, and the present tense verbs refer to what he is now writing. Still another group within this school of thought argues that both the present and the aorist tenses refer to the whole of 1 John and that the tense change is due more to stylistic variation that adds slightly more emphasis to the assertions being made by the author.[223] D. F. Watson sets forth a similar position based on rhetorical grounds. He argues that the use of the past tense was more vivid and that it is more striking to claim that all is finished than to intimate that it is about to be completed.[224] While the argument in favor of a stylistic use of an epistolary aorist is adequate to answer the question, it seems that the change of tense has the effect of moving the argument forward. When John uses *graphō* (I write) in the epistle, he tends to introduce a statement, but when he uses the aorist tense *egrapsa* (I wrote), it is used in the context of his discussion about statements (cf. 5:13). As a result, it is quite possible, if not probable, that John "uses the γράφω *[graphō]* clauses in vv 12–13 to lead into a threefold series of summary statements about orthodox belief, and the ἔγραψα *[egrapsa]* clauses in v 14 to preface the start of his further discussion of those statements, and to anticipate the body of teaching which is yet to come (vv 15–17 and 18 onward)."[225] This interpretation of the text also makes sense of the repetition of vv. 12–13 (with some variation) in v. 14 because of the manner in which the argument is pushed forward to the exhortation that follows.[226]

Three basic positions have been put forward to explain the meaning of the categories of children, fathers, and young men. The three-group position argues that John is addressing three groups of people based on physical age or spiritual maturity.[227] The advocates of the one-group position believe

---

[223] Brown, *Epistles of John*, 295–97. Brown goes into great detail in his discussion of this issue.

[224] D. F. Watson, "1 John 2:12–14 as *Distributio, Conduplicatio,* and *Expolitio:* A Rhetorical Understanding," *JSNT* 35 (1989): 105.

[225] Smalley, *1, 2, 3 John*, 78.

[226] Ibid., 77–80.

[227] Bruce, *The Epistles of John*, 58. R. Kysar, *1, 2, 3 John*, ACNT (Minneapolis: Augsburg, 1986), 52–53. Cf. also Thomas, "Exegetical Digest of 1 John," 143–48.

that John is using these terms rhetorically to describe the whole body of believers, due largely to the overlap of blessings that takes place in these verses.[228] The two-group position proposes that *teknia* and *paidia* are inclusive terms that John uses to describe those who have been loyal to the things that he has taught them. The terms *pateres* (fathers) and *neaniskoi* (young men) refer to the older and younger either in terms of age or spiritual maturity. Some think that the terms "fathers" and "young men" are indicative of leadership offices in the church, but this seems to read more into the text than it will support. The two-group position has the stronger support when John's inclusive use of *teknia* and *paidia* is considered (cf. 2:1,28), but it is best to use caution when attempting to make hard and fast distinctions about the meaning of these terms. Smalley notes:

> Knowing the Johannine mentality as we do, it is quite possible that our author is at this point being deliberately ambivalent. Almost certainly he is referring to his whole church when he calls his readers "children," but within that group he is in one sense recollecting and addressing the young and old in physical age; while in another sense he is referring to the spiritual privileges of Christian youth and maturity that should belong to all believers. ... In either case he is pointing out the riches of the orthodox faith belonging to the "fathers" and "young men" of his church, in stark contrast to the heresies which were being propagated by the other two groups within the Johannine community: those with too high a view of the nature of Jesus, and those with an inadequate understanding of his fully divine person.[229]

A third exegetical issue focuses on whether one should translate *hoti* (NIV "because") with a causal or declarative meaning. The causal understanding of the term implies that the readers of the epistle have the spiritual ability to respond to the challenge to live in the light and not fall prey to the charms of the world. Their spiritual position and maturity is the basis for John's encouragement and confidence. The NIV reflects this casual understanding. A second option is to understand *hoti* in a declarative sense. John has written these things to assure them of their place in the kingdom. These words are meant to assure them, in the face of a persuasive opposition, that they are the ones who have been forgiven, know the Christ, and have overcome the evil one. The fact that *graphō* is always followed by a direct object supports the declarative translation. But it is at this point that a helpful word can be given, using this particular issue as example, to guide those who wish to avoid those "exegetical fallacies." The difference of these

---

[228] This view goes back to Augustine and has been advocated by C. H. Dodd (*The Johannine Epistles* [New York: Harper & Brothers, 1946], 38–39) and I. H. Marshall (*The Epistles of John*, 138).

[229] Smalley, *1, 2, 3 John*, 70–71. Cf. also Thomas, "Exegetical Digest of 1 John," 149–51. Thomas provides a detailed description and critique of each position.

translations in the mind of the first-century reader might not have even been noticed. So fine a distinction would scarcely have been considered. Care should be taken and caution applied so that we do not see in a text what is really not there.[230]

The fourth issue to consider is the use of repetition. The most likely reason is for emphasis. As Sherman and Tuggy note, "John is here giving strong encouragement before presenting the exhortations to overcome temptations. By an emphatic reminder of who they are and what God has done for them, he provides the trust basis for exhorting them to live in the victory already won.[231] It is also the case that the use of repetition provides clear marker boundaries and sets these verses off as a distinct unit. Of course, the poetic and symmetrical nature of the verses would all but demand some degree of repetition.

2:12 The first and most fundamental word of encouragement that John can give to all members of the church is that in the past they were forgiven of their sins and that this forgiveness remains effective in their lives. "Have been forgiven" is in the perfect tense (John will use a perfect tense form six times in these verses). This forgiveness occurs because the death and resurrection of Jesus Christ made the mercy and grace of God available to those who repent of their sins and believe in the name of Jesus. This is the first reference to the "name" in the epistles (cf. 3:23; 5:13; 3 John 7), and it has a close relationship to John 20:30–31, the purpose statement of that Gospel. John asserts in v. 12 that real life is gained by virtue of the power of his (Jesus') name. This understanding may spring from a Semitic belief that the name stands for the identity of that person, and to know that name gives the person access to that power. "On account of his name" stands for the person and work of Jesus in its totality. What the person and work of Christ entails has been addressed in 2:1–2. As children of God, these believers have confessed the name of Jesus to be saved, and as a result of that confession they now have access to that name. It is this power that will give them victory as they stand against those who have departed from the community.[232]

2:13 John continues by addressing the "fathers" of the community, reminding them that they have known the one who is from the beginning,

---

[230] D. A. Carson, *Exegetical Fallacies* (Grand Rapids: Baker, 1984). Brown, *Epistles of John*, 301; Culpepper, *1, 2, 3 John*, 34; Smalley, *1, 2, 3 John*, 71. Brown does not translate the term. He uses a colon, which orients the reader to a declarative meaning but does not exclude a causal undertone (*Epistles of John*, 301). Cf. also M. de Jonge, C. Haas, and J. L. Swellengrebel, "A Translator's Handbook on the Letters of John," *BT* 22 (1): 111–18; and "On 1 John II. 12–14," *NTS* 6:236–41.

[231] Sherman and Tuggy, *Semantic and Structural Analysis*, 41.

[232] Brown, *Epistles of John*, 302; Culpepper, *1, 2, 3 John*, 35; Smalley, *1, 2, 3 John*, 72. Cf. also Thomas, "Exegetical Digest of 1 John," 151–53. Thomas seems to advocate the causal meaning, but he interprets that meaning in such a way that the content of the declaration—that John sees his readers as members of the faithful—remains.

Jesus Christ. The phrase "him who is from the beginning" could refer to the Father, but in this passage the reference is surely Christological. The connection of the "fathers" with "him who is from the beginning" is a rich allusion to the beginning of the Gospel based upon and rooted in the incarnation and ministry of Jesus, who was also there at the beginning of time and the beginning of the church. This declaration also reminds the readers of the importance of their knowledge about Jesus' earthly life. The knowledge they have is indicative of a deep, ongoing spiritual relationship ("have known" is in the perfect tense) that is grounded in the historical death and resurrection of Jesus Christ, not in intellectual speculation that perverts the true picture of who Jesus is, the eternal Son of God.[233] That he overtly draws attention to the Father in the latter part of this verse further supports the Christological understanding here.

The young men are to take heart because they have overcome the evil one (the devil). These believers have known what it is to overcome the temptations that the "evil one" places in front of them. "Have overcome" (perfect tense) particularly relates to the manner in which they have withstood the attempts to lure them away from the community. We must note that while it is likely that the term "young ones" refers to a specific group within the community, this reality should be a part of the life of every believer at any stage of spiritual development, for the Christian life is characterized by a constant battle against evil. This battle is shown in the ethical and spiritual struggle that is present throughout the epistle. The Christian can take heart in the midst of this battle because the victory is assured through the work of Jesus Christ on the cross and in the resurrection.[234]

The use of the term *poneron* ("evil one") suggests that the battle is against the one Scripture calls Satan, the personification of evil and all that is opposed to God. John is not thinking of evil in an abstract form. John describes this character, without using the term *Diabolos* or *Satanas,* as the one who has charge over the darkness, the place of confusion, death, and opposition to God (5:18–19; cf. 2:14; 3:12).[235] Schnackenburg asserts: "Just as Christ reveals the truth of God and champions God's cause in the struggle for the hearts and minds of people in this world, so is the evil one the representative of all that is opposed to God (5:18f.). He is an active aggressor, who, however, can never harm those who are born of God (5:18c)."[236] This security comes from the fact that "the evil one" has been defeated by Jesus Christ by victory over death and sin.[237] As a result, when someone is born of

---

[233] Culpepper, *1, 2, 3 John*, 35; Kysar, *1, 2, 3 John*, 54; Brown, *Epistles of John*, 303; Smalley, *1, 2, 3 John*, 74.

[234] Smalley, *1, 2, 3 John*, 75; Culpepper, *1, 2, 3 John*, 36.

[235] Smalley, *1, 2, 3 John*, 75.

[236] Schnackenburg, *The Johannine Epistles*, 117.

[237] See now J. E. Bruns, "A Note on John 16.33 and 1 John 2.13–14," *JBL* (1967): 451–53.

God, Jesus Christ secures victory over death for that person.

The final section of this verse arises out of an unfortunate versification in the NIV text (as also KJV, RSV, NASB, REB). Most editions of the Greek text begin v. 14 at this point. This text form creates an exact symmetry between 2:12–13 and 2:14. This portion of text contains two alterations from its form in 2:12. First, the author employs the term *paidia* rather than *teknia*. There is little significance to this change, and the NIV correctly translates both as "dear children."[238]

Second, in 2:12 John described the members of the community as those who had been forgiven on account of the name [of Jesus]. Now he characterizes them as those who have known (perfect tense) the Father. These two characteristics, the forgiveness of sins and the knowledge of the Father, are complementary. They are also necessary if one is to be part of the people of God. The interesting thing about these two descriptions is that they mirror exactly two of the promises of the new covenant made in Jer 31:31–34: knowledge of God and forgiveness of sins.[239] This passage again shows the deep continuity that exists between the Old and New Testaments. Those who are members of the new covenant community have the law of God written on their hearts, and they are taught by the Holy Spirit, who dwells within them.

To know the Father is to be like the Father. Spiritual maturity moves us into a deeper and fuller knowledge of our God with the result being familial resemblance. Children should resemble their Father. John believes they will.

2:14 The first part of the verse mirrors exactly what was said previously to the fathers in v. 13, except for the change in the verb tense of *graphō*. The NIV, as noted previously, does not reflect this change. The ambiguity over the identity of the one "who is from the beginning" remains, though it would seem again that the Son is in view (cf. 1:1). Even in this small way and somewhat veiled fashion, John is attacking the heterodox views about the person of Jesus Christ that are held by his opponents.

The final section of the verse, which focuses on the young ones, has a threefold structure. It includes the same material covered in v. 13 but also states these believers have been able to overcome the evil one. First, John affirms that these young ones are strong. This assertion could indicate that these believers were strong both physically and spiritually, but it is clear that contextually the reference is to spiritual strength. These young men are strong in the Lord (Deut 31:6; Josh 1:7). This strength comes from their faith in the Lord Jesus Christ, whose victory over the evil one gives them

---

[238] Smalley, *1, 2, 3 John*, 76.

[239] Brown, *Epistles of John*, 320; R. A. Culpepper, *The Gospel and Letters of John* (Nashville: Abingdon, 1998), 261.

the ability to triumph (1 John 5:4).

The second reason for their victory over the evil one is that the word of God abides (present tense) in them. The word "abides" probably refers to the word of life or divine message revealed by and in Jesus Christ, though it may refer to the love command that is described in 2:3–11. It would be unwise, however, to place unnecessary restrictions on the phrase. It is doubtful that this reference to the word refers to the Living Word Jesus Christ. It is through constant contact with the word of God that the believer has communion with the Father and gains direction and spiritual energy for the battle.[240] It is highly likely that John refers to the Old Testament and to the account of the life of Jesus in his Gospel. The believer's source of strength has not changed. The believer may still overcome (last of the perfect tense forms in vv. 12–14) the evil one through faith in Jesus Christ and careful study of and abiding in the Word of God.

4. Be Warned of Enemies of the Faith (2:15–28)

(1) Beware of the World (2:15–17)

[15]**Do not love the world or anything in the world. If anyone loves the world, the love of the Father is not in him.** [16]**For everything in the world—the cravings of sinful man, the lust of his eyes and the boasting of what he has and does—comes not from the Father but from the world.** [17]**The world and its desires pass away, but the man who does the will of God lives forever.**

In 2:15–17 the author moves from emphasizing the assurance that the members of the community have in their relationship with God to exhorting them about how they are to deal with the world that hates them and is opposed to God. He accentuates this change by using the present tense imperative form of *agapaō* to begin v. 15. Once again belief and behavior are linked together in John's assurances and exhortations. Smalley notes that the exhortations can be divided into the following three interconnected stanzas:[241]

15	Love of the world	Love of the Father
	▼	▼
16	comes from the world	comes from the Father
	▼	▼
17	the world passes away	the one who obeys remains forever.

This strophic description illustrates the logic of John's argument in these

---

[240] Brown, *Epistles of John*, 322; Smalley, *1, 2, 3 John*, 79.
[241] Smalley, *1, 2, 3 John*, 80.

verses. Those who are members of the believing community should see that the things of the world, though they are alluring, lead to death and not life. These verses provide apt commentary on the temptations of Eve and Adam in Genesis 3 and the Lord Jesus in Matt 4:1–11 (cf. Luke 4:1–13). The parallels are too striking to be insignificant.

2:15 John begins this verse by issuing the command that the believer is not to love the world or anything in the world. Initially this command sounds strange given the fact that John 3:16 says clearly and beautifully that God loves the world and the fact that 1 John 2:2 says the Son made atonement for the sins of the world. What is the difference? The difference is found in the way John uses the term *kosmos* in each instance. Contextual considerations are crucial. In these epistles and the Gospel, John employs this term in three distinct and basic ways: (1) the created universe (3:17; 4:17; John 1:10); (2) the world of human persons (John 3:16; 1 John 2:2); and (3) an evil organized earthly system controlled by the power of the evil one that has aligned itself against God and his kingdom (4:3–5; 5:19; John 16:11). In these verses John uses the third meaning. One should note that John is not advocating an ontological dualism or a dualistic cosmology in which the creation is evil. He is advocating a temporal, ethical dualism in which there is a constant battle going on between the realms of darkness and light.[242] That this dualism is temporal and not eternal is made clear by the transient nature of the world and its lust in v. 17.

The verb *agapaō*, used in this context to describe both the love of the world and the love of the Father could carry a different meaning in each usage. It is argued that when the word is used in its "Christian" sense it should be translated "love," but when it is used in a negative way it should be translated "take a fancy to" or "to place a higher value on." The difference in these uses is not the emotion that is felt by the individual but the application of that emotion, or attraction, in a positive or negative manner. When an individual believer fulfills the love command by showing compassion to a brother or sister (2:10), this love is properly motivated and properly directed. When people love the world, they are misapplying this human emotion in a way that will lead to their demise. In a sense love is neutral. The object of one's love or affection is decisive. One must be careful that this love is going in the right direction and that it acts in a manner consistent with Christian confession.[243] John charges us to love neither the world in general nor the things of the world in particular. The command is comprehensive. Our allegiance must not be

---

[242] Smalley, *1, 2, 3 John*, 80–81.

[243] Ibid., 82; Schnackenburg, *The Johannine Epistles,* 119. Cf. also Thomas, "Exegetical Digest of 1 John," 162–63. Thomas supports the view that the love for the world is the same type of love given to God, that it is a love of supreme devotion.

divided. Our affection must be focused and specific.

The correct application of love springs from the fact that the believer has a singular loyalty and commitment to the Father. This verse states clearly that one cannot love the world and love God at the same time. The absolute nature of this statement is striking and compels careful and serious reflection. The stakes are high. Because the Father's kingdom is at war with the kingdom of this world, the two will never coexist peacefully. To pledge allegiance to one side is to declare opposition to the other.[244]

2:16 This verse clarifies in vivid terms those things that come from the evil world and attempt to lead astray those who have believed in Jesus Christ. Again it must be emphasized that this condemnation of everything that is in the world is not a declaration that the world created by God is evil. John fully embraced the doctrine of the goodness of creation as taught in Genesis 1–2 (see John 1:1–18). Rather, it is a proclamation that humanity in its sinfulness has followed evil rather than good and has worshiped the created things rather than the Creator (Rom 1:20). The problem is not that God created the material things of the world. The problem is that people have made these things into idols. The three things listed in this verse—"the cravings of sinful man, the lust of his eyes and the boasting of what he has and does"—should not be seen as a comprehensive list of vices. These are avenues by which sinful humanity is especially prone to pervert the goodness of God's creation.[245]

John first mentions the "cravings" or "lust" (the NIV translates two occurrences of the Gk. word *epithymia* by these two English words) of "sinful man" (Gk. *sarx*, "flesh"). The terms John uses in the Greek text, *epithymia* and *sarx*, are basically neutral terms. *Epithymia* can be used to describe both positive and negative human desires (cf. 1 Thess 2:17, which relates Paul's "desire" to see his readers; Phil 1:23, where Paul relates his

---

[244] Kysar, *1, 2, 3 John,* 55; Smalley, *1, 2, 3 John,* 82. The interpreter also must again decide whether the genitive construction ἡ ἀγάπη τοῦ πατρὸς is objective or subjective. Due to the fact that it is in parallel construction where the world is the object of the verb ἀγαπᾶν on two occasions in this verse, one should interpret this as an objective construction. But Smalley, Brown, Culpepper, and others argue that it is more difficult to distinguish between the two meanings of the construction because the love that someone has for God can only come out of the love that God has shown the believer. These authors argue that this is an example of a place where the author employs a construction or term that can carry two meanings so that both can rightly be included in one's interpretation of the text. This decision may appear to be a nondecision to some, but when one considers this verse theologically, it makes perfect sense. Cf. Smalley, *1, 2, 3 John,* 83; Brown, *Epistles of John,* 306; Culpepper, *1, 2, 3 John,* 38.

[245] Smalley, *1, 2, 3 John,* 83; Brown, *Epistles of John,* 306; Schnackenburg, *The Johannine Epistles,* 120. Some commentators align these three sins with general categories of sin in the world. It seems that the best way to look at this verse is to see these as three general areas of sin that seem to plague people of every generation. They worked in the garden, they were used against Jesus, and we can expect their continued assault in our own personal battles with the evil one.

desire to be with Christ; and negatively Rom 1:24, which describes the "sinful desires" of the pagan heart). Most often it is used in the negative sense. The term *sarx* is not necessarily negative in that it may denote the idea of the whole person in his or her strengths and weaknesses. Yet it is obvious that in our present text John emphasizes the negative meaning of these terms that arises from the tendency of human beings to fulfill the natural desires they have that are contrary to God's will. We are not sinful because we sin. We sin because we are sinful. We enter the world with a nature and bent predisposed to sin (cf. Rom 3:9–20). The only remedy for this sin condition, which results in both physical and spiritual death, is to become a child of God through faith in Jesus Christ.[246] Schnackenburg argues that John has in mind "the overwhelming sexual desires which drive human beings to excess, the consequences of which can be devastating."[247] Although these types of desires must certainly be included, even emphasized in what John describes, one narrows the meaning of the phrase too much if this becomes the exclusive meaning of the text. John would include anything and any way in which humans improperly fulfill fleshly desires (overeating, drunkenness, etc.).

John then moves to address the "lust of his eyes," which can be seen as an aspect of the "cravings of the sinful man" that he previously discussed. The eyes in and of themselves cannot be said to be guilty of sinful desires. Our eyes are a precious gift from God (Prov 20:12). They are, however, often the means by which sinful desires are introduced into the mind of the individual.[248] Eyes are windows into the soul. "It is the eyes that lead most directly and quickly from the external observation to evil thoughts latent in the human heart" (cf. Mark 7:21–23).[249] This reality is affirmed in the teachings of Jesus, who in the antitheses in the Sermon on the Mount equates adultery with the lustful look (5:27–30). Again one must be careful not to limit this area of temptation to sexual desire. Dodd notes that the desire of the eyes can be understood as "the tendency to be captivated by the outward show of things, without enquiring into their real values."[250] This insight cuts to the heart of the issue in that all of these temptations of the world focus on enjoyment in the present without an analysis or understanding of the future ramifications. How an action, or its value, compares with the worth of the eternal things that come from God must always be factored into the equations of life.

The final temptation that John cites is the "boasting of what he [man] has

---

[246] Brown, *Epistles of John*, 308–10; Smalley, *1, 2, 3 John*, 83: Kysar, *1, 2, 3 John*, 56.

[247] Schnackenburg, *The Johannine Epistles*, 122.

[248] Smalley, *1, 2, 3 John*, 84.

[249] Schnackenburg, *The Johannine Epistles*, 122.

[250] Dodd, *The Johannine Epistles*, 41.

and does." This translation of the phrase *alazoneia tou biou* ("the pride or vain glory of life") focuses on an objective understanding of the genitive construction to condemn pride and boasting about having and doing things this worldly system deems important. Again one should not be too quick to dismiss the subjective genitive interpretation, for it is likely that John is also condemning the pride that results from giving false value to the things of the world.[251] This pride that results from and in worldly possession is an affront to God, for it leads to a glorification of the self and a failure to realize the dependence of humanity upon God, the Creator, for existence. In this area of temptation, individuals make idols of their livelihood, social standing, and any other status symbol that the world determines is important but that matters little to God.[252] Pride, prestige, power, and position count for nothing in the kingdom of God. The value system of this world is turned on its head when God provides the evaluation.

2:17 The heart of John's argument is now given. This final verse of the section "contrasts the outcomes of these two loves, two lives, and two orientations toward Life."[253] When compared with a life lived in the will of God, the things this life has to offer are really empty imitations of God's best. The things of the world seem to be of great value, but they are worthless when compared to the eternal blessings that come from doing the will of God. Jesus Christ in his death and resurrection has defeated the world that is opposed to God and has secured life eternal for those who believe.

John links the believer's confession of faith to his conduct by using the phrase "the one who does the will of God remains forever" to describe who will be a part of God's eternal kingdom. This idea of doing the will of God is closely linked to Jesus' mission in the Gospel, for there are several occasions where Jesus explains that he only takes action in accordance with the will of the Father (4:34; 5:30; 6:38; note particularly that involving eternal life for believers in 6:39–40; 7:17).[254] It is likely that John is again exhorting the readers to live as Jesus lived while he was on this earth, that is, solely focused on doing the will of the Father (2:6). As Culpepper notes, "Victory is assured, resistance is required."[255]

This passage has a clear eschatological focus that emphasizes that the things of the world, even the Earth itself, will one day pass from the scene, just as the darkness is passing away and the true light is already shining (2:8). The kingdom of God on earth was inaugurated in the death and resurrection of our Lord, and it will be established forever with his return. The

---

[251] Smalley, *1, 2, 3 John*, 85.

[252] Cf. Kysar, *1, 2, 3 John*, 56; Bruce, *The Epistles of John*, 61; Brown, *Epistles of John*, 312.

[253] Culpepper, *1, 2, 3 John*, 40.

[254] Smalley, *1, 2, 3 John*, 88.

[255] Culpepper, *1, 2, 3 John*, 41.

eschatological nature of this verse provides a fitting transition to John's discussion of the antichrists who have departed from the community in 2:18–19.[256]

(2) Beware of the Antichrists (2:18–28)

[18]**Dear children, this is the last hour; and as you have heard that the antichrist is coming, even now many antichrists have come. This is how we know it is the last hour.** [19]**They went out from us, but they did not really belong to us. For if they had belonged to us, they would have remained with us; but their going showed that none of them belonged to us.**

[20]**But you have an anointing from the Holy One, and all of you know the truth.** [21]**I do not write to you because you do not know the truth, but because you do know it and because no lie comes from the truth.** [22]**Who is the liar? It is the man who denies that Jesus is the Christ. Such a man is the antichrist—he denies the Father and the Son.** [23]**No one who denies the Son has the Father; whoever acknowledges the Son has the Father also.**

[24]**See that what you have heard from the beginning remains in you. If it does, you also will remain in the Son and in the Father.** [25]**And this is what he promised us—even eternal life.**

[26]**I am writing these things to you about those who are trying to lead you astray.** [27]**As for you, the anointing you received from him remains in you, and you do not need anyone to teach you. But as his anointing teaches you about all things and as that anointing is real, not counterfeit—just as it has taught you, remain in him.**

[28]**And now, dear children, continue in him, so that when he appears we may be confident and unashamed before him at his coming.**

Although the division of the previous sections of John's argument in this chapter has followed an easily discernible pattern, scholars disagree where this subunit of John's epistle should be divided. Scholars conclude the pericope at the end of v. 27, v. 28, and v. 29. I include 2:28 both with the conclusion of 2:18–27 and with the beginning of 2:28–3:10. Verse 28 functions as a connector (what linguists call a "heads-tail" connector) between sections. I include 2:28 here in part because of the use of *teknia,* which forms an inclusio with *paidia* in 2:18.[257] Smalley argues that 2:28 ends this section but that 2:29 also should be included because it provides the transition to the material that is discussed in chapter three.[258] First John 2:29, how-

---

[256] For a contrary perspective see Schnackenburg, *The Johannine Epistles,* 123; Brown, *Epistles of John,* 314.

[257] A significant argument for a chiastic structure of 2:18–28 is set forth by J. Breck, "The Function of ΠΑΕ in 1 John 2:20," *St. Vladimir's Theological Quarterly* 35 (1991): 203–6. The argument is not without its difficulties, but it helps explain the location and double (triple) use of χρῖσμα in vv. 20,27a,b.

[258] Smalley, *1, 2, 3 John,* 93–94.

ever, semantically fits better with 3:1 and what follows.

Brown offers helpful assistance in assessing various arguments concerning the literary structure of the passage. He acknowledges that some scholars see a chiastic structure in this section but notes that the text does not easily fit into any mold. He proposes arranging the text into four units based on a pattern of direct initial addresses to the audience that serve as markers. The first occurrence of a noun in direct address comes with the use of *paidia* ("children") in v. 18. The final three times the author addresses the congregation as "you" (plural) by placing the pronoun *hymeis* in an emphatic forward position in the sentence, with each instance being associated with an anointing or a message from Jesus Christ. This section is also held together by its focus upon the fact that it is the last hour. In the first subunit (2:18b–19) he speaks of the coming antichrist; in the second subunit (2:20–23), of the liar and the antichrist; in the third subunit (2:24–26), of the those who are trying to lead others astray with a final exhortation to resist the appeals of the ones who have left the community and to abide in Christ.[259] If v. 28 is taken with this final appeal, and thematically it does fit (remain in him ... continue in him), 2:18–28 forms an inclusio. Of course we acknowledge also that 2:28 is semantically related to 3:2! Perhaps John never intended for scholars to outline his epistle nicely and neatly.

In summary, John presents in great detail the nature of the deception that is being perpetrated by those who have left the community, and by so doing he passes on to every successive generation of believers "a study in the dangers, origin, and effects of the counterfeit teachings which constantly threaten to destroy the church."[260]

2:18 Verse 18 is chiastic in structure:

A This is the last hour.
  B Antichrist is coming
  B' Many antichrists have come
A' This is the last hour.

John begins this verse with the familiar use of *paidia* (dear or little children; cf. v. 13) to show that he is addressing the community as a whole. This usage also serves as a transition to a new section. He declares to them that it is the "last hour." While this is an anarthrous construction (i.e., without the definite article) in the Greek text *(eschate hora),* it seems clear both on grammatical and exegetical grounds that this must be seen as "the" final

---

[259] Brown, *Epistles of John*, 362–63. He notes that "scholars are almost evenly divided as to whether the unit should end with 2:27 or 2:28." He opts for 2:27 but notes John's love for hinge verses in part explains our dilemma. Allowing v. 28 to function as a "double hinge," swinging in both directions, would seem to solve the problem.

[260] Culpepper, *1, 2, 3 John*, 43.

hour, particularly when one takes into account the manner in which the hour is used in the Gospel.[261] This last hour, viewed as a theologically technical term, denotes a period of time, whether long or short, that will usher in the termination of all time and the revealing of the final salvation promised by God.[262]

In Christianity the consummation of the kingdom of God, inaugurated in the cross and resurrection of Jesus, will take place at the parousia (the return of the resurrected Lord Jesus Christ). The establishment of the kingdom will be opposed by the coming of the antichrist. That the antichrist can come paradoxically affirms that the Christ has come, for he cannot oppose that which has no reality. With the coming of God's Christ, a whole new dynamic is established. John's eschatology is flexible in that he both emphasizes the present experience of Christ that the believer has but also the promise of his return and the opposition he will encounter. Due to the fact that Jesus has inaugurated the kingdom, John can say with assurance that it is the last hour. It has been the last hour since the Son of God invaded the evil one's domain and dealt him a death blow in the cross and resurrection. The ending of that final hour, however, is unknown. John could say that the last hour has come "without being dogmatic about the precise chronology of the event, and the exact length of the 'hour.' "[263]

John asserts that it is the last hour because of the fact that there were many antichrists that had come. They were trying to lure members of the community into a world that is passing away (v. 17) and into the darkness. This term *antichristos* is found only in the epistles of John (2:18,22; 4:3; 2 John 7) and was likely coined by John himself.[264] The term is unique, and it bears different nuances of meaning. It is singular and plural, personal and impersonal. "Antichrist" carries a similar meaning to terms used both in the

---

[261] Brown, *Epistles of John*, 330. Brown explains that in BDF the rule states that predicate nouns are anarthrous and that the article may be used to indicate that the predicate noun is the only term in the construction that merits designation. This rule has caused some to argue that this phrase must be translated "a final hour." Others argue that this phrase is general in nature because abstract nouns are usually anarthrous. Brown argues that the more plausible explanation is that the absence of the article flows out of the fact that the author uses the "last" as if it were an ordinal number – "G John never uses an article with "hour" modified by an ordinal (BDF, 256; John 1:39; 4:6; 19:14)" (*Epistles of John*, 330).

[262] Smalley, *1, 2, 3 John*, 95; Bruce, *The Epistles of John*, 64.

[263] Smalley, *1, 2, 3 John*, 95–97.

[264] See the appendix on Antichrist for a more detailed examination of the background and meaning of the term. Americans in particular remain fascinated with the concept. Nineteen percent, at the end of the twentieth century, believed Antichrist was alive on the earth (*Newsweek* [Nov. 1, 1999]: 69). Brown, *Epistles of John*, 333–36 and Thomas, "Exegetical Digest of 1 John," 177–82 also provide detailed discussion of various interpretations of the meaning of this term in a useful format.

Synoptics[265] and Paul[266] to describe the situation that would precede the return of Jesus to earth. The focus in this verse is not the antichrist (singular) but the antichrists (plural) that had arisen to tear apart the community.

These individuals, as their designation indicates, are against Christ. They hold to a heretical Christology and are deceivers whose false views are put forward to lead believers astray and to oppose Christ. The following verses address their wrong thinking concerning his person.

There is little doubt that their view of his work was also defective. One form of the Christological error present in the community is that the secessionists (v. 19) are advocates of a docetic Christology that emphasizes the divinity of Jesus at the expense of his humanity (1 John 1:1–4; 2 John 7). It is also possible that there are those who emphasized the humanity of Jesus to the point that they failed to see that, as the Christ, he is God. (Both of these interpretations are possible based on where one places the emphasis in 2:22.)[267]

It takes wisdom and perception to understand which theological issues are open to discussion and honest disagreement and which ones are so clearly essential that schism must be preferred to compromise.[268] John examines the problem and rightly concludes that the proper understanding of the person and work of Jesus Christ is fundamental to Christianity and cannot be compromised. In a sense this debate has continued in discussions of New Testament theology throughout the twentieth century, in which there was a bifurcation of the Jesus of history and the Christ of faith. Critical scholarship has argued that these entities cannot be reconciled. It seems that John faced a similar issue in his day and argued forcefully that this divided, if not schizophrenic, Christology cannot be tolerated by the believing church.

The verse concludes with an inclusio through which John brings the reader back to the initial point of the verse. The rise of antichrists should not cause the believer to be dismayed or disheartened but should be an encouragement because it is a sign that the return of Jesus Christ is imminent. This antichrist activity is indicative of the reality that the real Christ has come and believers are living in a period of time when the kingdom of God has been inaugurated and awaits its final consummation.

2:19   The first part of v. 19 (like v. 18) is chiastic:

---

[265] Matt 24:24; Mark 13:22. Here the opponents of Jesus are called "false christs and false prophets."

[266] 2 Thess 2:1–12. Paul calls this individual "the man of lawlessness" and "the man doomed to destruction" (KJV, "son of perdition").

[267] Smalley, *1, 2, 3 John*, 99.

[268] Culpepper, *1, 2, 3 John*, 45.

A They went out from us
  B They did not really belong to us
  B′ If they had belonged to us
A′ They would have remained with us.

John begins by explaining that those who have left the community have done so at their own initiative and for our instruction. This contrast is amplified through the multiple uses of the first person plural and third person plural pronouns in the verse (they vs. us). The Greek construction *ex hēmōn* involves a play on the meaning of the preposition ("from") so that John can signify both "out of" (membership) and "part of" (origin). These people who left the community had shared in its external life but were never truly a part of its internal existence due to the fact that they had never truly been born from above.[269]

The reason for this assertion that they had never really been a part of the community is given in the form of a condition that is contrary to fact. Literally, "for if they were from us (but they weren't), they would have remained with us (but they didn't)."[270] The decision of the heretics to remove themselves from fellowship with the community gives evidence that they have never really believed the gospel and that their true inward devotion was to the world. John's reasoning in this verse is circular but flawless, given the presupposition that if they had been children of God they would have remained.[271] John has put forward the test of obedience and the test of love, and now he adds the test of perseverance. Bruce notes, "The perseverance of the saints is a biblical doctrine, but it is not a doctrine designed to lull the indifferent into a sense of false security; it means that perseverance is an essential token of sanctity."[272] John is confident that those who belong to God will remain with God and, by extension, with the community of faith. This verse is not meant to scare people into obedience but to strengthen the faith of the Johannine church, which had been torn apart by the actions of the dissenters. Once again it is clear that having one's name on the church roll does not necessarily mean that one's name is written in the Book of Life.[273]

The final clause reveals that this departure by the secessionists was according to the purposes of God, for in their leaving the true devotion of these people was revealed. This is a typical Johannine construction (*alla hina,* "but so that"), which in his Gospel pertains to the fulfillment of Scrip-

---

[269] Smalley, *1, 2, 3 John*, 102.

[270] D. E. Hiebert, "An Exposition of 1 John 2:18–28," *BSac* (1989): 81.

[271] Smalley, *1, 2, 3 John*, 103; Culpepper, *1, 2, 3 John*, 46.

[272] Bruce, *The Epistles of John*, 69.

[273] Ibid., 70.

ture or, more often, to a general aspect of God's plan (John 1:8,31; 9:3; 14:31; 15:25). The believers who have remained in the community can take heart that God has precipitated these events to remove this group that held to a heretical Christology so that the church would be purified and educated.[274]

2:20 Having discussed the reality of the antichrists that had departed from the community, John provides an emphatic word of encouragement to the members of the community by proclaiming that they were obviously standing firm in the truth and for good reason. The difference between the secessionists and the true believers is grounded in the fact that the faithful have received an anointing from the Holy One. Two questions are raised by this affirmation: (1) What exactly is the meaning and significance of the term, *chrisma* ("anointing")? and (2) To whom does the term Holy One refer?

A play on words is apparently taking place in this passage in which the terms *antichristos, christos,* and *chrisma* are all being used to explain the difference between the secessionists and the ones who have remained faithful to the Gospel. The believers should be encouraged because they have received an anointing from "the anointed one," here called the "Holy One." The term *chrisma* appears in the New Testament only here and in 2:27. The background for the anointing may be either Jewish or Greek, and the idea may refer to a figurative or literal event.[275]

In the Old Testament anointing was usually done for the purpose of consecration or the setting aside of an individual or object for a particular sacred purpose (Exod 29:7; 30:25; 40:15). Anointing later came to signify that the Spirit of God has come to dwell within an individual so that he can either rule or prophesy for God (1 Sam 16:13; Isa 61:1). This connection with the indwelling of the Spirit seems to provide the background for understanding the anointing of Jesus in the New Testament. Peter says in Acts 10:38 that God anointed him with the Holy Spirit, most likely illustrated at his baptism (Matt 3:16–17; Mark 1:10–11; Luke 3:21–22; John 1:32–34).

This Jewish-Christian background for understanding *chrisma* provides a

---

[274] Brown, *Epistles of John*, 340; Smalley, *1, 2, 3 John*, 104; 188–90; Westcott, *Epistles of St. John*, 72. The construction ὅτι οὐκ εἰσὶν πάντες ἐξ ἡμῶν is ambiguous in that the subject can either be the secessionists who have left the Johannine church or members of the Johannine congregation with the sense that "not all church members belong to us" (cf. KJV, NASB, RSV). The latter view is problematic in that it requires a change of subject that is unexpected and requires a different ordering of the words in the Gk. text that brings the negative particle to a position that immediately precedes πάντες. In the present situation the negation is separated from the noun by the verb and is, therefore, universal ("none").

[275] Smalley, *1, 2, 3 John*, 105; Thomas, "Exegetical Digest of 1 John," 192–93.

solid foundation for arguing that the term is here describing the gift of the Spirit to the one who believes. What Paul calls the baptism (1 Cor 12:13), John refers to as the anointing. Some have argued that this blessing of the Holy Spirit comes through a ritual act of anointing usually connected with baptism or the placing of oil upon a believer. There is nothing in the text, however, to indicate a ritual connection. The context of 2:18–28 (29) supports a spiritual understanding due to the fact that there is no mention of the act of anointing or baptizing. Second, the use of the term in v. 27 concerns the reception of doctrinal, spiritual truth. Third, the image of God's seed abiding in the Christian at 3:9 could form a parallel to the idea in our present verse in which God's indwelling Spirit acts as a teacher and a guide in all matters of truth.[276]

It could be argued, based on the Greek background of *chrisma,* that the ointment is the Word of God. The strength of this interpretation is that it establishes an objective standard against which doctrine can be measured and curtails the subjectivism that is possible when the Spirit of God is the only teacher. The main argument in favor of this view comes from the statement in v. 24 that what was heard from the beginning, namely, the word of God dwells within the believer (cf. also 2 John 2).[277] Although this view is attractive and may not be entirely out of place, it seems that the overall context of the passage and the connection of the Paraclete with knowledge of the truth would lead to understanding this term in connection with the Holy Spirit.[278] A connection between the word and the Spirit is possible in light of Old Testament teaching, where the Spirit is breath and can be placed in parallel with the word (Ps 33:6). Due to this cohesion between the Spirit and the word, it is best to see these entities as companions that always work together. The Spirit will never lead the believer in a direction that contradicts the teaching of the word of God.[279]

We are now faced with determining the identity of the Holy One. Is he the Father or the Son? The difficulty of determining the referent of the title is enhanced by the fact that John's Gospel states that the Paraclete is sent by Jesus (15:26; 16:7) and the Father (14:16,26). It should be noted that this passage is parallel to the anointing described in 2:27, which most likely comes from Jesus (cf v. 28). Still, this does not necessarily indicate that John would not say that the Spirit came from the Father in this verse.[280]

---

[276] Smalley; *1, 2, 3 John,* 106; Thomas, "Exegetical Digest of 1 John," 192–95; Brown, *Epistles of John,* 342–45.

[277] Dodd, *The Johannine Epistles,* 58–64; Smalley, *1, 2, 3 John,* 106.

[278] John 14:17; 15:26; 16:13. Cf. also Smalley, *1, 2, 3 John,* 106 and Schnackenburg, *The Johannine Epistles,* 151–54.

[279] Brown, *Epistles of John,* 346; Thomas, "Exegetical Digest of 1 John," 195.

[280] Brown, *Epistles of John,* 347.

In the Old Testament, especially in Isaiah, God is often called "the Holy One of Israel" (Ps 78:41; Isa 1:4; 5:19,24; 10:20; 12:6; 17:7; 29:19; 30:12,15; 31:1; 37:23; 41:14,16,20; 43:3,14; 45:11; 47:4; 48:17; 49:7; 54:5; 55:5; 60:9,14). The absolute use of *hagios* for God, though not as prevalent, also occurs in the Prophets (Isa 40:25; 43:15; Hos 11:9,12; Hab 3:3). In the New Testament God is described as holy (John 17:11; 1 Pet 1:16; Rev 6:10), though not through an absolute use of an adjective. Nowhere is the title "the Holy One" applied to God the Father. Still, one could argue that this passage about the giving of the Holy Spirit more closely resembles the two Paraclete passages where God is described as the one who gives him.[281]

The view that the Holy One refers to Jesus is held by a majority of scholars. One reason for this understanding is that there is a symmetry in describing the *chrisma* as coming from the *Christos*. In addition, there are several passages in the New Testament where Jesus is called the "Holy One of God" (Mark 1:24; Luke 4:34; John 6:69), and he is twice given the title "the Holy One" (Acts 3:14; Rev 3:7). These descriptions of Jesus as "the Holy One" tend to tip the balance in favor of understanding "the Holy One" to be a reference to Jesus in this passage. One must remember, however, that in the Johannine understanding of the Godhead this distinction is minimal due to the intimate fellowship that exists between the Father and the Son.[282]

The verse concludes with the statement that all believers know the truth ("the truth" is not in the Gk. text but is supplied from v. 21; see also the NLT).[283] John seeks to encourage these believers by explaining that they are the ones who truly know God and that it is this knowledge of God that enables them to understand the false nature of what the heretics are teaching. This instruction echoes the promise of the new covenant (Jer 31:31–34) that all who believe will have a real, intimate knowledge of God and that no man would have to teach them. Consequently, there is no need to be

---

[281] Ibid., 346–47.

[282] Ibid. 348; Thomas, "Exegetical Digest of 1 John," 195–96; Smalley, *1, 2, 3 John*, 108.

[283] Scholars are evenly divided over the exact form of the adjective πᾶς present in this sentence. The majority of MSS read πάντα, "all things," which would be the object of the verb (KJV). Several articles in favor of πάντα have been written in the past few years and should be consulted as one makes this decision. Cf. Thomas, "Exegetical Digest of 1 John," 197–98; Brown, *Epistles of John*, 348–49; J. Breck, "The Function of ΠΑΣ in 1 John 2:20," *St. Vladamir's Theological Quarterly* 35 (1991): 187–206; D. A. Black, "An Overlooked Stylistic Argument in Favor of πάντα in 1 John 2:20," *FNT* 5 (1992): 205–8; *TCGNT,* 641. Black makes an interesting argument in favor of πάντα that cannot be easily dismissed. But most scholars and translations favor the reading πάντες, "all," which would be the subject of the verb, as in the NIV. It seems that the more difficult nature of πάντες and the fact that πάντα could have been used to harmonize with the ideas of the Farewell Discourse favor the reading.

seduced by the esoteric teachings of the heretics who claim to have knowledge because real understanding comes only from the Holy One who gives it through His Spirit.[284]

2:21 John continues to praise and encourage believers in the community by explaining to them that, contrary to the claims of their opponents, they are the ones who know the truth and can identify the lie. This verse summarizes what John has been discussing in the previous verses by emphasizing that they know the truth and have no need of the esoteric knowledge claimed by the secessionists. John's argument is casual in nature. Because they have an anointing from the Holy One and because they know the truth, John can further explain both the nature of the truth and the nature of the lie. This is why he writes further. He is seeking to develop what he has previously written. Smalley explains, "It is because they possess an anointing, and can therefore discern the truth, that he is concerned to instruct them further in the gospel."[285]

Truth and error are incompatible. Indeed lies have their source in what is false, not in what is true. In this verse the truth is equivalent with the Christian gospel that has both theological content and ethical character. The truth and the lie (error) are mutually exclusive. They have no part with one another. John is no theological relativist in spiritual matters. As Smalley asserts: "The knowledge which John's orthodox readers possess, but which the secessionists (docetic or otherwise) lack, is the truth about the identity of Jesus: that he is the Christ, and that he is by nature one with man and one with God (cf. John 8:45; 14:6). This knowledge, moreover, is not simply intellectual; it is also part of a *relationship* between man and God through Christ."[286] The knowledge that the secessionists have does not make the believers ignorant; it makes the secessionists liars, confirming the assertion of v. 19 that they were never truly a part of the believing community.[287] These are strong but necessary words.

2:22 John's argument naturally flows from the lie that is not from the truth to the one who is "the liar." He speaks of those who have left the community and are propagating a false understanding of the person of Jesus. Those who do not believe that Jesus is the Messiah declare themselves to be on the side of the antichrist. It is interesting to note that this is the only place in the Johannine writings where liar *(pseustēs)* is used with the article as a title or designation of a known figure. When this point is taken with the Gospel of John, which defines a liar as the devil or anyone who claims to

---

[284] Brown, *Epistles of John*, 345–49; Bruce, *The Epistles of John*, 70–71; Smalley, *1, 2, 3 John*, 108.

[285] Smalley, *1, 2, 3 John*, 109.

[286] Ibid, 110.

[287] Cf. Schnackenburg, *The Johannine Epistles*, 144.

know God but does not accept the revelation in Jesus Christ (8:44,55), it seems that those who deny this revelation are classified as those who belong to the devil. This statement is not a general condemnation of all unbelievers but is likely a specific rebuke of these heretics, who have failed "to see the Godhead shine in the human life and death of Jesus."[288]

John now addresses directly the Christological error that leads people into the darkness. These false teachers have denied that Jesus is the Christ. It is certainly possible that there were those who, though attracted to Jesus, attempted to minimize his divinity, but it seems improbable that they would have been admitted to the community because the confession that Jesus is the Christ, the Son of God (John 20:31), would mostly likely be required for entrance (1 John 2:22,23; 3:23; 4:15; 5:1,5,13). It seems more probable, particularly when one takes into account the heresy of Cerinthus[289] that arose in this area, that the secessionists held to a Christology that diminished the human content of this confession of faith and denied the reality of the incarnation (cf. 4:2ff.; 2 John 7). Ignatius (d. 98/117) wrote against those who deny that Jesus is the Christ, the Son of God.[290] Irenaeus (Fl. ca. 175–ca. 195) attacked Cerinthus by name. Although it is not possible to know what the secessionists affirmed exactly/publicly (John does not tell us), it is clear that in some sense they denied that Jesus was the Christ, the Son of God in any vital and permanent incarnational understanding. They affirmed and accepted Jesus as significant and important in some manner, but their theology was wholly inadequate in its grasp of his person and ultimately of his work. As Marshall explains: "For John the height of heresy is to deny that Jesus is the Messiah, the Son of God and Savior. To reduce Jesus to the status of a mere man, or to allow no more than a temporary indwelling of some divine power in him is to strike at the root of Christianity. Modern thinkers may have more refined ways of stating similar denials of the reality of the incarnation. It may be doubted whether they are any more

---

[288] Bruce, *The Epistles of John*, 73; cf. also Culpepper, *1, 2, 3 John*, 49; Brown, *Epistles of John*, 351.

[289] Cerinthus probably lived around A. D. 100. He was a Gnostic Jewish-Christian who claimed that the divine emanation (or *aeon*) "Christ" came upon the man Jesus at his baptism in the form of a dove and left him at the crucifixion so that he died only as a man. As a result, the human and divine natures of Jesus were never properly united, and the Incarnation never really took place. There are some strong objections to a direct continuity between the secessionists and this individual, but it must be conceded that the Cerinthian heresy is similar to what John is attacking. For a more detailed discussion of this issue see Smalley, *1, 2, 3 John*, 111–13, and Marshall, *Epistles of John*, 157–58. Schnackenburg denies any Cerinthian connection (*The Johannine Epistles*, 19f.).

[290] Ignatius, *Letter to the Smyrnaeans*, in *The Apostolic Fathers*, 2nd ed. (Grand Rapids: Baker, 1989). Concerning Jesus he writes: "And he truly suffered just as he truly raised himself — not, as certain unbelievers say, that he suffered in appearance only. ... For I know and believe that he was in the flesh even after the resurrection" (pp. 110–11).

immune to John's perception that they take the heart out of Christianity."[291]

In the second half of the verse the liar, who denies the Incarnation, is called the antichrist. The designation of this person as the antichrist need not be a reference to the specific apocalyptic figure that will arise at the end of time. It may rather be a declaration that the one who opposes Christ by rejecting his true identity has taken on the "spirit of the antichrist" (4:3). The consequence of this action is that he denies the Father and the Son. The placing of this phrase in apposition to the title of antichrist shows the gravity of this false Christology. It is doubtful that anyone of the heretics had directly denied the Fatherhood of God, but by their refusal to believe that Jesus is the Christ they have shown that they have never truly known the Father, for Jesus and the Father are one (John 10:30). Denial or acceptance of God's revelation in the man, Jesus, is equivalent to a denial or acceptance of the Father.[292]

2:23 This emphatic statement about how one has a relationship with the Father develops what John said in the previous verse and shows the dire consequences of believing this Christological heresy. John begins by explaining the effects in negative terms and then moves to positive ones, preparing the way for the exhortation that is to follow. John's claim that anyone who denies the Son does not have or possess the Father asserts unequivocally that a person who denies the Son has no child-parent relationship with God.[293] Calvin puts it well, "The Father cannot be separated from the Son."[294] There is an exclusivity that cannot be denied. One enters into a relationship with the Father through a relationship with Jesus Christ. This unique saying as a whole is likely taken from the common Christian tradition that is reflected in the Synoptics (cf. Matt 10:32–33 and par.) and can also be found in John's Gospel (9:22; 12:42). The use of *echei* ("has") with a divine object, however, does not have this parallel, but it is used again in the epistles (1 John 5:12; 2 John 9). There are some approximations of this construction that occur in the Old Testament, but there is no word in Hebrew that matches the meaning exactly (Lev 26:12; Exod 20:3; Num 18:20; Deut 12:12). We have what appears to be "a Johannine adaptation of the covenant motif" in which the believer has God as Father through Jesus Christ. In addition, the construction comes from language that is used to describe the action of God in the New Covenant, whereby the people of God know him.[295]

The positive side of the argument is that the ones who confess the Son

---

[291] Marshall, *Epistles of John,* 159.

[292] Smalley, *1, 2, 3 John,* 114–15; Kysar, *1, 2, 3 John,* 63.

[293] Smalley, *1, 2, 3 John,* 115; Hiebert, "Exposition of 1 John 2:18–28," 85.

[294] Calvin, 260.

[295] Brown, *Epistles of John,* 353–54; Smalley, *1, 2, 3 John,* 115. It is interesting to note that this construction was used by those who followed John in the second century both among the orthodox and the heterodox (cf. Brown, *Epistles of John,* 354).

possess the Father, balancing perfectly the first part of the verse. The conscious and open confession that Jesus is Son of God who is both divine and human automatically results in a relationship with the Father. This mirrors the reciprocal relationship between the Son and the Father that was affirmed in v. 22. We are faced with either confessing or denying Jesus Christ. There is no middle ground. As Smalley notes, "The possibility of honest agnosticism about the person and work of Jesus does not seem to have occurred to John!"[296]

The foundation is established through a proper understanding of the person and work of Jesus Christ, as elucidated in vv. 22–23. John now returns to a discussion of abiding in the Son and the Father to exhort the believers to continue to live in a manner befitting one who has called Jesus Lord.

2:24–25 John begins his exhortation emphatically by using the personal pronoun, *hymeis* in a forward position. He emphasizes to the believers in the community that they are to make sure that what they have heard from the beginning remains in them. Placing this pronoun in a forward position also serves to draw a distinction between the true believers and the secessionists, who are liars and antichrists. What they have heard from the beginning most likely refers to the original apostolic message they heard at the time of and prior to their conversions (cf. 2:7). But we cannot exclude a possible reference to the teaching of Jesus himself (cf. Mark 1:14–15; Eph 2:17) or his preexistence with God the Father (1:1; John 1:1; 17:24). In addition, there is a connection between the abiding of the message in them and the abiding of the anointing. Both are continuous following their reception by the believer. The two work together as the Christian stays in communion with both the Father and the Son.[297]

John is so concerned that what they heard from the beginning remains in them that he repeats himself (this repetition is unfortunately not obvious in the NIV, which reduces it to "if it does"). Repetition reinforces the urgency of the teaching: Do not move away from the word you heard from us.[298]

The verse concludes with the promise that if this condition is met, the believer will continue to remain in the Son and in the Father. Three times in this verse some form of the word "remain" is used (again the NIV loses this emphasis). As with the first two parts of this verse, John uses the pronoun *hymeis* for emphasis and in a forward position. This relationship in which the Christian remains in God is vital, intimate, and constant. The order of

---

[296] Smalley, *1, 2, 3 John*, 117; Cf. also Brown, *Epistles of John*, 355; Hiebert, "Exposition of 1 John 2:18–28," 85–86; Culpepper, *1, 2, 3 John*, 50.

[297] Hiebert, "Exposition of 1 John 2:18–28," 86; Smalley, *1, 2, 3 John*, 118; Brown, *Epistles of John*, 355. Burge believes John had the fourth gospel in view when he penned these words (*Letters of John*, 130). This cannot be ruled out, but is probably more restrictive than is warranted.

[298] Smalley, *1, 2, 3 John*, 199; Marshall, *Epistles of John*, 160.

the Son and the Father places the emphasis on the person of Jesus Christ, through whom the believer has access to the Father. Smalley notes, "If this good news be allowed to direct the theological thought and moral practice of the individual disciple, the outcome is a deep fellowship with *both* the Son of God *and* God himself."[299]

The initial *kai* (and) in v. 25 indicates that John is relating a further blessing that comes from abiding in what we have heard from the beginning. This pledge (note the present tense form of *eimi*) is made available to all who believe that Jesus is the Christ, the Son of God. The antecedent of the pronoun "he" *(autos)* could be either the Father or the Son. Functionally, eternal life is a promise that comes to the believer from God through Jesus Christ. This interpretation makes sense given the mention of both the Father and the Son in v. 24 and the reciprocal relationship of the Father and the Son that John has stressed in this section of the epistle.[300]

John reveals the content of the promise that is made available to the Christian: eternal life. This promise echos the promises of life that Jesus makes in the Gospel (3:14–15,36; 4:14; 5:24; 6:40,47; 8:51; 17:2; 20:31). The reference to eternal life is both that of the future promise of eternal life with the Father and the Son and the present experience of abiding in God the Father and in Jesus Christ. No either/or interpretation is necessary. The eschatological perspective of both the Gospel of John and the epistle takes into account the present and future aspects of salvation unto eternal life, secured in the death and resurrection of Jesus the Messiah. In the present the abiding presence of Jesus Christ and the Father give evidence that the power of sin and death has been defeated and that the believer has moved from the darkness into the light and now possesses eternal life. This defeat of sin and death in the cross and resurrection also secures a future eternal dwelling place with the Father and the Son in the kingdom of God.[301]

2:26 M. Luther said, "Those who teach new doctrine rarely return."[302] John explains that the preceding exhortation to hold fast to their initial reception and understanding of Christ was meant to strengthen them in their quest to withstand the pressure to follow the secessionists away from the truth and down their pathway to destruction. The deceptive characteristics of the ones that John has previously called antichrists and liars again come

---

[299] Smalley, *1, 2, 3 John*, 119.

[300] Smalley, *1, 2, 3 John*, 121; Brown, *Epistles of John*, 358. Brown notes that the emphatic nature of the pronoun should lead one to the decision that Jesus is the antecedent, based upon the fact that Jesus has been the center of the controversy in the past few verses and that it is Jesus, not the Father, whom John needs to emphasize.

[301] Smalley, *1, 2, 3 John*, 121–22; Schnackenburg, *The Johannine Epistles,* 148; Hiebert, "Exposition of 1 John 2:18–28," 87.

[302] Luther, *LW,* 30:260.

clearly into view in this verse. They are not content to rush into error by themselves. Their goal is to bring as many as they can along with them. The use of the present tense participle alerts the readers to the reality that the secessionists are still a threat to the *koinonia* of the community and that they must be taken seriously.[303] Brown explains, "The secessionists are Antichrists embodying the apocalyptic expectation of the Antichrist; they are liars embodying the apocalyptic expectation of the Liar; even so they embody the great deception of the last times."[304]

2:27 Again John uses his familiar forward positioning of *hymeis* to emphasize the fact that the members of the Johannine community are to be distinct from those who have left the community.[305] He exhorts them to continue to stand strong in the faith by drawing upon the strength that is theirs through reception of the Spirit of God (the anointing), first mentioned in v. 20. The connection between the anointing the believers have received and the abiding nature of the message (v. 24) they have heard is brought to the forefront of this discussion so that they will understand that both of these abide in them and both of these will fortify them in their battle against the heretics. This connection would lend support to the idea that the abiding *chrisma* encompasses both the Spirit of God and the word of God.

This linkage of the Spirit and the word helps one to make sense of the difficult phrase that follows. It seems odd that John, given the didactic nature of this epistle, would say to the community that "you do not need anyone to teach you." John is not denying the importance and place of human teachers. The mere fact that he wrote this letter is sufficient proof. This claim that they have no need of someone to teach them echoes the promises that Jesus made in the Gospel that the Paraclete would lead them into all truth (John 14:16–17,26; 16:13). The ministry of the Spirit worked through the apostles (not the heretics) to bring the message of salvation that is found in the life, death, and resurrection of Jesus Christ, the Son of God. Here was the reliable truth they were taught. Additional revelation was not needed; indeed it could be deadly. Spiritual illumination of the received traditions was the pattern they should follow. In addition, it is the fulfillment of the promise of the new covenant in which all the members of the com-

---

[303] Robertson, *WP* 6:216. Schnackenburg, *The Johannine Epistles,* 149. Robertson notes that this is a connative use of the participle (NIV, "trying to lead astray") that is indicative of their intent to lead others in the community astray. John also uses the verb in 1 John 1:8; 3:7 and the cognate noun in 1 John 4:6; 2 John 7.

[304] Brown, *Epistles of John*, 358. This is the third of the four occasions on which John uses a form of the formula, "These things I write" (cf. 1:4; 2:1; 5:13).

[305] Cf. Smalley, *1, 2, 3 John*, 125–26; Brown, *Epistles of John*, 360–61; Thomas, "Exegetical Digest of 1 John," 21–218. It is possible to translate the last half of v. 27 as either one or two sentences. It seems that the NIV has adopted the most likely translation of the text, that it is one sentence. Smalley, Brown, and Thomas provide thorough discussions of this issue.

munity are taught by God (John 6:45) and no one needs to be taught by his neighbor, for the law of God will be written on their hearts, and they will know God.[306]

One other comment about this part of the verse should also be noted. It is also possible that John is making this declaration in an extreme form to give intensity to his statements about the power that is available to the believer through the anointing.[307] This statement also serves the purpose of keeping the members of the community away from the deceivers who claimed to be teaching new truths about God.[308]

John affirms that the anointing (Spirit), received by believing that Jesus is the Christ, the Son of God, teaches them the truth of the gospel. Using a typical Johannine motif of the positive-negative assertion, he explains that what the Spirit (John 14:17, "the Spirit of truth") teaches, in direct contrast to the teachings of the secessionists (liars, v. 22), is true and can be trusted without reservation.[309]

The final two clauses—"just as it [or he] has taught you, remain in him"—refer to the teaching that they had received in the past. It is possibly even a reference to the teaching of Jesus himself delineated in the Farewell Discourse (John 13–17), something that seems to be woven throughout John's argument in this chapter. This teaching encompasses the proper understanding of the reciprocal relationship that exists between the Father and the Son, the love command, the promise of the Paraclete (Spirit), and the promise that they would face hostility from the world that wars against God. The final command to remain in him also echoes the farewell discourse in which Jesus tells his disciples "remain in me" (15:4–7). To abide or dwell in Jesus is only possible when there is an intimate relationship with the Father through the Son (vv. 22–24), a reality possible only for those who have a proper understanding of the person and work of Jesus Christ, whose ethics are shaped by that understanding (cf. John 8:31), and who have received the anointing that is an assurance of their remaining in the truth.[310]

2:28 John continues the thought of v. 27 in the first part of this verse and concludes his focus on abiding or "continuing" in Christ, at least for the moment (it is resumed in 3:6; cf. also 3:15,17,24). "Dear children" forms an inclusio with v. 18, but it also serves as a transition to a new subject: the coming again of Christ. Abiding in him prepares believers for his appearing: abiding is our confidence; his appearing is our motivation.

---

[306] Cf. Culpepper, *1, 2, 3 John*, 52; Smalley, *1, 2, 3 John*, 125.

[307] Smalley, *1, 2, 3 John*, 125.

[308] Brown, *Epistles of John*, 374.

[309] Hiebert, "Exposition of 1 John 2:18–28," 89.

[310] Cf. Smalley, *1, 2, 3 John*, 128.

5. Live Like Children of God (2:28–3:10)

This is the fifth movement in section one of the epistle (1:5–3:10). The parent-child relationship is highlighted and complements the theme of love that follows in 3:11–5:12. Ten times from 2:29 to the end of the book (5:21) John uses the word "born." This is remarkable when one notes that the term does not occur even once in 1:1–2:28. John demonstrates that those born of God (his children) exercise faith toward God and love for one another as they await Christ's return. This observation leads some to see a major division break here, but we argue for a slightly different pattern.[311]

Although 2:28–29 is transitional, it also naturally links with 3:1–3 and its emphasis on the identity (and confidence) of the children of God. Those who are born of God have both an identity and responsibility that is consistent with their privileges as God's children. Six times John notes the believer's status as God's children (2:28; 3:1,2,7,10a,b). Three times he highlights their spiritual birth, which is the basis for this position as children (2:29; 3:9a,b). It is possible to see a shift in subject at 3:4.[312] A dual emphasis on Christ's appearances (the second time to make us like him [3:2] and the first time to deal with sin [3:5]), however, may indicate again that a hard and fast division is unnecessary. The two sections (2:28–3:3 and 3:4–10) clearly complement each other.

(1) Be Confident and Ready for His Coming (2:28–3:3)[313]

28And now, dear children, continue in him, so that when he appears we may be confident and unashamed before him at his coming.

29If you know that he is righteous, you know that everyone who does what is right has been born of him.

1How great is the love the Father has lavished on us, that we should be called children of God! And that is what we are! The reason the world does not know us is that it did not know him. 2Dear friends, now we are children of God, and what we will be has not yet been made known. But we know that when he appears, we

---

[311] See Sherman and Tuggy for a semantic structural defense for analyzing and dividing the epistle in this manner (*Semantic and Structural Analysis*, 53–54). M. E. Boismard identifies what he believes are formal parallels between 1 John 3:1–11 and 1 Pet 1:3–5,13–23. He argues that a common baptismal liturgy may be behind both ("Une liturgie baptismale dans la prima Petri," *RB* 63 [1956]: 182–208; esp. 200–204).

[312] So Marshall, *Epistles of John,* 175.

[313] As previously noted, scholars differ on where the new unit of thought begins exactly. Again, those who start this section with 2:28 are Brown, *Epistles of John*, 417–20; Bruce, *Epistles of John,* 77; Marshall, *Epistles of John*, 164–65; Stott, *Letters of John*, 120; and Burge, *Letters of John*, 143–44. Scholars who begin this section with 3:1 include Kysar, *1, 2, 3 John*, 69; and Smalley, *1, 2, 3 John*, 128.

shall be like him, for we shall see him as he is. ³Everyone who has this hope in him purifies himself, just as he is pure.

2:28 John's phrase "and now" *(kai nun)* marks the beginning of a new section in the epistle. The words both complete the previous verses and prepare the reader for an additional but complementary train of thought. Once again John's pastoral burden is revealed in his reference to his readers as "dear children" *(teknia),* a term of both general affection and intimate exhortation of responsibility (cf. 2:1,12). John is constant in his concern for his readers in light of the exigency of the situation they are facing.

John's admonition from v. 27 to abide *(menete,* present active imperative) in Christ is repeated in this verse.[314] He demands a continual, deepening relationship with Christ as a direct duty of their status as "dear children." In light of the false teachings that confront John's audience, it is a necessity that the children of God remain vibrant in their personal relationship with Christ. John's appeal to abide in Christ is not intended to frighten them into maintaining this relationship. Instead, John takes a more reassuring approach. He challenges them to continue faithfully in their present course. Motivation and exhortation are brought together. Admonition comes in the form of encouragement.

John states that the motivation behind this faithful abiding is eschatological in nature. The apostle wants his readers to remain true because of the certainty of Christ's return. The use of *ean* ("if"; NIV "when") does not cast doubt on the certainty of Christ's coming but merely the timing and circumstances surrounding the event. The fact is not in question; only the season of Christ's return is unknown.[315] Indeed, the Christian's hope rests on the certainty of this promised event.

John emphasizes the suddenness of Christ's return. The second coming of Christ will not be a process, but an instantaneous occurrence. John uses this same word ("appear," *phanerōthē)* to refer to Christ's incarnation (1:2; 3:5,8; John 1:31; 3:11; 7:4), his words and works (John 2:11; 17:6), his postresurrection appearances (3:2,8; John 21:1,14), and his second coming (2:28; 3:2). In each instance the emphasis rests on the factuality of Christ's appearance. Thomas points out that the word is only used of God the Son. It is never used of God the Father or God the Holy Spirit.[316] This observation

---

[314] The NIV obscures the connection of these two verses with its translation of "remain" in v. 27 and "continue" in v. 28. On the other hand, the KJV maintains the continuity between the verses by translating μένετε as "abide" in both verses.

[315] In a number of John's texts ἐάν means "whenever" (1 John 3:2; John 8:16; 12:32; 14:3). The emphasis rests on the certainty of the event and the uncertainty of its timing.

[316] Thomas, "Exegetical Digest of 1 John," 221.

is vital to John's arguments against those who want to deny the physical reality of Jesus Christ's life, death, and resurrection. John emphasizes that the Son of God will return physically and literally (just as he did the first time). The context also acknowledges the involvement of the Father in this grand event. God the Father again sends the Son, and his return will be a literal, physical second coming.

The promises of Jesus to the disciples that he would one day return unexpectedly (Matt 24:44; 25:13; Luke 12:40) cannot be underestimated at this point. Jesus' followers were urged to be prepared and to await the sudden return of Christ. Just as Jesus was made manifest as the incarnate Son of God in his earthly ministry, even so he will be made visible a second time when he returns in public glory. It is in that promise that the early church placed its hope and trust. One day they will be vindicated and rescued from the evil world in which they live and minister. It is that guaranteed promise of Christ's return that should help motivate and sustain today's believer.

John includes himself in the promise to the faithful (*schōmen*, "we may be") as he reveals the twofold benefit of abiding in Christ. Positively, the one who remains true will have confidence before him at his coming. The word "confidence" *(parrēsian)* connotes the absence of fear when speaking.[317] It carries the idea of boldness, openness, freedom, assurance, and courage. John uses the word four times in his epistle. Twice the term is used of the believer's confidence at the return of Christ (here and in 4:17), and twice John uses the term to refer to the confidence and freedom by which the believer can approach God in prayer (3:21; 5:14). In the immediate context the word describes standing before Christ at the time of his second coming without fear or shame. It is a confidence that stems from a personal, obedient, abiding relationship with the Coming One.[318]

Negatively, abiding in Christ is encouraged so that one will not be ashamed at the time of his coming. The verb translated "be ashamed" *(aischunthōmen)* appears only here in John's writings. It carries the idea of

---

[317] The word παρρησίαν was used in the Gk. political realm to describe the freedom of speech citizens of the democratic city-states enjoyed. It was one of the highest privileges of the full citizen, who was granted the right to speak with candor and without fear (Burdick, *The Letters of John the Apostle*, 208–9).

[318] The word also occurs nine times in John's Gospel. Vaughan notes: "It was the appropriate word to use of the entire freedom with which intimate friends unburden their hearts to one another. At least one ancient writer used it of the attitude of children to their father in contrast with the attitude of a slave to his master" (C. Vaughan, *1, 2, 3 John* [Grand Rapids: Zondervan, 1970], 69). See also W. C. van Unnik, "The Christian's Freedom of Speech in the New Testament," *BJRL* 44 (1961–62): 466–88; esp. p. 486.

shrinking back or being separated from God through guilt or shame.[319] One is reminded of the words of Jesus in Mark 8:38: "For whoever is ashamed of Me and My words in this adulterous and sinful generation, the Son of Man also will be ashamed of him when He comes in the glory of His Father with the holy angels" (NASB). Those who remain faithful to Christ will not have to withdraw from the Judge in shame or fear. Instead, they can stand with confidence before him at his coming (cf. Heb 9:24–28).

There are three primary terms in the New Testament used to denote the second coming of Christ: (1) *apokalupsis,* meaning "a revelation" or "an unveiling," signifies the disclosure of something previously hidden; (2) *epiphaneia,* meaning "an appearing," marks the visibility of Christ's physical return; and (3) *parousia,* meaning "a coming" or "an arrival," anticipates the personal return of Christ. Here John uses the word *parousia.* This is the only time he uses the word. This word was something of a technical term and marked the arrival of a king, ruler, or official with open splendor, dignity, and respect. It is a word early Christians frequently employed to distinguish the second coming of Christ and to mark the judgment that will accompany his return (cf. Matt 24:3,27,37,39; 1 Cor 15:23; 1 Thess 2:19; 3:13; 4:15; 5:23; 2 Thess 2:1,8–9; Jas 5:7–8; 2 Pet 1:16; 3:4,12). John's use of the word reminds the faithful saints that they can stand with confidence, unashamed at Christ's coming.

Of course, the overriding challenge in this verse is to abide in Christ. Only the one who continues, or abides, possesses this confidence and fearlessness. The Christian is challenged, as he awaits and anticipates the arrival of the King, to remain faithful in service. Those who are found faithful are those who will stand confidently before the King. On the other hand, those who do not abide in Christ will be ashamed and disgraced at his return.

2:29   The connection between vv. 28 and 29 lies in the fact that the One who will execute judgment in v. 28 is the One who is described as righteous

---

[319] The verb may be translated as either middle or passive. If translated in the middle voice, it means "to be ashamed." If translated in the passive voice, it carries the idea of being put to shame. Brown distinguishes between the two: "The passive reflects a legal situation where one is disgraced, while the middle has more the psychological aspect of the individual's feeling shame" (*Epistles of John,* 381). Those who favor the passive voice understand the verb to mean that God will openly put these unfaithful to shame for their refusal to abide in him (see Marshall, *Epistles of John,* 166–67; and Schnackenburg, *The Johannine Epistles,* 165). Those who favor the middle voice emphasize the personal shame involved in standing before God, having been unfaithful to him (see Westcott, *Epistles of John,* 82; and Brooke, *Johannine Epistles,* 66). Smalley seeks to find a balance in the two positions when he suggests both interpretations may be held together: "[John] could be saying that the person who has been faithful to the truth of Jesus need not, at the end, be ashamed in the presence of Christ, and (furthermore) will not be disgraced by him" (*1, 2, 3 John,* 131).

in v. 29.[320] As Smalley suggests, "The argument moves logically from the fact of judgment to the character of the judge; he is righteous."[321]

John uses two different words for knowledge in this verse ("If you know *[eidete]* ... you know *[ginōskete]*"). Without pressing the distinctions,[322] as did older commentaries, a nuanced difference may still be present. The former *(eidete)* is absolute and intuitive, "to be aware of the fact." The latter *(ginōskete)* is consequent, "knowledge learned or gained by experience." The combination of the two may indicate that the "absolute, intuitive knowledge that Christ is righteous is the basis of the logical conclusion that those who do righteousness have His very nature by their rebirth."[323] They know that Jesus the Son is righteous; therefore they know that those who behave righteously possess the righteous nature of their Father through spiritual birth.[324]

Marshall describes this righteousness as "correct, moral behavior, acceptable to God."[325] This specific righteousness is a distinct characteristic of the one who has been born of God. Likewise, it is a continual, life-characterizing righteousness that comes from having a personal, saving knowledge of him who is absolutely righteous.

John introduces in this verse a thoroughly Johannine concept that will repeatedly resurface in the remainder of his book. It is the idea of being born of God, of a spiritual new birth (3:9; 4:7; 5:1,4,18; cf. John 1:12–13; 3:3–8). In his Gospel John addresses the *experience* of the new birth. In his epistle the emphasis is more on the *evidences* of the new birth. John

---

[320] The "if" clause is not intended to create doubt in the reader's mind concerning the righteous nature of God. Instead, ἐάν is used as a third class conditional statement, which confirms the reality of what they already know (Hiebert, *Epistles of John*, 130).

[321] Smalley, *1, 2, 3 John*, 133.

[322] See Marshall, *Epistles of John*, 167, n.10.

[323] Thomas, "Exegetical Digest of 1 John," 222. Thomas identifies two possibilities for the mood of the verb γινώσκετε: (1) It is indicative. John wishes to state two facts about what his readers know. (2) It is imperative. John wishes his readers to apply in a practical way what they already know (ibid., 225).

[324] There is a question about the subject of the verb ἐτιν and the antecedent of the pronoun αὐτοῦ. While some scholars believe that they both refer to Christ (Westcott, *Epistles of John*, 83; Brooke, *Johannine Epistles*, 68–69; and Thomas, "Exegetical Digest of 1 John," 225), others identify both with the Father (H. Alford, *Alford's Greek Testament* [Grand Rapids: Guardian, 1976], 4:458; Plummer, *Epistles of S. John*, 119; Lenski, *Interpretation of the Epistles*, 445; Bruce, *Epistles of John*, 79; and Stott, *Letters of John*, 122). Still others take the first to refer to Christ and the second to the Father (D. Smith, "The Epistles of John," *EGT* [Grand Rapids: Eerdmans, 1970], 5:182; Law, *Tests of Life*, 384; Marshall, *Epistles of John*, 168, n. 13; and Robertson, *WP* 6:219). For a general overview of the pros and cons of each view, see Thomas, "Exegetical Digest of 1 John," 222–25. The latter or third position would seem the better option. The new birth is most naturally identified with the Father.

[325] Marshall, *Epistles of John*, 167.

describes the believer's new relationship with God as being analogous to that of a child to a father. This spiritual metaphor, which is common throughout the New Testament, has its roots in the Old Testament, where God's special people are viewed frequently as being in relationship with him.[326] John's use of new birth language is natural in his appeal for his readers (God's children) to manifest the nature of their Heavenly Father.

John's word order is something of a surprise. It would seem appropriate for John to suggest that everyone who has been born of God will do what is right and as a result will stand confidently before God at the parousia. Instead, he speaks first of doing what is right, which is the direct result of spiritual birth. His point is simply this: if a person does what is right, this is a sure sign of a new birth. This particular order, therefore, offers assurance to the child of God. For the child of God, faith precedes behavior, but right behavior is the natural result of proper belief.[327] As Stott affirms, "A person's righteousness is thus the evidence of his new birth, not the cause or condition of it."[328] Hence, believers can be assured of their acceptable status before God if their lives are marked by a godly righteousness, for only those who have truly experienced the new birth will "abide in him." Righteous living is a confirmation, an ethical expression, of an already existing relationship with God. Our lives, as children, resemble our Father's righteousness.

3:1 Having introduced the idea that believers are the children of God, John is reminded of the wondrous nature of God's love by which we are granted this privilege. The NIV loses something of the significance in the original by failing to translate the imperative "see" or "behold" *(idete)*. In a more accurate translation, the NASB reads, "See how great a love the Father has bestowed on us." The imperative calls for direct attention and reflection upon the amazing love God has bestowed upon his children.

The adjective *potapēn* translated "how great" (NIV) or "what manner" (KJV), which occurs only seven times in the New Testament, always implies astonishment. Admiration is usually conveyed as well.[329] Being a child of God stirs within John a sense of wonder, awe, and amazement. The expression carries both a qualitative and quantitative force, "what glorious,

---

[326] See Deut 1:31; 8:5; 14:1; 32:6; Ps 103:13; Prov 3:12; Isa 63:16; 64:8; Jer 31:9,20; Hos 11; Mal 1:6; 2:10. The primary emphasis in these texts rests in God's fatherly care for his children and their filial response of loving obedience in return (cf. Marshall, *Epistles of John,* 168).

[327] John's use of the perfect tense here (γεγέννηται: perfect active indicative) places emphasis on the continued results of being born again. While the action has been completed in the past, the effects continue into the present.

[328] Stott, *Letters of John,* 122.

[329] The word occurs in Matt 8:27; Mark 13:1 (2x); Luke 1:29; 7:39; 2 Pet 3:11; and 1 John 3:1. See Plummer, *Epistles of S. John,* 71.

measureless love."[330] Originally, the adjective meant "of what country." Stott captures this original sense when he writes, "The Father's love is so unearthly, so foreign to this world, that [John] wonders from what country it may come."[331] God's love is foreign to humankind in that we cannot understand the magnitude of such love. It astonishes, amazes, and creates wonder within those who properly reflect upon it.

John claims that this love is divine in nature. It is a love that originates only with the Father. As Hiebert states: "This love, originating with God, ever seeks the true welfare of those being loved; it is amazing indeed when we remember the personal destitution of those He loves. God's is a love that works visible, transforming results in the lives of its recipients."[332] Burdick adds: "God loves the sinner, not because He is drawn to him by his lovableness, but because, in spite of man's unloveliness, God sets His mind and will on seeking man's highest good. This is what is amazing about God's love."[333] It is a divine, initiated love that is active, for it seeks to bring sinners into the family of God.

The perfect tense verb "has lavished" *(dedōken)* is significant here and further accentuates the permanent results of this divine love. It is a gift from God the Father that cannot be earned or bought; it is given freely and cannot be withdrawn. Furthermore, God has not just shown his love to humans, but he has given it to them in such a way that it becomes a part of them. He lavishes, or imparts, permanent and abiding love to his children.

John's positioning of "the Father" *(ho patēr)* at the end of the clause draws attention to the divine initiative of this act. The word order is noteworthy. Literally, it is, "See what manner of love he has given to us, the Father." The fact that the Father would love "us" *(hēmin)* astonishes the apostle. John's use of "the Father" instead of "God" highlights the family relationship that is established by the Father's love. His role as the Heavenly Father illustrates and begins to explain why he loves the unworthy.

God's love provides the way for us to be called "children of God" *(tekna theou)*.[334] God's love transforms those who exercise saving faith into his children. They are now "called," or bear the name, "children of God." Furthermore, those who believe take on more than a mere title, for they actually become God's children *(kai esmen)*.[335] The words express a fact, a

---

[330] Hiebert, *Epistles of John,* 133.

[331] Stott, *Letters of John,* 122.

[332] Hiebert, *Epistles of John,* 133.

[333] Burdick, *The Letters of John the Apostle,* 230.

[334] For a detailed discussion concerning John's use of the ἵνα clause here, see Thomas, "Exegetical Digest of 1 John," 230–31.

[335] These words are omitted by the KJV, but strong Western and Alexandrian evidence argues for their authenticity and inclusion. See *TCGNT,* 711–12.

reality of relationship. We are members of a family; we are "God-children —a divine progeny."[336]

A difference of opinion exists as to the antecedent of the pronoun in *dia touto* ("for this reason" or "on account of this"). A literal translation would be, "For this reason the world does not know us because *[hoti]* it did not know him." The NIV translates the phrase as looking ahead to the *hoti* clause.[337] On the other hand, most commentators seem to understand the pronoun as looking back to that which has already been stated.[338] Because Christians are partakers in the divine love and have been designated the children of God, the world does not understand them. This latter view appears to be more appropriate in the immediate context. The child of God is unknown by the world because they have different fathers (i.e., God and Satan).

The "world" *(kosmos)* refers to the evil humanistic system that dominates the society around us, a hostile order that stands in opposition to God. Therefore it only makes natural sense that those in the world do not know (understand, comprehend) those who are born of God. The children of God are radically different from the children of this world.

A further explanation for this alienation between the world and the child of God is introduced by the concluding *hoti* ("because") clause. The world does not understand the child of God because it did not understand him. Opinions vary as to the antecedent of this pronoun. Suggestions include (1) God the Father,[339] (2) Jesus Christ,[340] or (3) God in Christ.[341] Looking back, the near antecedent is the Father. It would be easy to see a reference to Christ, however, and the reception he received at his first coming. At the same time, the hostile attitude of the world toward both the Father and the Son cannot be overlooked. In either case in light of the world's natural depravity and opposition to God, the child of God should anticipate rejec-

---

[336] H. E. Dana, *The Epistles and Apocalypse of John* (Kansas City: Central Seminary Press, 1947), 49; Marshall says, "The 'love package' contains our title to be called children of God" (*Epistles of John,* 170).

[337] Others who embrace this view include Brooke, *Johannine Epistles,* 81; Brown, *Epistles of John,* 391–92; and Smalley, *1, 2, 3 John,* 142. Brown's argument is especially strong.

[338] See G. Abbott-Smith, *A Manual Greek Lexicon of the New Testament* (Edinburgh: T & T Clark, 1937), 290; Westcott, *Epistles of John,* 96–97; Lenski, *Interpretation of the Epistles,* 450; Plummer, *Epistles of S. John,* 121; and Burdick, *The Letters of John the Apostle,* 231. Marshall advocates this position, though he notes "there is not a lot of difference in meaning between the two ways of understanding the sentence" (*Epistles of John,* 171, n. 25).

[339] Lenski, *Interpretation of the Epistles,* 451; Brooke, *Johannine Epistles,* 81; Alford, *Alford's Greek Testament,* 4:461; and Bruce, *Epistles of John,* 87.

[340] Law, *The Tests of Life,* 386; Stott, *Letters of John,* 123; Bultmann, *The Johannine Epistles,* 48; and Burdick, *The Letters of John the Apostle,* 231.

[341] Westcott, *Epistles of John,* 97.

tion and hatred. Such rejection by the world attests to the reality that the rejected are indeed children of God. Christ warned his disciples (including John) of the world's natural animosity toward his followers (John 15:18–16:4), and now the apostle communicates that same word of warning and encouragement to his audience. To be one of his is to be treated as he was treated, but to be treated in such a manner is to have assurance that we are his children.

3:2 The NIV translates John's personal address *agapētoi* as "dear friends." The better rendering is "beloved," which emphasizes the bonding love of the Father for his children. By using the first person "we," John also identifies himself with them as one of the beloved of God. John has an intense love for his readers because of their shared love in the Father. Smalley points out that John puts into practice "his own ethical demand of love within the brotherhood" (2:9–11; 3:11–17; 4:7–12).[342]

The writer's use of *nun* ("now") and *oupō* ("not yet") uncovers a stark contrast between the present and the future, the known and the unknown. On the one hand, John wants to accentuate the fact that we are the children of God here and now. At the same time, the full extent of what we will be has yet to be revealed. Although our present status as children of God is wonderful, our future state will be even more extraordinary. God has only begun a work in us that will not reach full fruition until the "not yet" has been fulfilled. John's "apostolic confession of ignorance" affirms that the exact nature and state of the children of God after Christ's return has not been revealed to him.[343] It will be disclosed only when he appears. "What we shall be" *(ti esometha)* remains veiled from our sight until his coming. Wild speculation and guesswork are futile and should be avoided.

The pronoun *ti* ("what") stresses the continuity between the believer's present state and his future state and also the quality of what lies in store for God's children. The verb "appear" *(ephanerōthē,* used three times in 2:28–3:3) guarantees that what we will be will be publicly displayed. The "not yet" will be even greater than the "and now."

Although the exact nature of the "not yet" has not been disclosed to John, he can affirm with certainty (1) the reality of Christ's appearance and (2) that when he appears we will be like him. The verb "know" *(oidamen)* carries an assurance, a certain knowledge concerning this particular aspect of the *parousia.* As in 2:29 the conditional aspect of *ean* ("if" or "whenever") does not cast doubt on the certainty of the event itself, but rather on the exact time of the event. John wants his readers to anticipate and be pre-

---

[342] Smalley, *1, 2, 3 John*, 144. For a unique punctuation of this verse see F. C. Synge, "1 John 3:2," *JTS* 3 (1952): 79. Kruse notes what he sees as the advantages of his rendering (*Letters of John*, 116, n. 112).

[343] Stott, *Letters of John*, 123.

pared for the event, even though they do not know the time of this occasion.

The unstated subject of the verb "appears" *(phanerōthē)* has created a division in scholarship about exactly what is to be manifested. Some scholars interpret the subject as the thought "what we shall be" stated in the preceding clause.[344] Hence, the NEB translates the verb as "it is disclosed." Yet others interpret the subject as masculine.[345] Thus the KJV and the NIV render the verb as "he shall appear" or "when he appears" (though the NIV offers an alternate reading consistent with the former view of "it"). From the immediate context it appears the better understanding is to see Christ as the subject, for it is at his appearing that "what we shall be" will be revealed.

Scholars also disagree concerning the antecedent to the words "like him" *(homoioi autō)*. While some suggest that the pronoun refers to God the Father,[346] others believe it refers to Christ.[347] Again, context appears to suggest the reference is to becoming like Christ. While it is true that the New Testament teaches that the believer is to be like God (Eph 5:1), more frequently it refers to our Christlikeness (Rom 8:29; 2 Cor 3:18; Phil 3:20–21). So when John states that "we shall be like him," his reference is to the promise that the Christian will be made like Christ. W. Alexander recorded that on the mission field, when native converts came to this phrase, the scribe laid down his pen and exclaimed: "No! It (sic) is too much; let us write, 'We shall kiss His feet.' "[348]

---

[344] See Alford, *Alford's Greek Testament,* 4:461; Plummer, *Epistles of S. John,* 119–20; Lenski, *Interpretation of the Epistles* 452; and Brown, *Epistles of John,* 394. Burdick lists two major reasons for this understanding: "(1) The proximity of the same verb in the first part of the verse ἐφανερώθη, "it has … appeared"), the subject of which is obviously the clause τί ἐσόμεφα, leads to the probable thought that the subjects of the two verbs would be the same: "What we shall be has not yet been manifested. We know that whenever it is manifested …" (2) The absence of both of the pronouns commonly used to refer to Christ (αὐτός, 2:2; ἐκεῖνος, 3:5,16) leads to the assumption that if the subject had been Christ, it would have been necessary to use one of those pronouns to make it clear that the subject of the second verb, φανερωθῇ, was not the same as the subject of the first verb, ἐφανερώθη" (*The Letters of John the Apostle,* 233).

[345] See Westcott, *Epistles of John,* 98; Brooke, *Johannine Epistles,* 82–83; Robertson, *WP* 6:220; Stott, *Letters of John,* 124; Bruce, *Epistles of John,* 87–88; Marshall, *Epistles of John,* 172, n. 29. In support of this view, Burdick lists the following "more weighty" considerations: "(1) The context shows that John is laying stress on the appearances of Christ. (2) The following verse (v. 3) is referring to Christ as the two pronouns αὐτῷ and ἐκεῖνος make clear. Therefore the αὐτὸν of v. 2b must refer to Christ, and, following the same line of reasoning, the subject of φανερωθῇ must be Christ. (3) It is more to be expected that John would identify the time of the believer's complete Christlikeness as being the second coming rather than the time when 'it is disclosed'" (*The Letters of John the Apostle,* 233).

[346] See Bruce, *Epistles of John,* 85–87; and Westcott, *Epistles of John,* 98.

[347] This view is obvious for those who hold that Christ is the subject of the appearance in the previous phrase. For a good summary of the pros and cons of both views, see Thomas, "Exegetical Digest of 1 John," 240–42.

[348] Quoted in Vaughan, *1, 2, 3 John,* 75.

There is also a question as to what verb the last *hoti* clause of v. 2 refers. The clause could qualify *oidamen* ("we know"). This would mean seeing him gives proof to the child of God that we know we will be like him. Understanding concerning our future resemblance to Christ is based on the fact that "we shall see him just as he is." Others suggest that the phrase qualifies *esometha* ("we shall be"). Being like him is the direct result or outcome of seeing him. "We shall be like him" because "we shall see him just as he is."[349] John's emphasis seems to rest here on what believers will be as opposed to how the transformation will take place. The better understanding is that our future likeness of Christ is based on the fact that we will one day see him as he is. The transformation idea is not absent, but it is not the primary one here.

The adjective "like" *(homoioi)* reminds John's readers that our transformation will be to a resemblance of Christ. We will not be made into little gods. As Smalley asserts, "[Like] implies spiritual unity, but not complete identity."[350] Burdick adds, "Believers can never be equal to Christ, since He is infinite and they are finite; but they can and will be similar to Him in holiness and in resurrection bodies."[351] Our face-to-face encounter with the risen Lord will complete our glorification process as we are transformed to be like him (cf. 1 Cor 13:12). On that day "the believer's yearning for inner Christlikeness will be fully realized."[352]

3:3 Now John reveals his reason for writing about the second coming of Christ. Our final state has an ethical and moral component for the present. With the use of the initial conjunction *kai* (absent in the NIV), John joins his previous eschatological thoughts with a moral, practical conclusion. There are practical implications associated with living the life of hope. Being born of God creates a vibrant hope for the future, one that motivates pure living in everyday life.

John's use of "everyone who" *(pas ho)*[353] seems to dismiss "the claims of some party or other who claimed special privileges or exemptions for themselves."[354] In this context John's inclusion defuses the proto-Gnostics who regarded themselves above any moral standard. Their life of sin exposed the falsity of their profession. John makes it clear that the posses-

---

[349] See Brooke, *Johannine Epistles*, 83; Plummer, *Epistles of S. John*, 122; Law, *The Tests of Life*, 388; and Marshall, *Epistles of John*, 172–73.

[350] Smalley, *1, 2, 3 John*, 146.

[351] Burdick, *The Letters of John the Apostle*, 234.

[352] Hiebert, *Epistles of John*, 138.

[353] John uses this phrase seven times in 2:29–3:10. This serves further as an evidence that 2:28–3:10 in general and 3:4–10 in particular (where it occurs five times) are semantic units. Note the very fine treatments of this in Brown (*Epistles of John*, 418ff.) and Burge (*Letters of John*, 143–44).

[354] Brooke, *Johannine Epistles*, 83. Brooke chooses to use the term "Gnostic" but does not place it in quotations.

sion of hope produces purity. There is no exception to the rule.

The hope *(tēn elpida)* John describes includes three primary factors: Christ's appearing, the believer's seeing him, and the believer's becoming as he is.[355] Defined in its New Testament context, hope involves a confident expectation of the future, a trust in God's provision, and the patience of waiting for him.[356] Our hope is founded upon Christ. There is nothing within the believer that creates hope and security for the future. The foundation for hope, now and forever, is Christ alone.

John declares firmly that anyone who possesses this hope "purifies himself" *(hagnizei heauton;* present active indicative), which denotes a continual moral purification process. It is now Christians' habit of life to pursue purity and holiness as we await the blessed hope of the return of Jesus (Titus 2:13). Furthermore, "himself" marks the conscious need for the believer to purify himself individually before a holy God. Although John makes clear in 1:7 that it is the blood of Christ that cleanses the believer from sin, he speaks here of self-purification. Both are true and essential to progressive sanctification, our growth in Christlikeness. As Hiebert affirms:

> That initial purification with its transforming result is the necessary antecedent to this personal self-cleansing in daily experience. The more intimate the believer's fellowship with God, who is "light" (1:5), the more conscious he becomes of his need to cleanse himself from all that is moral darkness (1:5–7). The more he contemplates this assured hope of being conformed to the image of Christ, the more eagerly will he strive for present personal purity (Phil. 3:13–14).[357]

Self-purification, through the power of the Holy Spirit, is a key component of the New Testament's teachings on the life of the believer (cf. 2 Cor 7:1; 1 Tim 5:22; Jas 4:8; 1 Pet 1:22).

The final words "just as he is pure" *(kathōs ekeinos hagnos estin)* reveals the supreme example for the striving believer to follow. "He" is translated from the demonstrative pronoun *ekeinos,* which in 1 John always refers to Jesus Christ (cf. 2:6). He is our pattern. As Hobbs asserts, "We are not to judge our lives by other peoples', but by Christ's, who is the standard or goal toward which we are to move."[358] *Hagnos* ("pure") refers to cleanliness and holiness of life. It expresses freedom from sin, which will be crucial to John's argument in the remainder of this section. As in 2:29, where John declared that "he is righteous," the apostle now affirms that "he is

---

[355] Thomas, "Exegetical Digest of 1 John," 244. This is the only occurrence of ἐλπίς in John's writings.

[356] Stott, *Letters of John,* 124–25

[357] Hiebert, *Epistles of John,* 140.

[358] H. H. Hobbs, *The Epistles of John* (Nashville: Thomas Nelson, 1983), 81.

pure." Lenski points out, "Purity is his inherent quality."[359] Furthermore, his unchanging nature guarantees his eternal purity. He is the eternally pure one. Thus John's ethical challenge is clear: since the Son is absolutely pure and we will be like him when he returns, we must strive to purify ourselves continually until that magnificent hour. Once again John's "abide in him" mandate is crucial to this purification process. To be purified we must remain close to the One who is wholly pure.

(2) Be Righteous and Do Not Sin (3:4–10)

⁴Everyone who sins breaks the law; in fact, sin is lawlessness. ⁵But you know that he appeared so that he might take away our sins. And in him is no sin. ⁶No one who lives in him keeps on sinning. No one who continues to sin has either seen him or known him.

⁷Dear children, do not let anyone lead you astray. He who does what is right is righteous, just as he is righteous. ⁸He who does what is sinful is of the devil, because the devil has been sinning from the beginning. The reason the Son of God appeared was to destroy the devil's work. ⁹No one who is born of God will continue to sin, because God's seed remains in him; he cannot go on sinning, because he has been born of God. ¹⁰This is how we know who the children of God are and who the children of the devil are: Anyone who does not do what is right is not a child of God; nor is anyone who does not love his brother.

Having marshaled the position that the practice of righteousness is evidence that one is a child of God, John now proceeds to show how being a child of God is incompatible with the practice of sin. He defines what it means to be righteous (2:29) and pure (3:3) from a negative standpoint: one does not live a life that is characterized by sin. This section, as indicated by the absence of a separating grammatical connection in v. 4, is not to be separated from the preceding section; and even though we identify a major divisional break at 3:10, it will also flow naturally into the argument of 3:11ff.

3:4 As in the previous verse, John uses the all-inclusive *pas* ("Everyone") to accentuate that there is no elite group that is above God's moral standards. While those who had left the church thought themselves to be above accountability, John emphasizes that no one is excluded from the following rule: literally, "Everyone doing [*poiōn*, a present tense participle] sin [*tēn hamartian*] also does [*poiei*, present tense indicative] lawlessness [*anomian*]." This truth is universal. There are no exceptions.

John makes an obvious contrast between this construction (*pas ho poiōn tēn hamartian*, "everyone who practices sin" [NASB]) and the expression in 2:29 (*pas ho poiōn tēn dikaiosunēn*, "everyone who practices righteous-

---

[359] Lenski, *Interpretation of the Epistles*, 454.

ness" [NASB]).[360] Not only does the child of God live a life marked by righteousness (2:29) and purity (3:3), but he abstains from a life characterized by the practice of sin. The word *poiōn* is used frequently in this section (vv. 3,4,7,8,9,10) to imply a continual practice of sin as well as a realization of sin's completeness.[361] In other words, it is a willful, habitual action.

In classical Greek the word for sin *(hamartia)* means to "miss the mark." It was used of a warrior who missed striking his opponent or of a traveler who missed the right path.[362] In the New Testament, however, *hamartia* is more active in nature. In other words, sin is an intentional breaking of God's moral standard. It is a willful rebellion arising from the deliberate choice of the individual, a direct violation of God's laws. Sin is "missing God's mark" (Rom 3:23); it is a direct offense against the known will of God.[363]

The NIV translation "Everyone who sins breaks the law" fails to capture the full significance of what John means. Kruse notes, "The word translated 'lawlessness' *(anomia)* is found only in this verse in 1, 2, and 3 John. It does not carry the idea of breaking the law, for the whole question of the law is absent from this letter; the word law *(nomos)* is not found at all in 1 John."[364] It is true that lawlessness is usually understood to be the violation of God's law.[365] But lawlessness is more than the absence of God's law for John. It is a willful rejection and an active disobedience against God's moral standard, which is a characteristic of the child of the devil.

Kruse, following De la Potterie, makes a compelling argument that "in the NT *anomia* as transgression of the law is completely absent." Rather, John equates "committing lawlessness" with "being of the devil" (v. 8). "Whoever commits *the* sin (i.e., the typical sin of heretics), he says commits not only a morally reprehensible act; he commits iniquity, thereby revealing that he is basically a son of the devil (v. 8), someone who is in direct opposition to Christ and God and who is under the control of Satan."[366]

John's emphasis here is vital to his argument against the false teachers.

---

[360] The contrast is also with the participle of the previous verse: ὁ ἔχων τὴν ἐλπίδα ("everyone who has this hope"). The contrast marks the distinct difference between the child of God, whose life is distinguished by righteousness and self-purification, and the child of the devil, whose life is marked by a habitual life of sin. See Brown, *Epistles of John*, 379 and Burge, *Letters of John*, 143 for their helpful comments.

[361] Robertson, *WP* 6:221.

[362] Thomas, "Exegetical Digest of 1 John," 247.

[363] Stott, *Letters of John*, 126.

[364] Kruse, *The Letters of John*, 117.

[365] Brown, *Epistles of John*, 398; also Lenski, *Interpretation of the Epistles,* 455.

[366] Kruse, *The Letters of John*, 117–19; see I. de la Potterie, "'Sin Is Iniquity' (1 John 3, 4)," in *The Christian Lives by the Spirit* (New York: Alba, 1971), 36–55.

From all indications the apostle is dealing with individuals who are indifferent to sin. They believed that they could engage in any and all kinds of sinful activities and still be in fellowship with God. In their line of reasoning, their acts were merely amoral. It was such licentious beliefs that John confronts. Sin is not amoral. It is not something to which one can be indifferent. On the contrary, sin is a willful disregard for God. It is a rebellious revolt against God's will. No one is excluded from the obligation to obey God; therefore the seccessionists were placing themselves, by their sinful acts, in direct opposition to God.[367] Sin in its very nature is "synonymous with being of the devil" (v. 8) and "the opposite of being just" (v. 7).[368] To live a life of sin is to align oneself with the world and the devil and to be at enmity with God. It is the very opposite of what righteousness is and entails.

3:5 John offers an added reason why the child of God is to strive to live without sin—the person and work of Christ. The apostle appeals to the common knowledge his readers possess by virtue of the spiritual "anointing" they have received (cf. 2:27). Implicit in this appeal to his hearers' basic Christian knowledge is an encouragement for them to conform their lives to the truth they already know.[369]

John's use of the demonstrative pronoun *ekeinos* ("he" or "that one") points back to the historical reality of Christ's incarnation. It also reveals the uniqueness of the Christ event. The apostle does not say, however, that Jesus "was born" but that he "appeared," "was manifested" (KJV) or made visible (*ephanerōthē;* cf. 1:2; 2:19,28; 3:2), which implies his preexistence even before the incarnation. It is important to note that John uses this word to refer to both the incarnation of Christ (1:2; 3:5,8) and his manifestation at the *parousia* (2:28; 3:2). Smalley makes a crucial observation when he writes, "The self-disclosure of God in his Son, for the purpose of dealing

---

[367] Other scholars have also suggested that the term "lawlessness" should be understood in more apocalyptic terms. E.g., Marshall writes that "the word was associated with the final outbreak of evil against Christ and that it signifies rebellion against the will of God. To commit sin is thus to place oneself on the side of the devil and antichrist and to stand in opposition to Christ" (*Epistles of John,* 176). He defends understanding lawlessness this way in a manner similar to De la Potterie (whom he cites, 176, n. 3) and Kruse: (1) John only uses the word here and never uses the word "law" in his epistle; (2) the thought goes back to John's reference to the antichrists of the final days; and (3) other NT texts use "lawlessness" in regard to the time just prior to Christ's return (Matt 7:22–23; 24:11–12; 2 Cor 6:14–16; 2 Thess 2:3). In essence, the point is that lawlessness is "a technical term for the Satan-inspired rejection of God and his law that will be manifest in the present age and will come to a climax before Christ's second coming" (C. Haas, M. De Jonge, and J. L. Swellengrebel, *A Translator's Handbook of the Letters of John* [London: UBS, 1972], 81). See also Smalley, *1, 2, 3 John,* 154–55; and Schnackenburg, *The Johannine Epistles,* 185–87.

[368] Kruse, *The Letters of John,* 118.

[369] Stott, *Letters of John,* 127.

with human sin, stretches from the preexistence of Christ to his exaltation in glory."[370]

"So that" (*hina,* "in order that") introduces the purpose of Christ's manifestation on the earth: to "take away our sins." John uses the plural form "sins" *(tas hamartias)* to denote the multitude of individual sinful acts humans commit. This plural use goes hand-in-hand with John's admonition to abstain from the practice of sin. The sinful nature of humankind is reflected in the individual sins they perform.

Christ came to "take away" individual sins. This verb *(airō)* can mean "to lift up," "to bear," or "to remove." While all three meanings have some connotation in the translation, the context seems to point to the expiatory nature of Christ's sacrifice. The aorist tense denotes the finality of this sacrificial act. One is reminded of the proclamation of John the Baptist in which the same word is used, "Behold the Lamb of God who takes away the sin of the world" (John 1:29). One of the goals of Christ's incarnation and sacrifice was the "effective removal of human sins."[371] Christ came to remove the individual acts of sin committed by his children.

The word order of John's added phrase "and in him is no sin" *(kai hamartia en auto ouk estin)* emphatically declares the sinlessness of Christ. Literally, the phrase could be translated, "And sin in him there is not," with the emphasis falling on sin. John's statement is more than the fact that Christ did not commit sin. He argues that Christ does not possess a sinful nature.[372] Furthermore, John uses the present tense verb "is" *(estin)* to assert that sinlessness is an eternal part of Christ's nature. His sinlessness is not limited to his preexistence, his incarnate life in the flesh, or his present exalted status. Instead, Christ is sinless—past, present, and future. Sinlessness is essential to his very personhood.

John maintains that Christ is the Righteous One (2:29), the Pure One (3:3), and the Sinless One (3:5). He is our atonement and advocate (2:1–2), and he is the supreme example and pattern of what his children should be and can be by abiding in him.

3:6 Verse 6 is a natural deduction from the previous verse. Since Christ came to take away sin, since there is no sin in him, and since the believer is to pattern his life after Christ, it is obviously true that the one who remains in him will not live a life of sin. As a matter of fact, John asserts that the one abiding in Christ cannot, that is, it is an absolute impossibility, to "keep on sinning." As before, John utilizes the all-inclusive *pas ho* ("everyone who"). This time, however, it is connected with a negative *(ouk),* which

---

[370] Smalley, *1, 2, 3 John*, 156. See also Westcott, *Epistles of John*, 124–28.

[371] Hiebert, *The Epistles of John*, 142.

[372] Burdick, *The Letters of John the Apostle*, 238.

combines to give the universal negative "no one."

The apostle distinguishes between two groups in this verse. The first class is characterized by their abiding relationship with Christ *(en autou)*. For this group abiding in Christ is the grounds for their abstinence from sin.

John's affirmation that "no one who lives ["abides, remains"] in him keeps on sinning" has been the center of much debate. What is John proposing here? Is the apostle suggesting that a believer does not commit acts of sin? What about his earlier statements that Christians do sin (1:8,10; 2:1–2)? How can this statement be balanced with these earlier assertions? Is John contradicting himself? These are all legitimate questions the serious biblical exegete must seek to answer.

Although numerous suggestions have been offered,[373] and none is completely satisfying, the most reasonable still seems to center on John's use of the present tense verb. John is not suggesting that the child of God will not commit a single act of sin. Instead, John is describing a way of life, a character, a prevailing lifestyle. Here the present tense verb contextually depicts linear, continual action. In other words, the believer will not live a life characterized by sin. From John's earlier statements it is obvious that the Christian, while enjoying a position or standing of sinlessness through identification with Christ, will sin on occasion and will need to seek God's forgiveness (1:9; 2:1–2). But what is also apparent from John's writings is that a genuine believer will not live in continual sin. As D. Smith writes,

---

[373] Thomas surveys nine possible interpretations and states both the pros and the cons of each view before offering his own interpretation. (1) The perfectionist view: the Christian does not commit acts of sin. (2) The limited view of sin: the Christian does not commit certain sins. (3) The Christian does not sin because what is sin in the life of the unbeliever is not so regarded by God in a believer. (4) The Christian does not sin in his new nature. (5) John is describing the theoretical or ideal and not reality. The ideal is, to a limited extent, true. (6) John is expressing himself by using exaggeration in this extremely controversial issue. (7) The Christian does not commit willful and deliberate sin. (8) The Christian does not commit habitual and consistent sin. Sin does not characterize his life. (9) The Christian who abides in Christ does not commit sin. When (or if) he sins, he is not abiding in Christ. In his conclusion Thomas offers a somewhat unique interpretation adapted from A. T. Robertson. It is the identification of the present tense of ἁμαρτάνει as a "progressive present." Simply put, this use depicts past action still in progress at the present time. In other words, John is saying "that an unbroken state of sinful behavior from the past into the present and continuing in the present, such as characterizes the children of the devil (cf. 3:10), is impossible for the one who has been begotten by God" ("Exegetical Digest of 1 John," 253–61). Kruse has an extended discussion on "Sinless Perfection" (*The Letters of John,* 126–32). He provides a fine overview but fails to provide a "satisfactory resolution of the tension between 2:1 and 3:6–9" (p. 132). For further discussion see J. Bogart, *Orthodox and Heretical Perfectionism in the Johannine Community as Evident in the First Epistle of John,* SBLD 33 (Missoula; Mont.: Scholars Press, 1977); P. P. A. Kotzé, "The Meaning of 1 John 3:9 with Reference to 1 John 1:8 and 10," *Neot* 13 (1979): 68–83; S. Kubo, "1 John 3:9: Absolute or Habitual," *AUSS* 7 (1969): 47–56; K. Inman, "Distinctive Johannine Vocabulary and the Interpretation of 1 John 3:9," *WTJ* 40 (1977–78): 136–44; H. C. Swadling, "Sin and Sinlessness in 1 John," *SJT* 35 (1982): 205–11.

"The believer may fall into sin but he will not walk in it."[374]

The second class of persons John characterizes are those who continue in sin. Of these John says that they have neither "seen him or known him." The one who lives the life of continual sin is also the one who is not abiding in him. Sin is the ruling principle of their lives. For them there is no abiding relationship with Christ. As a matter of fact, they have neither seen him nor know him. In contrast, it is clear that remaining in Christ is tantamount to seeing him and knowing him.

"Seen" and "known" are both in the perfect tense. To see *(heoraken)* him entails a spiritual vision brought about through a personal, saving relationship with him. The writer of Hebrews identifies this spiritual eyesight as faith: "Now faith is the assurance of things hoped for, the conviction of things not seen" (Heb 11:1, NASB). Earlier John referred to a literal seeing of Jesus in the flesh (1:2–3), but here the emphasis rests on seeing the true nature and purpose of the incarnate Christ. The one who sees Christ for who he is and embraces his redemptive work is the one who abides in him.

To know *(egnōken)* him is to enter into that personal, dynamic relationship with him. It is not a mere intellectual assent or innate comprehension, but rather it is a knowledge based upon experience. It is the subjective appropriation of who Christ is and what he has done for sinful humanity. The verb is ingressive, which means that this knowledge is obtained rather than naturally possessed. It is coming to know him more and more in a personal way.

The apostle asserts with absolute clarity that those who live in habitual sin have not seen Christ and do not know Christ. This is the same as saying they do not have a saving relationship with Christ. On the other hand, those who abide in him live a life marked by habitual righteousness and purity instead of lawlessness (rebellion) and disobedience. While the unbeliever lives in sin and has not seen or known Christ, the believer has terminated a life of sin for a life of abiding in him. The child of God has experienced a decisive break with sin. Sin no longer controls his life.

3:7 John's tender affection for his readers *(teknia)* causes him to remind them of the peril of their situation. As God's children they are to be on guard against those who want to lead them astray. The present imperative *(planatō)* carries the idea of "Let no one engage in deceiving you, i.e., even try it!"[375] Historically, the reference is to the false teachers who have attempted both doctrinal deception (2:26) and moral deception. As Stott points out, the subject of this deceit appears to center around the false teaching that one "could 'be' righteous without necessarily bothering to

---

[374] D. Smith, "The Epistles of John," *EGT* 5:184.

[375] Lenski, *Interpretation of the Epistles,* 459.

'practice' righteousness."[376] Bruce explains, "The false teachers with their sophistry were capable not merely of condoning sin, but of making it seem virtuous."[377] John's warning has been relevant throughout the history of the church until our own day.

The apostle's words of caution include a moral criterion for the professing believer: "He who does what is right is righteous" *(ho poiōn tēn dikaosunēn dikaios estin)*. Hiebert asserts: "The present tense participle makes clear that the test is not the performance of an occasional righteous deed but rather the habitual practice of 'righteousness.'"[378] Furthermore, "the righteousness" *(tēn dikaiosunēn)* indicates that a particular righteousness is in view. It emphasizes the completeness and unity of this righteous quality. Obviously the reference is to that righteousness that is characteristic of Christ. It is a distinguishing trait of God's family and is a product of regeneration. Notice that the practice of righteousness is not what makes the individual "righteous" *(dikaios)*, but it reveals the inner nature of the one who is practicing righteousness. One practices righteousness because of his righteous character. "By their fruit you will recognize them" (Matt 7:16). The individual's conduct is certain evidence of his nature. The one who practices righteousness does so because he has been granted the righteousness of God. In this sense John's regeneration language parallels the New Testament concept of justification. The believer does right because he possesses the imputed righteousness of Christ.

This righteousness is expected of the child of God because "he *[ekeinos, that one]* is righteous." This is, of course, a reference to the Son of God (cf. v. 8). John's use of "just as" *(kathōs)* does not imply that the believer is righteous to the same *extent* that Christ is righteous. Instead, Christ is the standard, the means, the motivation for the Christian's righteousness. As a child of God the believer seeks to live a life of Christlike righteousness. He seeks to be like Jesus.

John warns against the deception of the false teachers, who claim to be righteous based on some avowed esoteric knowledge but whose lives are marked by continual sin. In response the apostle warns his readers against the danger of being led astray by these heretical teachers. Righteousness is an inner quality that displays itself outwardly. The one who is truly righteous is the one who practices righteousness, a righteousness provided and displayed by Christ, the eternally Righteous One.

3:8 For the first time in the epistle John refers, specifically and directly, to the devil (cf. 3:12; 2:13–14; 5:18–19). John now contrasts the

---

[376] Stott, *Letters of John*, 128.

[377] Bruce, *The Epistles of John*, 91.

[378] Hiebert, *Epistles of John*, 144–45.

one who practices righteousness and is of Christ with the one who does what is sinful and is of the devil. As Thomas emphasizes, "The parallel clauses show the sharp contrast in the conduct and character of two classes of man. The former clause pictures a man whose righteous character underlies his righteous deeds. ... The latter clause pictures a man whose sinful conduct and character find their source in the devil."[379] In essence, both reflect the nature of their masters.

As before, the writer's use of the present active participle (*ho poiōn tēn hamartian,* "the one who practices sin" [NASB]) indicates a continual state of sin. One's life is a life of sin. John refers to a habitual life of sin, not just individual acts of sin (even though the individual acts reveal the inner character). Using the article *(tēn hamartian)* before the noun heightens the contrast between "the righteousness" of v. 7 and the one "who does what is sinful" of v. 8. As Burdick notes, "These are the distinguishing marks of the two families. The righteousness that John has in mind is the righteousness characteristic of God and coming from God; the sin referred to is the sin characteristic of the devil and which finds its source in him."[380]

The preposition "of" *(ek)* speaks of the source of this habitual sinfulness, that is, the devil *(tou diabolou).* Satan is the source, the spiritual father (John 8:44), of the one who continually practices sin. John uses the word "devil" four times in his epistle, all in this section (3:8,10). The name means "slanderer" or "accuser." He instigates sin, and those who live in sin are his children. He stands as the direct opponent of God and righteousness.

The further comment, "for the devil has been sinning from the beginning," identifies the devil as the originator of sin. The progressive present tense of the verb *hamartanei* depicts sin as continuous and ongoing. For the devil and his children, sin is a ceaseless way of life.

The time referred to as "the beginning" is somewhat debatable. It has been interpreted as the beginning of all creation, the beginning of the world, the beginning of sin, and the beginning of the devil's rebellion.[381] It would seem reasonable to conclude that John is referring to that period when Satan first sinned against God. To hold that sin existed prior to the devil's existence is untenable. Such a view would suggest that God created an evil being (Satan), that God created evil itself (making him the author of evil), or that God existed in some type of cosmic dualism between good and evil. Thus, "the beginning" is that period when the devil introduced sin through his own sinful rebellion. As Burdick comments: "Prior to the creation of the

---

[379] Thomas, "Exegetical Digest of 1 John," 266.

[380] Burdick, *The Letters of John the Apostle,* 242.

[381] There are other, though less popular, interpretations also. For a general overview of the various views, see Thomas, "Exegetical Digest of 1 John," 267–70. Thomas himself interprets the phrase to mean the beginning of human sinning, the fall of Adam.

first human beings, the devil was already sinning. It is he who introduced sin to the human race, and thus all who are sinning are his spiritual offspring."[382]

The prepositional phrase "for this purpose" (KJV; *eis touto*) reveals the intent of Christ's coming: he came to destroy the devil's works. As in v. 5, John's selection of "appeared" ("was manifested," KJV) as opposed to "was born" points to both the preexistence of the Son of God and the historical reality of his incarnation. The distinctive title "the Son of God," the first of seven occurrences in the epistle (3:8; 4:15; 5:5,10,12,13,20), emphasizes the deity of Christ and the severity of his conflict with the devil.

The NIV neglects the conjunction *hina*, "in order that," which introduces the divine purpose of the manifestation of the Son of God. A part of Christ's redemptive mission was to destroy the works of the devil. The verb "destroy" naturally looks to Christ's decisive victory over Satan on Calvary's cross (John 12:31; Heb 2:14). Satan is a defeated foe.

The devil's works *(erga)* are all those sinful and evil attitudes and actions of which he is the source. Everything the devil has done or will do was destroyed on the cross, and it will be on the basis of Christ's finished work that all of the devil's works will be ultimately destroyed at the final judgment (Rev 20:10–15). As Marshall correctly observes, "The task of Jesus was to undo whatever the devil had achieved, to thwart whatever he tries to do."[383] More specifically, in the immediate context the reference is to the removal of sin from the individual's life. Christ came to "loose" the sinner from the chains of sin. There is liberation in the cross. Deliverance can be obtained through the work of the incarnate Son of God. It is the characteristic of the devil to sin and of Jesus to save.[384]

3:9 John returns to the concept that the child of God will behave in a manner that is similar to his Father's nature. The one who is "born of God" will not continue in sin. The perfect participle *(gegennēmenos)* implies not

---

[382] Burdick, *The Letters of John the Apostle,* 243.

[383] Marshall, *Epistles of John,* 185. B. H. Carroll notes, "We are not theologians if we do not have correct views of a personal devil, between whom and our Saviour occurred the conflict of the ages on the cross" (*An Interpretation of the Evangelical Bible,* vol. 6 [Grand Rapids: Baker, 1973], 301). Kruse adds, "The devil's work is essentially trying to undo God's work by turning people aside from doing God's will, that is, causing them to sin" (*The Letters of John,* 123).

[384] Stott, *Letters of John,* 129. G. Aulen's *Christus Victor* is a fine historical survey of this atonement emphasis. His analysis does not capture the full or primary focus of the biblical witness concerning the atonement, but it is correct at significant points in what it affirms. Christ by his death on the cross did, indeed, defeat the devil (*Christus Victor* [New York: Macmillan, 1969]). For an orthodox treatment of the atonement, see L. Morris, *The Apostolic Preaching of the Cross* (London: Tyndale, 1955) and *The Cross in the New Testament* (Grand Rapids: Eerdmans, 1965). For the finest treatment overall to appear in many years see J. A. W. Stott, *The Cross of Christ* (Downers Grove: InterVarsity, 1986).

only a single past act of spiritual new birth but also the ongoing effects of being born of God. It is the one who has been born of God and continues to abide in Christ who is a child of God. Once again the apostle expresses a universal declaration (*pas,* "everyone") that allows no exceptions to the rule: "No one who is born of God will continue to sin."

John's word order (*pas ho gegennēmenos ek tou theou hamartian ou poiei,* lit., "everyone having been born from God sin not is doing") puts emphasis on the phrase "born of God." Westcott notes the importance of this order by affirming that the child of God "cannot sin, because it is of God, and of no other that he hath been born."[385] Because the child is born of God, he does not practice sin. This concept is a restatement of v. 6, where "abiding in Christ" explains one's abstinence from sin. Here the indicated source of power over sin is the regenerating power of God. John's point is clear: there is not a single regenerated person who lives a life of habitual sin. As in v. 6, the writer's use of the present tense accentuates that the child of God does not continually engage in sin.[386] John is not suggesting the believer is completely free from sin, but that the Christian's life is not characterized by sin, which is the mark of the follower of Satan, who has been sinning from the beginning (v. 8). The child of God does not behave in a manner that has the nature or character of sin.

The two conjunctions *(hoti ... hoti)* translated "because" both times reveal the two reasons for the incompatibility of sin and the child of God. First, the believer does not sin because "God's [lit. "his"] seed remains in him *(hoti sperma autou en auto menei).* The indwelling "seed" enables and motivates the sin-free living of the child of God. The metaphorical designation "his seed," which appears only here in John's writings, is variously interpreted.[387] Some interpret it as the Word of God, the regenerating agent that produces new birth (cf. Jas 1:18; 1 Pet 1:23–25). Others designate it as the divine nature or principle of life, which is implanted by God in the believer. Some understand the seed to denote God's offspring, that is, his children collectively. Still others identify the seed as the Holy Spirit (John

---

[385] Westcott, *Epistles of John,* 107.

[386] The debate concerning what John means when he says the child of God does not sin has been addressed earlier (see pp. 144–45; esp. n. 371). As before, John seems to be speaking of a habitual lifestyle as opposed to a single sinful act. For a further discussion regarding the differing viewpoints of what John means, see Burdick, *The Letters of John the Apostle,* 244–46.

[387] J. du Perez lists six different interpretations of "seed": Christ, children of God, the proclaimed word, the Holy Spirit, new life from God, and the new nature ("'Sperma auto' in 1 John 3:9," *Neot* 9 [1975]: 105–10). He defends new life from God as the best view, though he incorporates some facets of the other views also into his position. Thomas also lists six possibilities of interpreting "the seed." Besides those mentioned above, he includes the gospel message. For the pros and cons of each view, see Thomas, "Exegetical Digest of 1 John," 274–78; Brown, *Epistles of John,* 408–11; and the note on "God's Seed" in Kruse, *The Letters of John,* 124–26.

3:5–8). Smalley attempts to combine the two concepts of "Word" and "Spirit." He understands *sperma* to mean "the word of God which is received in faith by the Christian, and which (through the inward activity of the Spirit) leads to rebirth, and the experience of increasing holiness by living in Jesus."[388] Through both the Word and the Spirit, the Christian is born of God and enabled to live like Christ. This is an attractive option, but the natural parallelism with human reproduction is too strong. The believer cannot continue in sin because of the divine life that has been implanted through the new birth. A new nature, a divine nature, has been imparted to the believer. The life of God is now his life, and a life of sin is simply no longer possible.

One important note that must not be overlooked is the fact that the seed is planted firmly and eternally. The believer cannot continue to sin because God's seed remains in him. However the seed is understood, one cannot miss the eternal and life-changing effects of the seed. As Brown writes, "The exact identification is not so important, so long as we recognize that the author is talking about a divine agency for begetting God's children, which not only brings us into being but also remains and keeps us his children."[389] The believer does not continue in sin because of the implanted seed.

John's second reason for the believer's abstinence from sin is because "he has been born of God" *(hoti ek theou gegennētai)*. This statement is more sweeping than the first and emphasizes the incongruity between the life of sin and the new life of the child of God. Hiebert writes: "John insists that the believer's inability to continue in the practice of sin is due to the fact that he has been born of God. ... It is a moral incompatibility between the believer's old and new nature."[390] As Bruce maintains:

> The new birth involves a radical change in human nature; for those who have not experienced it, sin is natural, whereas for those who have experienced it, sin is unnatural—so unnatural, indeed, that its practice constitutes a powerful refutation of any claim to possess the divine life. John's antitheses are clearcut. While they are to be understood in the context of his letter and of the situation which it presupposes, any attempt to weaken them out of regard for human infirmity, or to make them less sharp and uncompromising than they are, is to misinterpret them.[391]

The life of the child who has been born of God is marked by the purity and righteousness of the One whom he follows. The child of God does not live a

---

[388] Smalley, *1, 2, 3 John*, 174.

[389] Brown, *Epistles of John*, 411.

[390] Hiebert, *Epistles of John*, 148.

[391] Bruce, *Epistles of John*, 92.

life of habitual sin because (1) the seed of God remains in him, and (2) he has been born of God. Although the Christian still falls prey to sinful acts, John insists that it is impossible for sin to become a believer's pattern of life.

3:10 This verse serves as both a summary and conclusion of what has gone before and a transition to what follows. Opinion is divided as to the antecedent of the phrase "by this" *(en toutō)*. Some believe it refers to what precedes.[392] Others see it as a transition to what follows,[393] and still others suggest it refers to both what precedes and what follows.[394] John uses the pronoun both ways in his epistle. Burdick points out, "It makes little difference since both the preceding and the following context speak of the same fact: the family of God is marked by the practice of righteousness."[395] What is crucial to John's transition is the identification of the members of two opposing families: the children of God and the children of the devil. This verse brings to a conclusion John's discussion in vv. 4–10 concerning the identifiable nature of the child of God. John reaffirms that both the child of God and the child of the devil can be identified by what they do. There are only two classes of people in John's diagnosis—those who are children of God and those who are children of the devil. John knows of no intermediate group. Sharp lines are drawn between those who practice sin and those who practice righteousness. One is fathered by the devil, and the other is fathered by God.

The apostle's twofold criterion for distinguishing the children of God and the children of Satan is stated negatively.[396] First, "anyone who does not do what is right is not a child of God" *(pas ho mē poiōn dikaiosunēn ouk estin ek tou theou)*. The absence of righteous character, as revealed by one's continual unrighteous conduct, indicates that the individual is not a child of God.[397] Moral conduct is a test of one's spiritual heritage.

Second, "anyone who does not love his brother" *(ho mē agapōn ton adelphon autou)* is not a child of God. This last phrase provides a transition to the theme of love that will dominate the second major section of the epistle (3:11–5:12), but it is not to be separated from its immediate application.

---

[392] See Robertson, *WP* 4:223.

[393] Brooke, *Johannine Epistles*, 90.

[394] Marshall, *Epistles of John*, 187.

[395] Burdick, *The Letters of John the Apostle*, 248.

[396] The apostle uses the same word (φανερά, "manifest") with which he has earlier referred to Christ's incarnation (3:5,8) and second coming (2:28; 3:2) and by which he identified the believer's yet-to-come final state (3:2). In the immediate context John suggests that one's outward manifestation reveals one's spiritual father.

[397] Once again John employs the linear tense of the present participle to denote the habit of not doing what is right. The child of the devil engages in a continual life of sin, as opposed to the child of God, whose life is characterized by righteousness.

As Plummer notes, "Love is righteousness in relation to others."[398] John's vertical-horizontal theme resurfaces. One who has been born of God treats his fellow brothers and sisters as family members. There is a common bond of love. Two of the apostle's major themes (righteousness and love) are joined together as evidence of the new birth. Those who fail to practice righteousness and/or neglect to love other Christians are not of the same spiritual heritage as the child of God. The family of God is marked by the practice of righteousness and love.

In summarizing this section of the epistle, the child of God is reminded of his unique calling and heritage. The believer's life is one marked by righteousness. Sin does not characterize the child of God. Our pattern is the Righteous One, Jesus Christ, who came to destroy the works of the devil and the power of sin. Those who have been born of God live a life that resembles the righteous life of Christ. The child has the distinguishing marks of his parent. Therefore the child comes to imitate, and even embody, the distinguishing marks of his parent.

---

[398] Plummer, *Epistles of S. John,* 128.

II. GOD IS LOVE (3:11–5:21)
  1. Love One Another: Part 1 (3:11–24)
     (1) Love in Action (3:11–18)
     (2) Live in Confidence (3:19–24)
  2. Test the Spirits (4:1–6)
  3. Love One Another: Part Two (4:7–21)
     (1) Love Others because God Loves You (4:7–10)
     (2) Love Others because God Lives in You (4:11–21)
  4. Obey God and Experience the Victory of Faith (5:1–5)
  5. Believe in the Son and Enjoy Eternal Life (5:6–12)
  6. Conclusion: The Confidence and Characteristics of the Child
     of God (5:13–21)
     (1) Know You Have Eternal Life (5:13)
     (2) Be Confident in Prayer (5:14–17)
     (3) Do Not Continue in Sin (5:18–20)
     (4) Keep Yourself from Idols (5:20–21)

II. GOD IS LOVE (3:11–5:21)

As argued in the introduction, this segment constitutes the second major section of the letter. There is a natural parallelism between 1:5 and 3:11 created by the phrase, "This is the message." The word *angelia* occurs in both verses and at no other time in the entire epistle. Further, as 1:5–3:10 gives greater attention to the theme "God is light," 3:11–5:12 focuses more on the theme "God is love."

It must be acknowledged that there is not a hard break between 3:10 and 3:11. Indeed, there is a common link built around the theme of love that allows for a smooth transition. The change is more one of emphasis, though new subject matter also is introduced.

1. Love One Another: Part 1 (3:11–24)

This section breaks at 3:18. Verse 18 serves as a summation of 3:11–18, and 3:19 introduces a new subject (confidence in prayer). The word truth *(alētheia)* occurs both in 3:18 and 3:19 and functions as a head-tail linkage.

Interestingly, the phrase *pas ho,* which dominated the previous section, occurs in this unit only at 3:15.

(1) Love in Action (3:11–18)

¹¹This is the message you heard from the beginning: We should love one another. ¹²Do not be like Cain, who belonged to the evil one and murdered his brother. And why did he murder him? Because his own actions were evil and his brother's were righteous. ¹³Do not be surprised, my brothers, if the world hates you. ¹⁴We know that we have passed from death to life, because we love our brothers. Anyone who does not love remains in death. ¹⁵Anyone who hates his brother is a murderer, and you know that no murderer has eternal life in him.

¹⁶This is how we know what love is: Jesus Christ laid down his life for us. And we ought to lay down our lives for our brothers. ¹⁷If anyone has material possessions and sees his brother in need but has no pity on him, how can the love of God be in him? ¹⁸Dear children, let us not love with words or tongue but with actions and in truth.

3:11 The NIV again fails to translate the conjunction *hoti* ("because"), which connects this unit with the previous thought. The absence of love in the life of a child of God is inconsistent with the message of love that has been proclaimed to them. The demonstrative "this" points forward to the subsequent "that" *(hina)* clause, "that we should love one another."

This message *(aggelia)*[1] of love is one these believers have heard from the beginning *(archēs)* of their Christian lives.[2] It is a message grounded in the very nature of God (4:7–8) and taught by Christ himself to his followers (John 13:34–35; 15:12,17). The original apostolic message affirmed that believers should love one another, a practice that is foundational to the Christian message.

Although the demand for obedience to love certainly applies to the world in general, this command to love is directed primarily to the community of

---

[1] The word "message," ἀγγελία, occurs only twice in the NT (here and in 1:5). It denotes a declaration or a proclamation, with the emphasis resting on the message itself and not the quality or source of the message (R. L. Thomas, "Exegetical Digest of 1 John," [© 1984 R. L. Thomas], 283).

[2] Once again the meaning of the word "beginning," ἀρχῆς, must be understood from the context. Thomas offers two solutions: (1) The word is used in an absolute sense, referring back to the beginning of the human race; and (2) the word is relative, referring back to their Christian beginnings, when they heard and received the apostolic message. From a contextual standpoint, the second alternative seems to be the most appropriate. John's use of the aorist verb ἠκούσατε ("heard") would appear to point to a recent reception of this message. But as evidenced by the apostle's Cain illustration in v. 12, the message also finds root as far back as creation itself. For immediate application, it seems that John is referring to the apostolic message they heard and received at salvation. See Thomas, "Exegetical Digest of 1 John," 283–84, S. S. Smalley, *1, 2, 3 John*, WBC (Waco: Word, 1984), 182, and I. H. Marshall, *The Epistles of John*, NICOT (Grand Rapids: Eerdmans, 1978), 189, n. 4.

faith.[3] The present tense of *agapōmen* ("we should love") calls for a continuous display of love in the family of God. Christian love is fundamental to being a child of God. Having established that believers are characterized by righteousness and abstinence from a life of continual sin, John now adds that they are also persons who love one another as a normal and consistent habit of life.

3:12   John cites Cain as an illustration of the absence of love, which marks the child of the devil. The apostle's choice of Cain (his only direct Old Testament reference in the entire epistle) demonstrates the antithetical natures of the children of God and the children of "the evil one."

Cain is identified as being "of the evil one" *(ek tou ponerou)*. Cain belonged to the evil one, to the devil, a thought that apparently is derived from Gen 4:7, where God warns Cain that "sin is crouching at your door." The adjective *ponerou* ("evil") indicates the active exercise of evil in one's behavior. Cain demonstrated the defining actions of his spiritual father (cf. 3:10). As Marshall writes, Cain "drew his inspiration from the evil one, the devil, who is himself the archetypal murderer (John 5:46)."[4]

Cain's conduct revealed his diabolical character when he "murdered his brother." John uses the word *esphaksen* ("to butcher, slay, murder"; lit., "to cut the throat") to portray the brutal violence of the event.

The unexpected rhetorical question, "And why did he murder him?" serves to expose the motive behind Cain's gruesome deed. The subsequent answer, "Because his own actions were evil and his brother's were righteous," contrasts the two deeds and character of the two brothers. The righteous acts of Abel provoked the jealousy of Cain, which digressed into hatred and eventually murder. As Stott affirms, "Jealousy—hatred—murder is a natural and terrible sequence."[5] The motivation behind Cain's initial envy illustrates the conflicting nature between good and evil. In essence, Cain murdered his brother Abel because the wicked person hates righteousness. Burdick adds, "Godlessness is disturbed by the condemning presence of righteousness in its midst, and it would remove the cause of its discomfort if it could."[6] In Cain's case the inner nature brought forth the outward action. Cain was on the devil's side and acted in accordance with his spiritual heritage.

3:13   The reference to the hatred exhibited by Cain introduces an additional aspect of this conflict between good and evil, namely, "God-prompted love and Satan-inspired hatred."[7] The hostility and enmity

---

[3] The reciprocal pronoun ἀλλήλου ("one another") marks the mutual operation of this love within the community of faith. Each family member seeks the welfare of others.

[4] Marshall, *Epistles of John*, 189.

[5] J. R. W. Stott, *The Letters of John*, rev. ed., TNTC (Grand Rapids: Eerdmans, 1988), 144.

[6] D. Burdick, *The Letters of John the Apostle* (Chicago: Moody, 1985), 262.

[7] D. E. Hiebert, *The Epistles of John* (Greenville: Bob Jones University Press, 1991), 154.

between righteousness and sinfulness, as emulated in the account of Cain and Abel (v. 12), will never end in this world. Hatred continues to be the reaction of the world toward the children of God. John uses the word "world" *(kosmos)* here as he did in 2:15, indicating that evil is an organized system in opposition to God and under the control of the devil.

John urges his readers not to be surprised by the world's hatred. The imperative construction of the verb *thaumazete* ("to wonder, marvel") with the negative assumes an action that is already in the process of occurring. Apparently, some of John's readers are surprised by the hostile attitude of the world around them. The apostle calls upon these believers to stop marveling at the hatred being displayed. "Because the hate of the world was an ever-present reality, so the Christian's response must be a cessation of continuous wonder."[8] This prohibition reflects the teachings of Jesus in John 15:18–21 (cf. also Matt 5:11–12; 1 Pet 4:13).

For the first and only time, the apostle addresses his readers as "brothers" *(adelphoi)*, a term denoting the unity that characterizes the community of faith.[9] John places himself on the same level as his hearers. As their brother, John knows what it means to be hated by the world.

The first class conditional clause "if the world hates you" *(ei misei humas ho kosmos)* presents this hostility not as a potential or foreseeable threat but rather as a present reality, a reality that is to be expected. Just as love is the defining characteristic of the child of God, so hatred is the natural response of the world toward righteousness. Smalley warns: "The child of God ... must be prepared for the enmity of the 'world.' For the fact is that those who belong to the world recognize neither God, nor those who belong to him."[10]

3:14 John's use of the emphatic "we" *(hēmeis)* marks the distinct contrast between the children of the devil who hate and the child of God, who is characterized by his love for the family of God. The apostle appeals to his hearers' personal knowledge for assurance of their new life in Christ. They know what the world does not know: that they have passed from death into life.

The perfect tense verb *metabebekamen* literally means "to take steps over," "to pass over," or "to move from one place to another." John employs the term to denote a permanent movement from one spiritual sphere, "out of

---

[8] Thomas, "Exegetical Digest of 1 John," 288.

[9] Although John uses this term only here as a direct address to his readers, a form of the word *adelphos* occurs in the Johannine epistles. *Adelehe* ("sister") occurs in 2 John 13. The word is a common reference throughout the NT (cf. 1 Cor 1:10–11; Heb 3:12; Jas 1:2). As we have seen, John employs two other "family" terms in his epistles: τεκνία and παιδία. John's choice of ἀδελφοί at this point parallels his reference to the brothers Cain and Abel.

[10] Smalley, *1, 2, 3 John*, 187.

death" *(ek tou thanatou)*, into the exact opposite region, "into life" *(eis tēn zōēn)*. The perfect tense distinguishes the permanent, abiding reality of the life they now experience. The distinct sphere has already been entered; the transfer has already occurred. The promise of John 5:24 is a present reality that begins at the moment of regeneration.

The conjunction "because" *(hoti)* modifies the verb "we know" *(oidamen)* rather than "we have passed" *(metabebekamen)*. In other words, eternal life is not earned by loving the brothers. Rather, loving the brothers (e.g., the Christian family) is evidence that one has made the transition from death to life. Loving the brothers is an avenue of assurance of eternal life, but it is not the means for obtaining it. As John has noted before, the Christian is one who loves others as Christ has loved them (John 13:34–35).

On the other hand, the absence of Christian love indicates that one has not passed into the state of spiritual life but remains *(menei)* in the realm of spiritual death. They walk in the darkness, not in the light. This state of spiritual death is one into which a person is born and continues to exist if regeneration does not occur (cf. Eph 2:1). Whatever one claims, the absence of love proves that one still remains outside the sphere of the life of God and in the realm of death and darkness (cf. 2:9–11). This statement serves as a stern warning for anyone at anytime who finds an absence of love in his heart. For those in the community of faith, it should be an occasion for soul searching and careful examination "to see whether you are in the faith" (2 Cor 13:5).

3:15 The apostle now parallels the hatred of the previous verse with the murderous action of Cain in v. 12. This sweeping declaration *(pas ho,* "everyone who") again provides no exceptions and offers no middle ground. "Anyone" who continually hates *(misōn,* present active participle) is in essence a murderer *(anthrōpoktonos,* lit., "man-killer"). The apostle may be drawing from the Sermon on the Mount at this point (Matt 5:21–22; 27–28), where Jesus equates one's inner attitude with overt actions.[11] The destructive nature of hatred is equivalent to the act of murder itself. Burdick notes, "Hatred is the desire to get rid of someone, whether or not one has the nerve or the occasion to perform the act."[12] Love and hatred are moral opposites, but hatred and murder belong to the same sphere of "death" noted in v. 14. The driving force that motivates the hater to commit murder

---

[11] H. H. Hobbs suggests, "Murder is in the heart before it is in the hand" (*The Epistles of John,* [Nashville: Thomas Nelson, 1983], 90). John simply does with murder what Jesus did with the Seventh Commandment: "Do not commit adultery" (Matt 5:27–28). The guilt of sin rests in the inner drive as well as in the outward performance of evil acts.

[12] Burdick, *Letters of John,* 266.

stems from Satan himself and is thus a distinguishing mark of his children.[13]

John adds a confirming note to his sweeping assertion: "and you know that no murderer has eternal life abiding in him." It does not require searching inquiry or research to confirm this fact. It is self-evident. The one who is governed by a spirit of hate does not possess eternal life.[14] This does not mean that the murderer cannot be transferred from the sphere of death to the realm of eternal life. Indeed, forgiveness is available to all who repent, including those who murder. This statement is one of present reality. No murderer possesses the eternal life that comes from "abiding in him."

3:16 Having shown that love is the evidence of life in the child of God, John now sets forth the supreme example of this love: the sacrifice of Jesus Christ. The pronoun *toutoi,* "this," looks forward to the ensuing *hoti* clause ("that Jesus Christ laid down his life for us"), which signifies that Christ's sacrifice is the supreme example of what genuine love entails.

The verb "we know" *(egnokamen)* refers to a knowledge that has been gained through diligent contemplation. It is an acquired understanding. The perfect tense emphasizes a historical encounter with Christ with ongoing results that affect one's present life. John's knowledge of the nature of this love was made known at Calvary, yet it is a love in which he continually grows and develops as God's child.[15]

The NIV does not translate the conjunction *hoti* ("that," NASB), which points to the laying down of Jesus' life as the supreme example of this love. As throughout 1 John, the pronoun *ekeinos* ("that one") refers to Jesus Christ (cf. 2:6; 3:3,5,7). The expression "He laid down his life for us" *(ekeinos huper hēmon tēn psuchēn autou etheken),* occurs only here in 1 John, but it is a common Johannine phrase (John 10:11,15,17,18; 13:37,38; 15:13). "Laid down" involves a deliberate, willful act that demonstrated his love "for us." His act was not one of mere martyrdom but an atonement (2:2), a designed self-sacrifice on behalf of others. Although the preposition *huper* ("for") is often used to refer to the substitutionary nature of the atonement (cf. John 11:50; 1 Cor 15:3; 2 Cor 5:21; Gal 3:13), John's pri-

---

[13] The word ἀνθρωποκτόνος ("murderer" or "man-killer") is used only twice in the NT, here and in John 8:44, where it refers to the devil as the "murderer from the beginning." It is evident that the one who hates has the same inner nature as his diabolical father.

[14] The adjective "eternal" (αἰώνιον) is both qualitative and quantitative. It is a quality of life that stems from the very nature of God himself; thus it is a present reality for the believer, not just a future hope. It is also eternal in that it is neither gained nor lost by physical death. It is eternal in its duration.

[15] The inclusion of the article with ἀγάπην, "love," highlights a particular love to which John refers, namely, the sacrificial love God demonstrated on Calvary.

mary concern is to stress the exemplary aspect of Christ's sacrifice.[16] As Hiebert explains: "Since one's life is an individual's most precious possession, Christ's willingness to lay down that life on behalf of others constituted the greatest possible expression of love."[17]

The use of "and" *(kai)* unites the example of Christ's love with his followers' actions. Kysar writes, "Christian love is not born from within the character of the individual but originates in Christ's act."[18] "We ought" *(hēmeis opheilomen)* is emphatic and accentuates the fact that just like him, "we ought to lay down our lives for our brothers."[19] John is not at all suggesting that his readers can in any way atone for the sins of the brethren. Instead, John's point is that Christians have an obligation to follow the example of their Lord even unto death if such an occasion presents itself. It is clear that to whichever sacrificial act John refers, the love of Christ's followers is to parallel the sacrifice of Jesus on Calvary. His is an example to imitate. As Kistemaker affirms, "When the honor of God's name, the advancement of his church, and the need of his people demand that we love our brothers, we ought to show our love at all cost—even to the point of risking and losing our lives."[20]

3:17 While laying down one's life for another is the supreme example of Christlike love, John moves to a more practical, everyday scenario to emphasize the type of love he describes previously. The adversative conjunction "but" *(de)*, absent in the NIV, introduces a negative example that contrasts the positive one of v. 16. Clearly, the more difficult call is to lay one's life down for another. It is a lesser demand to help a brother in need. The apostle knows, however, that not many are required to perform the heroic deed of giving one's life for another, but the opportunity to help a needy brother is constant. The challenge for John's hearers is to apply their Christian love to a context that is true to everyday life, one in which they repeatedly find themselves.

---

[16] The idea that Christ "laid down" (ἔθηκεν) can be pictured as taking off a garment. In other words, Jesus "took off" his life as if it were a garment. The emphasis rests on the voluntary nature of such an act. He willingly laid aside his life for others. Naturally, there is a substitutionary element involved in this understanding, but the primary emphasis here is on the exemplary aspect of Christ's love. For the pros and cons of this understanding, see Thomas, "Exegetical Digest of 1 John," 297. Other texts that emphasize the example aspect of the atonement include John 13:4; 15:13; and Rom 5:6–10.

[17] Hiebert, *Epistles of John*, 160.

[18] R. Kysar, *1, 2, 3 John*, ACNT (Minneapolis: Augsburg, 1986), 84.

[19] Instead of using δεῖ ("one must"), the apostle employs the word ὀφείλομεν ("one ought"). The reason for this choice appears to rest in the fact that δει leans toward "logical necessity" and ὀφείλω refers to "moral obligation." See G. Abbott-Smith, *A Manual Greek Lexicon of the New Testament*, 3rd ed. (Edinburgh: T & T Clark, 1937), 99.

[20] S. J. Kistemaker, *James and I–III John*, NTC (Grand Rapids: Baker, 1986), 310.

John's thought progresses through the use of three coordinated subjunctive verbs. The first two are in the present tense and express the inescapable responsibility of the child of God: He has the means to meet the need, and he sees the need. The third verb, an aorist, reveals the unwillingness of that one to fulfill his responsibility.

With the first verb the picture is that of one who possesses enough material to maintain life in this present world.[21] He has the means necessary to meet another's need. "And" *(kai)* introduces the second element of this negative example: observing the need to be met. The verb "sees" *(theōrē)* is more than just a casual, passing glance. Instead, the term denotes a continual, contemplative observation in which the beholder pauses "to appreciate and understand the circumstance of the case."[22]

The change from the plural in v. 16 ("brothers") to the singular here (*ton adelphon*) is deliberate and significant in that it makes the duty of helping a fellow member of the Christian community more individualized in its application. As Lewis observes: "It is easier to be enthusiastic about Humanity with a capital 'H' than it is to love individual men and women, especially those who are uninteresting, exasperating, depraved, or otherwise unattractive. Loving everybody in general may be an excuse for loving nobody in particular."[23]

In correspondence with John's negative example, the response to this need is one of conscious indifference. The neuter plural noun translated in the KJV "his bowels of compassion" *(ta splangchna)* and as "pity" in the NIV was regarded by the ancients as the seat of the emotions, the place where love and fear are felt. Figuratively, the word implies the emotions themselves. Brown argues that the most accurate translation may be simply "compassion."[24] Today, we would speak of "the heart." The verb "shuts out" *(kleisēi),* translated "has no [pity]" (NIV), suggests a deliberate neglect in spite of what he has observed. The verb literally means "to close or lock a door." Here it is employed figuratively to portray the erection of a barrier that encloses one's sympathetic feelings and isolates them from the needs of another. Robertson says it is the slamming of the door in the face of another's need.[25]

---

[21] "Material possessions" is lit. "life" or "means of life" (τὸν βίον). It covers both life itself and livelihood. It includes anything of value in this present era. It is not necessarily the wealthy of the Christian community to which John refers (although their responsibility may be even greater). Instead, John challenges all of those who have the necessities of life, who can come to the aid of those in need. The transition from laying down one's life in v. 16 to the sharing of one's livelihood in v. 17 is both natural and appropriate. Thomas, "Exegetical Digest of 1 John," 299–300.

[22] A. E. Brooke, *A Critical and Exegetical Commentary on the Johannine Epistles*, ICC (New York: Scribner's, 1912), 97.

[23] G. P. Lewis as quoted in Stott, *Letters of John*, 147.

[24] R. Brown, *The Epistles of John*, AB (New York: Doubleday, 1982), 450.

[25] Robertson, *WP* 5:226.

In essence, the concept is that of one who sees another Christian's need, has the means to meet that need, yet deliberately and hardheartedly turns his back on the needy brother (cf. Jas 2:15–16).

John's rhetorical question, "How can the love of God be in him?" challenges his readers to evaluate this pitiless response. The genitive case "of God" *(tou theou)* has been interpreted in three different ways: (1) as a subject genitive, referring to God as the author of this love (God's love); (2) as an objective genitive, speaking of God as the one being loved (love for God); and (3) as a descriptive genitive, a God-like love.[26] In addressing this issue, Hiebert suggests, "Whatever the intended meaning, in the operation of true Christian love, both the subjective and objective aspects of the 'love of God' are involved."[27] The one who possesses God's love demonstrates that love to others. And as Marshall declares: "Christian love is love which gives to those in need, and so long as we have, while our brothers have little or nothing, and we do nothing to help them, we are lacking in the love which is essential evidence that we are truly children of God."[28]

3:18 John's final appeal in this section is based on their common spiritual life, which reminds the readers of their spiritual new birth in the family of God.[29] His exhortation is expressed in a typical negative-positive fashion. Negatively, John contends, "Let us not love with words *[logō]* or tongue *[glossē]*." Including himself in this exhortation, the apostle challenges his readers to understand that love is more than making a good speech. John is not condemning kind or comforting words. The expression of such utterances without an outward manifestation of them, however, is mere noise and therefore worthless (1 Cor 13:1).

Positively, John insists that love is to be demonstrated in "actions *[ergō]* and in truth *[alētheia]*." Love expresses itself in deeds. The quality of truth is added because even actions can be hypocritical. The objective reality of love is that it expresses itself in one's actions. As Brown paraphrases, "Let us love, not by word of mouth but by real deeds."[30]

John's challenge in this section is for his readers to be genuine in their love. One of the distinguishing marks of the child of God is love, a love that originates in God, displays itself in actions of self-sacrifice, and is evidence of eternal life.

---

[26] Burdick, *Letters of John,* 270 and Thomas, "Exegetical Digest of 1 John," 300–302.

[27] Hiebert, *Epistles of John,* 162.

[28] Marshall, *Epistles of John,* 195.

[29] As a father encouraging his children, John goes back to the vocative, τεκνία ("little children"), to exhort his readers to display the love that has been implanted in their hearts (cf. 2:28; 3:7).

[30] Brown, *Epistles of John,* 451.

(2) Live in Confidence (3:19–24)

¹⁹**This then is how we know that we belong to the truth, and how we set our hearts at rest in his presence ²⁰whenever our hearts condemn us. For God is greater than our hearts, and he knows everything.**
²¹**Dear friends, if our hearts do not condemn us, we have confidence before God ²²and receive from him anything we ask, because we obey his commands and do what pleases him. ²³And this is his command: to believe in the name of his Son, Jesus Christ, and to love one another as he commanded us. ²⁴Those who obey his commands live in him, and he in them. And this is how we know that he lives in us: We know it by the Spirit he gave us.**

3:19–20³¹　In this section (3:19–24) John offers assurances that will arise in the heart of the one who possesses genuine love, that is, the child of God. Smalley is right when he suggests that the phrase in v. 19a governs the entire section: "This then is how we know that we belong to the truth."³² In addition to these assurances, John affirms that the believer can have confidence when approaching God in prayer.

Verses 19–20 are closely related in content and grammatical construction, but they present certain textual, grammatical, and exegetical difficulties.³³ The problems are essentially (1) the meaning of *peisomen* in v. 19 (translated "set ... at rest," NIV) and (2) the interpretation of the two *hoti* clauses in v. 20. These issues will be addressed as we proceed.

John seems to be making two primary points in vv. 19–20, which can be clearly identified in Burge's paraphrase of these verses:

19a:　　　"In this [the love and obedience we exhibit; vv. 11–18] we will know that we are of the truth."

19b–20:　"We will reassure our hearts in his presence whenever our hearts

---

³¹ Καὶ ("and") appears in brackets in the UBS Gk. NT, which indicates that the textual evidence is divided as to its inclusion at the beginning of v. 19. Although it is part of the Textus Receptus and is translated in the KJV, καὶ is omitted in more recent versions (ASV, RSV, NASB, NIV). One should take ἐν τούτῳ ("in this"), translated "This then," to refer forward to what follows as it does in most, if not all, of its thirteen occurrences in 1 John (2:3,5; 3:10,16,19,24; 4:2,9,10,13,17; 5:2). C. Kruse notes that though ἐν τούτῳ always points forward, "it does so in a way that carries forward the preceding discussion" (*The Letters of John*, The Pillar New Testament Commentary [Grand Rapids: Eerdmans, 2000],140).
³² Smalley, *1, 2, 3 John*, 199–200.
³³ For a detailed description and analysis of these difficulties, see Brown, *Epistles of John*, 453–60. I do not affirm Brown's statement that "the epistolary author is singularly inept in constructing clear sentences, and in these verses he is at his worst" (p. 453). R. Law (*The Tests of Life* [1914; reprint, Grand Rapids: Baker, 1979], 281) referred to this text as a *locus vexatissimus*. C. Vaughan says that "verses 19 and 20 are generally conceded to be the most difficult verses in the epistle" (*1, 2, 3 John* [Grand Rapids: Zondervan, 1970], 85).

condemn us, because (1) God is greater than our hearts, and (2) God knows all things." [34]

In this rendering the basis for the assurance that "we are of the truth" is the manifest love and obedience of the foregoing verses. The self-sacrificial, active love previously described offers evidence that one is "of the truth."

The NIV hides the fact that the verb "know" *(gnōsometha)* is in the future tense. This knowledge is an acquired knowledge based upon experience, and the use of the future tense "expresses the dependence of the knowledge upon the fulfillment of the specified condition."[35] Thus when the condition has been met, "we will know that we are of the truth" *(ek tēs aletheias)*. Marshall suggests that John is thinking of a time when a crisis (of belief) will come and we will want to be assured that we belong to God.[36]

The preposition "of" *(ek)* identifies the source of our obtained knowledge as "the truth." Used with the definite article, the truth is recognized as that truth which is distinctly God's truth as revealed in Christ and his gospel. As Stott observes: "Truth can only characterize the behavior of those whose very character originates in the truth, so that it is by our loving others 'in truth' that we know that we ourselves belong to it" [are of the truth].[37]

"And" *(kai)* adds a second aspect of this assurance (the first being that we are "[of] the truth"), which comes from the previously described love: "[It] shall assure our hearts before him." The difficulty of the translation of *peisomen* ("set ... at rest") stems from the hesitancy of most translators and commentators to give it its usual rendering, "to persuade." Following this interpretation, we should look to the second *hoti* clause of v. 20 for the content of the persuasion: "For God is greater than our hearts, and he knows everything."[38] Understood in this way, John "is reinforcing the exhortation to his readers not to close their hearts toward their fellow believers in need ... so that they do not succumb to the meanness in their hearts and refuse to offer material assistance. This persuasion is to be undertaken 'whenever our heart condemn us, that is, whenever their hearts object to legitimate calls upon their generosity when they are in fact in a position to respond.'"[39]

---

[34] G. Burge, *Letters of John*, The NIV Application Commentary (Grand Rapids: Zondervan, 1996), 164.

[35] B. F. Westcott, *The Epistles of John* (New York: Macmillan, 1905), 116.

[36] Marshall, *Epistles of John,* 197.

[37] Stott, *Letters of John,* 148.

[38] Kruse's argument is compelling in its defense of retaining "persuade, convince" as the understanding of πείσομεν (*Letters of John*, 140–41). Brown (*Epistles of John*, 455) also suggests that "to persuade" or "to convince" is the basic meaning of the verb and any other meaning is derived.

[39] Kruse, *Letters of John*, 141.

The use of the singular "heart" *(kardian,* the NIV translates it as a plural) describes the oneness of this experience among God's people. The word occurs four times in 1 John (all in 3:19–21). Here "heart" should retain the traditional meaning of the "seat of the emotions." The part conscience plays in the seat of emotions *(kardia),* however, should not be completely dismissed.[40] Furthermore, this assurance is experienced in the very presence of the omniscient and omnipresent God.[41]

The interpretation of the two *hoti* clauses in v. 20 has created one of the more difficult syntactical explications in the epistle.[42] One of the more widely accepted solutions is exemplified in the NASB translation "in whatever our heart condemns us; for God is greater than our heart and knows all things." This rendering makes the two clauses a continuation of v. 19 and takes the first *hoti* as *ho ti,* the neuter indefinite relative pronoun "whatever," combined with *ean* ("if" with the subjunctive verb), "if whatever," pointing out the diverse things that may cause our conscience to condemn us.[43] The second *hoti* clause would then be given the translation "for" (meaning "because"). Although not free from difficulties, this translation seems the most accurate in the context. In essence, John is arguing that we can persuade our hearts in his presence whenever our hearts condemn us.

Attempting now to bring all of this together, John identifies those things that may cause our conscience to condemn *(kataginōskei)* us.[44] When we refuse to love in action and truth (v. 18), God, who is greater than our hearts in kindness and generosity, motivates us to resist the hardness of heart that would refuse to show compassion to those in need (v. 17). Further, the fact that "he knows everything" reminds us "that any meanness of heart ... will not go unnoticed by an omnipotent God. As was the case in Deut 15:7–9, so too here, God knows what his people do, and judges them accordingly."[45] God, the final Arbitrator, knows our hearts better than we ourselves. God is able to judge because he is all-knowing.[46] His omniscience strengthens and

---

[40] Kruse, *Letters of John,* 139. Here we follow Kruse only in part.

[41] Some commentators give the phrase "before him" (ἔμπροσθεν αὐτοῦ) a more forensic force. The context of judgment in 1 John 2:28–3:3 would suggest that the assurance comes at the time of judgment. See Brown, *Epistles of John,* 455.

[42] Burdick lists at least ten possibilities for interpreting these two clauses (see *Letters of John,* 273–75). R. L. Thomas also provides a thorough investigation into the many possible understandings of these phrases (see "Exegetical Digest of 1 John," 310–16.

[43] Hiebert, *Epistles of John,* 167; Stott, *Letters of John,* 151.

[44] The verb καταγινώσκη ("to condemn") appears only here and in Gal 2:11. Law finds three elements of meaning in the word: to "accuse," to "declare guilty," and to "give sentence against." Law suggests that the second connotation is predominant in this verse (see *Tests of Life,* 391).

[45] Kruse, *Letters of John,* 141.

[46] Ibid. This understanding of this difficult text is indebted to the argument of Kruse, who notes his dependence on Hoskyns and Court (*Letters of John,* 140, n. 151). See J. M. Court, "Blessed Assurance," *JTS* 33 (1982): 508–17.

encourages us, but it also challenges us, for we know that he knows everything and will require an accounting of service done on his behalf (2 Cor 5:10).[47]

3:21–22 John's personal address "beloved" (*agapētoi;* cf. 4:1,7) expresses his concern for his readers who have experienced the struggle of a condemning heart. A reminder that they know the love of God would serve to comfort them. Keeping with his practice of placing positive and negative statements back to back, v. 21, which deals with the uncondemning heart, contrasts the thought of the previous verse, which addresses the heart that does condemn. Confidence before God results from a noncondemning heart and thus provides motivation for prayer.

The term "confidence" (*parrēsian*) means "boldness," "a freedom of speech," and "a frankness such as that a child has in approaching his father."[48] Although the confidence described in 2:28 is associated with the second coming of Christ, here the word deals with the Christian's uninhibited, free communion with God in prayer. The phrase "before God" (*pros ton theon,* lit., "toward God") portrays an intimate, relational, face-to-face encounter with the heavenly Father. At the same time, as Burdick reminds us, "it should be remembered that the confidence and boldness expressed by *parrēsian* contain nothing of impropriety or brashness. It gives no license to anyone to command God to act; it does not erase the distinction between God's infinity and our humanity."[49] Our confidence rests in his mercy and love, which have been extended to us.

The conjunction "and," which begins v. 22, seems to carry an epexegetical aspect (it explains the immediately preceding statement). If so, our confident fellowship with God is accompanied with a guarantee of answered prayer. The clause "whatever we ask" (*ho ean aitōmen*) is all-inclusive and leaves open both the content and the occasion for our requests. At the same time, this statement requires that both the immediate and remote context must be taken into consideration with this statement. The immediate context suggests that the one asking is the one who is striving to "obey his commands and do what pleases him" (v. 22b). Likewise, 5:14–15 states that the prayer is to be offered "according to his will." The guarantee of

---

[47] Other commentators have also taken this text not as an encouragement but as a warning to the believer, but not in exactly the same manner as Hoskyns, Court, and Kruse. For these scholars John is emphasizing the severity of God's judgment. H. Alford states, "Our conscience is but the faint echo of his voice who knoweth all things; if it condemn us, how much more He?" (*Alford's Greek Testament* [Grand Rapids: Guardian, 1976], 4:481); see also K. Grayston, *The Johannine Epistles,* NCBC [Grand Rapids: Eerdmans, 1984], 115–16).

[48] The word παρρησίαν occurs four times in 1 John (2:28; 3:21; 4:17; 5:14), and in each use it conveys the confidence a Christian has before God (Kruse, *Letters of John,* 142, n. 156). Also see commentary at 2:28.

[49] Burdick, *Letters of John,* 276.

answered prayer is based on the proper standing of the petitioner, which in return gives him confidence to approach God freely and openly.[50]

Both *aitōmen* ("we ask") and *lambanomen* ("we receive") are present tense verbs that describe a fact that is generally or always true.[51] God always answers the requests of his children. The "from him" *(ap' autou)* clearly refers to God the Father as the source of these answered prayers. It is "clear that these answers are not merely fortuitous circumstances but come from Him as His specific response."[52]

John adds that the promise of answered prayer is conditioned upon obedience and a willingness to please him. The causal conjunction *hoti* ("because") is not to be taken to refer to the ground on which answered prayer is based, but to the indicated condition for this guarantee. As Stott remarks, "Obedience is the indispensable condition, not the meritorious cause, of answered prayer."[53] The two verbs that confirm this precondition, "we obey" [keep; *teroumen*] and "[we] do" *[poioumen]* are both progressive presents and mark a defining characteristic of those whose prayers are answered. It is the continual obeying of God's commands and the striving to please him that precede our confidence before God in prayer. Such conduct provides "an objective, moral reason for the divine response; it does not simply depend upon the subjective ground of a worshiper's clear conscience."[54]

The apostle seems to distinguish between "the commandments" *(tas entolas)* and "those things that are pleasing to him" *(ta aresta enōpion autou poioumen)*. Although the commands appear to be those explicit demands of God's will, the things that please him are those spontaneous acts motivated by love and a desire to honor him above the specified commands. The believer desires to please him and bring glory to him in all manner of life and obedience (1 Cor 10:31). Such an attitude guarantees answers to prayer.

3:23 Having spoken of the need to obey God's commands, John now establishes the central command that is a summary of all the mandates. Fundamentally, there is only one comprehensive command conveyed in a dual form: an explicit belief in the Son, Jesus Christ, and an active love for

---

[50] Stott lists six conditions that must be met in order for prayer to be answered: prayer must be offered in Jesus' name (John 16:23–24), for God's glory (Jas 4:2–3), from a heart that does not cherish sin (Ps 66:18), from a forgiven and forgiving heart (Mark 11:25), with faith (Matt 21:22), and backed by an obedient life (1 John 3:22) (*Letters of John,* 153).

[51] Such use of the present tense is called "gnomic" presents instead of the more "progressive" presents. See C. F. D. Moule, *An Idiom-Book of New Testament Greek,* 2nd ed. (Cambridge: University Press, 1959), 8.

[52] Hiebert, *Epistles of John,* 170.

[53] Stott, *Letters of John,* 152.

[54] Smalley, *1, 2, 3 John,* 205.

one another. The two parallel verbs "believe" *(pisteusōmen)* and "love" *(agapōmen)* work together to form one primary command. As Lenski declares, "You cannot believe without loving nor love without believing."[55] The Christian life demands an essential union between faith and love.[56]

The command "to believe in the name of his Son, Jesus Christ" *(hina pisteusōmen tō onomati tou huiou Iesou Christou)* contains the first occurrence of the verb "believe" in the epistle.[57] While the manuscript evidence is somewhat divided as to whether "believe" is in the past or present tense, John seems to be pointing to the initial act of placing one's faith in Jesus Christ, in which case the past tense would be employed.[58] The content of this belief entails "the name of his Son, Jesus Christ." These words have "a creedal ring, being in fact a miniature confession of faith."[59] The preposition "on" or "in" is added in the English translations for clarity, but actually John uses a dative of personal relationship, which involves a personal commitment of oneself to "the name" of Jesus Christ. It is a personal identification with all that the bearer of "the name" entails.

The name in biblical usage is closely associated with the nature and personhood of the one who bears it. To believe in the name of his Son, Jesus Christ, is to place one's faith in all that Jesus is. "His Son" emphasizes the deity and unique sonship of this individual. "Jesus" is the Greek form of the Hebrew name "Joshua," which means "the Lord is salvation." It is his human name he was given at birth and which identifies him as totally human (Matt 1:21).[60] "Christ" is the Greek translation of the Hebrew word "Messiah" and affirms his role as the Old Testament Messiah. The double designation "Jesus Christ" represents the earliest of Christian confessions (Acts 2:36; 3:20; 5:42). To believe in the name of Jesus Christ is to place one's faith, one's trust, in him and all that he is—the Divine Son, the incarnate Deity, the sinless Human, the Messianic Savior, and all other facets of his unique nature

---

[55] R. C. H. Lenski, *The Interpretation of the Epistles of St. Peter, St. John and St. Jude* (Minneapolis: Augsburg, 1966), 479.

[56] A. Plummer suggests that this verse is the answer to those who from the previous verses want to argue that all that is required is to do what is right with little regard for what one believes. This insistence upon both faith and love reveals the necessity of both elements for a genuine salvation encounter and life (*The Epistles of S. John* [1886; reprint, Grand Rapids: Baker, 1980], 137).

[57] The verb occurs nine more times in the epistle (4:1,16; 5:1,5,10[3x],13[2x]) and will become a developing theme in the remaining chapters. The concept is present in his earlier teaching on the need to acknowledge Jesus as the Son of God and the danger of denying this truth (2:22f.; see Marshall, *Epistles of John,* 201).

[58] F. F. Bruce labels it an ingressive aorist, which means it reflects the decisive moment when the life of faith began (*The Epistles of John* [Grand Rapids: Eerdman's 1970], 100.

[59] Hiebert, *Epistles of John,* 172.

[60] The name "Jesus" is associated with his saving role. He had to be human to become the perfect sacrifice for sinful humanity.

and personhood. Belief is acceptance of the entirety of him.[61]

The second facet of this dual command is "to love one another as he commanded us" *(kai agapōmen allēlous kathōs edōken entolēn hēmin).* John uses the present tense in his command to love, which reminds his hearers that the practice of Christian love is a daily, continual expression. Furthermore, the reciprocal pronoun "one another" demands that love must be mutually displayed by members of the family of God. The added words "just as he commanded us" make clear that what is required is in exact conformity to the demands of Jesus (cf. John 13:34; 15:12,17). To be a child of God is to love one another. Thus, John insists that both faith and love stand as essential tests for the true child of God. Right belief and right action reveal the authenticity of one's faith.

3:24 In this final verse of this section, John resumes the thought of v. 22 (i.e., keeping God's commandments) and prepares for what follows in 4:1, testing the spirits. Thus, v. 23 serves as a parenthetical explanation of the central content of these commands and as a transition to a new subject. The pronouns John employs in v. 24 probably refer to God the Father.[62] With the words "those who obey his commands live in him, and he in them," the apostle again introduces a mutual "abiding" relationship for the one who obeys these commands. The one who is characteristically living in obedience experiences a reciprocal fellowship with God. The present tense verb "lives" *(menei)* indicates a close and permanent relational abiding between the child of God and the heavenly Father (see 2:24–28; also cf. John 15:1–6).

The pronoun in the expression *en toutō* ("by this" or "hereby" or "this is how") may point forward (to the indwelling presence of the Holy Spirit) or backward (to the keeping of his commands) as evidence of this reciprocal relationship. Most commentators agree that the more natural interpretation is to connect it with what follows (as reflected in the NIV translation).[63] In other words, the primary evidence of our mutual abiding experience in God is the presence of the Holy Spirit in our lives; for as Hiebert notes, "The Holy Spirit is the source from which the certainty of our relationship with God is drawn."[64]

---

[61] It appears evident that John is countering the heretical views of those who had infiltrated the church and held too low or too high a view of Christ's personhood (Smalley, *1, 2, 3 John,* 208).

[62] Hiebert emphasizes that John does not clearly distinguish between God the Father and God the Son. "Generally, [John] felt no need to press a rigid distinction since he always thought of the Father as working through the Son and the Son as revealing the Father" (*Epistles of John,* 173).

[63] Westcott and Burdick are two who suggest that the pronoun refers back to the keeping of the commands as the objective evidence of this relationship (Westcott, *Epistles of John,* 121; Burdick, *Letters of John,* 281).

[64] Hiebert, *Epistles of John,* 174.

The verb "we know" *(ginōskomen)* refers to knowledge obtained by drawing a conclusion based on facts.[65] When one possesses the Spirit of God, it is divine evidence of the reciprocal relationship, enjoyed and experienced (cf. Rom 8:16). The phrase "by the Spirit" *(ek tou pneumatos)* means "from the Spirit" and indicates the source of our knowledge. "The assurance is begotten by the Spirit."[66] The past tense translated "he gave us" *(edōken)* looks to the moment when the Spirit was given. In particular, it points to that instant when the Spirit is given to each believer at the time of their regeneration. John's mention of the Holy Spirit opens the door to his ensuing discussion in regard to the spirits (4:1–6).

In this section John provides the believer with certain assurances that accompany being a child of God. With these assurances comes the overwhelming truth that we can stand confidently before God in prayer and rest assured that he will answer our requests.

2. Test the Spirits (4:1–6)

[1]**Dear friends, do not believe every spirit, but test the spirits to see whether they are from God, because many false prophets have gone out into the world. [2]This is how you can recognize the Spirit of God: Every spirit that acknowledges that Jesus Christ has come in the flesh is from God, [3]but every spirit that does not acknowledge Jesus is not from God. This is the spirit of the antichrist, which you have heard is coming and even now is already in the world.**

[4]**You, dear children, are from God and have overcome them, because the one who is in you is greater than the one who is in the world. [5]They are from the world and therefore speak from the viewpoint of the world, and the world listens to them. [6]We are from God, and whoever knows God listens to us; but whoever is not from God does not listen to us. This is how we recognize the Spirit of truth and the spirit of falsehood.**

This chapter begins with a discussion of the conflict between the "Spirit of truth and the spirit of falsehood" (v. 6). *Agapētoi* ("Dear friends") serves as boundary marker at 4:1,7. The last verse of chap. 3 provides a typical Johannine head-tail transition by use of the word "Spirit." Believers have the Spirit of God, but there are other spirits in the world (4:3). Further, 4:2a and 4:6d form basically an inclusion. John has already dealt with the conflict between truth and falsehood (2:18–28), the conflict between the children of God and the children of Satan (2:29–3:12), and the conflict between

---

[65] Brown points out three tests of knowledge in this section: (1) Christ laid down his life for us (3:16); (2) we show the truth of love in our deeds (3:19); and from the Spirit whom he gave us (3:24) (*Epistles of John,* 465).

[66] Plummer, *Epistles of S. John,* 91.

love and hatred (3:13–24).[67] Given this conflict between the two spiritual realms, John exhorts his readers to test all spirits to determine their truthfulness and then gives the criteria for making this determination.

4:1 This passage parallels at many points 2:18–28, especially with its discussion of antichrist. John begins this section of admonishment with a compassionate, pastoral greeting "beloved" ("Dear friends," NIV; *agapētoi,* cf. also 2:7; 3:2,21; 4:7). He genuinely loves those to whom he is writing, and it is this sentiment that motivates him again to warn them of the dangers to the faith. His warning is clear: behind every statement is a spirit, a *pneuma,* but not every spirit is the Spirit of God.[68] Stott notes, "Neither Christian believing nor Christian loving is to be indiscriminate. In particular, Christian faith is not to be mistaken for credulity. True faith examines its object before reposing confidence in it."[69] John is interested in the source of the prophetic message.[70] One should not receive as true every prophetic pronouncement just because the prophets claim to speak with divine authority. Perhaps in their readiness to hear from God John's readers were unwisely open to what the false prophets had to say. The verb "test" *(dokimazete)* means "to prove, to examine," like coins that are being tested for genuineness and proper weight—something that should be done on a continual basis.[71]

The second person plural of "you" (in the imperatives "believe" and "test") makes it clear that all believers are to exercise the responsibility of discerning truth from error. "All of you test by proving the spirits ..." The testing was to be done in such a manner that hoped for the best, that what

---

[67] D. E. Hiebert, "An Exposition of 1 John 4:1–6," *BSac* (1989): 420.

[68] D. Burdick, *The Epistles of John* (Chicago: Moody, 1970), 66. The expression "of God" (ἐκ τοῦ θεοῦ) occurs six times in vv. 1–6. The use of the word ἐκ expresses source. Thus a believer is of God, who is his source.

[69] Stott, *Letters of John,* 156.

[70] Because the spirits are spoken of in the plural (τα πρεύματα), some discussion has ensued as to the nature of the spirits. Westcott notes: "There are many spiritual powers active among men. ... But some of these are evil influences belonging to the unseen order. They come to us under specious forms of ambition, power, honour, knowledge, as distinguished from earthly sensual enjoyments. All such spirits are partial revelations of the one spirit of evil which become (so to speak) embodied in men" (*Epistles of John,* 139). Stott is in agreement since "behind every prophet is a spirit, and behind every spirit either God or the devil" (*Letters of John,* 156). In other words, prophets, not the influencing spirits behind them, are the main topic in this passage. According to Thomas, "Whenever a plurality of spirits [*panti pneuma* (4:1), *pan pneuma* (4:2)] is implied or expressed, the reference is to human beings. The author's shifting of references from one to the other so quickly, sometimes within the same sentence, shows the close association between the human spirits and the two supernatural spirits which inspire them. Since the emphasis of the paragraph is upon the external phenomena by which the spirits are recognized, primary attention is focused on human beings, and the reference of the two occurrences of πνεῦμα *(pneuma)* in v. 1 is to men" ("Exegetical Digest of 1 John," 333).

[71] Hiebert, "An Examination of 1 John 4:1–6," 422.

was being tested would actually stand the test. The existence of true prophets made it necessary to discern and avoid the false, of which John says
there were "many." This particular task of the people of God is not new. In
Elijah's day there were the prophets of Baal and the prophets of Asherah
who were set in opposition to Elijah, who himself was a true prophet of
God (1 Kgs 18:1–22). Earlier Moses put forth clear instruction in determining a true prophet:

1. If what a prophet proclaims in the name of the Lord does not take
place or come true, that is a message that the Lord has not spoken. That
prophet has spoken presumptuously. Do not be afraid of him (Deut 18:22).

2. If a prophet or one who foretells by dreams appears among you and
announces to you a miraculous sign or wonder, and if the sign or wonder of
which he has spoken takes place, and he says, "Let us follow other gods"
(gods you have not known) "and let us worship them," you must not listen
to the words of that prophet or dreamer (Deut 13:1–5).

Paul also dealt with the importance of distinguishing between the spirit
of truth and error. The tendency to ascribe any unusual phenomenon to God
led Paul to encourage the Corinthians to test the spirits by evaluating
exactly what was said (1 Cor 12:1–3; 14:29).[72] Christians "needed to be
reminded that demonic activity could penetrate their churches."[73] Spiritual
activity is not necessarily Godly activity. We must be discerning. We must
listen and evaluate carefully the message and messenger against the infallible authority of Scripture.

In this case the anticipation of false prophets (*pseudoprophetai*) was not
imaginary or hypothetical. They were already among John's audience, and
in fact there were many (*polloi*) of them. Jesus had already warned his disciples about false prophets (Matt 7:15; 24:11,24; Mark 13:21–23). Similar
warnings can also be found from Paul (Acts 20:28–30), Peter (2 Pet 2:1–
22), and Jude (Jude 4–19). These false prophets have the world, that evil
system under Satan's control that opposes God, as their stage; and the scope
of their influence and work includes all of humanity.[74]

4:2–3 John not only gives the command to test and the reason for the
test ("Every spirit that does not acknowledge[75] Jesus is not from God,"

---

[72] Marshall, *Epistles of John*, 204.

[73] Ibid.

[74] Westcott, *Epistles of John*, 140. Stott challenges us to have biblical balance, avoiding "both
extremes, the superstition which believes everything and suspicion which believes nothing" (*Letters of John*, 157).

[75] There is a textual variant here. The NIV adopts the majority reading. This reading also is supported by B. E. Ehrman, "1 John 4:3 and the Orthodox Corruption of Scripture" *ZNW* 79 (1988):
221–43 (also G. Strecker, *The Johannine Letters*, Her [Philadelphia: Fortress, 1996], 135; Marshall, *Epistles of John*, 207–8. Brown (*Epistles of John*, 494–96) and R. Schnackenburg [*The
Johannine Epistles* (New York: Crossroad, 1992], 201–2) are representative of those who defend
the minority view, which reads "every spirit who annuls [*lyei*] Jesus is not from God."

v. 3), he now provides the actual test itself. Again it is Christological: What do you think about Jesus the Christ? John gives the way in which one can recognize *(ginōskete)*[76] "the Spirit of God." The test itself is comprehensive. Every spirit *(pan pneuma)* will either be approved or rejected based on the Christological test. Not only is the test comprehensive, but it is also confessional. The legitimacy of a prophet should be determined by the content of his message, his confession about Jesus. The verb "acknowledges" *(homologei)*[77] indicates an unwavering confession and "denotes not mere verbal acknowledgment but an open and forthright declaration of the message as one's own position."[78] It is the outward expression of inner faith. The content of the expression is crucial, and it must acknowledge that Jesus Christ is come in the flesh *(en sarki)*.[79]

John uses the phrase "Jesus Christ" eight times in his letters (1:3; 2:1; 3:23; 4:2; 5:6,20; 2 John 3,7). By it John emphasizes the genuine reality and abiding union of the incarnation. The man Jesus is God's Christ. Upon this truth the Christian faith stands or falls. The actuality of the incarnation is not secondary or optional. It is essential. The Spirit of God always gives honor to Jesus the Christ, the Son of God. John's concern with the mode of Christ's coming again reveals that he is battling a Docetic Christology of

---

[76] γινώσκετε, "know or recognize," can either be imperative, i.e., a command, or indicative. Since John uses ἐν τούτῳ (in this) to refer to what follows, and nowhere else in this letter does he connect ἐν τούτῳ with an imperative, then the indicative mood is to be preferred. See Plummer, *Epistles of S. John,* 95, Marshall, *Epistles of John,* 204, and Brown, *Epistles of John,* 491.

[77] The word ὁμολογεῖ means "to say the same thing, confess, or agree." It is not a mere statement of facts. Stott comments: "Even evil and unclean spirits recognized the deity of Jesus during his earthly ministry (e.g. Mk. 1:24; 3:11; 5:7–8; cf. Acts 19:15). But though they knew him, they did not acknowledge him" (*Letters of John,* 157). Plummer asserts that "we are not to suppose that all other articles of faith are unimportant ... but against the errors prevalent in that age this was the great safeguard" (*Epistles of S. John,* 95). Marshall says that "it is possible that John's opponents thought they could confess Jesus as Lord but without accepting the fact that he was the Word incarnate, and therefore John had to stress that the confession must be made in this particular form" (*Epistles of John,* 206). Calvin adds, "But let us remember what this confession contains. When the apostle says that Christ came, we infer that he was before with the Father. By this His eternal divinity is shown" (*The Gospel according to St. John,* Part 2 (11–21) and *The First Epistle of John,* CNTC [Grand Rapids, Eerdmans, 1988], 286).

[78] Hiebert, "An Examination of 1 John 4:1–6," 426.

[79] Westcott claims that the order of the phrase (ἐν σαρκὶ ἐληλυθότα) and the tense of the verb (per. act. part.) place a distinct emphasis on the "mode rather than the fact of Christ's coming ... and yet further, He came 'in flesh,' as revealing the nature of his mission in this form, and not only 'into flesh' (εἰς σάρκα), as simply entering on such a form of being" (*Epistles of John,* 141–42).

the false prophets.[80] Jesus himself was the incarnate Christ, and "far from coming upon Jesus at the baptism and leaving him before the cross, the Christ actually came in the flesh and has never laid it aside."[81] Therefore, no matter how convincing or eloquent the deceivers may be, they still must be judged by their own confession to Christ. The confession is crucial. It will affect every other aspect of one's theology and worldview. What one thinks about Jesus always has far-reaching ramifications.

"But" *(kai)* expresses the negative corollary. Failure to confess Jesus reveals that one is not of God *(ek tou theou ouk estin)*. Indeed this is the "spirit" (implied by the context) of the *antichristou*. By their refusal to confess the truth about Jesus, these false prophets now reveal their true colors. Theirs is a spirit that stands in hostile opposition to Jesus (cf. 2:18–28). John reminds his readers this is something they have already heard, so they should neither be surprised nor caught off guard. The spirit of the arch enemy of Christ is "now" in the world "already." His presence was active in John's day. It remains active in our day. It will continue until this age ends with the revelation of God's Christ, the true Christ (cf. 2:28–3:3).[82]

4:4 John now addresses his audience in tender terms as "dear" or "little children" *(teknia)*. He affectionately encourages them once again and emphasizes the fact that they are victors, that they have overcome. He reminds them of the true source and secret of their victory. They are not necessarily more intelligent or more skilled than the false prophets, but they are possessed and indwelt by one who is, the Holy Spirit. They have resisted those who have seduced or tempted them to accept false doctrine, and their victory is secured by the one who is in them (cf. 1 Cor 6:19–20).

The pronoun "you" *(humeis)* is placed first in the sentence and thus is emphatic. John is drawing a stark contrast between his readers, who are of God, and those who are the mouthpieces of the spirit of the antichrist.[83]

---

[80] As noted earlier in the discussion of 2:18–28, John is refuting Cerenthian Gnosticism (full-blown Gnosticism had not yet developed at this time). See Hiebert, "An Examination of 1 John 4:1–6," 426, and Plummer, *Epistles of S. John*, 95. Cerenthius (ca. A.D. 100) adhered to what is now referred to as a Docetic Christology. Adherents separate the two natures of Christ and regard the human aspects of his life as imaginary instead of being a necessary part of the incarnation. The Spirit of Christ empowered the human Jesus at his baptism but left him prior to the crucifixion. The principle behind these assertions was that if Christ suffered, he could not be divine. M. C. De Boer argues unconvincingly that 4:2 is speaking about the death of Jesus. This is too narrow. John is emphasizing the whole of the incarnation event ("The Death of Jesus and His Coming in the Flesh," *NovT* XXXIII, 4 [1991]: 326–46).

[81] Stott, *Letters of John*, 158.

[82] See the appendix "Antichrist" for a more thorough discussion of this issue. Burge notes: "In all five uses of "antichrist" in the Johannine letters, this denial of Jesus Christ is the antichrist's main interest (2:18–22; 4:3; 2 John 7)" (*Letters of John*, 175).

[83] Plummer notes that in the phrase νενικήκατε αὐτούς ("you have overcome them") John uses the masculine personal pronoun and "passes from the antichristian spirits to the false prophets who are their mouthpieces" (*Epistles of S. John*, 97). See also Brown, *Epistles of John*, 497.

The victory they have (*nenikēkate,* pertense) is a past victory that continues into the present. John does not specify the "one" in you. Given the explicit reference in 3:24 and the contrast of spirits in vv. 2 and 3, it seems clear that it is the Holy Spirit who is in view. He is greater, superior, to the enemy who opposes them. No cosmic dualism is found here! Their foe is one who is in the world, a reference to the one who is the prince of this world, the devil (cf. Eph 2:2).[84] The world is the devil's domain, and its philosophy is an expression of his values and agenda. He attempts to kill, steal, and destroy (John 10:10) but is rendered powerless by the greater Spirit of God who lives within the believer. Satan, Antichrist, and the false prophets are no match for God. As believers yield themselves to the one who lives within them, they experience continual victory in their daily battles with the forces of evil. This is a great promise that provides great comfort, assurance, and hope.

4:5   The difference between false prophets and true believers is their origin. The use of the word *kosmos* three times in this verse (six times in vv. 1–5)[85] only underscores the relationship between the deceivers and the prince of this world—Satan. They speak continually (*lalousin,* present tense) from the world, and their message reveals their source.[86] As Hiebert explains, "They draw the substance of their teaching from the godless world."[87] Further, their message is attractive to those who think like the world. Their words entice and capture those for whom the world is their home. "The world listens to those who speak its own language."[88] The words of these false teachers spring from the world, and "no stream rises above its source."[89] This is the precise reason that the world hears them. The world "recognizes its own people and listens to their message, which

---

[84] Westcott remarks that "the many false spirits represent one personal power of falsehood, 'the prince of the world' (John xii. 31, xiv. 30), the devil whose 'children' the wicked are (iii. 10) … the false prophets are representatives of the world" (*Epistles of John,* 144).

[85] Plummer notes that this repetition of "the world" is very characteristic of John's style (John 1:10; 3:17; 15:19; 17:14) (*Epistles of S. John,* 97). Burge points out the word occurs twenty-four times in John's letters (*Letters of John,* 176).

[86] Burdick, *Epistles of John,* 69. Burdick comments that John does not mean that they are talking about the world but that the world is the source of their message. It "springs from a secular, anti-Christian orientation."

[87] Hiebert, "An Exposition of 1 John 4:1–6," 433.

[88] Ibid.

[89] Lenski, *Epistles of St. Peter, St. John and St. Jude,* 490. Lenski goes on to say that the world "likes their speech; this their speech is the world's own language. It never rises any higher than that which the world considers wisdom. The world hears and nods with full approval whenever they speak. This is true to this day."

originates in its own circle and reflects its own perspective."[90]

4:6 John's declaration is reflective of the teachings of Jesus, who said in John 8:47: "He who belongs to God hears what God says. The reason you do not hear is that you do not belong to God." The opening pronoun "We" *(hēmeis)* is again emphatic, though interpreters are divided over its proper antecedent. The options are:

1. It refers to the apostles only.

2. It refers to the apostles and all other Christian teachers, as opposed to the false teachers.

3. It refers to all Christians.

Because the purpose of the paragraph is to instruct and encourage all believers, and the "we know" ("we recognize," NIV) in the last part of the verse *(ginōskomen)* is not distinctive, it would seem that it refers to all Christians.[91] Because all true believers "are from God" (v. 4) and all of them have the one "who is greater," then it maintains John's parallelism in thought to affirm "we all are from God." Still, that John would have at the forefront of his mind the apostles and other Christian teachers (view #2) does not have to be ruled out completely. People will gravitate to and have an affinity for that confession and teaching with which they are like-minded. Therefore one who affirms the world's message is from the world, and, likewise, one who affirms the message that Christ came in the flesh is of God. Whoever "knows God listens to us," and he is attracted to the apostles' message because of his abiding commitment and relationship to the true God.[92] This readiness to hear springs from a growing knowledge of the truth, which welcomes and appropriates the message of God's prophets.[93]

John summarizes his intentions and claims that this is how we know the Spirit of truth[94] from the spirit of falsehood *(ta pneuma tēs planēs)*.[95] The

---

[90] Stott, *Letters of John,* 160–61. See also Westcott, who claims: "The character of their speech and the character of their hearers are determined by their own character. They draw the spirit and the substance of their teaching from (out of) the world and therefore it finds acceptance with kindred natures" *(Epistles of John,* 145).

[91] Brown, *Epistles of John,* 499. Not only does Brown draw this conclusion but Lenski *(Epistles of St. Peter, St. John and St. Jude,* 491) and Bultmann *(Johannine Epistles,* 64) do as well. The "Apostles only" view is held by Plummer *(Epistles of S. John,* 145) and Stott *(Letters of John,* 158). The "Apostles and teachers" view is held by Westcott, *Epistles of John,* 145 and Bruce, *Epistles of John,* 106. Marshall holds to a combination of views and claims that the teachers are at the front of John's mind but that the rest of the church is not excluded *(Epistles of John,* 209, n. 19).

[92] "The hearer discerns the true message, and the teacher discerns the true disciple. And this concurrence of experience brings fresh assurance and deeper knowledge" (Westcott, *Epistles of John,* 145).

[93] Ibid.

[94] It is generally agreed that this is a reference to the Holy Spirit (cf. John 14:17; 15:26; 16:13). See Plummer, *Epistles of S. John,* 146; Westcott, *Epistles of John,* 146; Bruce, *Epistles of John,* 106; Stott, *Letters of John,* 159. Kruse, *Letters of John,* 152–55 has a helpful note on "The Role of the Spirit in 1 John." See also J. C. Coetzee, "The Holy Spirit in 1 John," *Neot* 13 (1979): 43–67. For an opposing view see Lenski, *Epistles of St. Peter, St. John and St. Jude,* 493.

[95] This phrase occurs only here in the NT.

spirits may be tested by first examining their confession, which comes through human instruments, and then by examining the character of their audience, who would give them credence. We can know the true from the false, the Spirit of God from the spirit of the antichrist. It is imperative that we be vigilant in this assignment.

3. Love One Another: Part Two (4:7–21)

This section is dominated and held together semantically by the concept of love. The word in some form occurs thirty-two times in 4:7–5:3 (forty-three times in the entire letter). "Dear friends" *(agapētoi)* serves as a boundary marker and prepares for a change in subject. Sherman and Tuggy also note a new type of argument appears: "It changes to poetic expression as the author presents his declaration 'God is love.' "[96] Though the theme of love extends through 5:3, a new emphasis appears in 5:1 that will be carried through to 5:13, the theme "believe." Therefore 4:7–21 is a unit dedicated to various facets of the subject of love. Love was also the theme of two earlier sections (2:7–11 and 3:11–24). Here it receives an even more extensive treatment, and John's discussion reaches something of a crescendo with the double affirmations that "God is love" (4:8,16). Additional themes are also addressed: spiritual birth (4:7), atonement (4:10), gift of the Spirit (4:13), and confidence at the judgment (4:17). Yet it is the theme of love that will weave these various theological threads into a beautiful tapestry.

(1) Love Others because God Loves You (4:7–10)

⁷Dear friends, let us love one another, for love comes from God. Everyone who loves has been born of God and knows God. ⁸Whoever does not love does not know God, because God is love. ⁹This is how God showed his love among us: He sent his one and only Son into the world that we might live through him. ¹⁰This is love: not that we loved God, but that he loved us and sent his Son as an atoning sacrifice for our sins.

4:7 This is the third and final time John appeals to the subject of brotherly love.[97] He first mentioned it in 2:7–11, where it is given as an indicator of one who is walking in the light. The second occurrence comes in 3:11–

---

[96] G. Sherman and J. C. Tuggy, *A Semantic and Structural Analysis of the Johannine Epistles* (Dallas: Summer Institute of Linguistics, 1994), 79. D. M. Scholer, "1 John 4:7–21," *RevEx* 87 (1990): 309–14 argues for a five-part structure in 4:7–21.

[97] Plummer contends that although it may appear at first glance that this section is unrelated to the former section, there are some links. First, the power to love one another and confess Christ as coming in the flesh "is the gift of the Spirit (vv. 2,12,13). Second, the selfishness of the antichristian spirit in vv. 1–6 is the same type of characteristic that would keep one from obeying the admonitions in this section. Still an obvious change in subject has occurred" (*Epistles of S. John,* 100).

18 (or even 3:10–24) and is mentioned as evidence that one is a child of God. "Dear friends" introduces a new subject, and it reestablishes warmth and affection following a very pointed and direct discussion. There is a pastoral warmth in the word *(agapētoi)* that would be welcomed. He loves them and will now challenge them to love others as well. The reflexive phrase "let us love one another" *(agapōmen)* occurs three times in this passage. Here in v. 7 it is an exhortation; in v. 11 it is a statement of duty, and in v. 12 it is a hypothesis.[98]

John's exhortation is for Christians to love Christians, although the importance of loving non-Christians is not to be excluded.[99] The basis for this love is God and his love;[100] in fact, it is because *(hoti)* love is from God *(hē agapē ek tou theou estin)*. Love flows from or out of *(ek)* God and has God as its spring or source.[101] Not only is this true of God, but all who love have been born *(gegennētai)* of God. Plummer argues that this refers to everyone, Christian or non-Christian.[102] In other words, inasmuch as anyone has even the smallest capacity to love, this comes by the grace of God.[103] Marshall tends to agree and claims that it is because all men are created in the image of God that they have the capacity to love, and it is the result of "common grace" that even nonbelievers can demonstrate even an incomplete kind of love.[104] But John's claim that everyone who loves is born of God and knows *(ginōskei)* God does not include these incomplete expressions of love.[105] He is referring to a particular kind of love that is found only in those who have been regenerated by Christ.[106] The perfect

---

[98] Stott, *Letters of John,* 162.

[99] Plummer, *Epistles of S. John,* 100. See also Westcott, *Epistles of John,* 147.

[100] Marshall rightly notes that this passage could possibly be misleading if not viewed in the proper context. "One might conclude that anyone who shows love is a child of God, regardless of whether he actually believes in Jesus Christ as the Son of God. This misunderstanding can only arise, however, if we take this statement and wrench it out of its context in the letter. John makes it plain enough elsewhere that the true child of God both believes and loves (3:23)" (*Epistles of John,* 211).

[101] Stott calls this the "most sublime of all biblical affirmations about God's being" (*Letters of John,* 163.

[102] Plummer, *Epistles of S. John,* 100.

[103] Plummer provides an example by stating, "If Socrates or Marcus Aurelius loves his fellowmen, it is by the grace of God that he does so" (ibid.).

[104] Marshall, *Epistles of John,* 212. Marshall continues, "Human love however highly motivated, falls short if it refuses to include the Father and Son as the supreme objects of its affection."

[105] Hiebert comments that this kind of love will "prompt the believer to reach out to the unsaved around him, but his God-inspired love cannot find mutual realization with unbelievers" ("An Exposition of 1 John 4:7–21," 71).

[106] Ibid. Hiebert contends that "the use of the definite article with "love" (ἡ ἀγάπη) centers attention on the kind of love John was urging, "the love" that has its source in God. It is not the natural love of the world for its own (John 15:19), nor the love of publicans for fellow publicans (Matt 5:46), but a self-sacrificing love motivated by goodwill and implemented in action."

tense of "born" would include the initial rebirth of the individual and the continuing effects this would have in their life, and the present tense of "know" emphasizes that the individual is continuing to grow in knowledge of God.[107] In other words, it is not the person's ability to love that causes the new birth, but his ability to love flows from his regeneration in Christ.[108]

4:8 John now turns from the positive expression of truth to its negative expression. He adds emphasis to the point in v. 7 by now stating the converse. Those who do not love do not know God. The absence of love in the life of an individual proves that he does not know God (*ouk egnō ton theon*). The one who does not love is a stranger to God. He never even began to have a relationship with God; that is, there was never a time when this person could have legitimately claimed that he knew God.[109]

The reason this is true is because God is love (*Theos agapē estin*). John has already stated that God is Spirit (John 4:24) and that God is light (1 John 1:5), and now he gives one more encompassing statement regarding the nature of God.[110] In this context John is saying that to know the love of God is to manifest his love.[111] Without this manifestation one could not possibly know, or ever have known, God or his love. Smalley provides three observations about John's description of God as love:

1. Its background is the Jewish (OT) understanding of God as living, personal, and active, rather than the Greek concept of deity which was abstract in character.
2. To assert comprehensively that "God is love" does not ignore or exclude the other attributes of his being to which the Bible as a whole bears witness: notably his justice and his truth.
3. There is a tendency in some modern theologies (especially "process" thought) to transpose the equation "God is love" into the reverse, "Love is God." But this is not a Johannine (or a biblical) idea. As John makes absolutely clear in this passage, the controlling principle of the universe is not an abstract quality of "love," but a sovereign, living God who is the source of all love, and who (as love) himself loves (see vv. 7,10,19).[112]

Because his very nature is love, mercy and goodness flow from God like

---

[107] Thomas, "Exegetical Digest of 1 John," 358.

[108] Marshall asserts: "[Human love] falls short of the divine pattern, and by itself cannot save a man; it cannot be put into the balance to compensate for the sin of rejecting God. Love alone, therefore, is not a sign of being born of God" (*Epistles of John,* 212).

[109] Thomas, "Exegetical Digest of 1 John," 358. See also Burdick, *Epistles of John,* 72.

[110] Marshall claims that "this statement is simply the clearest expression of a doctrine of the nature of God" (*Epistles of John,* 213).

[111] Bruce, *Epistles of John,* 107.

[112] Smalley, *1, 2, 3 John,* 239–40.

a beautiful river, as sunlight radiates from the sun. Love, real love (cf. 1 Cor 13), has its ultimate source and origin in God. It is not an abstract concept but concrete action, as John will now explain.

4:9 John states that believers are to love first, because love is the very nature of the God (v. 8) to whom they belong and of whom they are partakers and second (v. 9), because of the incredible manner in which God's love was displayed. This verse is clearly reminiscent of his magnificent statement found in John 3:16 (cf. also 1 John 3:16).

The sentence structure accentuates the nature and uniqueness of Christ.[113] The word *monogenēs* occurs nine times in the New Testament (Luke 7:12; 8:42; 9:38; Heb 11:17; and in John 1:14,18; 3:16,18; 1 John 4:9). Only John uses the term *monogenēs* (translated "one and only") to refer to Christ. The double use of the article (*ton huion autou*, "the Son of him") and (*ton monogenē*, "the one and only")[114] emphasizes the uniqueness and deity of Christ.[115] God sent (*apestalken*) his Son. The corresponding noun *apostolos* is typically rendered "apostle" and indicates one who is sent on a mission with a purpose, as a representative of another. This purpose is "that we might live through him." Life through and in the Son is a subject that greatly interests John. He refers to it no fewer than six times in vv. 9–16. The perfect tense of "sent" emphasizes the permanent consequences of this act.[116] The verb "live" (*zēsōmen*) implies that those to

---

[113] Westcott, *Epistles of John*, 149. "The order of the words in the whole clause is most impressive: 'in this that His Son, His only Son, hath God sent into the world,' into the world, though alienated from Him."

[114] There is some debate about the particular emphasis of the word μονογενής. According to Thomas ("Exegetical Digest of 1 John," 364) the word is derived from μόνος ("only") and γεννάω ("to beget"). Marshall says that in the OT the Hb. word *yaḥiḏ*, which means "single" or "only," is on occasion rendered in the Gk. ἀγαπητός but also sometimes by μονογενής (*Epistles of John*, 214, n. 8). This could mean that *monogenes* has some sort of nuance that pertains to being beloved. Marshall continues (contra Thomas) that the γενης part of the word has more to do with derivation (γένος) than with birth (γεννάω). The "English 'only begotten' arose from Jerome's use of *unigenitus* to replace the old Latin translation *unicus* in an effort to deny Arian claims that the Son was not begotten by God." Bruce translates the word "only begotten" and claims that the meaning combines the sense of begotteness and belovedness (*Epistles of John*, 108). Lenski asserts that "both 'His Son,' and 'the only begotten' avow the deity of the Logos" (*Epistles of St. Peter, St. John and St. Jude*, 501). Stott argues that the word "applied to Jesus Christ indicates His uniqueness; he is the Son in an absolute sense. No greater gift of God is conceivable because no greater gift was possible" (*Letters of John*, 165). Plummer comments that the proper translation should be "only born" (*Epistles of S. John*, 103). For him, "Christ is the only born Son as distinct from the many who have become sons." Kruse has a note on "*Monogenes*" and "the Son's Preexistence" (*Letters of John*, 158–60). He argues, unconvincingly, that μονογενής means simply "one and only."

[115] Hiebert, "An Exposition of 1 John 4:7–21," 74; also see E. Schweizer, "Zum religionsgeschichtlichen Hintergrund der 'Serdung-sformel' Gal. 4:4f. Rm. 8:3f. John 3:16f. 1 John 4:9," *ZNW* 57 (1966): 199–210.

[116] Plummer, *Epistles of S. John*, 102.

whom the Son was sent were in a condition of spiritual death, and his mission was to impart life to them.[117] This life only occurs through *(dia)* him since he is the true and only mediating agent between God and man (cf. 1 Tim 2:5).

4:10   In this verse the purpose in sending the Son is not the incarnation but the atonement[118]—God sent his Son to die. Further, God's love is primary, not ours. The death of Christ is extolled, not the birth. John, in concluding the verse with the phrase "our sin" *(tōn hamartiōn hēmōn),* is keenly aware of his own need as well as ours for this propitiatory act. Our act was to sin. God's was to love and send.

John begins the verse by choosing a parenthetical negative to emphasize the fact that man in his natural condition does not love God nor his Son whom he sent. But clearly and amazingly, God "loved us." And what incredible and unfathomable love it is: He sent his Son, and he sent him to die for us. "Amazing love, how can it be?" Love is always demonstrated by actions. It is not abstract; it is never complacent or static. John has already given the purpose for this demonstration of love: (1) to take away our sins (1 John 3:5) and (2) to destroy the works of the devil (1 John 3:8). This marvelous act was prompted not by man's love for God but God's love for man, so that "the sending of God's Son was both the revelation of his love (This is how God showed his love ... 9) and, indeed, the very essence of love itself (this is love ... 10). It is not our love that is primary, but God's (10), free, uncaused and spontaneous. All our love is but a reflection of his and a response to it."[119] The origin of love lies beyond human effort and initiative. Left to ourselves, we would not love him. We would hate him and oppose him. It took his boundless, sacrificial love to break our hearts of stone and bring us to himself.

(2) Love Others because God Lives in You (4:11–21)

[11]Dear friends, since God so loved us, we also ought to love one another. [12]No one has ever seen God; but if we love one another, God lives in us and his love is made complete in us.

[13]We know that we live in him and he in us, because he has given us of his Spirit. [14]And we have seen and testify that the Father has sent his Son to be the Savior of the world. [15]If anyone acknowledges that Jesus is the Son of God, God lives in him and he in God. [16]And so we know and rely on the love God has for us.

---

[117] Westcott, *Epistles of John,* 149. "The natural condition of men is spiritual death."

[118] See discussion of ἱλασμος in comments on 1 John 2:2 and also the appendix "Propitiation or Expiation: The Debate."

[119] Stott, *Letters of John,* 164. See also Plummer, "The superiority of God's love does not lie merely in the fact of its being Divine. It is first in order of time and therefore necessarily spontaneous" *(Epistles of S. John,* 102).

God is love. Whoever lives in love lives in God, and God in him. [17]In this way, love is made complete among us so that we will have confidence on the day of judgment, because in this world we are like him. [18]There is no fear in love. But perfect love drives out fear, because fear has to do with punishment. The one who fears is not made perfect in love.

[19]We love because he first loved us. [20]If anyone says, "I love God," yet hates his brother, he is a liar. For anyone who does not love his brother, whom he has seen, cannot love God, whom he has not seen. [21]And he has given us this command: Whoever loves God must also love his brother.

4:11 John now builds on his original admonition to love one another (v. 7). For the sixth time he uses this compassionate and affectionate greeting "Dear friends" *(agapētoi)* to exhort his readers. John is not so much introducing a new subject as he is adding to his prior discussion. Once one begins to understand the incredible price paid for sin and the magnitude of personal sin, he will understand the love of God and demonstrate it himself (John 13:31–35). The love God has shown becomes the motive for our responding to others properly.[120] John's use of "ought" *(opheilomen)* infers that there is an inner motivation and obligation to love others. Further, this obligation or debt cannot be postponed for any reason. It is one we rightly owe. John is insisting that loving God and loving others cannot be divorced, which is exactly what Jesus taught in Matt 22:37–40. John is writing to those who are recipients of God's love. Since God has loved them in this way, they have no option but to do the same. Burdick explains:

> The fact of God's matchless love lays upon us a continuing obligation (Greek present tense) to be loving one another. Not only is it true that we have received the nature of God by reason of our new birth and thus we should love, but we have the example of His love teaching us and persuading us to love each other.[121]

Those who are children of God must show mercy because he shows mercy (Luke 6:36), they must be holy since he is holy (1 Pet 1:15), and they must love since he loves.

4:12 This verse is striking both in its affirmation and order. Literally, the verse begins, "God no one ever has beheld." Hiebert notes: "The verb used here is not that used in John 1:18 (ἑώρακεν *[eōraken]*), which simply denotes the fact of having seen; the verb here (τεθέαται *[tetheatai]*) implies a careful observation or close scrutiny (the word "theater" is derived from it)."[122] No man has seen God in his unveiled essence, glory,

---

[120] The statement εἰ οὕτως ὁ θεὸς ἠγάπηοεν ἡμᾶς ("since God so loved us") is first class conditional.

[121] Burdick, *Epistles of John*, 74.

[122] Hiebert, "An Exposition of 1 John 4:7–21," 77.

and majesty. Indeed, we are incapable as finite sinful creatures of looking on God. It would certainly be our death. He can be seen, however, in the lives of those who demonstrate his love to others. There are no exceptions to who has seen God ("no one"), and there are no exceptions to the time frame ("has ever"). Jesus claimed that one who had seen him had also seen the Father (John 14:9), but this is not the kind of seeing referred to here. As Hiebert explains, "What Moses saw on Sinai (Exod 33:22–23) or Isaiah in the temple (Isa 6:1), were theophanies, revelations by which God made Himself visible to the eye."[123]

The second section of the verse opens with a third-class conditional sentence ("if we love one another") which leaves the possibility of not fulfilling the condition. Not everyone who professes to be a child of God manifests this kind of mutual love. But it is God's rightful expectation since it is the demonstration that God who revealed himself in Christ is also revealed in the lives of those in whom he "abides" (translated "lives"). In fact, this mutual love is the evidence that this has taken place. A person loves because God has come to dwell within him. This is how the love of God is brought to its goal.[124] The word translated "complete" *(teteleiōmenē)* can also be rendered "perfected." Both of these renderings seem to indicate a condition in which there is an elimination of inadequacies, but a more appropriate understanding would be that of achieving a goal—namely the practice of believers loving one another.[125] The love one has for other believers will demonstrate the fact that one is indwelt by God. The source for this kind of love is a personal and permanent union between God and the believer secured at the cross of Calvary.

4:13 John now provides a criterion that confirms that one has come to know personally God's love: the gift of his Spirit.[126] We know *(ginōsko-*

---

[123] Ibid. See also Kruse, *Letters of John,* 161–62; P. W. van der Horst, "A Wordplay in 1 John 4:12," *ZNW* 63 (1972): 280–82 and W. E. Sproston, "Witness to What Was *ap' archēs:* 1 John's Contribution to Our Knowledge of Tradition in the Fourth Gospel," *JSNT* 48 (1992): 43–65 for studies relating 1 John 4:12 to John 1:18.

[124] The phrase ἡ ἀγάπη αὐτοῦ is sometimes translated as an objective genitive, i.e., our love for God. But this would imply that human love toward God could be perfected. Not only is this incorrect, but this translation would not be in agreement with the present tense rendering of "if we continue to love one another." The subjective genitive rendering emphasizes God's love for us. A third position contends that it is a qualitative genitive which would describe a God-like love. A fourth would claim it refers to the mutual love between God and man. The subjective genitive is to be preferred, i.e., God's love for man, primarily since v. 9 speaks of God's love, and indeed the whole context seems to be about God's love. For a thorough treatment of the possible views, see Thomas, "Exegetical Digest of 1 John," 371–74.

[125] Following Hiebert, "An Exposition of 1 John 4:7–21," 78. See also Brown, "God abides in us and the love that comes from Him reaches perfection in our love for others" (*Epistles of John,* 521).

[126] The words Ἐν τούτῳ ("by this") are omitted in the NIV. But the phrase looks forward to the gift of the Spirit in connection with the ὅτι ("because") clause.

men) with a personal knowledge that we abide in him. Believers (note the plural) should be conscious of the indwelling Spirit. With a continuous and ongoing awareness, there is an intimate communion with God by his Spirit. It is the knowledge of this indwelling of the Holy Spirit that gives the believer assurance of his membership in the family of God. In harmony with what the apostle Paul asserts, "The Spirit himself testifies with our spirit that we are God's children" (Rom 8:16). "Has given" is in the perfect tense. It "denotes the resultant indwelling of the Spirit imparted at regeneration."[127] We receive the Spirit as gift, not obligation.[128]

4:14 For the third time John speaks of God sending his Son (vv. 9,10). Now he refers to God intimately as Father. Again John gives the core of the gospel message.[129] He begins with an emphatic "we" *(hemeis)* and proclaims that their message is rooted in historical reality and personal experience. John introduces another criterion (hence the use of the conjunction *kai*) for confirmation of the believers' union with God: adherence to the apostolic message. They bear "witness" to the Father's saving activity in the Son. There is some discussion as to the antecedent of "we."[130] The verse strikes with such force, however, that we believe the apostolic witness must be in view. It recalls the vivid testimony of the prologue itself (1:1–3). A strong affirmation of the message and mission of the incarnate Christ is clear. John is undergirding the fact that although "no one has seen God," "we have" seen his Son whom he sent. The use of *apestalken* ("has sent") refers to the actual sending and also to the purpose—the salvation of the world.[131] God had sinners in mind when he sent the Son of his love (cf. Col 1:13–14).

---

[127] Hiebert, "An Exposition of 1 John 4:7–21," 79. Marshall argues that the use of the perfect δέδωκεν as opposed to the aorist ἔδωκεν used in 1 John 3:24 is of no significance (*Epistles of John,* 219). The main emphasis remains the continuing presence of the Spirit in the Christian.

[128] The phrase ἐκ τοῦ πνεύματος can be a genitive of source (see Lenski, *Epistles of St. Peter, St. John and St. Jude,* 507 or Westcott, *Epistles of John,* 153). It can also be a partitive genitive, i.e., no source implied (see Brown, *Epistles of John,* 522). Marshall claims that this is a partitive genitive and asserts that it is referencing the charismatic gifts (*Epistles of John,* 219). Burdick argues that this passage is simply a reference to the presence of the Holy Spirit in the child of God (*Letters of John,* 328), which would seem to be the better understanding.

[129] Burdick asserts that this verse advocates an unlimited atonement: "His salvation was not intended for the elect only, but for all of lost humanity" (*Epistles of John,* 76; also see his *Letters of John,* 329). We addressed this at 2:2, noting our conviction that John affirms a general atonement. The atonement of Christ is unlimited in its provision (the world) and limited in its application (applied only to those who have faith).

[130] Westcott claims that this is a reference to the testimony of the entire church at large, embodied in the confession of its leaders (*Epistles of John,* 153). Brown (*Epistles of John,* 522–23) and Bruce (*Epistles of John,* 111) claim that it refers to John and his readers as opposed to those who had forsaken the fellowship of believers.

[131] Again, should there be something regarding the extent of the atonement here? "There is no limit to his mission to save, and no limit to its success, excepting man's unwillingness to accept salvation by believing on the Savior" (Plummer, *Epistles of S. John,* 104). See also Kruse and his note on "the Saviour of the World" (*Letters of John,* 164).

4:15   The message of love and truth are mutually inclusive. This confession provides further evidence that there is communion between God and the person making the statement. It also exposes the true from the false professor. It is a confession of public conviction and acknowledgment that reveals an inward commitment: "Jesus is the Son of God. I believe in him. I trust in him not just as the Savior of the world, but as my Savior. I personally trust in him as the Savior, the Son sent from God." Once again John affirms the mutuality of the divine relationship between God and man, "God lives in him and he in God." This is not just a statement regarding the status of Jesus as the Son. It is a confession that results in a reception of new life resulting in a commitment to obedient trust.[132] The natural reaction of someone who genuinely believes that Jesus is the Son of God is to join his life with his in all that means. The resultant obedience gives the necessary outward evidence that there is true fellowship with God. To live or abide in God ("live" is present tense) is a vital, intimate, continuous, and growing reality. The believer has a new and invisible power for the fulfillment of his work on earth: "God is in him." He realizes that his life is not on earth, that he belongs essentially to another order: "he is in God."[133]

4:16   John now gathers together several of his previous thoughts. The "we" again is emphatic. He clearly refers to himself and all of his readers and affirms that they know and believe. These two Greek words, *egnōkamen* ("know") and *pepisteukamen* ("rely"), are so closely connected that they form what should be considered something of a "compound verb," since they both concern the object of love.[134] They are both in the perfect tense, which signifies that the result of these two characteristics is an abiding reality. There is a definite order and emphasis in the verbs. Knowledge is prior to and explained by faith. Faith must have content. "Keep the faith" is nonsensical. "Faith in what?" is always the crucial question. When one abides in the love of God, his knowledge of God grows, and his faith in God grows. The more we love him, the more we understand him, and in turn we trust him more and our faith increases. Westcott says:

> We must have a true if limited knowledge of the object of faith before true faith can exist; and true faith opens the way to fuller knowledge. A general faith in Christ and self-surrender to Him prepared the disciples for a loftier apprehension of His character. The actual experience of love includes the promise of a larger manifestation of its treasures.[135]

---

[132] Marshall, *Epistles of John,* 220. See also Burdick, *Epistles of John,* 77.

[133] Westcott, *Epistles of John,* 155.

[134] Thomas, "Exegetical Digest of 1 John," 381.

[135] Westcott, *Epistles of John,* 155. Hiebert notes, "In John 6:69 these two verbs are used in reverse order, thus indicating that in spiritual matters "the growth of knowledge and the growth of faith act and react on each other" ("An Exposition of 1 John 4:7–21," 82, quoting in part Brooke, *Johannine Epistles,* 122).

Faith and love are at the same time fruit and evidence of one who is indwelt by God. It is this indwelling that makes the fruit possible.

Divine-human mutuality is once again expressed here. Bruce notes: "The love which dwells in the community of God's children and which they show to one another is His love imparted to them. More than that: the God of love imparts Himself to His people, so dwelling within them that they, in their turn, dwell in His love and dwell in Him."[136] Indeed this is a fulfillment of the prayer of Jesus: "I have made you known to them, and will continue to make you known in order that the love you have for me may be in them and that I myself may be in them" (John 17:26). When we remain in this love, we live in God because God is love (cf. v. 8). It must be stated that the previous characteristics and qualifications are still required. Speaking of the love of God, as many often do, is not enough. The confession of the incarnate Christ and acknowledgment of his atonement and Lordship are necessary. Without this combination, this mutual abiding is not possible. The fact that the word "abide" *(menō)* occurs three times in the Greek text underscores this point.

4:17 John now expands his discussion by incorporating the theme of judgment. He also refers to what he has just written.[137] The clear message is that the love one has for God has an effect on the future. The confession of Jesus as Lord and the mutual abiding between God and the believer allow for God's love to have its full expression.[138] It is in his close union with God (referring to the mutual relationship) that a believer's love is made complete or perfected in order that he will have no fear in the day of judgment. The "function of love in the believer's life is the impartation of a bold confidence that will enable him to stand before the judgment seat of Christ without fear or shame."[139] On that day the believer need not fear because Christ has atoned for his sins. The atonement also has a present effect since "in this world we are like him" (lit., "just as that one is, we also are in this world"). This does not mean that we have attained his perfection, but we stand in relation to God the same way that Christ does, and in this

---

[136] Bruce, *Epistles of John,* 112.

[137] There are basically three ways to understand the phrase ἐν τούτῳ ("in this way"): (1) it can refer to the preceding statements regarding the mutual abiding between God and the Christian (see Plummer, *Epistles of S. John,* 151), (2) it can refer to the clause immediately following, i.e., confidence in judgment is an indicator of God's perfect love (see Lenski, *Epistles of St. Peter, St. John and St. Jude,* 510), or (3) it can refer to the ὅτι clause and give a reason for the exhibition of perfected love (see Brown, *Epistles of John,* 526–27). We follow Brown, though it is obvious John builds on what he has just written.

[138] Hiebert, "An Exposition of 1 John 4:7–21," 84.

[139] Burdick, *Epistles of John,* 78.

way we are like him.[140] Those who are indwelt by God have a relationship with their Judge that is characterized by love. It is this love that allows the believer to have confidence when looking toward that day of judgment.

4:18   John begins this verse with an affirmation. The reason that the believer need not fear is that the relationship between him and God through Christ is based on love, and in love "there is no fear." The word "fear" begins the sentence and is thus emphatic. Literally John says, "Fear not is in love." The believer can have full "confidence" based on this assertion. John uses the word *phobos* (fear), which can mean either a good fear (respect) or bad fear (dread).[141] It is this latter type of fear to which he is referring. There should be no dread in the life of the one in whom God dwells. In fact the claim here is that love and fear are mutually exclusive. This is made even more evident by the use of the strong adversative *alla,* "but." There is a drastic disparity between the two entities. They cannot coexist because perfect love "drives out fear." Robertson calls this phrase a powerful metaphor and notes that this can mean "to turn out-of-doors."[142] The evil of fear is cast out of those in whom God's love is being perfected. This is because fear "has to do with punishment." John's use of *kolasin* ("punishment") in this context clearly is a reference to eternal punishment. The fear of this punishment is already being felt by the one whom John is describing. This individual is deficient in love, which would cast out the fear. This deficiency of love causes one to dread the day of judgment for fear of permanent departure from the presence of God.[143] Therefore if one fears this day, he is not being perfected in love.

4:19   The sentence once more begins with an emphatic "we" *(hēmeis)*. The comparison is being made between our love for God and God's love for us. His love is prior. Plummer gives three reasons why this fact is significant:

1. Our love owes its origin to God's love.

---

[140] Thomas refers to this as "one of the most perplexing issues of the Epistle" ("Exegetical Digest of 1 John," 390). The reason for this is that the likeness between Christ and the believer is not qualified, i.e., in righteousness, in suffering, etc. In other places believers are encouraged to walk as he walked (1 John 2:6), to lay down one's life as he did (1 John 3:16), or to be pure like he is (1 John 3:3). Here it appears to mean the very existence and nature of the believer is the same as Christ's. Likeness in character is certainly affirmed. Likeness in love may best fit the context (Hiebert, "An Exposition of 1 John 4:7–21," 85).

[141] The word δειλία also means "fear" in the sense of dread or angst. Another word for the more positive kind of fear, i.e., respect, is εὐλάβεια, which in the NT always refers to this kind of fear of God. John uses φόβος, which can mean both. The context determines the meaning to be the negative kind of fear.

[142] Robertson, *WP* 6:235.

[143] John chooses not to adhere to his contrastive method. In other words he does not attempt to say anything about those who fear not. "And rightly, for the absence of fear proves nothing: it may be the result of ignorance, or presumption, or indifference, or unbelief, or inveterate wickedness" (Plummer, *Epistles of S. John,* 106).

2. Love is characterized by fear when there is a doubt it will be returned. We have no fear of this since God's love was prior to ours.

3. Affection can easily flow from a heart filled with gratitude for God's initiation of love toward us.[144] Yes, we love but only because he loved us first. Remember: he sent his Son to die for you.

4:20 The inward character of an individual is revealed when he lies about his love for God. He declares that he loves God but fails to demonstrate that love in his treatment of fellow Christians. One may possibly claim to love God and deceive others since God cannot be seen and others are not able to prove the truth of the declaration. The visible manifestation of an individual's love for God, however, will eventually show up in his dealings with his brothers and sisters in Christ, who indeed are very visible.

The phrase "whom he can see" *(hon hēoraken),* which is expressed in the perfect tense, pictures a permanent condition that continues from the past. The unloved brother has been and continues to be in sight, while God has been and remains out of sight. This is no sporadic occasion but a constant and sustained situation. It is not just unlikely, but it also is impossible for a man to love God if he fails to love his brother. Love for God and hatred for a brother cannot coexist in the same heart. They are mutually exclusive and completely incompatible. The concern here is not with the individual's attempt to love, that is, he tried and failed, but his complete unwillingness and inability since he does not have the love of God in him in order to accomplish the task in the first place. The words "God" and "brother" are juxtaposed to emphasize the fact that one must have the same love for both.

Jesus had already made it clear that to love God and to love one's neighbor are mutually inclusive (Mark 12:29–31). John very clearly acknowledged this existence of the potential for people to claim verbally to know God and to be indwelt by him and yet treat others who have made this same commitment with disdain. John has not hidden his own contempt for this kind of hypocrisy and in fact has already stated that to behave this way puts the perpetrator in kinship with Cain (1 John 3:18).

4:21 Loving one's brother is not just a spiritual requirement; it also is a command. The reason that it is impossible for the inconsistency stated in 4:20 to remain is that the command to love God and the command to love one's brother are two parts of one command. They are inseparable. In fact, the use of "and" *(kai)* to begin the verse connects it with the prior verse. The phrase *ap' autou* ("From him," trans. "he has ...") is a reference to God the Father as the final source of the commandment. Disobedience to this commandment demonstrates a false love toward God that results in fail-

---

[144] Plummer, *Epistles of S. John,* 107.

ure to love the brethren. As Paul wrote: "The entire law is summed up in a single command: 'Love your neighbor as yourself'" (Gal 5:14). Of course, Paul and John therefore agree with their Lord (Mark 12:31).

4. Obey God and Experience the Victory of Faith (5:1–5)

¹**Everyone who believes that Jesus is the Christ is born of God, and everyone who loves the father loves his child as well. ²This is how we know that we love the children of God: by loving God and carrying out his commands. ³This is love for God: to obey his commands. And his commands are not burdensome, ⁴for everyone born of God overcomes the world. This is the victory that has overcome the world, even our faith. ⁵Who is it that overcomes the world? Only he who believes that Jesus is the Son of God.**

There is some question about whether 5:1–5 belongs with the previous section (4:7–21) or begins a new section. Those who maintain the former argue that this passage further elaborates the theme of love.[145] For example, the word "love" *(agapē)* in its various forms occurs five times in vv. 1–3. Others, however, see 5:1 as providing a new section, with faith being the primary topic.[146] Obviously, the two themes are related (especially in John's writings), and here they are combined without a strict break in thought. For John, true faith always leads to love for God and others, and true love always results in obedience. Interwoven then throughout this section are three characteristics of the genuine child of God: (1) right belief (5:1,5); (2) righteousness or obedience to God's commands (5:2–3); and (3) love (5:1–3). There is a coherence to this section that may be reflected in the form of a chiastic structure.

> A   the one who believes that Jesus is the Christ (5:1a)
>   B   is born of God (5:1b)
>   C   love those born of the Father (5:1c)
>   C' love the children of God (5:2)
>   B' everyone born of God (5:4)
> A' the one who believes that Jesus is the Son of God (5:5)[147]

---

[145] Brown, *Epistles of John,* 565; Bultmann, *Johannine Epistles,* 76; Marshall, *Epistles of John,* 226; Schnackenburg, *Johannine Epistles,* 227; Smalley, *1, 2, 3 John,* 235; Strecker, *Johannine Letters,* 174.

[146] Bruce, *Epistles of John,* 116; Plummer, *Epistles of S. John,* 110; Westcott, *Epistles of John,* 176.

[147] A. Culpepper argues that 5:1 forms an inclusion with 5:5, since the titles "Son of God" and "Christ" also appear in the fourth evangelist's purpose statement (John 20:30–31) ("The Pivot of John's Prologue," *NTS* 27 [1980/81]: 25–26). Although this observation is correct, it is uncertain as to whether these commonalties are intentional structural devices in 1 John the way they are in John's Gospel. Sherman and Tuggy argue for a chiastic arrangement (*Semantic and Structural Analysis,* 92–93).

5:1 John states that all who believe that Jesus is the Christ (i.e., the Messiah) have been born of God. As the book has already indicated, this requirement includes believing specifically that "Jesus Christ has come in the flesh" (4:2), that he is God's Son, and that he is the Savior of the world (4:14–15). One should not think that John is promoting mere intellectual assent as the requirement for being a child of God, since the second half of the verse indicates that Johannine faith includes an ethical dimension. That is, faith and love are inseparable (cf. 3:23).[148] The phrase "Jesus is the Christ" corresponds to 2:22 and is possibly an early creedal formulation.[149]

The text goes on to declare that those who have faith in Jesus as the Messiah are "born of God." Thus faith is a sign of sonship. John has previously mentioned the theme of sonship in this epistle. He states that being born of God leads to right behavior (2:29), prevents one from habitually sinning (3:9–10), and causes one to love others (4:7). In the fourth Gospel we read that faith is not only a sign but also a condition of the new birth: "To all who received him, to those who believed in his name, he gave the right to become children of God" (John 1:12). Marshall writes: "Here, however, John is not trying to show how a person experiences the new birth; his aim is rather to indicate the evidence which shows that a person stands in the continuing relationship of a child to God his Father: that evidence is that he holds to the true faith about Jesus."[150] The perfect tense of the verb *gegennētai* suggests a past action with results that continue in the present. In other words, Smalley concludes, "The regenerate Christian (past) must constantly live out (present) his faith in Jesus as Messiah, and also give his sustained allegiance to the love command."[151]

Having already stated that the true believer is a child of God and therefore has God as his Father, John now declares that the believer will not only love God but also God's child or offspring. That is, he will not only love the parent but also the child of the parent. Plummer offers two syllogisms to help understand John's logic:

Every one who believes the Incarnation is a child of God.
Every child of God loves its Father.
Therefore every believer in the Incarnation loves God.

Every believer in the Incarnation loves God.
Every one who loves God loves the children of God.
Therefore every believer in the Incarnation loves the children of God.[152]

---

[148] Strecker states, "In the Johannine writings, dogmatics and ethics cannot be played off against one another; instead, every faith statement has an ethical quality" (*Johannine Letters,* 174).

[149] O. A. Piper, "1 John and the Didache of the Primitive Church," *JBL* 66 (1947): 438.

[150] Marshall, *Epistles of John,* 227.

[151] Smalley, *1, 2, 3 John,* 266–67.

[152] Plummer, *Epistles of S. John,* 110.

The Greek term translated "father" (NIV) is literally "the one who has begotten" *(gennēsanta),* and "his child" is literally "the one begotten from him" *(tov gegnnēmenon ex auto).*[153] John is stating that a believer must love his heavenly Father and the other offspring of his heavenly Father (i.e., Jesus and/ or his brothers and sisters in Christ).[154]

5:2 Having already stated in the previous verse that everyone who is born of God loves God's children, John now explains how we can know if we are truly accomplishing this task. What follows in v. 2, however, is somewhat unexpected. The word order is indeed surprising. John declares that love directed toward God and carrying out his commands serves as the basis of the knowledge that one loves the children of God. This logic seems to be the reverse of what John has previously used. Elsewhere he has argued that love for others is the basis on which love for God is discerned. For example, in 4:20 John argues that one cannot love God, whom he cannot see, without also loving his brother, whom he can see (cf. 3:14–15,17–19). But here love for God's children follows one's love and obedience to God.

As in the previous instances, there is some debate about whether the phrase *en toutō* (lit., "by this"; NIV, "this is how") refers to what precedes or what follows. If one argues that it refers to the preceding sentence, v. 2 would simply be "an application of the rule in v. 1b."[155] In 1 John this phrase can refer to what precedes (3:19), although this is the exception to John's normal usage.[156] Marshall, agreeing that *en toutō* refers to what precedes, claims that "we love" in this context should be taken as an obligation, "we ought to love."[157] The verse can be paraphrased thus: "By this principle, namely, that we must love our father's [other] children, we know that we ought to love the children of God whenever we love God and keep his commands." The relationship between v. 2 and v. 1, however, seems to be one of explanation and not so much application. Also taking *en toutō* as referring to what precedes does not do justice to the *hotan* ("when") clause.[158] Also, if Marshall is correct, John has reversed what he enunciated

---

[153] The verse can be translated literally as follows: "Everyone who believes that Jesus is the Messiah has been begotten of God, and everyone who loves the one who begets, loves the one who is begotten of him."

[154] Brooke states, "Every one who loves the father who begat him naturally loves the other children whom his father has begotten. ... Those who are 'born of God' must love all His children, as surely as it is natural that any child should love his father's other children" (*Johannine Epistles,* 127–28).

[155] Schnackenburg, *Johannine Epistles,* 228; also C. H. Dodd (*The Johannine Epistles* (New York: Harper and Brothers, 1946), 125, who translates the verse: "By this we know that, when we love God, we love the children of God."

[156] See 2:5; 3:10,16,24; 4:2,9,10,13,17, where *en touto* refers to what follows.

[157] Marshall, *Epistles of John,* 227–28.

[158] Ibid. 227. The NIV "by loving God and carrying out ..." is lit. "when we love God and carry out ..."

in v. 1: if we love God, we also love his children.

It is better to interpret the verse straightforwardly. John is arguing once more that love for others is grounded in the love of God (cf. 4:8,16,19). When we love God, we will keep his commands, which also involves having love for others (3:11; 4:7,21). Therefore love for God and love for others are interrelated. Each feeds and strengthens the other, though love for God is the basis for any and every other manifestation of love. Smalley argues, "For the fact is that each kind of love (for God, and for others) demonstrates the genuineness of the other, and reinforces it. Brotherly love is proof of the love of God; but the reverse is also true."[159] Just as it is impossible to love God without loving God's children, it is impossible to love God's children without loving God (cf. 4:21).

John claims that Christians must love God and carry out his commands. In one sense to love God is to carry out his commands. The expression "carrying out his commands" is unique in the New Testament. The usual phrase in 1 John is "keeping his commands" (cf. 1 John 3:22; 5:3). John may be stressing the need for obedient living against those of his congregation who slighted moral conformity to God's word.

5:3 Love for God is real only when God's commands are kept. Obedience is not only the outcome of loving God but also a part of it. Or, as Stott succinctly comments, "Love for God is not an emotional experience so much as a moral commitment."[160] The NIV correctly interprets the construction *he agapē tou theou* ("the love of God") as an objective genitive (i.e., our love for God).[161] The idea of showing love to our Lord by keeping his commands is frequently found in John's Gospel. For example, John 14:15 reads, "If you love me, you will obey what I command" (also see 14:21,23–24,31; 15:10).

John adds that God's commands are not "burdensome."[162] This does not mean that God's laws are not exacting or demanding. Rather, it means that God's laws are not oppressive or crushing. They are not a terrible weight we cannot bear. God's moral standards are high, but God gives the Christian grace to be able to live up to that standard (cf. 4:4). "Love-prompted obedience is not a crushing burden that exhausts the believer's strength and destroys his sense of freedom in Christ."[163] In Matthew, Jesus rebukes the Pharisees because they "tie up heavy loads and put them on men's shoul-

---

[159] Smalley, *1, 2, 3 John*, 268. Plummer writes, "Love to God and love to the brethren confirm and prove each other" (*Epistles of S. John*, 111).

[160] Stott, *Letters of John*, 176.

[161] Many translations leave the phrase ambiguous in Eng. as it is in Gk., rendering it "love of God."

[162] Gk. βαρεῖαι. This word only occurs here in 1 John.

[163] Hiebert, "An Exposition of 1 John 5:1–12," 220.

ders" (Matt 23:4). Jesus does not weigh down his people with meaningless laws that do not affect the heart. He gives commands that reveal to us the heart of God and direct our hearts to God. Jesus offers us an easy yoke and a light burden: "Come to me, all you who are weary and burdened, and I will give you rest. Take my yoke upon you and learn from me, for I am gentle and humble in heart, and you will find rest for your souls. For my yoke is easy and my burden is light" (Matt 11:28–30).

5:4 For the eighth and final time in his letter, John addresses an aspect of the new birth by use of the word *gennaō* (2:29; 3:9 twice, 4:7; 5:1 three times; 5:4). Everyone[164] who has been born of God is able to keep God's commands because he has been given power by God to overcome the negative influences that would prevent such obedience. Because of the new birth, the believer is given supernatural power to withstand the forces of the world. As the epistle states earlier (cf. 2:15–17; 3:1,13; 4:1–6), "world" often has an ethical dimension representing humanity, which is at war with God and his people.[165] Just as Jesus states that he has overcome the world in John's Gospel (16:33b), here believers are said to overcome the world.

The translation of v. 4 in English obscures the Greek wordplay. The NIV translates the Greek verb *nikaō* as "overcome" but translates the Greek noun *nikē* as "victory."[166] A translation that keeps the root the same in English would read: "For everyone born of God conquers the world. This is the conquering that has conquered the world, even our faith."[167] John uses the present tense, which indicates that believers are currently experiencing the victory.[168]

It should be noted that v. 4 contains the only occurrence of the noun *he pistis* ("the faith") in the Johannine writings. Every other time he favors the verb *pisteuo* ("believe"). It seems clear from the context that his use of "faith" differs slightly from the Pauline usage and stresses the idea of confession, the confession that Jesus Christ is the Son of God.[169] Marshall

---

[164] John switches from the masculine in v. 1 (πᾶς) to the neuter in v. 4 (πᾶν). Plummer indicates that the neuter is used here to emphasize not the victorious person but the victorious power (*Epistles of S. John*, 112). Westcott states that John uses the abstract (i.e., neuter) form "in order to convey a universal truth" (*Epistles of John*, 179).

[165] Bultmann states, "That 'world' here means the world not only divorced from God but also hostile to him at the same time, is shown by the talk about a victory over it, which of course presupposes a war between God and world" (*Johannine Epistles*, 77). Westcott says, "Under the title 'the world' St. John gathers up the sum of all the limited, transitory powers opposed to God which make obedience difficult" (*Epistles of John*, 179).

[166] The word νίκη occurs only here in the NT.

[167] A form of νικάω occurs four times in vv. 4 and 5.

[168] Hiebert states, "The present tense verb presents this victory as a continuing experience gained through continuing struggle against 'the world'" ("An Exposition of 1 John 5:1–12," 220).

[169] Bultmann, *Johannine Epistles*, 78; Marshall, *Epistles of John*, 229; Smalley, *1, 2, 3 John*, 271; Westcott, *Epistles of John*, 180.

writes, "The fact that we hold the true faith from our hearts is the means whereby the power of the new world operates in us and enables us to overcome the world."[170] The particular nature of the victory is variously understood.[171] It could refer to (1) Christ's once-for-all victory on the cross over Satan, sin, and the world;[172] (2) the believers' victory over the heretics;[173] or (3) the victory that occurs at the conversion of the individual believer.[174] R. Brown finds it difficult to decide between these three choices and admits, "I see no way to be certain as to which past action John means here."[175] Ultimately, these three elements are all included in the final victory. The ground of our victory is Christ's death and resurrection. From that work believers will have victory over all that is in opposition to God. Daily victory is also granted to the individual believer, but he must exercise faith in Christ and be active in his pursuit of God.

5:5   Several commentators see 5:5 as beginning a new section,[176] while others break the section midway through v. 4.[177] It appears unnatural to break at 5:4 and best to take 5:5 with the previous section, since the theme of overcoming is continued.[178] Furthermore, the theme of "believing" forms an inclusion in this section (cf. v. 1 and v. 5).[179]

Another evidence that v. 5 belongs with the previous section is that it basically reiterates the truth found in v. 4 and in some sense serves as a summation of vv. 1–4. In v. 4 it was faith that overcame the world, and in v. 5 the content of overcoming faith is unpacked. Faith that overcomes is only faith that believes that Jesus is the Son of God (cf. 2:22; 4:15). In v. 1 belief in Jesus as the Christ was emphasized. In v. 5 it is Jesus as the Son of God that is affirmed. Verses 1 and 5 may indeed be a type of inclusio.[180]

---

[170] Marshall, *Epistles of John,* 229. Calvin notes, "But as God does not arm us for one day alone, and as faith is not of a day's duration but is the perpetual work of the Holy Spirit, we are already partakers of victory, as if we had already finished the war" (*Gospel according to John and First John,* 301).

[171] Gk. νικήσασα is an aorist participle.

[172] So Marshall, "To believe that Jesus has been victorious is to have the power that enables us also to win the battle, for we know that our foe is already defeated and therefore powerless" (*Epistles of John,* 229). Also Schnackenburg, *Johannine Epistles,* 230; Westcott, *Epistles of John,* 180.

[173] Stott, *Letters of John,* 177.

[174] Brooke, *Johannine Epistles,* 131; Hiebert, "An Exposition of 1 John 5:1–12," 221.

[175] Brown, *Epistles of John,* 571.

[176] Bultmann, *Johannine Epistles,* 79; Marshall, *Epistles of John,* 230; Schnackenburg, *Johannine Epistles,* 230; Smalley, *1, 2, 3 John,* 272.

[177] Brown, *Epistles of John,* 592; Strecker, *Johannine Letters,* 181.

[178] Brooke, *Johannine Epistles,* 131; Bruce, *Epistles of John,* 116; Dodd, *Johannine Epistles,* 123; Hiebert, "An Exposition of 1 John 5:1–12," 220; Stott, *Letters of John,* 174; M. M. Thompson, *1–3 John* (Downers Grove: InterVarsity, 1992), 129; Westcott, *Epistles of John,* 176; *UBSGNT.*

[179] K. L. Hansford, "The Underlying Poetic Structure of 1 John," *JTT* 5 (1992): 167.

[180] A. Culpepper, "The Pivot of John's Prologue," *NTS* 27 (1980/81): 25–26. See earlier comments at 5:1, n. 149.

In v. 5 John rhetorically asks who is able to overcome the world except he who believes that Jesus is the Son of God. The interrogative pronoun "who" *(tis)* individualizes the question, asking for the personal identification of one who overcomes the world. Whereas in v. 1 the content of true faith affirmed that Jesus is *the Christ,* here true faith affirms that Jesus is the *Son of God,* which suggests that John considered these two titles virtual synonyms. Such a confession was aimed at countering the heretical tendencies of the false teachers because they denied that Jesus was the Son of God. For John, saving faith must have as its foundation belief in the incarnation of the Son of God and all that entails the entire career of the Son. As Hiebert asserts, "This article of faith underlies all the other parts of the Christian message; to destroy this truth is to destroy the whole gospel and effectively to nullify God's provision for victory over sin and the world."[181] On the other hand, acceptance of the apostolic message assures the believer of the victory.

John has already encouraged his readers in their dealings with the false teachers: "You, dear children, are from God and have overcome them, because the one who is in you is greater than the one who is in the world" (1 John 4:4). In Rev 12:11 we also see comfort given to those who persevere: "They overcame him by the blood of the Lamb and by the word of their testimony; they did not love their lives so much as to shrink back from death."[182] Paul similarly assures us that "in all these things we are more than conquerors through him who loved us" (Rom 8:37) and that we should thank God because "he gives us the victory through our Lord Jesus Christ" (1 Cor 15:57).

Stott aptly summarizes this section: "Christian believers are God's children, born from above. God's children are loved by all who love God. Those who love God also keep his commands. They keep his commands because they overcome the world, and they overcome the world because they are Christian believers, born from above."[183]

5. Believe in the Son and Enjoy Eternal Life (5:6–12)

⁶This is the one who came by water and blood—Jesus Christ. He did not come by water only, but by water and blood. And it is the Spirit who testifies, because the Spirit is the truth. ⁷For there are three that testify: ⁸the Spirit, the water and the blood; and the three are in agreement. ⁹We accept man's testimony, but God's testimony is greater because it is the testimony of God, which he has given about his Son. ¹⁰Anyone who believes in the Son of God has this testimony in his heart. Anyone who does not believe God has made him out to be a liar, because he has

---

[181] Hiebert, "An Exposition of 1 John 5:1–12," 222.

[182] Cf. Rev 2:7,11,17,26; 3:5,12,21.

[183] Stott, *Letters of John,* 177–78.

not believed the testimony God has given about his Son. [11]And this is the testimony: God has given us eternal life, and this life is in his Son. [12]He who has the Son has life; he who does not have the Son of God does not have life.

Verses 6–12 are semantically united around the theme of witness or testimony. A form of the word *martus,* "witness," occurs no fewer than nine times. John's purpose is to demonstrate that there is more than adequate evidence to prove that Jesus is the Son of God who provides eternal life to all who believe in him. Testimony presents itself from different but unified voices. John's polemic in this section focuses in particular on the career of Jesus from baptism to crucifixion. There is a clear refutation of the Cerinthian type of proto-Gnosticism that plagued the churches of Asia Minor at the end of the first century. There is not a clear break between vv. 12 and 13, though v. 13 functions very much like a summary statement of the entire book. It provides a bridge between the "God is love" section (3:11–5:12) and John's concluding concerns (5:13–21), though its close connection to v. 12 and the concept of [eternal] life must not be ignored.

Jesus is the one who came by water and blood, a fact to which the Spirit testifies. Since it is God who has given these witnesses (the Spirit, the water, and the blood), the believer should readily embrace them. Those who believe God's testimony have a God-given assurance that confirms this truth in their hearts, and they are granted eternal life as a result. Those who reject God's testimony in effect call God a liar and cut themselves off from eternal life.

5:6 In 5:11 John has explained that orthodox faith is based on the revelation and reality that Jesus is the Christ, the Son of God (5:5). He now underscores the reliability of this confession by providing witnesses. John states that Jesus "is the one who came by water and blood" and "he did not come by water only, but by water and blood."[184] This passage was no doubt clear to the original audience but, unfortunately, is somewhat obscure to us.[185] Three main interpretations of this passage have been offered.

1. The "water and blood" refer to baptism (water) and the Lord's Supper (blood).[186] This interpretation, which goes back to the time of the Reform-

---

[184] Literally translated the second half of the verse reads: "This is the one who came through water and blood, Jesus Christ. Not in the water only but in the water and in the blood."

[185] Plummer calls this text "the most perplexing passage in the Epistle and one of the most perplexing in N.T." (*Epistles of S. John,* 113).

[186] Strecker argues that the author's shift in prepositions from διά ("by") to ἐν ("in") "introduces a change in the system of theological coordinates, and that in the phrase ἐν τῷ ὕδατι καὶ ἐν τῷ αἵματι it is no longer simply the baptism and death of Jesus (including its atoning effect), but also the two community sacraments of Baptism and the Lord's Supper that are the object of the instruction" (*Johannine Letters,* 183; also cf. Westcott, *Epistles of John,* 182). More probably, however, the shift in prepositions is merely stylistic (so Bruce, *Epistles of John,* 131, n. 5; Bultmann, *Johannine Epistles,* 79, n. 1; Marshall, *Epistles of John,* 232, n. 6; Schnackenburg, *Johannine Epistles,* 234; Smalley, *1, 2, 3 John,* 280).

ers,[187] is not without its difficulties. First, John is concerned with combating false teachers who denied the human nature of Jesus. It is therefore unlikely that John would now switch topics. Second, John uses the past tense (*ho elthōn,* "the one who came") which reflects a past, completed event in history, whereas baptism and the Lord's Supper are recurring observances.[188] Third, although water seems to be a likely synonym for baptism, the same is not true for blood and the Lord's Supper.

2. The "water and blood" are parallel to John 19:34–35, which speaks of a spear being thrust into Jesus' side at the crucifixion that produced "blood and water."[189] Again, although this view can be found as far back as Augustine, it remains problematic. First, the order has been reversed. First John speaks of "water and blood," but the Gospel of John reads "blood and water." Second, if "water and blood" refer to the spear thrust, then how can it be said that Jesus "came" by them? Whereas the Gospel of John indicates that "blood and water" came from Jesus, here it is said that Jesus came "by" water and blood. Third, this view does not account for the statement in v. 8 that affirms that Jesus "did not come by water only, but by water and blood."

3. The "water and blood" refer to the terminal points in Jesus' earthly ministry: his baptism (water)[190] and his crucifixion (blood). This is the best interpretation and is followed by most scholars. Historically, Jesus "came" into his power by the "water" of his baptism and even more so by the "blood" of his cross. Unlike the previous two views, this explanation fits the historical context of John's epistle. John writes this letter to counter the Gnostic tendencies of the false teachers. These false teachers, who at one time were part of the fellowship (2:19), were denying the humanity of

---

[187] Hiebert (*Epistles of John,* 235). Interestingly, neither Luther nor Calvin held this view. Luther acknowledges that "most interpreters turn their attention to the two sacraments ... yet I simply take this statement to mean Baptism, provided that it is applied in the right way, so that the very sprinkling of the blood of Christ comes to me" (*LW,* 30:314). Calvin wrote: "I do not doubt that by the words 'water and blood' he refers to the ancient rites of the Law ... by blood there was expiation and a pledge of full reconciliation with God. ... There is no ambiguity about the blood by which Christ reconciled God; but how He came by water may be queried. It is improbable that it refers to baptism" (*Gospel according to John and First John,* 302).

[188] Brown, *Epistles of John,* 573; Hiebert, "An Exposition of 1 John 5:1–12," 223; Marshall, *Epistles of John,* 231; Schnackenburg, *Johannine Epistles,* 232; Smalley, *1, 2, 3 John,* 277; Stott, *Letters of John,* 180; Strecker, *Johannine Letters,* 182; Westcott, *Epistles of John,* 181.

[189] Brown, *Epistles of John,* 578; M. M. Thompson, *1–3 John,* NTCS (Downers Grove: Inter-Varsity, 1992), 134.

[190] B. Witherington III, takes "water" as referring to the physical birth of Jesus ("The Waters of Birth: John 3.5 and 1 John 5.6–8," *NTS* 35 [1989]: 160). M. C. De Boer interprets "through water and blood" epexegetically ("through water, that is, blood"; "Jesus the Baptizer: I John 5:5–8 and the Gospel of John," *JBL* 107 [1988]: 103). Kruse (*Letters of John,* 178) takes water as a reference to Jesus' ministry of baptism, and not his experience of baptism.

Jesus, and so John emphasizes the reality of the Incarnation. John's further qualification that Jesus came "not by water only, but by water and blood" is likely a direct renunciation of the false teaching (perhaps that of Cerinthus) that claimed that Jesus was born an ordinary human being but became God's special agent when the heavenly Christ descended upon him at his baptism. The heavenly Christ abandoned him before his death and, consequently, it was only the earthly Jesus who died on the cross. In seeking to refute this teaching, John emphasizes that it was Jesus Christ who experienced both baptism and crucifixion. Marshall eloquently explains the importance of John's teaching.

> As soon as we reduce the death of Jesus to that of a mere man, so soon do we lose the cardinal point of the New Testament doctrine of the atonement, that God was in Christ reconciling the world to himself; in the last analysis, the doctrine of the atonement means that God himself bears our sins and shows that the final reality in the universe is his sin-bearing, pardoning love, but if Jesus is not the Son of God, his death can no longer bear this significance. So-called theologies, which reduce talk of the incarnation to the status of myth, may be attractive to modern men, but they take away our assurance that God's character is sin-bearing love.[191]

In support of Jesus' historical life and death, John appeals to the testimony of the Spirit. The witness of the Spirit is needed because Jesus' divinity is a scandal and a stumblingblock to the world. The Spirit can be trusted since he is the truth and therefore speaks God's truth (John 14:17; 16:13). The Spirit speaks through the Word, convicting the heart of the individual. Jesus makes a similar statement in John's Gospel concerning the role of the Spirit: "When the Counselor comes, whom I will send to you from the Father, the Spirit of truth who goes out from the Father, he will testify about me" (John 15:26).

5:7–8 Having previously mentioned the witnesses of the Spirit, John now appeals to the threefold testimony of "the Spirit, the water and the blood."[192] The "water and blood" have the same meaning as they did in v. 6.[193] These three bear witness to the truthfulness of the person of Jesus

---

[191] Marshall, *Epistles of John,* 233–34.

[192] Although Spirit, water, and blood are all neuter nouns (πνεῦμα, ὕδωρ, and αἷμα), John introduces them with a clause in the masculine plural (ὁι μαρτυροῦντες, "witnesses").

[193] Brooke, *Johannine Epistles,* 137; Hiebert, "An Exposition of 1 John 5:1–12," 227; Marshall, *Epistles of John,* 237; Plummer, *Epistles of S. John,* 116; Smalley, *1, 2, 3 John,* 282. Some claim that even though the water and blood in v. 6 are historical, in v. 8 they are symbolic, referring to the sacraments (so Bultmann, *Johannine Epistles,* 80–81; Schnackenburg, *Johannine Epistles,* 235–38) or at least admit a secondary allusion to the sacraments (so Brown, *Epistles of John,* 584–85, 599; Bruce, *Epistles of John,* 212; Dodd, *Johannine Epistles,* 130–31; Stott, *Letters of John,* 182).

as the Christ. "Water" and "blood" are personified because the Spirit is regarded as personal.[194] The Spirit is given priority because it is the Spirit who testifies through the water and the blood.

These three witnesses are said to be one.[195] By this phrase John is "implying that the Spirit, water and blood converge on the same point, and work together toward the same result: that of establishing the truth that Jesus is Messiah and Son of God."[196] It is likely that Deut 19:15—"A matter must be established by the testimony of two or three witnesses"—has influenced the author's defense in presenting three witnesses.[197]

Excursus: Johannine Comma

In versions following the (so-called) *Textus Receptus* or Received Text (KJV and NKJV) there is an additional section of v. 7 known as the *Comma Johanneum* or the Johannine Comma (Gk., comma = sentence or clause). Here vv. 7 and 8a read, "For there are three that testify in heaven: the Father, the Word and the Holy Spirit, and these three are one. And there are three that testify on earth: the ..." Why do most modern versions demote this additional section to a mere footnote? Are modern versions deliberately less Trinitarian than classic translations such as the KJV? The question involved in deciding whether this verse is authentic is not based on the truthfulness of the statement but on the external manuscript evidence. In other words, just because a statement is true does not make it Scripture. One must look at why and how the Johannine Comma came to be adapted into the Greek Edition of the New Testament known as the *Textus Receptus* (A.D. 1633). This is not a question of the *inspiration* of the text but of the *transmission* of the text. John's letter, whatever the original, is inerrant. What must be established is what the autographs actually said.

The oldest textual witnesses of this text occur in Latin manuscripts of the seventh century. With its eventual acceptance in the Latin Vulgate (Clementine edition, 1592), the Johannine Comma began to appear in many other translations and versions. It only appears in eight Greek manuscripts (minuscules), none of which can be dated before 1400. Furthermore, it is clear that the text has been translated from Latin back into Greek, and in four of the eight manuscripts the Johannine Comma appears only in the margin of the text. If the text is authentic, then its disappearance in the early manuscripts is an absolute mystery. Why would the church be so careless as to let such a valuable text be forgotten?

It should be noted that not only does the manuscript evidence strongly favor the omission of this passage, but the same is true concerning the testimony of the

---

[194] Marshall, *Epistles of John*, 237, n. 20; Smalley, *1, 2, 3 John*, 281.

[195] Gk. καὶ οἱ τρεῖς εἰς τὸ ἕν εἰσιν, lit., "and the three are into the one." Brooke notes, "They all work towards the same result, the establishing of the truth that Jesus is the Christ, the Son of God" (*Johannine Epistles*, 137).

[196] Smalley, *1, 2, 3 John*, 282. Strecker comments, "In the context of Johannine terminology this probably means not only that their testimony agrees but primarily that it corresponds to the one truth" (*Johannine Letters*, 192).

[197] Also see Deut 17:6; Matt 18:16; John 8:17; 2 Cor 13:1; 1 Tim 5:19.

early church. Not one Greek or Latin Church Father ever quotes this passage in the first four and a half centuries. This is especially revealing in light of the many controversies revolving around the Trinity (especially Sabellianism and Arianism). If the Johannine Comma was a part of the original text, then what would be a better passage to quote in order to prove the Trinity? Nicea (A.D. 325) and Chalcedon (A.D. 451) almost certainly would have taken advantage of it. The absence of such usage causes one to doubt seriously the authenticity of this passage.

Erasmus, a prominent New Testament Greek scholar of the fifteenth century, rejected the Johannine Comma in the first two editions of his Greek New Testament (1516, 1519). Soon, however, he began to receive criticism for his omission of the Johannine Comma. The Englishman E. Lee was one of Erasmus's constant critics. After being criticized by Lee for several years, Erasmus wrote to Lee the following reply, "If a single manuscript had come into my hands, in which stood what we read (sc. In the Latin Vulgate) then I would certainly have used it to fill in what was missing in the other manuscripts I had. Because that did not happen; I have taken the only course which was permissible, that is, I have indicated (sc. In the Annotationes[198]) what was missing from the Greek manuscripts."[199]

Later, Lee suggests that Erasmus was negligent and that if he only had looked at other manuscripts he would have certainly found a copy that contained the Johannine Comma. Erasmus again explained to Lee that he had diligently consulted many manuscripts. He continues: "What sort of indolence is that, if I did not consult manuscripts which I could not manage to have? At least, I collected as many as I could. Let Lee produce a Greek manuscript in which is written the words lacking in my edition, and let him prove that I had access to this manuscript, and then let him accuse me of indolence."[200] Shortly thereafter, a Greek manuscript containing the Johannine Comma was shown to Erasmus.[201] It is almost certain that this manuscript was produced simply to induce Erasmus to include the Johannine Comma in his Greek New Testament. Even though Erasmus suspected this Greek manuscript to have been based on the Latin, there is doubt as to whether Erasmus knew that the manuscript had been created for the purpose of encouraging him to include the Johannine Comma.[202] In the third edition of his Greek New Testament, Erasmus included the extra text (although he omitted the passage from later editions).

After Erasmus included the additional words of 1 John 5:7 in his Greek New Testament, others began to accept it without question. It was later included in Stephanus's edition (1550), which was a precursor to the *Textus Receptus*—the basis for the KJV.

Is the Johannine Comma Scripture? The evidence seems to say no. Is the Johannine Comma truthful? Is it sound theology? Yes. It is not necessary, how-

---

[198] I.e., in the footnotes.

[199] Quoted in H. J. De Jonge, "Erasmus and the Comma Johanneum," *ETL* 56 (1980): 385.

[200] Ibid., 386.

[201] The text (now minuscule Gregory 61) had been copied from Codex Britannicus or Codex Montforianus (early sixteenth century).

[202] See De Jonge, "Erasmus and the Comma Johanneum," 381–89.

ever, to place the Johannine Comma in the text of Scripture. The Trinity can be adduced from many other texts of Scripture (e.g., Matt 28:18–20; 1 Cor 12:4–6; 2 Cor 13:14; Eph 1:3–14; 4:4–6). We are warned in the Bible neither to take away nor add to its words. On this basis it is best to leave out the disputed words.[203]

5:9 John continues his argument concerning the witness to Jesus as the Son of God, the Messiah, by stating that this threefold witness is of divine origin. In other words, God's own authority and approval have been stamped on the truth of the Gospel concerning Jesus Christ.

John uses an argument from the lesser to the greater. Since we believe the testimony of man, how much more should we believe the testimony of God (cf. John 5:36)? In Jewish jurisprudence the testimony of two or three witnesses was sufficient to be received as the truth; how much more if God himself offers three divine witnesses to prove his case? As Smalley comments, "The testimony of God, whose divine being incorporates the divinity of the Son and the Spirit (vv 7–8), is superior in status and force to the testimony of man because it is more trustworthy."[204] Therefore John's point is that we should accept God's testimony precisely because it is *God's* testimony about *his Son.*

What exactly is the testimony given by God? The most likely answer is that John is referring back to the threefold testimony in v. 8.[205] This interpretation fits with the perfect tense of the verb (*memarturēken*, "he has testified"). God has testified concerning his Son in the past through the Spirit, water, and blood, and this testimony is still valid today.[206]

5:10 John now discusses belief and unbelief. The one who believes in God's Son is the one who affirms God's testimony concerning his Son. Therefore, according to John, believing in Jesus as the Son of God is equivalent to accepting God's testimony about his Son (v. 9).[207] The result is that the Christian has God's testimony "in his heart."[208] This phrase suggests

---

[203] Lengthy discussions of this textual issue are found in Brooke, *Johannine Epistles*, 154–65; Brown, *Epistles of John,* 775–87; Marshall, *Epistles of John,* 236–37, n. 19; Schnackenburg, *Johannine Epistles,* 44–46; Strecker, *Johannine Letters,* 188–91; Westcott, *Epistles of John*, 202–9.

[204] Smalley, *1, 2, 3 John*, 283.

[205] Dodd, *Johannine Epistles*, 132; Marshall, *Epistles of John,* 240; Stott, *Letters of John,* 184; Westcott, *Epistles of John*, 185.

[206] Stott states, "The perfect tense indicates the continuing validity (in itself and through the Spirit) of God's historical testimony to Christ" (*Letters of John,* 184).

[207] According to Hiebert the articular participle (ὁ πιστύων, "the one who believes") "involves not merely an acceptance of the truthfulness of the message but also a personal trust in or committal to the One to whom witness is borne" ("An Exposition of 1 John 5:1–12," 228).

[208] Gk. ἐν ἑαυτῷ, lit., "in himself." Marshall takes the phrase ἔχει ἐν ἑαυτῷ to mean "hold fast" (*Epistles of John,* 241, n. 39). He writes, "It is, therefore, more likely that John is simply stating that to believe in the Son of God is to accept and keep God's testimony" (p. 241).

that John is referring to the inner testimony of the Spirit in the heart of the believer. As Smalley claims, "The inward witness of God's Spirit shows the Christian that he was right to believe in Jesus; and this 'internal testimony' (of the Spirit) balances and complements the external and historical witness of the 'water and blood,' the baptism and death of Jesus, which marked the limits of his earthly ministry (vv 6–8)."[209] Or as Plummer succinctly puts it, "The external witness faithfully accepted becomes internal certitude."[210]

John turns his attention from those who believe in Jesus and therefore accept God's testimony to those who reject God's testimony. All who reject God's testimony make God out to be a liar. Brooke forcefully comments:

> There is no room for ignorance or misconception. To reject the witness is to deny the truthfulness of God. He has spoken and acted deliberately, and with absolute clearness. The testimony has been borne. The things were not done in a corner. The witness must therefore either be accepted or rejected. It cannot be ignored or explained away.[211]

This is because belief in the Father cannot be separated from belief in his Son (cf. 1 John 2:22–25). The charge of making God out to be a liar is obviously a serious one.[212] Early in this epistle John similarly stated that "if we claim we have not sinned, we make him [God] out to be a liar and his word has no place in our lives" (1:10). John is likely countering the heretical teachings of those who have left the community. It would also serve as a warning to those of the community who might be considering the same. "It is inconsistent to profess belief in God, as John's opponents did, and yet to disbelieve what God has said."[213] "Has made" and "has not believed" are both perfect tense verbs indicating a past event with continuous results.[214]

5:11 The demonstrative pronoun "this" *(hautē)* points forward to the rest of the verse. As with the previous verse, the nature of this "testimony" involves God's witness concerning his Son. Strictly speaking John does not state the content of God's testimony concerning his Son but the result of

---

[209] Smalley, *1, 2, 3 John*, 285–86. Also see Brooke, *Johannine Epistles*, 139.

[210] Plummer, *Epistles of S. John*, 117.

[211] Brooke, *Johannine Epistles*, 139.

[212] Schnackenburg writes, "This contradiction of God is so awesome, so catastrophic, for those who deny him, because they reject the witness God has given to his Son. With the rejection of the only Son of God the unbelievers pronounce their own death sentence" (*Johannine Epistles*, 240).

[213] Marshall, *Epistles of John*, 241.

[214] Westcott: "When the crisis of choice came he refused the message: he made God a liar: he did not believe on His testimony: and the result of that decision entered into him and clings to him" (*Epistles of John*, 187).

that testimony, which is nothing other than "eternal life."[215] Therefore "the question whether we accept God's testimony or not is not a merely academic one. Our answer to it will determine whether or not we participate in eternal life."[216]

The last part of this verse is perhaps the main point.[217] God's testimony concerning his Son does result in eternal life, but the point to stress is that this eternal life is only obtainable "in his Son." God's testimony is that his Son is the only means by which one can receive the gift of eternal life, which by implication means that God has given his divine approval on the earthly ministry of his Son. In the current theological context, John is clearly and convictionally a "theological exclusivist" with respect to salvation. This conviction is affirmed here in v. 11 and restated with greater force in v. 12.

5:12 This verse consists of a further explication of the last phrase of the previous verse. In parallel clauses John states the relation between having the Son and having life. To possess the Son is to possess life in all its fullness. Holding to the biblical faith means possessing Christ himself, as well as the life the Father grants to those who trust his Son as Lord and Savior. Ultimately, what matters is our relationship to the Son. This life is not something only to be received in the future but is a present possession ("has," *echei* = present tense). It should be noted that eternal life is not earned or merited, but rather it is a gift that is given by God to those who have the Son.

Conversely, if we reject the Son, we do not have life. As was stated above, John uses a parallel phrase to balance out the first part of the verse; however, there are two small but significant changes. The first is the addition of *tou theou* ("of God") to "the Son." John reminds his readers that the Father and the Son are inseparable and that it is impossible to have God as one's Father without also acknowledging Jesus as his Son.[218] The second is

---

[215] Smalley notes that eternal life "is qualitative, not quantitative; it is the highest kind of spiritual and moral life, irrespective of time, which God enables the believer to share in relationship with Jesus" (*1, 2, 3 John*, 287). Vaughan adds: "The concept of life" or "eternal life" dominates the thought of I John. The epistle begins (1:2) and ends (5:20) with references to it, and the stated purpose of the author was to give believers assurance of possessing it (5:13)" (*1, 2, 3 John*, 124). See also the note on "eternal life" in Kruse (*Letters of John*, 184–87).

[216] Marshall, *Epistles of John*, 241.

[217] Schnackenburg, *Johannine Epistles*, 241, "Since divine testimony is always related to the Son (vv. 9c,10c), this last statement is still part of the *martyria*. Indeed, it only now makes v. 11b comprehensible."

[218] Marshall, comments, "John says, 'does not have the Son of God,' thereby indicating once again the enormity of the offense, and the impossibility of having God as Father without accepting his Son" (*Epistles of John*, 242, n. 44). N. Alexander adds, "Whatever else the 'Sonless' man has, he does not have life" (*The Epistles of John: Introduction and Commentary*, TBC (New York: Macmillan, 1962), 124).

that the words *tēn zoēn* ("life") are placed before the verb. The second half of the verse literally reads, "The one not having the Son of God life does not have." This shift stresses the fact that those who reject God's Son also reject the life the Father gives. They are without [eternal] life and are spiritually dead (cf. Eph 2:1–7). Earlier John similarly stated, "No one who denies the Son has the Father; whoever acknowledges the Son has the Father also" (cf. John 3:36).

John has again stressed the importance of believing in Jesus as the Son of God, the Messiah. Eternal life is not possible apart from such belief. The words of Jesus once again ring true, "I am the way and the truth and the life. No one comes to the Father except through me" (John 14:6).

6. Conclusion: The Confidence and Characteristics of the Child of God (5:13–21)

This is the final section of John's first epistle.[219] It consists of John's purpose for writing his epistle (5:13), teaching about prayer (5:14–17), a summary section about the believer's knowledge and sin (5:18–20), and a warning to flee false religion (5:20–21). The theme of knowledge or confidence pervades this section.

(1) Know You Have Eternal Life (5:13)

¹³I write these things to you who believe in the name of the Son of God so that you may know that you have eternal life.

5:13 "These things" could refer specifically to John's teaching in vv. 1–12[220] or may indicate John's reason for writing the entire epistle.[221]

---

[219] Some argue that 5:13 is still part of the main body and that the conclusion does not begin until 5:14 (so Bultmann, *Johannine Epistles*, 83; Dodd, *Johannine Epistles*, 133; Smalley, *1, 2, 3 John*, 274–75.). Yet even Smalley admits that this verse "is transitional, in that it looks back to the subject matter of vv 5–12, and also provides a summary conclusion (to 1 John in its entirety) which leads into the closing remarks of vv 14–21" (p. 289). Marshall similarly states that v. 13 "sums up the Epistle as a whole, but in function it serves to link verses 5–11 with verses 14–21" (*Epistles of John*, 243, n. 1). Sherman and Tuggy argue: "In 5:13–21 John makes a Final Appeal to the readers' emotions so that all the previous appeals aimed at affecting their behavior will be heeded. In 5:13 he explicitly presents his purpose along with further descriptions of the benefits of living together according to Christ. Then pointedly and succinctly he gives the Final Appeal summarizing the letter: avoid anything that is not according to Christ (5:21). … Coherence is evidenced by the unit's being a summary of the whole letter" (*Semantic and Structural Analysis*, 98).

[220] Brooke, *Johannine Epistles*, 142; Schnackenburg, *Johannine Epistles*, 247; Stott, *Letters of John*, 186. Interestingly, each of these authors includes v. 13 in the closing section of 1 John and not with the previous section as might be expected.

[221] Bultmann, *Johannine Epistles*, 83; Marshall, *Epistles of John*, 243, n. 1; Plummer, *Epistles of S. John*, 120; Smalley, *1, 2, 3 John*, 290; Strecker, *Johannine Letters*, 198; Westcott, *Epistles of John*, 188.

Although there are close links in thought and language to vv. 1–12,[222] there are at least four reasons for choosing the latter option. First, the author shifts to the first person singular pronoun ("I") for the first time since 2:26. Second, the theme of assurance of salvation is one that appears frequently in this epistle. Third, many of the themes found in 5:13 are continued in 5:14–21 (e.g., know, eternal life, and Son of God). Fourth, there is a close parallel between 5:13 and John's purpose statement for the Fourth Gospel (20:31), which reads, "These [things] are written that you may believe that Jesus is the Christ, the Son of God, and that by believing you may have life in his name."[223]

What is the purpose for John's writing this epistle? John writes this epistle "so that" *(hina)* his readers might know they have eternal life. Earlier he stated, "We write this to *(hina)* make our joy complete" (1:4), and "I write this to you so that *(hina)* you will not sin" (2:1). Both of these verses also give some indication of John's purpose for writing this epistle. Now, at the conclusion of his epistle, John not only gives a reason for why he writes to his audience, but he now gives the (main) reason why he writes, "I write[224] these things to you ... so that you may know *[eidete]* that you have eternal life." It is apparent that many in the church were being led astray by false teachings and made to doubt whether they really possessed eternal life. John therefore assures his readers that they can and *should*[225] have confidence that they possess eternal life even now ("have," *echete*, present tense).

John writes to those "who believe in the name of the Son of God" and not to the heretics who were deceiving God's people.[226] This fact indicates that "John was therefore writing not to persuade unbelievers of the truth of the Christian faith but rather to strengthen Christian believers who might be tempted to doubt the reality of their Christian experience and to give up their faith in Jesus."[227]

---

[222] The theme of "eternal life" in v. 13 is related to the discussion about life in vv. 11–12 as is the theme of believing in the "Son of God" (vv. 5,10,12).

[223] Brown adds the argument that "1 John 5:13 constitutes as inclusion with the 'we are writing this' of the epistolary Prologue (1:4) which looks ahead to all that follows" (*Epistles of John*, 606). Sherman and Tuggy see an inclusio at 5:13 and 5:20, with both verses addressing eternal life through the Son (*Semantic and Structural Analysis*, 100).

[224] John uses an epistolary aorist (ἔγαψα, cf. 2:21 and 2:26).

[225] Smalley maintains that John's purpose clause functions as an indirect imperative. "Believers can be sure of possessing eternal life ... and therefore they must be certain" (*1, 2, 3 John*, 290).

[226] In the Gk. the phrase "to those who believe in the name of the Son of God" occurs as the end of the sentence and is deliberately emphatic (so Marshall, *Epistles of John*, 243, n. 2; Thompson, *1–3 John*, 139).

[227] Marshall, *Epistles of John*, 243.

(2) Be Confident in Prayer (5:14–17)

¹⁴**This is the confidence we have in approaching God: that if we ask anything according to his will, he hears us. ¹⁵And if we know that he hears us—whatever we ask—we know that we have what we asked of him.**

¹⁶**If anyone sees his brother commit a sin that does not lead to death, he should pray and God will give him life. I refer to those whose sin does not lead to death. There is a sin that leads to death. I am not saying that he should pray about that. ¹⁷All wrongdoing is sin, and there is sin that does not lead to death.**

5:14 Not only can a believer have assurance of salvation, but he also can have assurance that God will hear his prayers and answer them. Moreover, it is the gift of eternal life that allows the believer to come directly before God with boldness or confidence. The truth of vv. 14ff. is the natural result growing out of the truth of v. 13. John has already used the term "confidence" *(parrēsia)* three other times in this epistle. Twice (2:28; 4:17) it appears in connection with the coming judgment; and once (3:21–22), in connection with the issue of approaching God in prayer. Again, as in the previous three occurrences, the term "confidence" is applied to a believer's status before God.²²⁸

John states that "if we ask anything … he [God] hears us." Whereas the condition of answered prayer in 3:22 is that "we obey his commands and do what pleases him," here it is that our petitions should be "according to his will." In his Gospel, John records Jesus making similar statements. In 15:7 Jesus encourages us to "ask whatever you wish, and it will be given to you." Again there is a condition: "If you remain in me and my words remain in you." Also on several occasions Jesus indicates that he or the Father will do whatever we ask if we ask it in his "name" (14:13–14; 15:16; 16:24,26).²²⁹ Smalley writes, "The fundamental characteristic of all truly Christian intercession is that the will of the person who offers prayer should coincide with God's will."²³⁰ This does not mean that if a believer is sincere God will answer his prayer. Sometimes our desires are not God's desires for us. Sometimes what we want is not what our heavenly Father wills. Faith will accept that God's will is best, and it will trust his plan and purpose, even if it does not understand at the time.

---

²²⁸ The Gk. does not specifically indicate that the believer's confidence is "in approaching God" but merely says it is "with him" (πρὸς αὐτόν). The NIV is undoubtedly correct, however, in assuming that the pronoun refers to God.

²²⁹ Praying in Jesus' "name" is often viewed as being equivalent to praying according to God's will.

²³⁰ Smalley, *1, 2, 3 John*, 295. Vaughan adds: " 'According to his will'… seems to be the most inclusive way of setting forth the fundamental condition of effectual prayer. The statement implies that we recognize the infinite wisdom of God's will and subordinate our desires to it. Rightly seen, this is not a fetter to our freedom but a safeguard to it" (*1, 2, 3 John*, 130).

The believer has confidence when he prays according to God's will. Having faith, then, is not the only prerequisite for obtaining what we ask for in prayer. Many pray believing that God will answer their prayers simply because they trust that he will answer them. James warns believers to be careful how they pray: "When you ask, you do not receive, because you ask with wrong motives, that you may spend what you get on your pleasures" (Jas 4:3). Stott aptly reminds us:

> Prayer is not a convenient device for imposing our will upon God, or for bending his will to ours, but the prescribed way of subordinating our will to his. It is by prayer that we seek God's will, embrace it and align ourselves with it. Every true prayer is a variation of the theme "your will be done."[231]

The promise of making our petitions according to the will of God is that "he hears us." This does not mean that God simply acknowledges that we have prayed but that he hears us favorably or, even better, answers us favorably (cf. John 9:31; 11:41–42). What an encouragement for the believer to pray! In a sermon on this verse, C. H. Spurgeon powerfully gives us the following exhortation: "Brethren, if there be a God, and if this Book be his Word, if God be true, prayer must be answered; and let us on our knees go to the sacred engagement as to a work of real efficacy."[232]

5:15 This verse further expands the thought of v. 14. John assures the believer that he can know (*oidamen,* repeated twice in this verse) that God will hear and answer a prayer that is according to God's will. Because of the context, the use of "if" *(ean)* cannot indicate an uncertainty.[233] In v. 14 John has made it clear that God does hear the prayer of a believer. The text says that for "whatever" *(ho ean)* the believer asks, God will hear him. It should be noted, however, that the "whatever" of v. 15 is conditioned by the "according to God's will" of v. 14.

The second "know" of this verse is that the believer knows that God will grant him his request. Because God hears and listens to us, we can also be sure that God will respond positively to our petition. Often, however, we do not have what we desire because we do not ask God (Jas 4:2). But when we do come to God in prayer, we must come in faith. Jesus says in Mark 11:24, "Whatever you ask for in prayer, believe that you have received it, and it will be yours." The present tense "we have" *(echomen),* and not the future

---

[231] Stott, *Letters of John,* 188. Similarly, Dodd comments: "For prayer rightly considered is not a device for employing the resources of omnipotence to fulfill our own desires, but a means by which our desires may be redirected according to the will of God, and made into channels for the forces of His will" (*Johannine Epistles,* 134).

[232] C. H. Spurgeon, "Praying and Waiting," in *The Metropolitan Tabernacle Pulpit,* vol. 10 (Pasadena, Tex.: Pilgrim, 1969), 607.

[233] The use of ἐάν ("if") with an indicative verb (οἴδαμεν, "we know") has no parallel in the Johannine literature (cf. Luke 19:40; 1 Thess 3:8).

("we will have"), indicates that God grants our requests immediately, even though his answer may not be immediately revealed. As Plummer notes, "Our petitions are granted at once: the results of the granting are perceived in the future."[234]

5:16 In vv. 14 and 15 John gives the reader assurance that God will answer prayer. Now he gives a specific encouragement to pray that God would restore a fellow believer ("brother") who is sinning. There is, however, one limitation to such a prayer. If this person's sin involves "a sin that leads to death," prayer should not be offered.

John has often mentioned the theme of sinning in this epistle (e.g., 1:7–10; 2:2,12; 3:3–5,8–9; 4:10). The believer is not without sin (1:8), but at the same time he is not characterized by an ongoing sinful lifestyle (3:8–9; 5:18).

When a Christian "sees"[235] his brother sinning a sin that does not lead to death, he is to pray for that person. The verb translated "he should pray" *(aitesei)* is a future tense verb (lit., "he will pray"), which "expresses not the writer's command but the Christian's inevitable and spontaneous reaction."[236] The result is that God will grant the sinning brother "life" *(zōēn)*.[237]

But not every sinner is granted life as a result of answered prayer. The praying Christian can have confidence if the person's sin is not of the sort that leads to death. For those whose sin is of this nature John states, "I am not saying that he should pray about that."[238] John does not strictly forbid

---

[234] Plummer, *Epistles of S. John,* 121.

[235] Smalley states, "The resulting activity of prayer rests on visual evidence, not suspicion" (*1, 2, 3 John,* 299). Likewise, Plummer comments, "The supposed case is one in which the sinner is seen in the very act" (*Epistles of S. John,* 121).

[236] Stott, *Letters of John,* 188.

[237] The NIV correctly assumes that God is the subject of the verb "he will give" (δώσει). Others maintain that the verb is too closely connected with the previous verb, "he will ask" (αἰτή-σει), and therefore insist that the second verb also refers to the praying Christian (Brooke, *Johannine Epistles,* 146; Bultmann, *Johannine Epistles,* 87, n. 16; Plummer, *Epistles of S. John,* 122; Stott, *Letters of John,* 189; Strecker, *Johannine Letters,* 202, n. 23). Appeal for this interpretation is also based on Jas 5:20, which states, "Whoever turns a sinner from the error of his way will save him from death and cover a multitude of sins." Even those who hold to this view acknowledge that it is ultimately God who is granting life through the praying Christian. On the other hand, "To say that a human being could impart eternal life would seem foreign to Johannine thought, strictly theocentric as it is" (Schnackenburg, *Johannine Epistles,* 249).

[238] P. Trudinger's article "Concerning Sins, Mortal and Otherwise: A Note on 1 John 5, 16–17" (*Bib* 52 [1971]: 541–42) suggests that ἐρωτήσῃ (translated "pray") in v. 16 does not refer to prayer offered to God on behalf of someone but "asking questions about the various gradations and gravities of sin." Instead the Christian is "to intercede for the brother who is a sinner in order that he may be restored to life and not suffer spiritual death." Such an interpretation, however, is highly improbable.

prayer for such a person, but it is clear that he is in doubt about its efficacy.[239]

What exactly is the "sin that leads to death"? That John's readers understood the precise distinction between "a sin that does not lead to death" and a "sin that leads to death" is likely.[240] For the modern reader, however, such precise understanding is difficult, if not impossible, to attain. From the outset it is safe and contextually appropriate to reject any interpretation that refers to a physical death, since "death" is contrasted with spiritual (or "eternal") life.[241]

There are three main interpretations of "a sin that leads to death."[242]

1. *A Specific, Deadly Sin.* This view maintains that there are certain sins which, if committed, are unforgivable. All sins are punishable, but some sins are so heinous that those who commit them have no hope of ever obtaining eternal life. The Old Testament makes a distinction between inadvertent sins committed in ignorance and deliberate sins committed arrogantly or "with a high hand" (Lev 4:2,13,22,27; 5:15,17–18; Num 15:27–31; Deut 17:12). Offering the correct sacrifice to God could cleanse the sinner of the sin committed in ignorance, but deliberate sins could only be removed by death.[243] A similar distinction is made in this text between what later came to be called "mortal" (deadly) and "venial" (nondeadly)

---

[239] Schnackenburg goes so far to say that the "idea of mortal sin implies nothing about the possibility or impossibility of repentance" (*Johannine Epistles,* 250). On the other hand, Brown comments, "Since this verse follows the reference in 5:14 to asking "according to God's will," it is patent that he does not think that prayers in reference to deadly sin would be according to God's will" (*Epistles of John,* 613). Brown explains that such a position is consistent with other texts in the Bible where God's mercy is purposefully withheld from some (e.g., Deut 3:26; 1 Sam 3:14; Isa 22:14; Jer 14:11; John 17:9).

[240] Stott says, "John's readers were no doubt familiar with the expression, but commentators since the sub-apostolic fathers have debated its meaning" (*Letters of John,* 189).

[241] Texts often cited that speak of physical death include Num 18:22; Deut 22:26; Isa 22:14; *Jubilees* 33:12–18; Acts 5:1–11; 1 Cor 5:5; 11:29–30.

[242] Besides the many commentaries written on 1 John also see I. A. Busenitz, "The Sin Unto Death," *Master's Theological Seminary Journal* 1 (1990): 17–31; A. H. Dammers, "Hard Sayings—II: I John 5,16ff," *Theol* 66 (1963): 370–72; Kruse, *Letters of John,* 193–94; D. M. Scholer, "Sins Within and Sins Without: An Interpretation of 1 John 5:16–17," in *Current Issues in Biblical Interpretation: Studies in Honor of Merrill C. Tenney,* ed. G. F. Hawthorne (Grand Rapids: Eerdmans, 1975): 230–46; M. M. Thompson, "Intercession in the Johannine Community: 1 John 5:16 in the Context of the Gospels and Epistles of John," in *Worship, Theology and Ministry in the Early Church: Essays in Honor of Ralph Martin,* ed. M. J. Wilkins and T. Paige, JSNTSup 87 (Sheffield: Academic Press, 1992); T. Ward, "Sin 'Not Unto Death' and Sin 'Unto Death' in 1 John 5:16," *The Churchman* 109 (1995): 226–37.

[243] For a discussion see W. Kaiser, *Toward Rediscovering the Old Testament* (Grand Rapids: Zondervan, 1987), 132–33. Kaiser believes this sin involves "blasphemy against the Lord and contempt for the Word of God (Num 15:30). ... All sins could be forgiven in the OT, and atonement was available for all types and categories of sin except blasphemy against God and his Word."

sins.[244] Certain designated sins, such as murder, idolatry, injustice, apostasy, adultery, and fornication, were sometimes considered to be "mortal sins." These sins pushed one over the edge and beyond the reach of God's grace.

Although the Old Testament's distinction between lesser (unintentional) and greater (deliberate) sins possibly has some bearing on this text, the view that John is referring to some specific sin cannot be sustained from the context of 1 John.

2. *Blasphemy against the Holy Spirit.* This view is based on Jesus' testimony against the Pharisees, who are said to have committed such a sin (Matt 12:32). This sin "was a deliberate, open-eyed rejection of known truth."[245] It was verbal, knowledgeable and continual. It was claiming that Jesus' mighty works were done not by the Spirit of God but by the power of Beelzebub. Jesus states that such a sin "against the Holy Spirit will never be forgiven; he is guilty of an eternal sin" (Mark 3:29).

Similarly, we are warned in 1 Sam 2:25, "If a man sins against another man, God may mediate for him; but if a man sins against the LORD, who will intercede for him?" Hebrews 12:16–17 states that Esau hardened his heart to the point that repentance was impossible.

Although John probably does not have Jesus' reference to the blasphemy against the Holy Spirit in mind, this view at least makes a correlation with the other texts in Scripture that support the idea that some people have hardened their hearts to the point that prayer will not even help them.

3. *Total Rejection of the Gospel.* Whereas the first view contended that specific sins are envisioned in the sin that leads to death, this view holds that the text is referring to total apostasy, the rejection of Jesus Christ as the Son of God and denial of the faith. Plummer states that it "is possible to close the heart against the influences of God's Spirit so obstinately and persistently that repentance becomes a moral impossibility."[246]

In connection with this view scholars appeal to the so-called apostasy texts of Hebrews. For example, Heb 6:4–6; 10:26–27 states:

> It is impossible for those who have once been enlightened, who have tasted the heavenly gift, who have shared in the Holy Spirit, who have tasted the goodness of the Word and the powers of the coming age, if they fall away, to be brought back to repentance, because to their loss they are crucifying the Son of God all over again and subjecting him to public disgrace. ... If we deliberately

---

[244] The specification of "seven deadly sins" came about from this distinction.

[245] Stott, *Letters of John,* 191.

[246] Plummer, *Epistles of S. John,* 122. He continues, "'Sin unto death,' therefore, is not any act of sin, however heinous, but a state or habit of sin willfully chosen and persisted in: it is constant and consummate opposition to God" (p. 123).

keep on sinning after we have received the knowledge of the truth, no sacrifice for sins is left, but only a fearful expectation of judgment and of raging fire that will consume God's enemies.

Some scholars more specifically identify this sin with the false teachers who have left John's community (cf. 2:19). For example, Brown notes that John calls the one whose sin "is a sin not unto death" a "brother" while the one whose sin "is a sin unto death" is unnamed. Therefore, "since in Johannine dualism eternal life is possessed only by those who believe in the name of God's Son, the sin unto death is a sin by nonbrothers, i.e., those who do not believe in the name of God's Son."[247] These "secessionists," as Brown refers to them, have refused "to believe in Jesus as the Christ come in the flesh and as the Son of God," and therefore "the author discourages (and implicitly forbids) prayer for them."[248] The strength of this view is that it seeks to interpret 5:16 based on the context of John's epistle.

The question then arises whether a true Christian can apostatize? It seems clear from John's epistle that such is not a possibility. John has already stated that a believer cannot persist in sin because God's seed remains in him (3:9), and he will go on to say that a believer cannot continue in sin because God keeps him safe, not allowing the evil one to harm him (5:18). It does not seem likely that he who cannot "continue in sin" (5:18) is able to commit a "sin that leads to death" (5:16). Furthermore, in 2:19 John indicates that in leaving the true faith, the false teachers demonstrated that they were never really true believers: "They went out from us, but they did not really belong to us. For if they had belonged to us, they would have remained with us; but their going showed that none of them belonged to us." John is confident the true believer will remain.

All three of the above views have something positive to offer to the interpretation of 5:16. Likewise, each of them has its own difficulties. Nevertheless, the third view makes the most sense in the context of 1 John and offers the fewest difficulties.[249]

5:17 So that he might clear up any misunderstanding, John indicates

---

[247] Brown, *Epistles of John,* 617. Stott argues that both types of sinners are actually unbelievers since even the so-called "brother" is said to need "life" from God. "This means that, although his sin does not lead to death, he is in fact dead, since he needs to be given life. For how can you give life to one who is already alive?" (*Letters of John,* 191). Stott argues that "normal" unbelievers have simply not believed in Christ and that the "unto-death" unbelievers have not believed in Christ <u>and</u> have taught or believed the false teachers.

[248] Brown, *Epistles of John,* 618.

[249] The following questions still remain unanswered: (1) How do we know when a person commits a sin that leads to death? (2) Is John saying that there are no circumstances in which we are to pray for such a person? Unfortunately, John does not give answers to these questions and therefore makes it difficult for us clearly to apply this text today.

that he is not soft on sin by stating "all unrighteousness is sin."[250] No act of unrighteousness is so trivial that it can be ignored or neglected. He has previously declared that sin is "lawlessness" (*anomia,* 3:3) and here states that it is "unrighteousness" *(adikia).* The former speaks of rebellion against God, and the latter denotes a violation of God's standard of what is right.

It should be noted that although most of the scholarly debate is devoted to understanding the "sin that leads to death," John's real concern is to encourage believers to pray for those whose sin "is not to death." Thus, John again states that "there is a sin that does not lead to death." "The words are added to show the wide scope which is given for the exercise of Christian sympathy and intercession."[251]

(3) Do Not Continue in Sin (5:18–20a)

18We know that anyone born of God does not continue to sin; the one who was born of God keeps him safe, and the evil one cannot harm him. 19We know that we are children of God, and that the whole world is under the control of the evil one. 20We know also that the Son of God has come and has given us understanding, so that we may know him who is true.

Verses 18–20 continue on the theme of assurance or confidence (5:13,15), but a transition is made from assurance in prayer to the believers' knowledge and proper attitude toward sin (5:18), the world (5:20), and the Son of God (5:20). Each of these three verses begins with the verb "we know" *(oidamen),* which indicates an intuitive knowledge. These verses function as summary statements, reiterating John's main points in his epistle. Verse 18 also reaches back to the previous section as John demonstrates that he is in no way indifferent to sin, as some might (wrongly) have argued, since he speaks about "a sin that does not lead to death." Rather, John reminds his readers that no one who is born of God continues in sin, since Jesus protects him from the evil one's influence. Verse 20 actually connects well with John's surprise ending in v. 21 and provides a natural antithesis to his warning concerning idolatry.

5:18 John maintains that "anyone (lit., "everyone") born of God does not continue to sin." This means that there should be no exceptions to this general rule. Verse 18 reiterates the truths found in 3:6,9 that the believer

---

[250] Stott, "In distinguishing between sin that leads to death and sin that does not lead to death, he is not meaning to minimize the gravity of sin" (*Letters of John,* 193). Likewise Schnackenburg states, "He does not want to belittle failure to keep the commandments, for that shows that they do not know God (2:3ff.)" (*Johannine Epistles,* 251–52). Also see Brown, *Epistles of John,* 619; Plummer, *Epistles of S. John,* 123.

[251] Westcott, *Epistles of John,* 192.

does not continue in sin (see comment on those verses).[252] The use of the perfect participle ("born of God," *gegennēmenos*) suggests a permanent relationship begun in the past with continuing results from this new birth. One of these results is the God-given ability not to fall into long-term, habitual sinning. As Smalley asserts, "John is affirming, new conduct should follow from new birth."[253]

The reason why the child of God does not continue in sin is because "the one who was born of God keeps him safe."[254] The identity of "the one who was born of God" is not immediately clear. Some insist that it refers to the believer, since the same verb was used to characterize the believer earlier in this verse.[255] Most scholars, however, believe that John is referring to Jesus Christ based on the following reasons:[256] (1) John logically shifts from the perfect tense to the aorist tense (when referring to believers), referring to the birth of Jesus, a specific event in history. (2) If "the one who was born of God" refers to the believer, the text would need a reflexive pronoun ("the one who was born of God keeps himself safe").[257] (3) The idea of a believer being kept (or protected) by Jesus is found elsewhere in the New Testament (John 17:12; 1 Pet 1:5; Jude 24; Rev 3:10). It is therefore Christ's protection of the believer that allows the believer to keep the commands of God (3:24; 5:3).

Consequently, because of Christ's protection of the believer, "the evil one cannot harm him." The word translated ("harm") literally means "touch" *(haptetai)*. That is, the evil one is not permitted to touch the believer to the point of doing harm to him. Sin and its consequences are to

---

[252] The Gk. literally reads "does not sin" (ἁμαρτάνει, present active indicative). The NIV (correctly) inserts the words "continue to" into the text for the following reasons: (1) The present tense often carries with it a durative or progressive sense; and (2) John has earlier stated, "If we claim to be without sin, we deceive ourselves and the truth is not in us" (1:8) and that a "brother" may be guilty of sinning "a sin that does not lead to death" (5:16). If John means that Christians do not sin in any way, then he contradicts what he said previously in these verses. Rather, John is indicating that Christians do not sin in such a way as to be characterized by such behavior. They sin, but they are not in bondage to sin as to be controlled by its powers. "Sin and the child of God are incompatible. They may occasionally meet; they cannot live together in harmony" (Stott, *Letters of John*, 194).

[253] Smalley, *1, 2, 3 John*, 302.

[254] The NIV renders the adversative ἀλα ("but") with a semicolon, thus weakening its force.

[255] Brown, *Epistles of John*, 622; Schnackenburg, 252–54.

[256] Brooke, *Johannine Epistles*, 149; Bruce, *Epistles of John*, 126; Bultmann, *Johannine Epistles*, 88; Dodd, *Johannine Epistles*, 138; Smalley, *1, 2, 3 John*, 303; Stott, *Letters of John*, 194; Strecker, *Johannine Letters*, 208–9; Westcott, *Epistles of John*, 194.

[257] It should be noted that some Gk. manuscripts do contain a reflexive pronoun (ἑαυτόν, *heauton*, "himself"), but Brooke does not favor this reading since it is unlikely that ἑαυτόν would have been changed to the more difficult reading of αὐτόν (*Johannine Epistles*, 148–49). Also Burdick, *Letters of John*, 393; Stott, *Letters of John*, 194.

be taken seriously, but in Christ the child of God is given supernatural power to overcome sin and to obey the will of God. Stott comments, "The devil does not touch the Christian because the Son keeps him, and so because the Son keeps him, the Christian does not persist in sin."[258]

5:19 What was expressed in v. 18 is now enunciated in terms of a general principle. "We know that we are the children of God,[259] and that the whole world is under the control of the evil one." This is the second "we know" of vv. 18–20. God's people are comforted with the certainty that God is their Father and that he will protect them.

The second half of the assertion is that "the whole world is under control of the evil one."[260] Again, John's use of "the world" represents human society under the power of evil and at war with God and his people. "The evil one does not 'touch' the Christian, but the world is helplessly in his grasp."[261] There are only two possible positions. Everyone is either "of God" or "under the control of the evil one."[262] Neutrality is not possible.

5:20a John now gives the third ground for Christian confidence in vv. 18–20. Ultimately, a believer's assurance in grounded in the person and work of Jesus Christ, the Son of God. He states, "We know that the Son of God has come." Even though the verb "has come" *(ekei)* is present tense in the Greek, it has the force of a perfect.[263] Not only can we be sure that Christ came but also that he also "has given us understanding." Against the heretics who only claimed to have the proper understanding of things, John assures his readers that through faith in Christ they can take confidence in the truths of Christianity. The term *dianoia* ("understanding") occurs only here in John's writings and contains the notion of "reasoning which leads to perception."[264]

True believers are given this insight or understanding "so that they might know him who is true." John uses the word "true" three times in rapid succession. It should be noted that John does not say "so that they might know the truth," which might come across as abstract and be susceptible to Gnos-

---

[258] Stott, *Letters of John*, 195.

[259] Lit., "We know we are *of God*" (ἐκ τοῦ θεοῦ). The NIV adds "children of" to the verse (cf. 2:16; 3:9–10; 4:1–4,6,7; 5:1,4,18). The opposite is to belong to the evil one or the devil (3:8).

[260] Lit., "the whole world lies (κεῖται, *keitai*) in the evil one." Stott, *Letters of John*, 195–96, states that the world "is not pictured as struggling vigorously to be free but as quietly lying, perhaps even unconsciously asleep, in the embrace of Satan."

[261] Ibid., 196.

[262] Marshall argues that "mankind is divided into two camps, those who belong to God and those who belong to the evil one" (*Epistles of John*, 253).

[263] Smalley comments that this functional perfect indicates "the continuing effects of a past event (the incarnation)" (*1, 2, 3 John*, 306).

[264] Ibid. He also suggests that John is hesitant to use related terms such as γνῶσις ("knowledge") and νοῦς ("mind") "because of their potential misuse by heretics."

tic teachings. Rather, John proclaims that the object of this Christ-given knowledge is personal. John switches verbs for his second use of "know" (from *oidamen* to *ginōskōmen*), the latter focusing on experiential knowledge.[265] The phrase "him who is true" refers to God, the ultimate reality, and is contrasted with the "idols" of v. 21 (cf. John 17:3; 1 Thess 1:9).

(4) Keep Yourself from Idols (5:20b–21)

And we are in him who is true—even in his Son Jesus Christ. He is the true God and eternal life.
[21]Dear children, keep yourselves from idols.

5:20b Christians are said to be "in him who is true—even in his Son Jesus Christ" (cf. 1:3; 5:11). Being "in Christ" is the means by which the believer enjoys communion with God. Jesus is the mediator not only of the knowledge of God but also of intimate fellowship with God. As John has stated earlier, to know the Father is to know the Son (2:23). But one cannot know the Father without belief in his Son, who is the revealer of the truth.

The final phrase of this verse reads, "He is the true [i.e., real] God and eternal life." This phrase raises the problem: who is the antecedent to the pronoun, "he," Jesus or God the Father?[266] The arguments that it refers to Jesus include the following:[267] (1) "Jesus Christ" is the nearest antecedent to the pronoun. (2) It would be repetitive to state that God is "true" after having already stated that "who are in him who is true" earlier in the verse.[268] (3) Jesus was designated as the source of eternal life in 1:2 (cf. 5:12; John 11:25; 14:6). (4) First John 5:6 begins in the same way as this phrase *(houtos estin)*, and there it clearly refers to Jesus Christ. (5) John has referred to Jesus as "God" on other occasions (John 1:1,18; 20:28). Marshall rightly comments, "It is fitting that at the climax of the Epistle, as at the beginning and climax of the Gospel of John (Jn. 1:1; 20:28), full deity should be ascribed to Jesus."[269]

Others maintain that the text most naturally refers to God (the Father) for the following reasons: [270] (1) The word *houtos* does not necessarily refer to

---

[265] Smalley: "Whereas οἴδαμεν at the beginning of the sentence means 'we know' as a fact, ἵνα γινώσκωμεν ... signifies the ability to "know" in terms of an experiential relationship" (p. 306).

[266] The Gk. οὗτός lit. means "this (one)."

[267] Those who adopt this view include Brown, *Epistles of John*, 626, 640; Bruce, *Epistles of John*, 128; Bultmann, *Johannine Epistles*, 90; Marshall, *Epistles of John*, 254, n. 47; Plummer, *Epistles of S. John*, 128; Schnackenburg, *Johannine Epistles*, 262; Thompson, *1–3 John*, 147.

[268] Plummer states, "The Father having been twice called 'the true One' in the previous verse, to proceed to say of Him "This is the true God' is somewhat tautological" (*Epistles of S. John*, 128).

[269] Marshall, *Epistles of John*, 254, n. 47.

[270] Brooke, *Johannine Epistles*, 152; Dodd, *Johannine Epistles*, 140; Smalley, *1, 2, 3 John*, 308; Stott, *Letters of John*, 198; Westcott, *Epistles of John*, 196.

the closest antecedent (cf. 2:22; 2 John 7[271]) and therefore can refer back to God the Father. (2) It is John's style to repeat what has already been stated and then add to it. (3) The Father can more properly be described as the source of life (John 5:26[272]). Westcott paraphrases his understanding of the verse, "This Being—this One who is true, who is revealed through and in His Son, with whom we are united by His Son—is the true God and life eternal."[273] Although it is difficult to be absolutely certain, this second view is not as strong as the first. It is best to see this as the meaning: Jesus is the "true God and eternal life."

5:21 John does not end his epistle with a typical farewell but with a stern warning: "Dear children, keep yourselves from idols." This warning, however, is motivated by John's love for his readers. It also nicely contrasts with the last part of v. 20. Again he addresses them tenderly and affectionately as "Dear children" (*teknia*, cf. 2:12,28; 3:7,18; 4:4). It may appear that John's final address is somewhat anticlimactic, but in reality it confirms a very important truth he has been establishing in this last section of the epistle and in the entire epistle itself: Reject the false and embrace the real.

John commands his readers to keep or guard themselves "from idols." What are these "idols" (*eidolon*) against which the author is warning?[274] Many suggest that since the Roman Empire and its rampant paganism was dominant in the first century, John is warning against worshiping pagan idols that were such a large temptation to John's non-Jewish audience. Against such an interpretation are the following reasons: (1) The literal use of "idols" (*eidolon*) is rare in the New Testament. (2) It does not fit with the context of the epistle but would represent a change in thought. There-

---

[271] In both of these examples, however, οὗτός, in a sense, does refer back to the nearest antecedent if the entire clause is taken as the antecedent. In 2:22 it refers to "the one denying that Jesus is the Christ" (ὁ ἀρνούμενος ὅτι Ἰησοῦς οὐκ ἔστιν), and 2 John 7 refers to "the ones not confessing Jesus Christ having come in the flesh" (οἱ μὴ ὁμολογοῦντες Ἰησοῦν Χριστὸν ἐρχόμενον ἐν σαρκί).

[272] "For as the Father has life in himself, so he has granted the Son to have life in himself."

[273] Westcott, *Epistles of John*, 196.

[274] Brown considers the following ten possible interpretations of εἰδώλων: (1) Plato's designation of the "unreal"; (2) the images of pagan deities; (3) an abbreviated description of food dedicated to idols; (4) a compromise with paganism; (5) the mystery religions and their practices; (6) Gnostic ideologies or philosophies; (7) Jewish worship in the Jerusalem temple; (8) various sins; (9) anything that takes the place of God; and (10) teachings proposed by the false teachers (Brown's choice) (*Epistles of John*, 627–28). Also see J. Hill, who defends view (2) ("'Little children, keep yourselves from idols': 1 John 5:21 Reconsidered," *CBQ* 51 (1989): 285–310) and J. N. Suggit, who offers and defends an eleventh view. Suggit translates the verse, "Keep yourselves away from ghosts" ("1 John 5:21: TEKNIA, ΦΥΛΑΕΑΤΕ ΕΑΥΤΑ ΠΟ ΤΩΝ ΕΙΔΩΛΩΝ," *JTS* 36 [1985]: 386–90). He states that by this John "means to warn them against the imaginations of Docetics and those who deny the reality of the human life and the risen body of Jesus Christ" (p. 389).

fore, it is best to take "idols" as "anything which occupies the place due to God"[275] (cf. 1 Thess 1:9). This wider understanding of idolatry fits well with other texts of the New Testament (cf. Eph 5:5; Col 3:5).

In specific application and concern John, no doubt, would have in mind the "idols" of the heretical teachers who speak about a Jesus who is less than God. John is very disturbed by the false teachers that the god they proclaim is not merely less than perfect or close to what he holds but is altogether an idol. That is, their god is not real but the god of men's imaginations. As Marshall argues, "Having emphasized that Jesus is the true God, John warns against being misled into worship of any other alleged manifestation or representation of God."[276] Applying this text for today, Dodd gives the following exhortation: "It behooves the individual Christian to be on his guard against any such God-substitute, whether it be a political idea, or some fashionable cult, or merely the product of his own 'wishful thinking.'"[277]

Jesus Christ is the Son of God, who provides eternal life to anyone who comes to him in faith. He is the true revelation of God. Anything else is a counterfeit and a false substitute. On this truth one can be certain. On this truth John brings his letter to a close.

---

[275] Westcott, *Epistles of John*, 197.
[276] Marshall, *Epistles of John*, 255.
[277] Dodd, *Johannine Epistles*, 142.

2 John

INTRODUCTION

Second John is the second shortest book in the New Testament. It has only 245 words in the Greek text and would have easily fit on a single piece of papyri. Today we might call it (and 3 John) a "postcard epistle." It is an excellent example of hortatory (or exhortation) discourse, for the author's intent is to motivate his audience to action. The recipients must continue to walk in the truth, love one another, and be on guard against false teachers (e.g., the deceiver and the antichrist of v. 7).

The letter follows the normal epistolary pattern of the New Testament period with opening (salutation), body, and closing. The body of the epistle (vv. 4–11) consists of three sections that comprise the heart of the correspondence. Verse 4 introduces a commendation similar to that in other letters of the Greco-Roman culture. The two constituents that follow (vv. 5–6 and 7–11) contain three commands; one is located in vv. 5–6, and the other two are in vv. 7–11.[1] Although there are only two imperatives in the epistle: "watch out" (*blepete*) in v. 8 and "do not take" (*lambanete*) in v. 10, "Love one another" in v. 5 virtually bears an imperatival force, in part because of the close proximity of the word "command," which occurs four times in vv. 4–6.

John also builds this epistle around unifying key words. In these thirteen verses John repeatedly uses "truth" (five times), "love" (four times), "commandment" (four times), "walk" (three times), "teaching" (three times), and "children" (three times). He also utilizes a rare word, "antichrist," which appears in Scripture only in 1 and 2 John (see 1 John 2:18,22; 4:3; 2 John 7).

In essence, John tells his children to (1) walk in the truth, (2) obey the commandments, (3) love one another, and (4) guard the teachings of Christ so that they will not be deceived by antichrist. The spiritual safety of the believing community is confidently affirmed, being further heightened by the fact that John begins and ends his letter with a reference to their election or chosen position (vv. 1,13).

A first century letter, whether Christian or non-Christian, was different in form and structure from modern correspondence. Actually, the ancient pattern makes more sense because it identified the author at the outset. Jewish or Greek, an ancient epistle began with a salutation or word of introduction that followed a threefold formula of: (1) the name of the sender, (2) the name of the recipient, and (3) a word of greeting. The salutation was by no means merely perfunctory or insignificant. It would often establish the mood of the epistle and contain in "seed form" major themes or concerns the author wished to address.

1. The Salutation (vv. 1–3)

(1) The Sender (v. 1a)

[1]The elder,

1a This epistle is anonymous with the author providing as simple and

---

[1] G. E. Sherman and J. C. Tuggy, *A Semantic and Structural Analysis of the Johannine Epistles* (Dallas: International Academic Books, SIL, 1994), 105, 108. D. F. Watson has analyzed 2 John in the context of Greco-Roman rhetorical conventions. He concludes that the letter "conforms well to the conventions of the letter genre and Greco-Roman rhetoric with regards to matters of invention, arrangement and style ... 2 John is the product of the careful interweaving of the Greco-Roman rhetoric, especially as it pertains to the deliberative species, and epistolary conventions of parenetic-advisory letter, creating a reasonable attempt to persuade the audience to adhere to the commandment of love as the advantageous course of action to take in the face of the exigence posed by the secessionist" ("A Rhetorical Analysis of 2 John According to Greco-Roman Convention," *NTS* 35 [1989]: 129–30). Both discourse and rhetorical analysis, when utilized with appropriate caution, are proving to be fruitful avenues for further study of Holy Scripture. Their fruits are especially attractive when their observations and conclusions are mutually supportive of each other.

direct an identification as is found in the New Testament (this also is true of 3 John). This introduction of the author as "the elder" is unique to 2 and 3 John. "The elder" *(ho presbuteros)* emphasizes his position and personal relationship with the recipients of the letter. This is more important than his name. No doubt those receiving this letter were quite familiar with the author, and his title conveys the respect and authority he held with the "chosen lady and her children."

In its basic use "elder" simply means "an old or aged man." As utilized in the context of the Christian community, the word took on the meaning of one who possessed authority and leadership by virtue of his character, integrity, and moral standing. An elder[2] was a man whose life was exemplary and thus an example (1 Pet 5:3) worthy of the church's imitation.

The fact that the apostle John was by now an old man and that he also held a special position and authority as the last surviving apostle makes this title especially fitting. He had no need to assert his apostleship. That was common knowledge and he could appeal to them in a more tender fashion. His standing with those to whom he was writing was well established.

(2) The Recipient (vv. 1b–2)

To the chosen lady and her children, whom I love in the truth—and not I only, but also all who know the truth— [2]because of the truth, which lives in us and will be with us forever;

1b This is a unique designation for the recipient of a New Testament letter, and it has engendered significant discussion. Interpreters are divided over exactly who *eklektē kuria kai tois teknois autēs* is, and the following views have been offered:

1. It is a figurative reference to a local church and its members. Verse 13 would likewise refer to another local church.

2. It is a reference to the church universal (a view favored by Jerome).[3]

3. The recipient is an individual lady and her children.

The majority of scholars, especially recent ones, have favored the first option, believing the phrase to be a metaphorical or symbolic means of

---

[2] The word "elder: usually appears in the plural in the NT designating a plurality of leadership as a common pattern in the first century church (cf. Acts 11:30; 14:23; 20:17,18; 1 Tim 4:14; 5:17; Titus 1:5; Jas 5:14; 1 Pet 5:1). There is no warrant for reading into the word the idea of a monarchical bishop who exercised authority over a particular region. The weight of the NT is against this understanding. See G. Bornkamn, *TDNT* 6:651–83; L. Coenen, *NIDNTT* 1:188–201. Also note the discussion of R. Brown, *The Epistles of John,* AB (New York: Doubleday, 1982), 647–51.

[3] Jerome, "Letter cxxiii," in *Nicene and Post-Nicene Fathers,* 2nd Series, 6:234.

identifying a local church and its members.[4] This probably is the wisest option. Regardless of how one interprets these words, however, the basic application of the epistle remains unchanged. What the author would expect in belief and behavior of a lady and her children he would also expect of a local church and its members.

"Chosen Lady" is a term of endearment and respect. Lady *(kuria)* is the feminine form of "lord." Marshall notes that there may be a hint of the church as the bride of Christ (Eph 5:25–27; Rev 19:7–8) "so that her children are the spiritual offspring of the Lord and his church."[5] She is "chosen" because God elected her to belong to himself. God called the lady and those who comprise her family to be his own. The fact that she is chosen ["by God" is clearly implied] indicates the initiative of her election was with God and that her privileged position is not accidental. The spiritual status believers enjoy is the result of God's grace and goodness.

Two key words drive the early part of this letter: love *(agapē)* and truth *(alētheia)*. John wishes to establish an intimate connection with his readers considering the circumstances that have prompted this letter. His expression of love would certainly appeal to their heart and emotions and make them more receptive to the words he would share. "I" is emphatic, and "love" is in the present tense. "Whom I, myself, love as a constant expression of my

---

[4] The literature on the precise meaning of the "chosen lady" is extensive. I. H. Marshall points out that older scholars such as Plummer, Smith, Ross, and Morris understood the phrase as a literal designation of a woman and her children (*The Epistles of John,* NICOT [Grand Rapids: Eerdmans, 1978], 60, n. 5). D. E. Hiebert has recently made a strong case for this understanding, arguing that this is the most natural interpretation. He supports his position by noting that "the simplicity of the letter, the writer's reference to having met some of her children (v. 4), the mention of her sister's children (v. 13), the reference to the elect lady's house (v. 10), as well as the analogy of the third epistle, which certainly is addressed to an individual." Following the view of Athanasius (ca. A.D. 296–373), he believes "cyria" *(kuria)* to be her personal name (*The Epistles of John* [Greenville: Bob Jones University Press, 1991], 282–83). D. Burdick is also sympathetic to this view (*The Letters of John the Apostle* [Chicago: Moody, 1985], 415–17). E. S. Fiorenza has even argued that the elect lady is a woman who heads her own house-church and that the elder has "no power to command but 'begs' or 'entreats'" (*In Memory of Her* [New York: Crossroad, 1987], 248). J. Lieu makes a similar observation but offers no specific evidence (*The Theology of the Johannine Epistles* [New York: Cambridge, 1991], 3). In opposition to this view A. E. Brooke lists at least four arguments: (1) the general character of the epistle implies a group of believers; (2) the language of vv. 1–3 and the conclusion of v. 13 fits a community better than an individual; (3) perhaps most significant, the interchange of singulars and plurals in vv. 4,5,8,10,12 and the language of v. 5 indicates teaching for the whole church, not just an individual (*The Johannine Epistles,* ICC [Edinburgh: T & T Clark, 1948], 167–70). J. R. W. Stott adds in this context, "There are no obviously personal references in this letter, as there are in the third, viz. to Gaius, Diotrephes and Demetrius" (*The Letters of John,* rev. ed., TNTC [Grand Rapids: Eerdmans, 1988], 204). He also notes the consistent use of the second personal singular in 3 John. Brown also provides a good survey of the various interpretive offerings (*Epistles of John,* 652–55).

[5] Marshall, *Epistles of John,* 60–61.

heart" is what John is saying. Even if the letter contains some "hard sayings," his affirming love should move them to hear what he has to say.

If love would appeal to their hearts, then truth would appeal to their minds. The neglect of this epistle throughout the history of the church has been unfortunate because no letter more beautifully balances the twin Christian graces of "love" and "truth." Paul admonished the Ephesians to speak the truth in love (Eph 4:15) in the context of each member of the body doing his part as the church grows and matures. John's concern is certainly corporate, but it is also relational and individual. John loves this community personally and devotedly. As a good elder his heart is knit to theirs. This is not mere sentiment and emotion. Truth is the framework, the principle, that guides and gives genuine meaning to his expression of love. In the absence of truth, true love is not present. John knew that both love and truth are essential and not optional.

John will go on to explain that love walks in obedience to God's commands and is expressed in relation to one another (in this context note Paul's magnificent description of love in 1 Cor 13:4–8). Truth, interestingly, is related to both belief and behavior. John's interest in truth is not so much philosophical as it is spiritual and personal. Truth is that which is embodied in Jesus Christ (John 14:6), who he is and what he has done. John is especially concerned with the person of Christ in this letter (v. 7).

Truth mattered to John. If deception and error slip into a fellowship, the results are always tragic and devastating. The reason for this commitment to the truth is that the truth has seized them as a permanent and abiding reality.

In the past John and his fellow witnesses came to "know the truth." The result of that experience has stayed with them to the present and will remain with them forever. "All" is used in a general sense and is not specific. John is simply affirming that those who "know the truth" as a practice of their Christian faith do love each other.

2 In a sense John provides his own commentary concerning the significance of the aorist tense of the word "know" in v. 1. Two things are affirmed: (1) the truth lives or remains *(menousan)* in us as the community of faith devoted to the Father and his Son, Jesus, and (2) this truth literally "with us will be unto the ages" (eternally). The truth of God the Father revealed in his Son Jesus is truth that has an abiding reality. It has come to stay. It is dynamic and personal, for it lives in us. God's revelation of himself is something we now possess as our very own. It is also ours in assurance. Smalley points out that this phrase "adds an important eschatological dimension."[6] "With us" is brought to the front in the Greek text. It is the truth that will be with us, truth that is eternal, truth that is abiding and unchanging because its source is the one

---

[6] S. S. Smalley, *1, 2, 3 John*, WBC (Waco: Word, 1984), 320.

true God. Hiebert writes, "In saying 'with us,' John again joins himself with those who have this blessed assurance for the future."[7] Our security is as sure as the truth and character of God. His truth will forever remain in us and with us as a constant companion. As we renew and appropriate this wonderful truth on a daily basis, we equip ourselves to stand against the deceivers and false teachers who would snatch away the abundant reward God has for his children (v. 8).

(3) The Greeting (v. 3)

[3]Grace, mercy and peace from God the Father and from Jesus Christ, the Father's Son, will be with us in truth and love.

3 Though he has followed the pattern of a typical first century letter, John's greeting is filled with Christian graces and a subtle but significant theological affirmation. John's greeting is similar to those in Paul, though his inclusion of "mercy" is paralleled only in 1 Tim 1:2 and 2 Tim 1:2 (see also Jude 2). John does not express a wish in this greeting, for he is confident these Christian blessings "will be with us," which appears first in the Greek text for emphasis. John again identifies himself with his audience as one who, like them, is a recipient of God's favor.

John offers a triple blessing, beginning with grace *(charis)*. "Grace" is God's unmerited and undeserved kindness, which he freely bestows on persons who are unworthy of such attention. It is everything a holy and righteous God does for sinners that they do not deserve. Mercy *(eleos)* occurs only here in the entire Johannine corpus. It speaks of God's compassion and pity, his tenderness and readiness to forgive sin. Peace *(eirēnē)* is a Hebrew concept emphasizing wholeness and well-being of life in all its aspects. It conveys ideas such as safety, rest, and the absence of hostility (cf. Rom 5:1; Phil 4:9). Grace is God doing for us what we do not deserve, mercy is his not doing to us what we do deserve, and peace is God giving us what we need based upon his grace and mercy. The word order is significant. God's grace is always prior. Mercy and peace flow from it.[8]

John points out that these Christian graces come *from* God the Father and *from* Jesus Christ, the Father's Son. The repetition of the preposition "from" is important. It places the Father and Son on an equal standing and at the same time distinguishes their separate personhood. Jesus Christ is

---

[7] Hiebert, *Epistles of John*, 293.

[8] Grace, mercy, and peace are important words in the rich vocabulary of the Christian faith. On "grace" see W. Zimmerli and H. Conzelmann, *TDNT* 9:372–402 and H. H. Esser, *NIDNTT* 2:115–24; on "mercy" see R. Bultmann, *TDNT* 2:477–485 and H. H. Esser, *NIDNTT* 2:593–601; on "peace" see G. Von Rad and W. Foerster, *TDNT* 2:400–417 and H. Beck and C. Brown, *NIDNTT* 2:776–83.

God the Father's Son, but he is also God. Spiritual blessings flow equally from the Father and the Son. What we receive from the Father we receive from the Son. What we enjoy from the Son we likewise enjoy from the Father. Any theology that would set the Father in opposition to the Son is faulty theology. There is a oneness of essence and purpose as God the Father and God the Son unite in extending grace, mercy, peace, love, and truth to their children.

God's title as Father takes on new meaning in the coming of his Son, in the person of Jesus Christ (John 1:14,18). God is a good Father who desires to have a loving, intimate, and personal relationship with all people. The beautiful relationship that exists between the Father and the Son is a picture of the relationship God desires to have with us.

"Jesus" is the human name of our Lord, the Greek counterpart to the Hebrew "Joshua." The name is descriptive of why the Son came into the world and took upon himself a sinless human nature (Matt 1:21), for it means "the Lord saves." Christ is equivalent to the Hebrew "Messiah" and means "the anointed one." Jesus is God the Father's Son, his Messiah/Christ.

The greeting closes with the repetition of the words "truth and love." The placement of these words here allows John to emphasize their importance through bracketing (see v. 2) and prepares the readers for the main theme of the epistle. To maintain a healthy and growing community the church must exhibit a fidelity to the truth that knows no compromise, and they must love one another in a way that knows no boundaries. Grace, mercy, and peace "flourish in an environment where truth and love prevail. Truth unites the Christian community when it faces the common foe of falsehood; it is evident among Christians when they demonstrate their unity in showing love toward one another."[9]

2. Walking in Truth and Love (vv. 4–6)

The body of the epistle evenly divides into two parts: (1) vv. 4–6 and (2) vv. 7–11. The first section is structured around significant vocabulary such as "walk(ing)," "truth," "command(ed)," "beginning," and "love." The word "truth" provides a bridge or connection between vv. 3–4.

Coherence and contrast tie the body of the letter together. The letter's three commands (implied in v. 5 and overtly stated in vv. 8–10) develop out of the twin themes of truth and love. The first command to "love one another" is basic to the Christian worldview because it was "from the beginning" (v. 5; also v. 6). The second command, "watch out" (v. 8),

---

[9] S. J. Kistemaker, *James and I–III John,* NTC (Grand Rapids: Baker, 1986), 376.

comes immediately after John exposes the false teachers and their defective Christology. It serves as an internal protection against loss of reward that results when one embraces false teaching (loss of truth). The third command, "do not take him" (v. 10), demands a complete rejection and severance from the wicked actions (disobedience) of the false teachers. It serves as an external defense against those enemies who are outside the Christian community.

There are also several significant contrasts that unite the body of the letter. Sherman and Tuggy suggest five:

1. Those who walk in truth (v. 4a) vs. those who reject the truth (v. 7) and fail to continue in the teaching of Christ (v. 9);
2. The command received in the beginning (vv. 5c, 6b) vs. the teaching which has gone beyond Christ (v. 9);
3. Work to be rewarded (v. 8) vs. wicked works (v. 11);
4. Those who continue in Christ vs. those who do not (v. 9);
5. Those who refuse to welcome a false teacher vs. those (at least hypothetically) who welcome a false teacher (vv. 10–11).[10]

John's letter is both a message of exhortation and a message of warning.

(1) Walking in Truth (v. 4)

⁴It has given me great joy to find some of your children walking in the truth, just as the Father commanded us.

4 The elder begins the heart of the epistle on a positive note, with a word of encouragement and an expression of personal joy. He wishes to continue the warm affection established with his readers in the opening three verses, thereby preparing them for the harsh warnings that will follow. Many a minister would do well to follow the wise strategy we see here (note Paul's similar approach concerning the "Onesimus affair" in his letter to Philemon).

John rejoices because of a good report he has received concerning these believers (see 3 John 3). There is a depth of intensity to the joy John has experienced upon discovering that members of this community are walking in truth.[11] "Find" is in Greek a perfect tense (lit., "I have found"), suggesting that the time of John's discovery was in the past but also that he believes their walking in the truth continues.

How did John discover these things about the chosen lady's children? The text does not say. Perhaps he had actually met some of them and discovered firsthand their commitment to obey the Father. News may have reached him by a report from visitors or traveling missionaries. Regardless

---

[10] Sherman and Tuggy, *Semantic and Structural Analysis,* 109.

[11] There is no definite article before "truth."

of how the information arrived, this community had cultivated a reputation for devotion to the truth of God.

Some students of Scripture have emphasized the word "some" and taken it to mean that certain children were walking in the truth but that others were not. John may only be referring to those children whom he had actually met, however, and that they constitute "some" of the total fellowship. Given the positive and encouraging thrust of v. 4, to read a negative judgment between the lines seems unnecessary and unwarranted.[12]

"Walking in the truth" indicates that truth is both what we believe and how we live. It is doctrine and duty, creed and conduct. The wonderful Baptist preacher Vance Havner used to say: "What we live is what we believe. Everything else is just religious talk."

John notes that walking in the truth is a commandment we received from the Father. It may be that he is alluding to 1 John 3:23.[13] Any other attempt to specify a canonical reference is difficult to support. It may be that John's intent is simply to stress the ultimate source (the Father) of the message (to love one another) and to remind us to whom we are ultimately accountable.[14]

(2) Walking in Love (vv. 5–6)

5And now, dear lady, I am not writing you a new command but one we have had from the beginning. I ask that we love one another. 6And this is love: that we walk in obedience to his commands. As you have heard from the beginning, his command is that you walk in love.

5 Verse 5 contains a vocative, a form of address. The word "dear" is not in the original text, although its addition captures the elder's intent. Understanding "lady" as referring to a local congregation, the words that follow are for the whole body of believers. The gentle and sensitive approach taken by John again ensures that he will gain a receptive hearing.

"And now" has a logical force flowing from the previous commendation of v. 4. Since they are walking in the truth, John is confident they will wel-

---

[12] R. Brown provides a strong argument for the positive understanding on three points: (1) the author probably would not speak of those not walking in the truth as "children" of the chosen lady; (2) this verse is basically a thanksgiving concerning the healthy status of the church; and (3) his concern for any improvement in their situation comes in the next verse (*Epistles of John*, 661). Actually any serious concerns expressed by the author do not come until vv. 7ff. Still, Brown's overall argument is sound and supports our understanding of the text.

[13] This would support the priority of 1 John.

[14] Burdick notes that there is no specific command in Scripture to walk in truth but that John may have in mind the "general teaching of Scripture." He alludes to such texts as John 3:21 and 1 John 1:6; also Exod 20:1–17; Mic 6:8; 1 Pet 1:15–16 (*Letters of John*, 423). This interpretation has much to commend it.

come his call to "love one another." John does not have a new word for this congregation. This sets him apart from the "deceivers" of v. 9, who boast of something more, something new. John is not one who believes old is always bad and new is always better. Truth is truth regardless of its age, for all truth ultimately finds its source in God.

The command "we have had from the beginning" (a favorite and recurring phrase in the epistle of 1 John) is simple and worthy of being repeated: "We should love one another." What John means by "from the beginning" may bear the same meaning in each instance, although each occurrence should be evaluated in context. Here John seems to be referring to the origin of the Christian faith itself embodied in the person of Jesus Christ. On the night of his betrayal he admonished the disciples saying, "A new commandment I give: Love one another" (John 13:34). "Love" *(agapōmen)* is a present tense verb, so John calls for consistent expression of the "love ethic" toward one another. Seeing that these words were voiced by our Savior the night before he died adds special weight to them. In using the word "ask," John appeals to their heart. Genuine affection undergirds the request.

Verses 4 and 5 should be linked closely together. Walking in the truth (obedience) and love for one another go hand in hand. The absence of one will ensure the absence of the other. In addressing the issue of love Marshall notes: "Christians must love one another. This is the basis of Christian living to which all believers constantly need to be recalled. For the elder it meant practical, *costly caring* [emphasis mine] for the needy, even readiness to sacrifice oneself for the sake of others (1 John 3:16–18), but at the same time it included real affection for one's fellow-believers."[15]

6 John is rapidly approaching the main purpose of the epistle, and he gently, yet strategically, moves his readers forward. "He" has great joy in them (v. 4), and the command to love one another is one that is obligatory for John also (v. 5).

The command to love one another is strengthened in vv. 5–6 through the literary device of chiasmus:

A command (5b)
  B love (5d)
  B′ love (6a)
A′ commands (6b)

Love is a multifaceted concept in John that receives different emphases depending upon the need of the audience. The initial phrase of v. 6 raises an important question: Who is the object of "this love"? Is it God, each other, or both God and fellow believers? If John is focusing upon the believer's rela-

---

[15] Marshall, *Epistles of John,* 67.

tionship to the Father, we prove our love by obeying him (cf. 1 John 5:3). If our brothers and sisters in Christ are intended, we show our love for them by keeping God's commandments (cf. 1 John 5:2). It seems best to combine these two options and see the whole family of God as the object of love made evident by obedience to the commands of God. "Walk" is in the present tense and thus conveys the idea of consistency of life. Because we love God, we want to please him. When we love others, we are obeying him.

The alternate use of "command" (singular) and "commands" (plural) has arrested the attention of numerous scholars. The word *commandment* would seem to imply a specific referent in mind: "walk in the truth," "love one another." *Commandments* represent the broader requirements and expectations of God.[16]

Verse 6 ends ambiguously. The phrase "heard from the beginning" is clear enough. It most probably refers to the beginning of their Christian experience, an experience rooted in the gospel message itself. The Greek text, however, ends not with the word "love" but the word "it." A translation that reads "his command that you walk in it" is more true to the original text. The question then is to what does "it" refer? Three options are possible: (1) command, (2) love, and (3) truth. "Command" is the most logical since it is the nearest antecedent, but this creates a tautology (e.g., This is the commandment ... that you walk in the commandment).[17] Most commentators opt for "love," with some marshalling a chiastic argument for support (love - commands - command - it [love]).[18] Von Wahlde points out, however, that nowhere in the entire Johannine corpus is there an example of the phrase "to walk in love." He proceeds to argue for "truth" as the antecedent of "it" in spite of the fact that it appears forty-six words earlier. He notes that clearly the major theme of 2 John is truth and the true message about Jesus. Hence the idea of "it" referring to "truth" prepares the way for the heart of the epistle (vv. 7–11), and it allows John to conclude this section by returning it the idea of walking in truth.[19]

---

[16] U. C. von Wahlde has noted that "the plural of *commandment* always occurs in instances of general exhortation whereas the singular is used in cases where a specific command is referred to. This provides a consistent explanation of the usage throughout the Johannine literature. Thus the singular is used with "walking in truth" (a single commandment) in v. 4; with "loving one another" in v. 5 (a single commandment); and with "walking in it" in v. 6e (a single commandment); but the plural is used in the general exhortation of v. 6b" ("The Theological Foundation of the Presbyter's Argument in 2 John [2 Jn. 4–6]," *ZNW* [1985]: 216). John uses the singular in 1 John 2:7,8; 3:23; 4:21; 2 John 4,5,6. He uses the plural in 1 John 2:3,4; 3:22,24; 2 John 6. Note also John 13:34; 14:15,21; 15:10,12.

[17] Brown, *Epistles of John,* 667–68; Brooke, *Johannine Epistles,* 174.

[18] F. F. Bruce, *The Epistle of John* (Grand Rapids: Eerdmans, 1970), 140; Burdick, *Letters of John,* 424; Marshall, *Letters of John,* 68; J. R. W. Stott, *The Letters of John,* rev. ed., TNTC (Grand Rapids: Eerdmans, 1988), 210.

[19] Ibid., 217–24. Note also the extensive discussion of Brown, *Epistles of John,* 666–68.

3. Guarding the Truth about the Son (vv. 7–11)

The elder now comes to the heart of his message. This pericope confronts a docetic heresy, an incipient or proto-Gnosticism that denied (or radically reinterpreted) the cardinal doctrine of the incarnation. Verses 7–9 parallel 1 John 2:18–27; 4:1–3. It would seem that in all three texts the same group of false teachers is in view. Because of distance and the immediate danger of infiltration by these deceptive prophets, John writes with a sense of urgency and in a tone quite different from the earlier portions of the letter. Two imperatives mark the strategy that must be employed: (1) "Watch out" (v. 8) and (2) "do not take him into ..." (v. 10). Special attention must be given to the historical context of John's counsel, especially the latter admonition in v. 10. It has too often been taken out of context, with unfortunate and inappropriate results.

(1) The Deceivers and the Antichrist (v. 7)

⁷Many deceivers, who do not acknowledge Jesus Christ as coming in the flesh, have gone out into the world. Any such person is the deceiver and the antichrist.

7 Verse 7 begins with a coordinating conjunction *(hoti)* absent in the NIV text. It means "because" or, perhaps more accurately in this instance, "for." It links the two sections together (vv. 4–6 and 7–11). The church is walking in truth and loving one another, something that brings "great joy" (v. 4) to the heart of the elder. Danger is lurking about, however, in the form of false, deceptive teaching that could divide and disrupt the church.

The danger is real and immediate. Many deceivers have defected, leaving the confines of the believing community and going forth into the world. "World" *(kosmos)* in this context may stand for that evil, organized system in hostile opposition to God (cf. 1 John 2:15–17). It also may simply refer to the world at large. Stott thinks the statement is a deliberate "reminiscent of the mission of Christ and of his apostles. Christ was being aped by antichrist."[20] Here are Satan's missionaries on assignment.

The error of the false teachers struck at the very heart of the Christian faith: the doctrine of Christ and, specifically, the incarnation. Their failure to pass the Christological test is evident, for they failed to "acknowledge Jesus Christ as coming in the flesh."

Caution must be exercised in identifying the deceivers of 2 John. Full-blown Gnosticism did not appear until the second century. What we encounter in John's epistles is an incipient, early stage of development. It does seem clear that John was dealing with some type of docetism that "denies the fleshiness of Jesus Christ."[21] *Dokeō* in Greek means "to seem or appear." Influenced by neo-

---

[20] Stott, *Letters of John,* 210.
[21] D. M. Smith, *First, Second, and Third John* (Louisville: John Knox, 1991), 144.

platonic dualism, docetism taught that a dichotomy existed between "evil matter" and "good spirit," which had significant implications for Christology. The Christ-spirit or Son of the Father (uniquely emphasized in 2 John) could not become contaminated with evil flesh. At worst, it would only assume it temporarily. At best, the Christ-spirit would give an appearance of taking on the physical, but in reality this would be an illusion or apparition.[22]

Much has been made of the fact that John uses the present tense in this Christological confession. Literally the verse reads, "Jesus Christ coming in flesh." "Coming" is a present active participle. This stands out in remarkable contrast to the affirmation of 1 John 4:2, where the text states that "Jesus Christ *has* [emphasis mine] come in the flesh." There the perfect active participle is used.[23] The key, it seems, is to discover what John is affirming. Here in 2 John the emphasis falls on the abiding reality of the incarnation. First John 4:2 teaches that the Christ, the Father's Son (v. 3), has come in the flesh. Second John affirms that the wedding of deity and humanity has an abiding reality (cf. 1 Tim 2:5).[24] The ontological and essential nature of the incarnation that would receive eloquent expression one thousand years later in the writing of St. Anselm (1033–1109) in his classic *Cur Deus Homo* is already present in seed form in the tiny and neglected letter of 2 John.[25]

---

[22] "The deceit so roundly spoken against has to be a failure to assert the Christological faith of the John circle, here primarily concerned to affirm the reality of Jesus Christ as fully human. We are right to call the opponents docetists without knowing precisely what subtle distinctions their teaching embraced" (G. S. Sloyan, *Walking in the Truth* [Valley Forge: Trinity, 1995], 64–65).

[23] G. Strecker believes the change in tense is significant and argues that the opposition confronted in 2 John is different from the defectors of 1 John. In 1 John there is Christological error. In 2 John there is eschatological confusion. Second John is looking forward to the second coming of Christ, not back to the incarnation. The elder affirms "a future eschatological expectation, directed toward a messianic reign to be established on the earth. ... He is concerned with earthly reality, the empirical fact of the substance of apocalyptic hope. The "deceivers," by contrast, deny the real substance of the apocalyptic expectation" (*The Johannine Letters,* Her, ed. H. Attridge [Minneapolis: Fortress, 1996], 233–36). Though ably argued, this view has not received strong support. It discovers a problem that was real enough in the late second and third century and then relocates it in 2 John, where it does not belong.

[24] Brooke argues that by use of the present tense "the confession is taken out of all connection with time and made timeless. In the First Epistle stress was laid on the historical fact and its permanent consequences. Here the writer regards it as a continuous fact. The Incarnation is not only an event in history. It is an abiding truth. It is the writer's view that humanity has been taken up into Deity. The union is permanent and abiding" (*Johannine Epistles,* 175).

[25] "Therefore, none but God can make this satisfaction. ... But none but man ought to do this, otherwise man does not make the satisfaction. ... If it be necessary, therefore, as it appears, that the heavenly kingdom be made up of men, and this cannot be effected unless the aforesaid satisfaction is made, which none but God can make and none but man 'ought to make, it is necessary for the God-man to make it'" (Anselm, *Cur Deus Homo in St. Anselm's Basic Writings* [Las Salle: Open Court, 1962], 244–45). J. Calvin (1509–64) understood the essential nature of the incarnation similarly when he wrote in Book Two, chap. 12 on *The Knowledge of God The Redeemer:* "1. Only he who was true God and true man could bridge the gulf between God and ourselves. 2. The Mediator must be true God and true man. 3. Only he who was true God and true man could be obedient in our stead. 4. The sole purpose of Christ's incarnation was our redemption" (*Institutes of the Christian Religion,* 2 vols., in The Library of Christian Classics [Philadelphia: Westminster], 1:464–67).

John identifies the false teachers in harsh and uncompromising terms: "this one is the deceiver *(planos*[26]*)* and the antichrist *(antichristos)*." Westcott points out, "The idea of the 'deceiver' is mainly relative to men: that of 'antichrist' to the Lord."[27] "Deceiver" addresses their actions. They lead astray and place in danger those who believe their message. It is not accidental that John uses the word twice in this verse, at the beginning and the end. Their numbers are many and their message destructive (cf. v. 8). Yet their true colors are seen in what they stand against: they are *antichristos*. They are in active opposition to Christ. They proclaim a message of heresy and error. Although it is clear that John anticipates the coming of an eschatological embodiment of evil, the Antichrist, here in 2 John he affirms that his forerunners have already made their debut. His concern is their false message and attack on the person of Jesus Christ. They are *against* the Lord. The idea of one who attempts to take the place of Christ is not addressed here.[28]

The elder was well aware of the fact that what one believes about Jesus will impact other areas of his theology. Indeed it will shape his entire worldview. The beliefs one holds about the Bible, God, humanity, creation, sin, and salvation will be shaped by what is believed about Jesus Christ. These traveling missionaries were false teachers who posed great danger for the church. As Polhill asserts, "They are assuming the guise of Christian teachers but are actually the enemies of Christ."[29]

(2) Warning to Be on Guard (vv. 8–9)

[8]Watch out that you do not lose what you have worked for, but that you may be rewarded fully. [9]Anyone who runs ahead and does not continue in the teaching of Christ does not have God; whoever continues in the teaching has both the Father and the Son.

8 Verse 8 is a call to vigilance in light of the danger addressed in v. 7. The verse itself has several textual issues that must be addressed, though the NIV rendering is well supported.[30]

"Watch out" is the only Johannine use of *blepete* to signal a warning.[31] Jesus used the word several times to warn his disciples about those who

---

[26] A. T. Robertson notes the word πλάνος [from which we get our word "planet"] means "wandering, roving" (WP, 6:252).

[27] B. F. Westcott, *The Epistles of St. John* (New York: Macmillan, 1905), 229.

[28] See in the appendices a fuller analysis of the origin and theology of antichrist.

[29] J. Polhill, "An Analysis of II and III John," *RevExp* LXVII, No. 4 (1970): 464.

[30] Marshall summarizes the issue and supports the NIV text (*Epistles of John,* 72, n. 11). See also the judgment of K. Grayston, *The Johannine Epistles*, NCBC (Grand Rapids: Eerdmans, 1984), 155. Hiebert provides commentary on each of the possible readings (*Epistles of John,* 304).

[31] Grayston, *Johannine Epistles*, 154.

might deceive them (Mark 8:15; 12:38; 13:23; cf. also Heb 3:12). As noted earlier, *blepete* is a present active imperative. The elder's audience must be on constant guard. There is no place for complacency. There is always a seductiveness to false teaching that can lure one into a stupor if he is not careful.

John is concerned that they not lose the things for which they have labored so that a full reward might be received. This verse must be interpreted in the context of what follows in vv. 9–11. Even then the theological issue at stake is not perfectly resolved. Some scholars believe loss of salvation is in view, especially when v. 9 is considered. Others, however, believe the danger is a loss of reward in the context of Christian service. They think vv. 10–11 support this interpretation. The tension one senses at this point is reminiscent of the warning passages of Hebrews (Heb 2:1–4; 3:7–4:13; 5:11–6:12 [esp. 6:4–6]; 10:19–39 [esp. 10:26–31]; 12:14–29). How the verse is understood certainly will be influenced by the theological commitments one brings to the text.

It does seem clear that for John perseverance is the proof of possession. To stay with Christ gives the clearest evidence that one belongs to Christ. To cling to him and him alone is the surest and only path to receiving all that God has provided. John is pastoral at this point of the letter. Entailed in the warning is also a word of encouragement. If you remain alert and on guard, you will stay with Christ and receive a full reward. Standing with him proves you truly belong to him. To turn aside and give an ear to false teaching can only result in loss. To walk away and not continue with Christ proves you never received him in the first place (v. 9).[32]

9 The dual themes of warning and promise now come to a climax. The phrase "runs ahead" translates the present active participle of *proago*. It means "to go beyond," "to go too far," "to go or run on ahead," "to be progressive." Used figuratively, John may be borrowing from the vocabulary of the Docetists, who fancied themselves as advanced or enlightened thinkers.

When someone adds to the biblical testimony of Jesus Christ, a subtraction from the truth of who he is and what he did is inevitable. John knows this very well and condemns these self-professed progressives in the stron-

---

[32] Marshall says, "It is hard to be sure that he [the elder] excludes the possibility of genuine believers embracing heresy" (*Epistles of John,* 72). Stott, on the other hand, says, "The thought is not of their winning or losing their salvation (which is a free gift), but rather their reward for faithful service" (*Letters of John,* 213). T. Schreiner has investigated how the tension between God's threats and promises might be more profitably understood. He concludes "that God's electing and sustaining grace is such that His sheep will never perish. They never perish precisely because they listen [continue!] to the Good Shepherd's voice which effectively admonishes and warns them lest they fail to follow Him and perish" ("Perseverance and Assurance: A Survey and Proposal," *SBJT,* Vol. 2, No. 1 [1998]: 32–62).

gest terms. The elder would not say that all advancement or progress is bad, but any development in theology that does not continue (*meno,* "to abide or remain") in the teaching (*didache,* "doctrine") of Christ[33] is to be condemned and rejected without compromise. These "spiritual know-it-alls" have run on ahead and left both the Son and the Father behind. There has been no true progression but a fatal and flawed digression.

The elder could not state in clearer terms the intimate relationship that exists soteriologically between the Father and the Son. Without question there is no place in his theology for any type of universalism or inclusivism. Anyone who rejects the apostolic witness to Jesus Christ forfeits any potential relationship with the one true God. The elder's perspective on this is in perfect harmony with what Jesus himself said and taught (John 14:6). To reject the Son is to reject the Father who sent him (1 John 4:10). John's interest is not mere sterile orthodoxy but vital, experiential truth. To abide in the teaching of Christ is to walk in the truth (v. 4). To deny the teaching about Christ is to walk in error.[34] In a real sense it is to call the Father a liar and reject his witness concerning his Son (John 5:37–38).

There is a positive side to the antitheses John constructs, and he closes v. 9 with that emphasis. The genuine believer abides, remains in the orthodox teaching about Christ. He affirms his unique person and divine work and rests in it. The result is that he has both the Father and the Son. This is the third time in this short letter the elder has used the word "Father" and the second time he has emphasized the Father-Son relationship (cf. v. 3). This union cannot be separated or redefined. It is vital to Christian orthodoxy and experience. We receive both together or we receive neither. The exclusivity of this Christian claim could not be stronger.

(3) Warning to Refuse Assistance to False Teachers (vv. 10–11)

[10]If anyone comes to you and does not bring this teaching, do not take him into your house or welcome him. [11]Anyone who welcomes him shares in his wicked work.

---

[33] "Teaching of Christ" is either a subjective genitive (teaching from Christ) or an objective genitive (teaching about Christ). The context strongly favors the latter. Bultmann notes, "It is more probable, that 'of Christ' is an objective genitive, since the author hangs everything on his christology, i.e. on the doctrine about Christ, as v. 7 shows" (*Johannine Epistles,* 113). Burdick, Marshall, Smalley, and Strecker also agree with this judgment, though it is surprising to discover the majority of commentators understand the construction in the subjective sense.

[34] "John is not condemning advanced thinking; he is not saying that Christian doctrine must be a static thing in which there is no advance; but he is saying that Jesus Christ must be the touchstone of all thinking, and that which is out of touch with Christ can never be right" (W. Barclay, *The Letters of John and Jude* [Edinburgh: The Saint Andrew Press, 1958], 167).

10 Having laid the theological foundation, John moves to provide practical instruction. This verse, perhaps more than any in the epistles of John, is open to abuse and misunderstanding if removed from its immediate context. So strong is its prohibition that some have deemed it unloving and worthy of rejection. C. H. Dodd believes the elder is addressing an emergency situation, but even taking that into consideration, he feels compelled to reject his counsel.[35] Barclay affirms Dodd's judgment that "emergency regulations make bad law and that love must find a way."[36] These judgments, however, totally miss John's point and do not consider the historical situation. The elder is not demanding that they refuse to engage in conversation with someone who is spiritually confused. He is not saying you cannot invite them into your home for a visit where you confront them with the claims of Christ. What he is saying is that we are not to provide support and aid (e.g., a place to stay and money) to anyone who is spreading false teaching and disseminating error.

"If anyone comes" assumes the reality of what is asserted. "The Greek wording suggests that the possibility of such an 'invasion' is more than hypothetical."[37] "Do not take" is a present imperative. They must not open their homes to any such persons and give them a base of operation to spread their heresy. The unloving thing would be to assist and accommodate their error. A strong stand of opposition to these evangelists of error is essential for the health of the church.

"Do not welcome him," though often used as a word of greeting, functions here as a farewell. We cannot pray God's blessing upon those who deny the Lord and reject the faith.[38] We may and should pray for their conversion and that the Holy Spirit would remove their spiritual blindness.

11 This verse is interesting in the original text. More literally it says, "For the one saying to him rejoice, fellowships in his evil works." "Shares" *(koinōneo)* is a present tense verb denoting continuous action. Wicked *(ponēros)* is placed at the end of the verse for emphasis. The word translated "welcome" *(chairein)* means something like "God bless" or "may it go well." It is an expression of affirmation and support. John says there is to be no encouragement whatsoever. Showing hospitality or verbal agreement would be to participate in their evil work. Although there is to be no rudeness on the part of a believer, neither is there to be the slightest encourage-

[35] Dodd, *Johannine Epistles,* 152.

[36] Barclay, 169. Note also the contributions of Brown, *Epistles of John,* 691–93. His partial support of Dodd is unfortunate.

[37] C. C. Black, *The First, Second and Third Letter of John,* in The New Interpreters Bible, vol. XII (Nashville: Abingdon, 1998), 454. John uses εἴ with the indicative.

[38] See the appendix "Welcoming False Teachers into Your Home" for a historical and practical analysis of this issue.

ment to these teachers who spread the cancer of false teaching. The issue of truth is crucial. It must be preserved at all cost. To act in any other manner would be to invite spiritual suicide.[39]

4. The Conclusion (vv. 12–13)

[12]I have much to write to you, but I do not want to use paper and ink. Instead, I hope to visit you and talk with you face to face, so that our joy may be complete.

[13]The children of your chosen sister send their greetings.

12–13 Second and Third John close in a similar fashion. In both the elder's pastoral heart shines. John desires for this congregation to have as their last thoughts from this letter his affection and love. He has much to communicate to them because his concern for them is great. Indeed putting it down on paper (papyrus), though helpful, is not sufficient. He must come and see them.

There is a beautiful Greek idiom in v. 12. "Face to face" is literally "mouth to mouth" *(stoma pros stoma)*. The intimacy of the desired meeting is evident. All ministers of the church should care for their people with such heartfelt love and commitment.

One cannot but notice the contrast between the reception John anticipated and the rejection of the deceivers. John's visit would result in a fullness of joy for all. "May be complete" is a perfect passive participle and speaks of the joy being experienced in the most complete and full measure.[40] John has great confidence in this people. He believes in them and their devotion to the truth concerning Christ.

The letter closes with either a greeting from a sister church or the elect lady's actual sister. This affectionate word adds support to the elder's letter. It also adds a further personal communication. Like John's recipients, she is also chosen *(eklektēs)*, the object of God's gracious pleasure. Thus the letter ends with a reference to the same idea with which it began (inclusio). "The affectionate tone and the restraining of further advice (v. 12b) so that it may be given in person (v. 12c) for the completion of their mutual happiness (v. 12d) corresponds to the love expressed in vv. 1 and 4 (and, in fact, throughout the letter)."[41] Second John was meant to warn. The epistle was motivated by love.

---

[39] D. Jackman, *The Message of John's Letters* (Downers Grove: InterVarsity, 1988), 185.

[40] "Our" joy is to be preferred over "your." See Hiebert, *Epistles of John,* 313, n. 69.

[41] Sherman and Tuggy, *Semantic and Structural Analysis,* 120.

3 John

───────────── **INTRODUCTION** ─────────────

Third John is the shortest book in both the New Testament and the Bible. It is only 219 words in the Greek text. Third John and 2 John are rightly described as "twin epistles," though they should be viewed as fraternal and not identical. There are both similarities and differences between the two as the following charts indicate:

Similarities in 2 and 3 John

1. The author describes himself as "the elder" (2 John 1; 3 John 1).
2. The recipients are those whom he "loves in the truth" (2 John 1; 3 John 1).
3. The recipients are the occasion of "great rejoicing" (2 John 4; 3 John 3).
4. The recipients "walk in the truth" (2 John 4; 3 John 3).
5. The elder has received good reports about both (2 John 4; 3 John 3,5).
6. Both letters contain a warning (2 John 8; 3 John 9).
7. The elder desires to see both face to face (2 John 12; 3 John 14).
8. Others sent their greetings (2 John 13; 3 John 14).

235

The structure of the two letters overall is also quite similar. The brevity of each would have allowed them to fit on a single piece of papyrus paper.

The Structure of the Two Letters

2 John	3 John
Greeting/Salutation	Greeting/Salutation
vv. 1–3	vv. 1–4
An exhortation to love	An exhortation to love
vv. 4–6	vv. 5–8
Warning concerning false teachers	Warning concerning Diotrephes
vv. 7–9	vv. 9–10
Charge to reject the false teachers	Commendation to receive Demetrius
vv. 10–11	vv. 11–12
Conclusion with greetings	Conclusion with greetings
vv. 12–13	vv. 13–14

There are also some significant differences between the two letters. Again, a comparative chart is helpful in clearly identifying these.

2 John	3 John
Written to a lady and her children (feminine; a church) 2 John 1	Written to an individual (male) 3 John 1
Some children walk in truth 2 John 4	Gaius and the elder's children walk in truth 3 John 3–4
A request follows the "great joy" affirmation 2 John 5	The "great joy" declaration has witnesses 3 John 3
The problem is with many deceivers (from without) 2 John 7	The problem is with one (Diotrephes from within) 3 John 9
Written to one considering entertaining the wrong visitors	Written about one refusing to entertain the right visitors

2 John 10–11	3 John 10
Do not receive false teachers 2 John 10–11	Welcome strangers 3 John 5
Truth is the major emphasis	Love is the major emphasis
Anyone not abiding in the teachings of Christ does not have God 2 John 9	Anyone who does evil has not seen God 3 John 11
Anyone who continues in the teaching has both the Father and the Son 2 John 9	Anyone who does what is good is from God 3 John 11
No personal names (like 1 John)	Three personal names (Gaius, Diotrephes, Demetrius)[1]

Third John is a personal letter that revolves around three individuals: Gaius (the recipient), Diotrephes (the troubler), and Demetrius (probably the bearer of the letter). Like its twin 2 John, it follows the ancient epistolary form more closely than any of the other New Testament letters. It contains a word of exhortation to Gaius, encouraging him not to imitate the bad example of Diotrephes but to continue the good work he is doing receiving and supporting the traveling teachers/missionaries.[2] The letter follows the basic epistolary pattern with an introduction (vv. 1–4), body (vv. 5–11), and a conclusion (vv. 13–14). A prominent structural feature is the repetition of the address "Dear Friend" *(agapēte)* in vv. 2,5,11 (cf. 2 John 5). This is followed in each case by a direct personal comment. In v. 2 there is a prayer or

---

[1] Aspects of these comparisons were gleaned from R. Funk, "The Form and Structure of II and III John," *JBL* 86, no. 4 (1967): 424–30 and J. Polhill, "An Analysis of II and III John," *RevExp* LXVII, no. 4 (1970): 461–71.

[2] G. Sherman and J. C. Tuggy, *A Semantic and Structural Analysis of the Johannine Epistles* (Dallas: Summer Institute of Linguistics, 1994), 124. Using rhetorical categories, D. Watson classifies the letter as "epideictic rhetoric ... because Gaius does not need to be persuaded of the necessity of extending hospitality, but only to adhere more clearly to that conviction" ("A Rhetorical Analysis of 3 John: A Study in Epistolary Rhetoric," *CBQ* 51 (1989): 500. Watson also points out that "3 John is a mixed letter, for it exhibits characteristics of several types of letters including the friendly, the requesting, the advisory or paraenetic, the commendatory, the praising, the encouraging, the vituperative, and the accusing" (p. 482). Funk ("Form and Structure of II and III John," 430), S. S. Smalley (*1, 2, 3 John*, WBC [Waco: Word, 1984], 342), and B. Olssen call 3 John "the most secularized letter in the New Testament" ("Structural Analyses in Handbooks for Translators," *BT* 37, no. 1 [1986]: 124).

wish for the welfare of Gaius; in v. 5 there is a commendation of his work; and in v. 11 there is personal counsel expressing desired behavior. The negative *motivational basis* (vv. 9–10) has neither "Dear Friends" nor a positive personal comment and is thus very different in content from the rest. Therefore, it is set off from the *appeal* paragraphs of the *body*.[3]

Though vv. 1–4 clearly function as the salutation, it is possible to outline the letter for teaching purposes around the four (counting the elder) personalities of the book. Verses 1–8 contain a multifold commendation of Gaius. Verses 9–10 condemn the high-handed and malicious autocracy of Diotrephes. Verses 11–12, taken as a unit, praise the godly Demetrius. Verses 13–14 close with a glimpse into the heart of the elder. Four men and their reputations (growing out of their behavior) constitute the sum and substance of 3 John.[4]

John again constructs this letter with the building blocks of key word repetition: "beloved" (four times; vv. 1,2,5,11); "truth" or "true" (seven times; vv. 1,3 [twice],4,8,12 [twice]); "witness" (five times; vv. 3,6,12[three times]). The elder is understandably concerned that his authority is being challenged. He fears the powerplay of Diotrephes may succeed and that others might be influenced by him. He will come if necessary for a face-to-face meeting where he will personally deal with the situation. In the meantime, John seeks to enlist the support of Gaius. He praises him for his past labors and encourages him to continue. Demetrius comes to Gaius both as the bearer of the letter and a reinforcement in the crisis. Third John provides insight into a personality conflict that arose at the end of the first century and the strategy adopted by the elder to resolve it. Clearly then there is much that is valuable for our consideration in this letter. The church has neglected it for too long—at its own expense.

1. The Greeting (vv. 1–4)

Third John follows the typical pattern of the ancient epistle (as does 2 John; see comments at v. 1). The author wishes to establish positive and friendly affection with his reader. Adopting the letter writing style of the day, the greeting consists of three basic parts: (1) identification of the author and his recipient (v. 1), (2) a blessing or expression of good wishes (v. 2), and (3) a greeting or word of praise (vv. 3–4).

---

[3] Sherman and Tuggy, *Semantic and Structural Analysis,* 124.

[4] For other structural/outline assessments see Funk, "Form and Structure of II and III John," 429, Smalley, *1, 2, 3 John,* 343, R. Brown, *The Epistles of John,* AB (New York: Doubleday, 1982), 739–51, 788–95.

(1) The Sender (v. 1a)

[1]The elder,

1a This letter begins in the same way as 2 John with the author simply identifying himself as the elder (see the comments on 2 John 1). He writes on his own authority[5] and with a sense of authority. The elder, whom I believe to be John the apostle, rightly held a position of theological, moral, and pastoral leadership over the churches of the Lord Jesus Christ. The apostle Peter used a similar title when addressing a group of elders in his first epistle (1 Pet 5:1). Men of respect and authenticity with a solid "track record" could rightly identify themselves by this term *(ho presbuteros)*.[6]

(2) The Recipient (v. 1b)

To my dear friend Gaius, whom I love in the truth.

1b The letter is addressed to a man named Gaius. This is the only epistle of John addressed to an individual by name. In this regard it is similar to Paul's letter to Philemon. "Gaius" was a common name in the Roman Empire of the first century, and three men by that name appear in the New Testament: Gaius of Corinth (Rom 16:23). Gaius of Macedonia (Acts 19:29), and Gaius of Derbe (Acts 20:4). Because the name was common, it is unlikely the Gaius of 3 John should be identified with any of these.[7] To my "dear friend" *(tō agapētō)* appears four times in the letter and at significant locations (vv. 1,2,5,11). The term appears on six occasions in 1 John.[8] "Dear friend" is probably too weak to convey the affection the term bears. The elder desires to express deep and genuine love for this man. Gaius[9] is near and dear to his heart. He is loved by John.

To reinforce his affection and go beyond typical convention the elder

---

[5] This is seen in his use of the first person singular in vv. 1,2,3,4,9,10,13,14; cf. C. Kruse, *The Letters of John* (Grand Rapids: Eerdmans, 2000), 220.

[6] For a lengthy discussion of the various positions on "the elder" see Brown, *Epistles of John*, 648–51. Brown believes the elder was "a disciple of the disciples of Jesus and thus a second-generation figure who served as a transmitter of the tradition that came down from the first generation" (p. 650). His influence would be more along the lines of "a prophetic witness" (p. 651). The view of this respected scholar and those who follow him are not convincing.

[7] I agree with Brown (*Epistles of John*, 702), A. E. Brooke (*The Johannine Epistles*, ICC [Edinburgh: T & T Clark, 1912], 182), and others that the tradition in the *Apostolic Constitutions* (7.46.9) that John ordained Gaius as bishop of Pergamum is without sufficient evidence. That it is an accurate tradition is certainly possible. The information available is simply not adequate to make a firm judgment.

[8] 1 John 2:7; 3:2,21; 4:1,7,11.

[9] Smalley (*1, 2, 3 John*, 344) notes that Gaius's name is Roman in origin and that he was possibly a former pagan; he rightly affirms that the communities over which John exercised oversight were no doubt Jewish and Gentile in makeup.

adds (lit.) "whom I myself love in truth." The "I" is emphatic. John has in mind a love which is a companion to the truth of the Christian faith.[10] Truth is an important theme, for it is mentioned seven times in this brief letter (vv. 1,3,[twice],4,8,12[twice]). Love does not function as some disconnected emotion with no substance or content. Without truth it will devolve into mere sentimentalism. Love and truth are necessary companions. They go together. They work together. They must stay together. John expresses sincere love flowing from both heart and head, a love rooted in him who is the "truth" and "true God" (John 14:6; 1 John 5:20).

(3) The Blessing (Prayer-Wish) (v. 2)

[2]Dear friend, I pray that you may enjoy good health and that all may go well with you, even as your soul is getting along well.

2 After an initial greeting, John moves to express his good wishes for Gaius in the form of a brief prayer. He begins by again expressing his love and affection through the second use of *agapēte* ("dear friend"). In Greek concerning "all things" is put first in the sentence for emphasis: "Concerning all things [John] prays that [Gaius] may prosper and be in health just as his soul prospers" (my translation). The word "prosper" (translated "all may go well with you" in the NIV) can mean "to have a good journey." Here it is used metaphorically.[11] John asks God for the best in every way for Gaius. Further, he specifically prays for "good health."[12] It is clear that Gaius was a man with a clean bill of health spiritually. That he was also in good health physically is not so certain given John's request. It should be noted that to pray or wish for someone "good health" was a common feature of the letters of this day. Brown points out we need some type of contextual clue to see a definite and specific request for the good health of someone who is ill.[13] What we can be certain of is that Gaius was thriving spiritually. He was in the best sense of the phrase a man of God.

John's prayer-wish should give us pause. What if such a prayer was made to God for me and it was answered? What condition would I find myself in physically and spiritually? Compare your bodily health to your spiritual health. Dare we hope or pray for ourselves or others in this manner? The order is not insignificant. The spiritual is indeed "the standard of measurement for the physical."[14]

---

[10] I. H. Marshall, *The Epistles of John,* NICOT (Grand Rapids: Eerdmans, 1978), 82.

[11] Ibid., 83.

[12] The word is ὑγιαίνειν. In English the word has come over as "hygiene" (see also Luke 5:31; 7:10; 15:27).

[13] Brown, *Epistles of John,* 703.

[14] D. E. Hiebert, "An Exposition of 3 John 1–4," *BibSac* (1987): 62.

(4) Word of Praise (vv. 3–4)

³It gave me great joy to have some brothers come and tell about your faithfulness to the truth and how you continue to walk in the truth. ⁴I have no greater joy than to hear that my children are walking in the truth.

3 There is ample evidence that Gaius was "soul healthy." The elder had received a report from itinerate teachers concerning Gaius. It was a source of "great joy" *(echarēn lian)* to the elder.[15] The report was that Gaius was in the truth and walking in the truth. The emphasis is twofold. First, he was faithful in what he believed. Second, he was faithful in how he lived. In doctrine and deed Gaius was commendable, praiseworthy, and consistent. To walk in the truth is to conduct one's life in the truth. It is to flesh out in conduct one's confession. Loyalty to Christ and the gospel marked his life.[16] Gaius continued to do the truth he had been taught.

4 Verse 4 reinforces v. 3. It also carries the word of praise *(exordium)* a step further. In v. 3 the elder has "great joy." In v. 4 he now has "no greater joy."[17] The elder is enthusiastic and emphatic in his joy over what he hears concerning Gaius. The life of Gaius and his service for the Savior are of the greatest joy to John. "Children" of course is plural and is regularly used by Paul in referring to his own converts (1 Cor 4:14; Gal 4:19; Phil 2:22).[18] That the elder views Gaius as one of his children could indicate he was responsible for leading Gaius to faith in Christ.[19] It is also possible John simply has in mind all believers who are under his pastoral care.[20] Regardless of the view taken, John's point is clear. He experiences supreme joy when it is reported to him that those under his watchcare are walking in the truth. To walk in the truth means to know it, believe it, and live it. As Stott writes: "Whoever walks in the truth is an integrated believer in whom there is no dichotomy between profession and practice. On the contrary, there is in him an exact correspondence between creed and conduct."[21]

---

[15] "Joy" is a theme that is emphasized at the beginning of all three letters of John (1 John 1:4; 2 John 4; 3 John 3–4). Kruse points out "this is one piece of evidence which suggests that one person wrote all three letters (*Letters of John*, 221, n. 6).

[16] Bruce, *Epistles of John*, 148. "Faithfulness … expressed itself in practice" (D. Burdick, *The Letters of John the Apostle* [Chicago: Moody, 1985], 449).

[17] Smalley notes μειζοτέραν ("greater") appears only here in the New Testament (*1, 2, 3 John*, 348). Brown says the word is a "Hellenistic double comparative … the least one may say is that the Presbyter is being emphatic" (*Epistles of John*, 706).

[18] Marshall, *Epistles of John*, 84.

[19] This is the view of Bultmann, Kistemaker, and Westcott.

[20] So Brooke, Brown, Bruce, Burdick, Lenski, Grayston, Smalley, and Stott.

[21] J. R. W. Stott, *The Letters of John*, rev. ed., TNTC (Grand Rapids: Eerdmans, 1988), 224. See also our comments at 2 John 4.

2. Commendation of Gaius's Hospitality (vv. 5–8)

[5]Dear friend, you are faithful in what you are doing for the brothers, even though they are strangers to you. [6]They have told the church about your love. You will do well to send them on their way in a manner worthy of God. [7]It was for the sake of the Name that they went out, receiving no help from the pagans. [8]We ought therefore to show hospitality to such men so that we may work together for the truth.

The body of the epistle can be divided into three fairly even sections, each revolving around the main characters of the letter. The elder continues his praise of Gaius, specifying his faithfulness in showing hospitality to traveling teachers/missionaries (vv. 5–8). He then addresses the arrogant and abusive behavior of Diotrephes (vv. 9–10). He concludes with a word of praise for Demetrius (vv. 11–12). Within this last section is the main exhortation of the book: "Do not imitate what is evil but what is good."[22] We will basically follow our more "biographical analysis," which still takes into account rhetorical and discourse insights.

5 For the third time John calls Gaius his "dear friend" *(agapēte)*. He praises him for his faithfulness in showing hospitality to Christian brothers who are traveling about preaching the gospel, even though he did not know them personally.[23] "You are faithful" *(piston poieis)* means literally "a faithful thing you do." Hiebert notes: "The present tense is a compliment to Gaius, indicating that the expected hospitality is in keeping with his established practice, which John highly appreciated. He characterizes it as 'a faithful thing, an act becoming a faithful man.'"[24] That Gaius would treat strangers in this faithful manner is a further testimony of the fact that he was walking in the truth. He did not know them, but did know they were from John and that they proclaimed the same gospel of Jesus as he did. That was enough for Gaius. To provide food, lodging, money, encouragement,

---

[22] Watson breaks vv. 5–12 into two sections: (1) vv. 5–6 *(narratio)* and (2) vv. 7–12 *(probatio)*, 486–500. Sherman and Tuggy argue unconvincingly that the body has "a major chiastic structure" *(Semantic and Structural Analysis,* 127–28).

[23] Kruse notes, "When one reads 3 John alongside 2 John, it becomes apparent that two groups of missionaries were moving around among the churches" *(Letters of John,* 222).

[24] D. E. Hiebert, "An Exposition of 3 John 5–10," *BibSac* (1987): 195. Also see Brown's extended discussion of πιστὸν ποιεῖς and its "possible theological overtones" *(Epistles of John,* 708). He believes "Gaius is praised for acting as a true believer, conformable to a faith *(pistis)* that is showing itself in works."

and stand for them before the community was his pleasure.[25]

6 It was natural, perhaps obligatory, for the itinerate teachers to report back to the home base their reception and treatment by Gaius. They provided a glowing report worthy of the elders' earlier accolades. John informs Gaius that before the church they gave witness of his love. A form of the word translated "told" *(martureō)* occurs five times in the letter (vv. 3,6,12[three times]). "Church" *(ekklēsia)* occurs three times in this letter (vv. 6,9,10) and only in 3 John in the Johannine material, excluding Revelation. Here it refers to a local body of believers, most likely the church in which the elder himself was a member. "Love" *(agapē)* describes the acts of hospitality extended by Gaius to the stranger. No doubt at personal sacrifice, he had cared for and assisted these traveling evangelists. In word and deed he had ministered graciously to their needs (cf. 1 John 3:16–18). Thus he displayed true Christian love. His actions stood in stark contrast to those of Diotrephes.

The last phrase of v. 6 is somewhat complex grammatically though the meaning is clear. Literally the verse reads "whom well you will do sending them forward worthily of God." The phrase "whom well you will do" is an idiom meaning "please." It is a polite request.[26] In it John expresses his confidence that Gaius will continue the good work he is already doing. "Sending them forward" became something of a technical term in the context of the missionary work in the early church.[27] These brothers were on

---

[25] B. J. Malina, "The Received View and What It Cannot Do: III John and Hospitality," *Sem* 35 (1986): 171–94 is an excellent article about hospitality in the Mediterranean/Near Eastern world. Kruse provides an excellent summary of the article (*Letters of John*, 215–16):

Hospitality might be defined as the process by means of which an outsider's status is changed from stranger to guest. … [It] is not something a person provides for family or friends but for strangers. They need such hospitality, for otherwise they will be treated as nonhuman because they are potentially a threat to the community. Strangers had no standing in law or custom, and therefore they needed a patron in the community they were visiting. … Hospitality was not reciprocated between individuals … but it was reciprocated between communities. And it was to the strangers' own community that they were obliged to sing the praises of their hosts if they had been treated well (cf. 3 John 5–8) and to which they would report adversely if they had not been welcomed properly (cf. 3 John 9–10). Communities would repay hospitality to strangers from another community if that community had treated their own people well. Letters of recommendation were important in the matter of hospitality. Their function was to help divest the stranger of his strangeness. … To refuse to accept those recommended was to dishonor the one who commended them, and in the Mediterranean culture of the first century the one dishonored had to seek satisfaction or bear the shame heaped upon him by the refusal of his commendation.

This helps us greatly in putting III John into its proper *Sitz im Leben* (life setting).

[26] Marshall, *Epistles of John,* 85; Hiebert, "An Exposition of 3 John 5–10," 198.

[27] The word is προπέμψας (cf. Acts 15:3; 20:38; 21:5; Rom 15:24; 1 Cor 16:6, 11; 2 Cor 1:16; Titus 3:13). See Hiebert, "An Exposition of 3 John 5–10," 198; Kruse, *Letters of John,* 223; Brown, *Epistles of John,* 711; Polhill, "An Analysis of II and III John," 467–68.

assignment for the gospel. As faithful missionaries and ministers of the
Word, it was right to help them as they moved on to their next assignment.
"In a manner worthy of God" probably modifies both the work of Gaius and
the traveling missionaries.[28] All partners are to do their share in a way that
is worthy of the God they serve. Nothing less than their best is expected (cf.
1 Cor 10:31).

7 This verse (and v. 8) provides the rationale for Gaius's help in v. 6:[29]
"For on behalf of the Name they went forth" (my translation). "The Name"
of course is the name of Jesus Christ.[30] These missionaries have gone out
representing and proclaiming the Lord Jesus Christ as Savior. Though it
may be subtle and inferential, the exclusivity of the gospel is certainly in
view. There is one Name and only one Name that they proclaim. Interestingly, this is the only time the Lord Jesus is mentioned in 3 John (and indi-
rectly at that).

"They went forth" affirms they were sent out. In context it is from John
that they have come. But it is for Jesus, the Name, that they go.[31] As they
went, they received nothing from the pagans. The word for "pagans" *(eth-
nikōn)* is usually a reference to the Gentiles. Here it is used of unbelievers
as a whole in contrast to Christians. The traveling emissaries of Jesus Christ
did not seek to finance the work by appeals to the lost for their money. They
depended, and rightly so, on the generosity and gifts of fellow believers.
Polhill points out: "Peripatetics were not exclusive to Christianity. Hellenistic street preachers often took advantage of hospitality and even expressed
pride in their success at fleecing the countryside. This is probably why 'they
received nothing from the heathen' (v. 7), so as not to be identified with that
sort of abuse. The same sort of refusal to claim provisions in order to avoid
all possible stumbling blocks was practiced by Paul as Corinth (1 Cor 9:15–
18)."[32]

8 John offers his third and final reason for Gaius and others to help
traveling evangelists who preach the gospel of Jesus Christ. "We" is gram-

---

[28] Brown, *Epistles of John,* 711.

[29] Brooke, 185. Kruse identifies three reasons it was appropriate for Gaius to assist the traveling
missionaries: (1) it was for the sake of the Name; (2) they received nothing from the pagans; and
(3) by helping these in their ministry, we become fellow workers for the truth (*Letters of John,* 223–
24).

[30] "Name" is a metonymy for Jesus Christ (cf. Acts 5:40–41; 9:16; 15:26; 21:13; Rom 1:15;
Phil 2:9). See Brown for interpretative options of how "the Name" should be understood (*Epistles
of John,* 711–12). His decision to see "the Name" as representing both the name of God and Jesus
is plausible, but not convincing.

[31] Kruse notes that " the expression 'go out' *(exerchomai)* is found four times altogether in the
Johannine letters, and in the other three places it is used in reference to the secessionists" (*Letters
of John,* 223–24).

[32] Polhill, "An Analysis of II and III John," 467. See also Stott, *Letters of John,* 226–27.

matically emphatic. "Ought" *(opheilomen)* speaks of an obligation. It is our dutiful responsibility. The verb is present tense and speaks of a continual obligation. Unlike the false teachers of 2 John 11, who deny "the Name" and therefore should be refused hospitality, these men are faithful to "the Name" and deserve assistance. As we support such persons, "we become coworkers in the truth" (a more accurate translation than the NIV). We may not physically go where they go, but when we support them, we go with them anyway. We work together, as one, for the truth. Some give support and some are sent. Both are essential.

Brown provides a fine summary of what it means to be coworkers for the truth:

> Jesus is the truth; those who believe have dwelling within them the truth revealed in Jesus; it is not an inert principle; and there is a Spirit of Truth within the believer interpreting the Truth: This Spirit bears witness on behalf of Jesus; and the Spirit does this in and through Christians (John 15:26–27). Missionaries who "set out for the sake of the Name" are allowing the truth that is within them to find a voice and are the instruments of the Spirit of Truth. By helping them as an act of love, Christians like Gaius are coworkers of the truth.[33]

Would that our God would multiply both "the sent" and "the supporters." Gaius is a wonderful model for the latter.

3. Condemnation of Diotrephes' Behavior (vv. 9–10)

[9]I wrote to the church, but Diotrephes, who loves to be first, will have nothing to do with us. [10]So if I come, I will call attention to what he is doing, gossiping maliciously about us. Not satisfied with that, he refuses to welcome the brothers. He also stops those who want to do so and puts them out of the church.

The letter now takes a striking and unexpected turn. Everything has been positive and glowing through v. 8. A situation, however, came to the elder's attention that demands a response. Indeed if it were not for this problem, it is unlikely 3 John would have been written. Diotrephes has refused the missionaries sent from John. This would have been embarrassing to John and culturally shameful.[34] To do nothing would be to accept the dishonor leveled at him by Diotrephes and to allow a spiritual crisis to go unchecked. John was of no mind to allow either. One of the "sons of thunder" now responds in a way that is in keeping with his old nickname.

9 John begins this section of the letter by informing Gaius that he had

---

[33] Brown, *Epistles of John,* 715.

[34] Malina, "The Received View and What It Cannot Do," 171–89; also Kruse, *Letters of John,* 225. Both Malina and Kruse are to be commended for their excellent contribution at this point.

written a previous letter to a church, but he had encountered trouble from a man named Diotrephes. This is the only mention of Diotrephes in the New Testament, and so our knowledge of him is limited. We can, however, construct a basic outline. His name was probably not all that common,[35] and it would indicate he had come out of the pagan world.[36] He had a position of leadership in a local church in the city or area where Gaius lived. Whether they were members of the same church is not stated, but given the information we have in 3 John it would seem unlikely. The elder had written an earlier letter to "the church" (not Diotrephes). That letter is probably lost. Its contents can only be vaguely surmised.[37] It would seem to have contained recommendations for traveling teachers sent from John that would encourage the church of Diotrephes to extend to them hospitality. Apparently Diotrephes either intercepted the letter or, once it was read, led a movement to reject the elder's appeal.[38]

Why did Diotrephes reject John's letter and the teachers he sent? John provides his judgment in the text with unreserved boldness: "The one loving to be first among them, Diotrephes, does not receive us" (literal translation). The verb translated "loves to be first" (philoprōteuon) is unique and found only here in the New Testament. The word has an interesting etymology.[39] The NKJV translates it "who loves to have the preeminence." Colossians 1:18 states that only Christ rightly deserves the preeminence (prōteuōn). Diotrephes usurped for himself the position only our Lord should hold. He loved being the leader and exercising authority. Amazingly, even the apostle John had nothing he wanted. "He will have nothing to do with us" (ouk epidechetai hēmas) is literally "he will not receive us." His refusal to provide hospitality for the traveling missionaries was not just a rejection of them. It was also a rejection of the elder himself. Kruse notes, "This way of thinking is common in the Fourth Gospel, where to receive

---

[35] So Brown (Epistles of John, 716), and Stott (Letters of John, 228) who appears to follow Findlay on this point. R. Schnackenburg says the name "was not unusual" (The Johannine Epistles [New York: Crossroad, 1992], 297).

[36] The exact meaning of his name (which bears no significance to the conflict) is interesting. Stott (Letters of John, 228), Robertson (WP 6:263) and Burdick (Letters of John, 454) say it means "Zeus-reared, nursling of Zeus." Brown opts for the more general "God-nurtured" (Epistles of John, 716).

[37] G. Strecker's position that the letter is 2 John is unlikely and not widely held. The simple fact that there is no request for hospitality in 2 John is sufficient to set aside his view (actually 2 John encourages refusal and hospitality to the deceivers and antichrists) (The Johannine Letters, Her [Philadelphia: Fortress, 1996], 253–54).

[38] Ἔγραψά τι is literally "I wrote something" and indicates the letter was probably of modest size (see Hiebert "An Exposition of 3 John 5–10," 203; Marshall Epistles of John, 88, n. 1).

[39] See Kruse's (Letters of John, 226) fine discussion of the word in his text and at n. 16; also Brown, Epistles of John, 717.

the ones sent is the same as receiving the one who sent them (cf. John 5:23; 12:44–45; 13:20; 14:24)."[40] Diotrephes wished to put space between himself and John, between "his church" and John's influence. Plummer adds: "Perhaps the meaning is that Diotrephes meant to make his church independent [for whatever reason]: hitherto it had been governed by S. John from Ephesus, but Diotrephes wished to make it autonomous to his own glorification. Just as the antichristian teachers claimed to be first in the intellectual sphere (2 John 9), so the unchristian Diotrephes claimed to be first in influence and authority."[41]

John addresses the spiritual aspect of the problem from his perspective: Diotrephes is prideful and self-interested. This still leaves unanswered the precise nature of the conflict. Historically what was the particular issue that caused the conflict? Numerous interpretations have been offered, which I will briefly summarize.

1. *Conflict over ecclesiastical authority.*—Diotrephes was perhaps the first monarchical bishop (so Harnack, who did not believe the elder was the apostle John) who acted dictatorially and abused his powers.[42] J.-W. Taeger takes the opposite position and argues that it was the elder who was guilty of pushing his authority on another church.[43] Brown believes Diotrephes was caught in the middle of the secessionist schism reflected in 1 and 2 John. Without sufficient information to decide, he simply shut the doors to all.[44]

2. *Conflict over doctrinal orthodoxy.*—Diotrephes was guilty of the heresy condemned in 1 and 2 John.[45] E. Käsemann turns the argument around and says it was the elder who was guilty of heresy and that Diotrephes was the defender of the orthodox tradition. Strecker also defends this position.[46]

3. *Conflict due to misunderstanding.*—R. Price provides a complex reconstruction (as well as an overview of competing theories) that sees two groups of missionaries coming from the elder. One had adopted a heretical (docetic) Christology without the elder's knowledge. They came to

---

[40] Kruse, *Letters of John*, 227. See also M. M. Mitchell, "Diotrephes does not receive us": The Lexicographical and Social Context of 3 John 9–10," *JBL* 117 (1998): 229–320.

[41] A. Plummer, *The Epistles of S. John* (1886; reprint, Grand Rapids: Baker, 1980), 149.

[42] A. von Harnack, "Über den dritten Johannesbrief," *TU* 15 (1897): 3–27.

[43] J.-W. Taeger, "Der konservative Rebell: Zum Wilderstand des Diotrephes gegen den Presbyter," *ZNW* 78 (1987): 267–87. See also M. R. Storm, "Diotrephes: A Study of Rivalry in the Apostolic Church," *ResQ* 35 (1993): 193–202.

[44] R. Brown, *The Community of the Beloved Disciple* (New York: Paulist, 1979), 160–61; also Brown, *Epistles of John*, 738.

[45] W. Bauer, *Orthodoxy and Heresy in Earliest Christianity* (Philadelphia: Fortress, 1971), 93; also B. Bonsack, "Der Presbyteros des Johannes," *ZNW* 79 (1988): 45–62.

[46] E. Käsemann, "Ketzer und Zeuge: Zum johanneischen Verfasserproblem," *ZTK* 48 (1951): 292–311; Strecker, *Johannine Letters*, 261–63.

Diotrephes' church, who rightly refused them but wrongly assumed they represented the elder's teaching. A second orthodox group came from the elder to Diotrephes who again rejected them assuming they also held to a defective Christology. In reverse order the elder penned a lost letter (see 3 John 9), 3 John, 2 John and 1 John. The elder and Diotrephes were reconciled between 3 John and 2 John.[47]

J. Lieu believes it is impossible to attempt any "confident reconstruction."[48] This is wise counsel. It does seem we may conclude that the issue was not doctrinal. There is not a hint of doctrinal controversy in the letter, and it is scarcely imaginable that if this were the problem the elder would not have mentioned it. It would seem the problem was personal and spiritual. Diotrephes[49] arrogantly refused the elder's request to provide hospitality to the brothers (v. 10). We do not know the reason. His refusal did, however, raise the issue to an ecclesiastical level as well as one of personal respect and honor for the elder. Given his responsibilities for the churches under his watchcare, John would need to respond, and respond he did.

10 John lodges four specific charges against Diotrephes in this verse: (1) he is gossiping maliciously about us; (2) he refuses hospitality to the traveling teachers; (3) he prevents others in the church who want to from doing so; and (4) he attempts to put out of the church those who extend hospitality.[50] "If" is not intended to cast doubt. It means "whenever."[51] When he comes, he will bring up and address the actions ("works," *erga*) of Diotrephes (probably intended to be a public rebuke; cf. 1 Tim 5:20). These actions include "gossiping maliciously" *(logois ponērois phluarōn)*. The verb "gossiping" occurs only here in the New Testament and is in the present tense. Diotrephes was making evil accusations, unjustified charges. He was talking nonsense and "spouting silliness." There was an emptiness to what he said[52] as well as a vicious and wicked intent. John no doubt deemed his opponent's words to be slanderous and without foundation.

There is a digression in Diotrephes' behavior. What began as ambition

---

[47] R. M. Price, "The Sitz-im-Leben of Third John: A New Reconstruction," *EvQ* 61 (1989): 109–19.

[48] J. Lieu, *The Second and Third Epistles of John* (Edinburgh: T & T Clark, 1986), 163; also Schnackenburg, *Johannine Epistles,* 297; Polhill, "An Analysis of II and III John," 470.

[49] Polhill refers to Diotrephes as a "sinister figure" ("An Analysis of II and III John," 468). It is difficult to contain one's laughter (tragic though it is) at the personal comment of A. T. Robertson (*WP* 6:263) concerning Diotrephes: "Some forty years ago I wrote an article on Diotrephes for a denominational paper. The editor told me that twenty-five deacons stopped the paper to show their resentment against being personally attacked in the paper."

[50] Polhill,"An Analysis of II and III John," 468; Kruse, *Letters of John,* 227.

[51] Burdick, *Letters of John,* 455; Smalley, *1, 2, 3 John,* 357.

[52] C. Rogers, Jr. and C. Rogers III, *The New Linguistic and Exegetical Key to the Greek New Testament* (Grand Rapids: Zondervan, 1998), 603–4.

("he loved to be first") moved to arrogance ("he refused the elder"), then to accusations (of no substance), and finally to action. First, "he did not receive the brothers." He acted exactly the opposite of Gaius (vv. 5–8). Second, he went further and attempted to stop others who would, even to the point of putting them out of the church. "Stops" *(kōluei)* means to "forbid" (NASB), "prevent," "hinder." It is a present tense verb that may indicate repeated action (iterative present). "Puts them out" *(ekballei)* is also in the present tense.[53] It is a strong word and is used in John 9:34–35 of the Pharisees throwing out from the synagogue the blind man Jesus had healed.[54] The autocracy and dictatorial behavior of Diotrephes was extreme. No doubt the church suffered under his heavy-handedness as would be the case anytime a Diotrephes type rises to power.[55]

4. Consistency of Demetrius's Testimony (vv. 11–12)

[11]Dear friend, do not imitate what is evil but what is good. Anyone who does what is good is from God. Anyone who does what is evil has not seen God. [12]Demetrius is well spoken of by everyone—and even by the truth itself. We also speak well of him, and you know that our testimony is true.

These verses comprise the didactical climax of the epistle. Here the first imperative in the letter appears, "imitate" *(mimou)*. Two commands are contained in v. 11. Verse 12 provides supporting evidence in the person of Demetrius, who probably carried the letter to Gaius. If someone is to be mimicked or followed (and we all mimic someone), let it be Demetrius (or Gaius) and not Diotrephes.

11 The verse begins with the familiar "Dear friend" *(agapēte)*. This is the last of its four uses in the epistle (vv. 1,2,5,11). Here it serves both as a term of endearment and transition as John returns to personally address Gaius.[56] The verse is also chiastic in the use of evil *(kakos)* and good *(agathos)*. "Do not imitate" *(mimou)* is a present imperative. We derive our English word "mimic" from it. Paul is also fond of the word (e.g., 1 Cor 11:1; 1 Thess 1:6). With the negative "not" *(me)* it could imply the stopping of an action already in progress. Given the previous description of Gaius in vv. 5–6, however, this is unlikely. Rather it is a general admonition to do

---

[53] It may be conative, "he is trying to" (B. F. Westcott, *The Epistles of John* [New York: Macmillan, 1905], 241), or factual, e.g., "he is putting them out" (Marshall, *Epistles of John*, 91, n. 16).

[54] Kruse, 228, n. 23.

[55] Stott wisely comments: "Self-love vitiates all relationships. Diotrephes slandered John, coldshouldered the missionaries and excommunicated the loyal believers—all because he loved himself and wanted to have the preeminence. Personal vanity still lies at the root of most dissensions in every local church today" (*Letters of John*, 231).

[56] Sherman and Tuggy, *Semantic and Structural Analysis*, 134.

the good[57] as you are already doing and especially to continue the good work of providing hospitality to the traveling missionaries. Westcott says, "He who does good proves by his action that his life springs from God as its source: he who does evil has not made the first step towards participation in the Divine Nature."[58] Ultimately the child of God imitates the Savior, the Lord Jesus (1 Cor 11:1). He is our supreme example. Yet it is the case we all need earthly flesh and blood examples to imitate (mimic) as well. We should ever be mindful on whom we set our eyes. We must also be mindful of those who have set their eyes on us!

12 John now provides an example (in addition to Gaius) of one who does good and is from God. It is most probable Demetrius[59] was the bearer of 3 John and that this verse served as his recommendation. A threefold witness (a form of the word *martus* occurs three times in this verse) is brought forward on Demetrius's behalf (cf. Deut 17:6; 19:15). First, he is well spoken of by everyone, "an expression found in several places in the New Testament (Acts 6:3; 10:22; 16:2; 22:12; 1 Tim 5:10; Heb 11:2,4,3,39)."[60] The verb "well spoken" *(memarturētai)* is in the perfect tense and "implies that the testimony to Demetrius had been given over a period of time, and it was still effective."[61] Everyone *(pantōn)* is an amazing declaration. It is doubtful everyone (e.g., pagan unbelievers) agreed with Demetrius's views or appreciated the stands he took. It was the case, however, that all who knew him knew him to be a man of character and integrity.[62] Second, he had the witness of "the truth itself." Demetrius's devotion to the truth of the gospel was self-evident. His life was consistent with the truth of the Christian

---

[57] "Both the adjective 'good' *(agathos)* and the verb "to do good" *(agathopoieō)* are found only here in the Johannine letters" (Kruse, *Letters of John*, 232). Kruse's view that "the good" should be limited to providing hospitality for the missionaries is too restrictive. It was certainly the contextual application most immediate in John's mind, but it is difficult to imagine he would not affirm a wider application. The example of Demetrius in v. 12 supports our position.

[58] Westcott, *Epistles of John*, 241. The suggestion of T. Horvath that whoever does good, believer or unbeliever, "is from God and shares in faith" is fundamentally in error and requires no refutation ("3 Jn 11: An Early Ecumenical Creed?" *ExpTim* 85 [1973–74]: 339–40). I would agree with his assessment that "it seems that v. 11b is the foundation of all that is said in 3 Jn."

[59] The only other Demetrius mentioned in the NT is the silversmith at Ephesus (Acts 19:24,28) who caused Paul no small problem. There is no basis for identifying them as one and the same. All we know of this Demetrius we glean from this one verse. The fourth century tradition (*Apostolic Constitutions* 7.46.9) that John made him bishop of Philadelphia does not have sufficient historical support to be deemed credible (cf. Smalley, *1, 2, 3 John*, 360).

[60] Kruse, *Letters of John*, 233.

[61] Smalley, *1, 2, 3 John*, 361; also Brown, *Epistles of John*, 722.

[62] Marshall restricts "everyone" to every Christian who knew him, but perhaps especially from those in the elder's immediate circle" (*Epistles of John*, 93). Smalley concurs with this view (*1, 2, 3 John*, 361). This interpretation is not without merit. Burdick's opinion that *everyone* "is hyperbole, not exaggeration" is not compelling (*Letters of John*, 458).

faith. There was a marvelous match between the two. Third, he had the testimony of the elder and his church on his side. The "we" is emphatic and should be understood to include the entire community who had sent Demetrius out.[63] Given this sterling recommendation, Gaius would have more than adequate motivation to receive Demetrius and extend to him the gracious hospitality for which he was so well known.

5. The Benediction (vv. 13–14)

[13]**I have much to write you, but I do not want to do so with pen and ink.** [14]**I hope to see you soon, and we will talk face to face.**
Peace to you. The friends here send their greetings. Greet the friends there by name.

John's concluding remarks (vv. 13–14a) are almost identical to those at the end of 2 John 12. Wishing to maintain rapport with Gaius to the end, "he closes the letter in an appropriate manner. This is in keeping with how letters are usually ended, affecting the audience's emotions in such a way as to produce a good feeling about what was said."[64]

13 John's heart is both full (for Gaius) and burdened (because of Diotrephes). What he needed to say could not be put on a single sheet of papyrus or in a longer letter for that matter. An overflowing heart must give way to a bolder course of action. Yes, he would come and confront Diotrephes (v. 10). He would also come and enjoy the company of Gaius as well.

14 This verse is quite similar to the conclusion of 2 John (see 2 John 12 and the comments there). The word "soon" (*eutheōs*) is the only significant difference. It is probably added because of the urgency of dealing with Diotrephes. John plans to come and come quickly to Gaius. He will not allow the problem with Diotrephes to fester and perhaps grow worse. There is wonderful pastoral wisdom in John's approach. "Face to face" is again a translation of the idiom "mouth to mouth" (*stoma prōs stoma;* see also 2 John 12). The elder is the only New Testament writer to use this phrase.[65] John wants a personal conversation with Gaius. No letter can substitute for his presence. John loves him and loves him dearly. If God will allow it, he will soon be on his way to see his precious friend.

The conclusion[66] of the letter is typical, yet there is still substance in

---

[63] Stott sees the "we" as referring only to John (*Letters of John,* 233).

[64] Sherman and Tuggy, *Semantic and Structural Analysis,* 137.

[65] Paul uses πρόσωπον πρὸς πρόσωπον in 1 Cor 13:12, which does literally translate "face to face" (Kruse, *Letters of John,* 216). Kruse also notes that "face to face rather than by letter is typical of the friendly letter tradition of the first-century Mediterranean world" (p. 234).

[66] Eng. texts include this portion of text with v. 14; Gk. texts in contrast begin v. 15 at this point.

what the elder says. Unlike 1 or 2 John, there is an expression of peace (but note 2 John 3). For Gaius this was especially appropriate considering the situation with Diotrephes.[67] Peace *(eirēnē)* is a wonderful Christian grace that has several facets.[68] Objectively we have peace with God through the Lord Jesus (Rom 5:1). Subjectively we can enjoy that peace that transcends understanding through the Lord Jesus (Phil 4:9). John adapts the well-known and common Jewish greeting and benediction and communicates to Gaius his personal prayer for wholeness and blessing in his life.[69]

"Greet" is placed toward the front of the sentence for emphasis (lit., "Greet you the friends"). Those who are members of the elder's church send them "hellos" as well. This would indicate they are aware of the Diotrephes matter and that they stand with John. If their opinions matter, it should be known they favor John in the dispute. This is the only place in the New Testament that believers are called "friends." This may reflect the words of Jesus in John 15:13.

Finally, the elder entreats Gaius to also greet the friends and to do so by name *(kat' onoma)*. Burdick points out a possible twofold reason for the specificity of the request: "First, it was more personal and more readily conveyed John's warm affection to them, and second, because of Diotrephes' stranglehold on the church, the greetings could not be conveyed in a corporate fashion."[70] John thus ends his letter as he began it: on a positive note. The Diotrephes affair has grieved him and caused him sorrow and embarrassment. Nevertheless, he is hopeful about what will unfold in the future. The gospel will prevail. Right will win out. Such confidence should characterize all who live their lives under "the Name." He will honor our faithfulness. We should not grow weary in doing good on his behalf.

---

[67] Burdick, *Letters of John,* 460.

[68] See John 20:19,21,26; Rom 15:23; 16:20; 2 Cor 13:11; Gal 6:16; Eph 6:23; 1 Thess 5:23; 2 Thess 3:16; Heb 13:20; 1 Pet 5:14.

[69] Marshall notes that the presence here of peace may "compensate for the absence of an opening greeting" *(Epistles of John,* 94). If so, John felt no need to do so in 1 and 2 John.

[70] Burdick, *Letters of John,* 460; also Marshall, *Epistles of John,* 94–95.

Excursus: Propitiation or Expiation: The Debate Over *Hilaskomai*

In the New Testament there are four occurrences of the Greek word ἱλάσκομαι *(hilaskomai)* or its derivatives, which relate to Christ's atoning work.[1]
Hebrews 2:17 asserts that Jesus Christ became "a merciful and faithful High
Priest ... to make propitiation for the sins of the people." John twice writes in his
first epistle that Jesus Christ is "the propitiation for our sins" (1 John 2:2; 4:10).
The apostle Paul declares that God "set forth" Jesus Christ "to be a propitiation
by his blood, through faith, to demonstrate his righteousness" (Rom 3:25). Since
propitiation means the "turning away of the wrath of God by an offering," its use
in these passages entails a definite view of God's wrath, the purpose and effect of
Christ's death, and, to a degree, the authority and inerrancy of Scripture.[2]

For this reason, its traditional understanding has not gone unchallenged.
Beginning with the seminal work of C. H. Dodd, some modern scholars object to
the traditional concept of propitiation. They insist that "expiation," meaning "the
cancellation of sin" or "the removal of sin from God's sight,"[3] represents the
more accurate rendering of the *hilaskomai* word group.[4] On both sides of the
debate there is agreement that in classical and koine Greek the *hilaskomai* word
group meant "to propitiate," "to placate," or "to appease" an angry deity.[5]
L. Morris states, "Whatever may be the biblical usage there can be no doubts as
to the prevailing use in all non-biblical writings."[6] Neither is there any dispute
that *hilaskomai* underwent an important change in meaning when adapted from
pagan sources for use in the Bible. Morris comments:

> Among the heathen, propitiation was thought of as an activity whereby the
> worshipper was able himself to provide that which would induce a change
> of mind in the deity. In plain language he bribed his god to be favorable to
> him. ... It has long been recognized that the use of the ἱλάσκομαι word-
> group in the [Bible] is not the same as that in profane sources. ... The
> Bible writers have nothing to do with pagan conceptions of a capricious
> and vindictive deity, inflicting arbitrary punishments on offending wor-

---

[1] The ἱλάσκομαι word group appears elsewhere in the NT but infrequently. In Luke 18:13 the
publican prays, "God be merciful to me [lit., 'be propitiated for me'] a sinner!" The same word
(ἱλάσκομαι) translated "propitiation" in Rom 3:25 is translated in Heb 9:5 as "mercy seat." An
adjectival form of the word is found in Matt 16:22 (Peter's rebuke of Christ), where it is translated
by the idiomatic expression "Far be it from you," and in the quotation from Jer 31:34 in Heb 8:12,
where it is rendered, "For I will be merciful to their unrighteousness."

[2] L. Morris, "propitiation," in *Evangelical Dictionary of Theology,* ed. W. Elwell (Grand Rapids: Baker, 1984), 888.

[3] Ibid.; also see J. I. Packer, "What Did the Cross Achieve? The Logic of Penal Substitution,"
TB 25 (1973): 23, n. 21.

[4] See C. H. Dodd, *The Bible and the Greeks* (London: Hodder & Stoughton, 1935); A. T. Hanson, *The Wrath of the Lamb* (London: SPCK, 1959).

[5] Even those at the forefront of advocating the change readily acknowledge this fact. See Dodd,
The Bible and the Greeks, 82; F. Buchsel and J. Hermann, "ἱλάσκομαι" *TDNT,* 3:314ff.

[6] L. Morris, *The Apostolic Preaching of the Cross* (1955; reprint, Grand Rapids: Eerdmans,
1976), 126.

shippers, who must then bribe him back to a good mood by the appropriate offerings. [C. H.] Dodd's important work makes this abundantly clear.[7]

On the matter of the extent of this change in meaning, agreement ends. Dodd and those who follow him want to eliminate completely from the biblical usage of *hilaskomai* and its derivatives all vestiges of divine wrath or propitiation, believing such concepts to be "crude" and "unworthy of the God of Israel."[8] Morris, while agreeing that in the Bible "pagan ideas of wrath and propitiation" nevertheless believes they go too far in concluding that "all ideas of wrath and propitiation are absent from it."[9] He replies:

> When we reach the stage where we must say, "When the LXX [Septuagint] translators used "propitiation," they did not mean "propitiation," it is surely time to call a halt. No sensible man uses one word when he means another, and in view of the otherwise invariable Greek use it would seem impossible for anyone in the first century to have used one of the ἱλάσκο-μαι group without conveying to his readers some idea of propitiation.[10]

Morris had this incongruity in mind when he asks, "If the LXX translators and the New Testament writers did not mean propitiation, why did they ... use words which signify propitiation and are saturated with propitiatory associations?"[11] D. Hill likewise cautions, "In so far as Dodd is concerned to maintain that ideas of celestial bribery and of capricious, vindictive anger on the part of Yahweh are absent from the [Bible], his work commands grateful agreement. But, this must not be taken to mean that all ideas of divine wrath are foreign to [the Bible]."[12] J. Walvoord also rejects Dodd's conclusion, finding that the "Biblical terminology in both the Old and New Testaments ... does not sustain a complete departure from the ... concept of propitiation."[13]

Behind this attempt to substitute "expiation" for "propitiation" lies a radical reinterpretation, if not an outright denial, of the biblical concept of God's wrath. Packer comments on the replacement of "propitiation" in Rom 3:25 with "expiation" in many modern translations, asserting that "the effect of this change is not to bring in a sacrificial motif that was previously absent, but to cut out a reference to quenching God's anger that was previously thought to be present."[14] To adopt "expiation" is to move away from a conception of wrath as a personal attitude of a holy God to one that treats wrath as an automatic, impersonal, and inexorable process of cause and effect. Hanson affirms this conclusion by declaring, "If you think of the wrath as an attitude of God, you cannot avoid some theory of propitiation. But the wrath in the New Testament is never spoken of as being propiti-

---

[7] Ibid., 129, 183.

[8] Dodd, *The Bible and the Greeks,* 87, 93-4.

[9] Morris, *Apostolic Preaching of the Cross,* 148.

[10] Ibid., 173.

[11] Ibid., 148.

[12] D. Hill, *Greek Words and Hebrew Meanings: Studies in the Semantics of Soteriological Terms* (London: Cambridge University Press, 1967), 24–25.

[13] J. Walvoord, "Propitiation," *BibSac* 119 (1962): 104–5.

[14] Packer, "What Did the Cross Achieve?" 23, n. 21

ated, because it is not conceived of as being an attitude of God."[15] Rather, "wrath" in the New Testament has been transformed "from an attribute of God into the name for a process, which sinners bring upon themselves."[16] Dodd also depersonalizes God's wrath. He claims, for example, that Paul has retained the concept of the wrath of God in Romans "not to describe the attitude of God to man, but to describe an inevitable process of cause and effect in a moral universe."[17] It is precisely this recasting of God's wrath that has opened the way to avoid an understanding of propitiation.[18] After all, only an angry God needs propitiating.

J. R. W. Stott suggests that the "crucial question" dividing scholars over the proper interpretation of the *hilaskomai* word group "is whether the object of the atoning action is God or man."[19] If God is the intended object, "then the right word is 'propitiation' (appeasing God);" if, however, man is the intended object, then "the right word is 'expiation' (dealing with sin and guilt)."[20] Dodd's view of God's wrath necessarily commits him to reject propitiation with its Godward focus (it being unnecessary to "propitiate" an impersonal force) in favor of expiation (which has a decidedly manward focus). Dodd believes the early church Fathers had "little inward sense for the Hebrew and biblical ideas that formed the atmosphere of Paul's thinking," and they erred in translating *hilaskomai* as "propitiation."[21] The Reformers, on the other hand, labored under grievous cultural misconceptions and, consequently, could not help reading into the biblical text "current or traditional ideas" which effectively rendered words like *hilaskomai* "unintelligible" to them. Dodd offers "expiation," not as a competing or a different interpretation of the *hilaskomai* word group, but as the correct and originally intended one that he has rescued from the errors of the past.

A related idea underlying their advocacy of "expiation" relates to their view of Scripture. Dodd's reasons for rejecting wrath as God's personal reaction to sin is rooted in his "underrating" both the authority and the nature of divine revelation. He explains:

> It is only to a God not yet fully conceived in terms of moral personality that the primitive numinous terror can be directed. The idea of an angry God is a first attempt to rationalize the shuddering awe which men feel before the incalculable possibilities of appalling disaster inherent in life, but it is an attempt which breaks down as the rational element in religion advances. *In the long run we cannot think with full consistency of God in*

---

[15] Hanson, 192.

[16] Ibid., 21, 37.

[17] C. H. Dodd, "The Epistle of Paul to the Romans," MNTC (London: Harper & Brothers, 1984), 23.

[18] Ibid.

[19] J. R. W. Stott, *The Cross of Christ* (Downers Grove: InterVarsity, 1986), 169.

[20] Ibid.

[21] Dodd, *The Epistle to the Romans,* 60–61.

terms of the highest human ideals of personality and yet attribute to Him
the irrational passion of anger[22] [emphasis supplied].

Scripture, according to Dodd, records the development or "evolution" of men's thinking about God. Because of this progress "the way [was] open[ed] for a further development in which anger as an attitude of God to men disappears and His love and mercy become all-embracing."[23] It is difficult to conclude apart from this defective view of Scripture that Dodd (and other proponents of "expiation") would have detected such a dramatic shift in meaning away from propitiation.

When propitiation is set aside, it is not surprising that the doctrine of penal substitution also becomes a casualty. G. W. H. Lampe, in rejecting penal substitution, states: "It is high time to discard the vestiges of a theory of Atonement that ... finds nothing shocking in the idea that God should crucify sinners or the substitute who took their place. It is time, too, to stop the mouth of the blasphemer who calls it 'sentimentality' to reject the idea of a God of retribution."[24] Lampe finds reprehensible this particular theory because it assumes that "God inflicts retributive punishment," an idea unseemly to him since "retribution is impersonal; it considers offenses in the abstract." He rejects outright the proposition that "the Father of mankind ... deal[s] with His children on the basis of deterrence and retribution." He adds that "to hang the criminal is to admit defeat at the level of love."[25] Herein lies the linkage among the concepts of atonement, wrath, and propitiation. No one who rejects penal substitution could consistently render *hilaskomai* or its derivatives by the word "propitiation," for propitiation implies wrath and wrath requires satisfaction. The use of the word itself virtually compels the adoption of penal substitution.

How did C. H. Dodd come to conclude that *hilaskomai* means "expiation"? He begins his analysis of the word group by detecting in its profane usage, that is, classical and koine Greek, a dual meaning. While he admits that "to propitiate" is the primary one, he finds "to expiate" to be a definite, although secondary meaning."[26] This is foundational to his entire argument. He determines along the way that the "secondary meaning" of "to expiate" overtakes and actually eclipses the primary meaning "to propitiate."[27]

---

[22] Ibid. 24.

[23] Ibid.

[24] G. W. H. Lampe, "The Atonement: Law and Love," in *Soundings,* ed. A. R. Vidler (London: Cambridge University Press, 1962), 187ff.

[25] Ibid.

[26] Dodd, *The Bible and Greeks,* 82.

[27] Buchsel and Hermann make the identical argument to the same effect. They propose that "through cultic use, this expansion of meaning was quite natural. The cultic action denoted by the words was designed to make God gracious again to the sinner. Hence it also cleansed from sin, or expiated his sin. Materially the effect on God could not be separated from the effect on man or his sin. The two were wrought and achieved together. In purpose and effect the cleansing of the sinner and the expiation of his sin are so essential a part of the cultic action that they came to be expressed along with propitiation in the term used for this action. Hence, the meaning of the term, though complex, is ultimately consistent. ... The most striking thing about the development of the terms, however, is that words which were originally used to denote man's action in relation to God cease to be used in this way in the NT and are used instead of God's action in relation to man" (*TDNT,* 3:316–17).

To resolve the ambiguity created by the alleged dual meaning of the *hilasko-mai* word group, Dodd examines the LXX usage to see what predominated in Hellenistic Judaism.[28] He divides his analysis of the LXX usages into three distinct groupings. The first consists of passages in which the LXX translators used a word other than *hilaskomai* or its cognates to translate the Hebrew word *kipper* ("to make atonement"), which is rendered by words of the *hilaskomai* class an overwhelming majority of the time (83 out of 105 times).[29] In this first group Dodd finds that the LXX translators rendered *kipper* "by words which give the meaning 'to sanctify,' 'purify' persons or objects of ritual, or 'to cancel,' 'purge away,' or 'forgive sins.'" He concludes from this that, "We should therefore expect to find that they regard the ἱλάσκομαι class as conveying similar ideas" (i.e. of expiation, but not propitiation).[30]

Dodd's second grouping includes passages in which the LXX translators used *hilaskomai* or its cognates to translate a word other than *kipper*. Here Dodd encounters a problem, for in four passages the rendering by a cognate of *hilasko-mai* unmistakably conveys the "ordinary classical and Hellenistic sense" of "to propitiate."[31] Three of these, Dodd explains, represent "exceptional" usages deliberately expressing the LXX translators' "contempt for its [the ἱλάσκομαι word group] standard meaning in pagan usage, as unworthy of the God of Israel." Dodd simply reinterprets the fourth to mean "made an act of expiation" because otherwise "the story is one of 'propitiation' in the crudest sense."[32] Thus he concludes that, with the exception of these four passages, the *hilaskomai* word group was used to translate Hebrew words (other than *kipper*) "which fall into one or the other of two classes: (i) with human subject, 'to cleanse from sin or defilement,' 'to expiate'; (ii) with divine subject, 'to be gracious' 'to have mercy,' 'to forgive.'" The latter class he declares "to be an entirely new usage [of *hilasko-mai*], with no pagan parallels."[33]

Dodd's final grouping involves the majority of passages in which the LXX translators used *hilaskomai* or its cognates to render *kipper*. In summarizing the results of his analysis under this third grouping, Dodd states unequivocally that "the LXX translators did not regard [*kipper*] (when used as a religious term) as conveying the sense of propitiating the Deity, but the sense of performing an act whereby guilt or defilement is removed, and accordingly rendered it by ἱλάσκομαι in this sense." Thus, bringing together the results of his evaluation of each of the three groupings, Dodd concludes: first, with regard to all but the four "exceptional" passages, "we have at the most faint echoes or reminiscences of a dead meaning." In other words, Dodd holds that in the hands of the LXX translators the *hilaskomai* class of words completely lost the sense of "to propitiate," and second, "Hellenistic Judaism, as represented by the LXX, does not regard the

---

[28] Dodd, *The Bible and Greeks*, 82.
[29] Ibid.; see Morris, *The Apostolic Preaching of the Cross*, 161ff.
[30] Dodd, *The Bible and Greeks*, 84.
[31] The four passages are Zech 7:2; 8:22; Mal 1:9; and Ps 105:30.
[32] Dodd, *The Bible and Greeks*, 87–88.
[33] Ibid., 88–89.

cultus as a means of pacifying the displeasure of the Deity, but as a means of delivering man from sin, and it looks in the last resort to God himself to perform that deliverance, *thus evolving a meaning of ἱλάσκομαι strange to nonbiblical Greek*"[34] (emphasis supplied).

As might be expected, Dodd treats identically the four occurrences of the *hilaskomai* word group in the New Testament that refer to Christ's death. Of Heb 2:17, Dodd summarily remarks, "Christ is represented as performing an act whereby men are delivered from the guilt of their sin, not whereby God is propitiated."[35] Likewise, regarding Rom 3:25, Dodd asserts that the "meaning conveyed (in accordance with LXX usage, which is constantly determinative for Paul) is that of expiation, not that of propitiation." On this particular text, Dodd unabashedly says, "Most translators and commentators are wrong."[36] However, he has "less confidence appealing to LXX usage" in the case of 1 John 2:2 and 4:10 because "the Johannine Epistles are probably less influenced by the LXX than any other New Testament writings, nor does their language ... betray any substantial signs of Semitism."[37] Dodd concedes, therefore, that "we should not be surprised to find that [John] followed the prevailing nonbiblical usage of ἱλάσκομαι and used ἱλασμός (the nominative form of ἱλάσκομαι) in the sense of 'a propitiatory offering.'"[38] Nevertheless, Dodd rejects this meaning, declares that these passages portray Christ in terms of a "divinely supplied means of canceling guilt and purifying the sinner," and in summary fashion says, "The Johannine usage thus falls into line with Biblical usage in general."[39] He concludes his discussion by remarking, "The common rendering 'propitiation' is illegitimate here as elsewhere."[40]

---

[34] Ibid., 93.

[35] Ibid., 94.

[36] Ibid. See Dodd, *Epistle of Paul to the Romans*, 54–55.

[37] Ibid., 94.

[38] Ibid., 95.

[39] Buchsel and Hermann offer a similar interpretation of these passages. Regarding Heb 2:17, they comment: "At Heb 2:17 the task of Jesus as High-priest is ... to expiate the sins of His people, to rob them of their validity and significance before God. We are not to think here either of making God gracious or of an ethical conquest of sin in man." Of 1 John they remark: "John is obviously following the OT. ἱλασμός does not imply the propitiation of God. It refers to the purpose which God Himself has fulfilled by sending the Son. Hence it rests on the fact that God is gracious. ... The meaning, then, is the setting aside of sin as guilt against God." They attribute a number of consequences to this, including "the *subjective* (emphasis supplied) result of ἱλασμός in man is παρρασια (confidence) before the divine judgment ... or victory over the consciousness of sin"; it also "begets love (for the brethren)"; and, "the overcoming of sin as guilt cannot be separated in fact from the overcoming of sin as transgression, which in John is lack of love." Concerning Rom 3:25 they assert: "The ἱλάσκομαι contained in ἱλάστηριον naturally does not mean 'to propitiate,' as though God were an object. This is excluded by the fact that it is God who has made the ἱλάστηριος what it is. In this whole context God is subject, not object. This is in keeping with Paul's doctrine of reconciliation. Only men, or the sins of men, can be object of ἱλάσκομαι. To [be] sure, we cannot support this statement by Paul's use of ἱλάσκομαι elsewhere, since there is in Paul no other instance of the word or its derivatives. Nevertheless, the statement is incontestable" (see *TDNT*, 3:315–23.

[40] Dodd, *The Bible and the Greeks*, 95.

If Dodd represents proponents of "expiation," Morris likewise represents advocates of "propitiation." In his classic *Apostolic Preaching of the Cross*, he writes, "We readily agree that pagan ideas of wrath and propitiation are absent from the biblical view of God, but Dodd seems to say that all ideas of wrath and propitiation are absent from it."[41]

Morris begins his argument by overturning Dodd's claim that the *hilaskomai* word group possessed a dual meaning in pagan usage, that is, "to propitiate" but with "to expiate" being a definite, although secondary, meaning. He responds:

> Even a man who thinks that men were moving away from early, crude ideas can find no instance wherein ἱλάσκομαι, etc., reflects this trend. It is difficult to resist the conclusion that, while the general trend ... may have been in evidence, yet the word group under consideration was not used to express it. In other words, while men may have been modifying their ideas about the nature of the gods, when they used ἱλάσκομαι, etc., it was to convey the older thought of propitiation rather than some later development.[42]

He notes that Dodd relies on just two equivocal examples. In response Morris comments, "The most ... that can be said in favour of the view that these words may contain an expiatory meaning is that the two passages ... could well be interpreted in this way."[43] But, he contends, since they in no way demand this interpretation and "in view of the otherwise consistent usage of the [profane] sources, we must draw the conclusion that, when a first century Greek heard the words of this group, there would be aroused in his mind thoughts of propitiation."[44]

However, Morris's main objection to Dodd's analysis, and one that strikes at the very heart of his conclusions, concerns Dodd's disregard for the context of the passages in which the *hilaskomai* word class appears.[45] He argues that because Dodd "totally ignores the fact that in many passages there is explicit mention of the putting away of God's anger; ... his conclusions cannot be accepted without serious modification."[46] In particular, Morris has in mind Dodd's opinion that *hilaskomai* and its derivatives completely lost the sense of 'to propitiate' in its use in the LXX. Morris notes that there are more than twenty words (in the OT) that express the idea of wrath as it applies to Yahweh and that these are so frequent that there are over 580 occurrences one must consider.[47] So pervasive is the concept of God's wrath in the Old Testament that, according to Morris, "there is no important section of which it can be said 'Here the wrath of God is unknown.'"[48]

---

[41] Morris, *Apostolic Preaching of the Cross*, 148.

[42] Ibid., 146.

[43] Ibid., 147.

[44] Ibid.

[45] Hill offers the same objection. He charges that Dodd "omitted all discussion of contexts from his study and thereby deprived himself of an important guide to interpretation" (*Greek Words and Hebrew Meanings*, 25).

[46] Morris, *Apostolic Preaching of the Cross*, 138.

[47] Ibid., 149–50.

[48] Morris, *Apostolic Preaching of the Cross*, 174.

Morris argues persuasively that Dodd's redefinition of God's wrath simply does not fit the facts. God's wrath is described by the biblical writers in intensely personal terms. "It is difficult to imagine how the prophets and psalmists could possibly have expressed more strongly the personal character of the wrath of God."[49] Disaster may in fact inevitably result from man's sin, but not "by some inexorable law of an impersonal Nature [Dodd's position], but because a holy God wills to pour out the vials of His wrath upon those who commit sin."[50] A depersonalized wrath also robs God's mercy of much of its meaning. Morris explains, "It is largely because wrath is so fully personal in the Old Testament that mercy becomes so fully personal, for mercy is the action of the same God who was angry, allowing His wrath to be turned away."[51] But he adds, "The removal of this wrath is not due to man's securing such an offering that God is impressed and relents, but to God Himself. This alone is sufficient to show that we are not dealing with the pagan idea when we speak of propitiation."[52] Thus, whereas Dodd eliminates this Old Testament concept of God's wrath from his analysis of the LXX, Morris states his "conviction that ἱλάσκομαι and its cognates include as an integral part of their meaning the turning away of wrath ... partly on the fact that, quite apart from the words themselves, there is a formidable body of evidence that the wrath of God was a conception to be reckoned with on the Old Testament view."[53]

His conviction also depends "on the words themselves." Like Dodd, Morris delves into the relationship between *hilaskomai* and *kipper,* since the two words are "nearly synonymous in meaning, or at least the LXX translators thought so."[54] He goes further than Dodd and examines the meaning and usage of *kipper* in the Old Testament. The usage of *kipper,* he notes, "divides naturally into two sections, according as atonement is thought of as coming by a cultic action or by noncultic means."[55] Though significantly smaller, the noncultic section is the more important group because it tends to show "what the verb means in itself quite apart from the conventional use of the cultus" and which, Morris believes, probably will "differ somewhat from the [cultic] use."[56]

From his evaluation of the noncultic use of *kipper* in the Old Testament, Morris concludes that *kipper* "usually bears the meaning 'to avert punishment, especially the divine anger, by the payment of a *kopher,* a ransom,' which may be of money or which may be of life."[57] In each case "the essence of the transaction is the provision of an acceptable substitute."[58] Thus he finds that noncultic *kipper* denotes a substitutionary process. Morris says, "This is so plain as to need no

---

[49] Ibid., 152.
[50] Ibid.
[51] Ibid.
[52] Ibid., 177.
[53] Ibid., 178.
[54] Ibid., 160.
[55] Ibid., 160–61.
[56] Ibid., 161.
[57] Ibid., 166.
[58] Morris, *Apostolic Preaching of the Cross.*

comment in the cases where life is substituted for life, and the principle is really the same when the sentence is commuted for a money payment."[59]

In its cultic usage, however, *kipper* "acquired a technical meaning which completely overshadowed any other. In most places it means 'to accomplish reconciliation between God and man' without anything to indicate how that reconciliation is held to be obtained."[60] Still, Morris insists the cultic usage retained the ideas of wrath and propitiation on the basis of the word's noncultic usage, the continuity of the cultic and noncultic usages seen in several passages in the Old Testament, and from the "general impression produced by the sacrificial system, that an offering of a propitiatory character is being made."[61] On this matter Morris says, "It is not so much from consideration of details as from the general sweep of the whole that conviction [i.e., the cultic usage of *kipper* also includes the concepts of wrath and propitiation] is obtained."[62]

That the LXX translators chose *hilaskomai* to render *kipper* in the overwhelming majority of instances confirms the propitiatory content of both verbs. In discussing the connection between the two, Morris says that "it would seem that the verb *kipper* carries with it the implication of a turning away of the divine wrath by an appropriate offering. The meaning accords well with the general usage of ἐξιλάσκομαι, and it seems clear that this verb is used so often to translate *kipper* precisely for this reason."[63] The LXX translators rendered *kipper* with a word so laden with propitiatory significance precisely because they believed *kipper* itself possessed this same significance. Conversely, because the LXX translators apparently understood *kipper* to refer to averting the divine wrath, they selected the appropriate Greek term to express this idea. Morris acknowledges, as Dodd's work makes abundantly clear, that "εξιλάσκομαι in the LXX is a complex word," but he convincingly argues that "the averting of anger seems to represent a stubborn substratum of meaning from which all the usages can be naturally explained."[64] Thus, in the final analysis, "the words of the ἰλάσκομαι group as used in the LXX *were not eviscerated of their meaning, nor were they given an entirely new meaning*. Rather there is a definite continuity, and in particular the removal of wrath seems to be definitely in view when this word group is used"[65] (emphasis supplied).

Morris concludes his analysis of the concept of propitiation in the New Testament, not by examining the four key *hilaskomai* passages, but with an extended

---

[59] Ibid., 148.

[60] Ibid. 167.

[61] Ibid., 170.

[62] Ibid.

[63] Ibid. Though this is a somewhat difficult statement to grasp, Morris's point seems to be that the LXX translators would not have chosen a word like ἰλάσκομαι, which was unquestionably heavily freighted with propitiatory significance in its pagan usage, to translate *kipper* unless it, too, carried and conveyed similar ideas. At the same time, given the undisputed propitiatory meaning attached to ἰλάσκομαι and its derivatives in its usage in profane sources, their choice of this word class reflects their understanding that it, in fact, possessed propitiatory meaning.

[64] Ibid., 173.

[65] Ibid.

discussion of God's wrath revealed therein. For Morris the necessity of such an approach is evident:

> In the New Testament, as in the Old, a good deal depends upon our conception of the place and nature of the wrath of God. If this wrath is regarded as a very real factor so that the sinner is exposed to its severity, then the removal of the wrath will be an important part of our understanding of salvation; whereas if we diminish the part played by the divine wrath we shall not find it necessary to think seriously of propitiation.[66]

Morris points out, "There is neither the same richness of vocabulary nor the same frequency of mention in the New Testament treatment of the wrath of God as in the Old"; yet "for the early Christians the divine wrath was just as real as it was for the men of the old covenant."[67] As in his discussion of the LXX, Morris rejects Dodd's view that wrath in the New Testament represents the "inevitable process of cause and effect in a moral universe."[68] Jesus' own words preserved in the Gospels and those of the apostles make this claim untenable. Morris adopts as his own the statement of H. W. Robinson that "this wrath of God is not the blind and automatic working of abstract law [as Dodd would have it]—always a fiction, since 'law' is a conception, not an entity, till it finds expression through its instruments. The wrath of God is the wrath of divine Personality."[69]

Turning to the four occurrences of the *hilaskomai* class of words in the New Testament, Morris contends that the context of each passage requires the meaning "propitiation." Regarding Rom 3:25 he comments: "The thought of God's wrath is never out of sight. ... It is in this context that the critical passage 3:21–26 must be studied. ... for Paul has brought heavy artillery to bear in demonstrating that God's wrath and judgment are against the sinner."[70] Moreover, he notes there is no other term than this one in vv. 21–26 to express the turning away of God's wrath. Morris thinks this term is necessary since "wrath has occupied such an important place in [Paul's] argument leading up to this section [3:21–26] that we are justified in looking for some expression indicative of its cancellation in the process which brings about salvation."[71] Countering Dodd's position, Morris argues that "more than expiation is required [here], for to speak of expiation is to deal in sub-personal categories ... whereas the relationship between God and man must be thought of as personal in the fullest sense."[72] Finally, he draws upon the single noncultic usage of *hilasterion* in the LXX, found in *4 Macc* 17:22, to bolster the inference that the word has a propitiatory meaning.[73] On the parallel

---

[66] Ibid., 178.

[67] Ibid.

[68] Dodd, *Epistle of Paul to the Romans,* 50; Morris, *Apostolic Preaching of the Cross,* 179.

[69] H. W. Robinson, *Redemption and Revelation* (London: Hodder & Stoughton, 1942), 269.

[70] Morris, *Apostolic Preaching of the Cross,* 199–201.

[71] Ibid., 201.

[72] Ibid.

[73] *4 Macc* 17:22 refers to the death of the seven Maccabbee brothers in this way: "They having as it were become a ransom for the nation's sin; and through the blood of these righteous men and their propitiatory death (or the propitiation of their death) the divine Providence delivered Israel that before was evil entreated."

between the two verses he argues that the propitiatory significance of the word in *4 Maccabbees* strongly supports a similar significance in Rom. iii 25, especially as in both cases the wrath of God is viewed as active, blood is shed, death is vicarious, and God is involved in the whole process."[74]

In Heb 2:17 there is no explicit or implicit reference to God's wrath, so that in interpreting *hilaskomai* in this passage Morris believes one "must be guided by the plain meaning of the term in contexts where the wrath is unmistakable." Though grammatically the verse presents some difficulty,[75] he concludes, "There is no really good reason for denying to ἱλάσκομαι ... its usual significance."[76] Morris notes that "even Dodd can say" with respect to the *hilaskomai* derivative in 1 John 2:2 that "in the immediate context it might seem possible that the sense of 'propitiation' is in place."[77] For Morris the crucial interpretive issue is that "Christ is said to be 'an Advocate with the Father,' and if we sinners need an advocate with God, then obviously we are in no good case. ... Under these circumstances we may well speak of Christ turning away the wrath of God, and thus ἱλασμός is a natural word in the context."[78] Also, the coincidence of language between this verse and Rom 3:25 (i.e., the mention in both of "righteousness" and Christ's blood) suggests that the same idea of propitiation is present. Finally, with regard to 1 John 4:10, Morris favors giving *hilaskomai* its usual significance, since to do so creates "one of those resounding paradoxes which mean so much for the understanding of the Christian view of sacrifice. It is to God Himself that we owe the removal of God's wrath." Otherwise, "the verse is much less striking."[79]

In sum, Morris rejects the idea that *hilaskomai* and its derivatives possessed a secondary meaning of "to expiate" in profane sources. Rather, he sees a consistent usage of the term throughout both biblical and nonbiblical writers, although he readily admits a transformation of the term away from crude, pagan concepts of propitiation in its biblical usage. His analysis of the LXX leads him to conclude that the *hilaskomai* word group in fact retained the sense of "to propitiate"; it was neither stripped of this meaning nor given an entirely new meaning. He

---

[74] Morris, *Apostolic Preaching of the Cross,* 198. Hill joins Morris in this. He says, "The remarkable community of thought between 4 Macc. 17:22 and Rom 3:21f. creates a strong presumption that ἱλαστήριον in the latter is used, as in the former, with 'propitiatory' significance" (*Greek Words and Hebrew Meanings,* 42–43).

[75] The grammatical difficulty concerns an accusative of sin following ἱλάσκομαι, which would seem to support the interpretation "to expiate." Morris treats this construction as an accusative of general respect for two reasons: first, because of its infrequency in both profane and biblical writers; and, second, because in the NT period the accusative often replaced or substituted for prepositional phrases with little if any change in meaning. Thus, he says, "It seems best to take the accusative in Heb. ii 17 as an accusative of general respect and to understand the meaning of the expression as "to make propitiation with regard to the sins of the people'" instead of "to make propitiation for the sins of the people" (*Apostolic Preaching of the Cross,* 202–5).

[76] Ibid., 205.

[77] Ibid., 206.

[78] Ibid., 206–7.

[79] Ibid., 207.

bases his conclusion on both a careful etymological analysis of *hilaskomai* and *kipper* and on the pervasive references to God's wrath (over 580), which form the setting and context for these words. Morris criticizes Dodd's approach for ignoring the context of crucial passages and for embodying a deficient, and depersonalized, view of God's wrath. The latter, he correctly observes, removes the necessity of seriously considering propitiation. Morris examines the four New Testament passages in light of his earlier analysis of the LXX and within each particular context. In each case he argues that "propitiation" represents the better and more correct translation.

If the essence of the dispute over the proper translation of the *hilaskomai* word group was etymological only, then the results of the work of Morris, Hill, Stott, and Packer, among others, could hardly be resisted, for they have demonstrated beyond question the inadequacy of Dodd's work insofar as he holds that *hilaskomai* and its cognates lost any trace of the sense "to propitiate" when adapted for use by the LXX translators. But the real heart of the controversy lies elsewhere. Stott insightfully notes, "It is discomfort with the doctrines of wrath and propitiation, which has led some theologians to reexamine the biblical vocabulary."[80] It appears that the primary, but by no means only, reason for this "discomfort" is their rejection or, at least, radical reinterpretation, of God's holiness and his wrath, which is "in fact his holy reaction to evil."[81] Commenting on this matter, E. Brunner declares that modern opposition to forensic language (i.e., wrath and propitiation) in relation to the cross derives from the "fact that the idea of the Divine Holiness has been swallowed up in that of the Divine Love; this means that the biblical idea of God, in which the decisive element is this twofold nature of holiness and love, is being replaced by the modern, unilateral, nomistic idea of God."[82]

Motivated by a passion of an "all-embracing love" and a desire to rescue God's character from the debasement attached to the "irrational passion" of anger, modern scholars propose to replace "propitiation" with "expiation." Yet the consequences of such a move, as Brunner notes, are nothing short of revolutionary: "the dualism of holiness and love ... of mercy and wrath cannot be dissolved, changed into *one* synthetic conception, without at the same time destroying the seriousness of the biblical knowledge of God, [and] the reality and mystery of revelation and atonement."[83] J. Denney offers a similar assessment when he writes, "If the propitiatory death of Jesus is eliminated from the love of God, it might be unfair to say that the love of God is robbed of all meaning, but it is certainly robbed of its apostolic meaning."[84] To embrace "expiation" is to denigrate the reality of God's holiness by denying his wrath against sin. It is, as well, to lessen his grace, for "unless we give a real content to the wrath of God, unless we hold that men really deserve to have God visit upon them the painful

---

[80] Stott, *The Cross of Christ* 169.
[81] Ibid., 103.
[82] E. Brunner, *The Mediator* (London: The Lutterworth Press, 1934), 281–82.
[83] Ibid., 519.
[84] J. Denney, *The Death of Christ* (London: Hodder & Stoughton, 1950), 152.

consequences of their wrongdoing, we empty God's forgiveness of its meaning."[85]

"Propitiation" is the proper translation because it preserves the basic usage of *hilaskomai* by both nonbiblical and biblical writers and because it addresses the concept of God's wrath, which is so prominent in the Old and New Testaments. Indeed, the "use of the concept of propitiation witnesses to two great realities, the one, the reality and the seriousness of the divine reaction against sin, and the other, the reality and the greatness of the divine love which provided the gift which should avert the wrath from men."[86] It is not that the idea of expiation is denied, for it is present in and subsumed by the idea of propitiation, which embodies both a Godward and a manward aspect. Rather, the concern is to maintain this twofold nature of God revealed in the Bible so as not to destroy "the seriousness of the ... knowledge of God, [and] the reality and the mystery of revelation and atonement."[87]

---

[85] Morris, *Apostolic Preaching of the Cross,* 212–13.
[86] Ibid., 211.
[87] Brunner, *The Mediator,* 519.

APPENDIX 1

The Origin and Theology of the Term "Antichrist" in the Epistles of John

The term "antichrist" is unique to John, appearing only in 1 John 2:18,22; 4:3; 2 John 7. John's interest in the concept is primarily theological and Christological, not political or eschatological.

John refers to the false teachers as "antichrists" (2:18), noting that they have the spirit of the Antichrist (4:3). They rejected that true knowledge of God comes through the revelation of God in the person of Jesus Christ, by means of the Incarnation. They spurned the human life of Jesus as the revelation of God.[1] Therefore the origin of any doctrine of "Antichrist" is of necessity related to the belief that there is a "Christ." In the context of Christianity, of course, Jesus of Nazareth is that Christ.

John's explicit references to the "antichrist" reveal several important facts:

1. The Johannine community had been told that an opponent of Christ would come. He is the Antichrist, an eschatological figure of evil. Though John is the only author of Scripture to use the term "antichrist," he makes it clear the concept, and the term itself, was already being used in the early church (cf. 2:18).

2. "Many antichrists have come" (reflecting the warning in Mark 13:22 of "false christs and false prophets" and "deceivers"; cf. 2:26 and 2 John 7). John clearly makes a distinction between many "antichrists" (plural) and "Antichrist" (singular), between the many who have come and the one who is to come.

3. The antichrists had left the church because they did not belong to the community of the faith. They were unregenerate and energized by an evil force (4:3).

4. The antichrists were of the world (that evil, organized system that under the rule of Satan is the opponent of God), not of the Christian community (4:1–5; 2 John 7).

5. The heretics claimed a unique knowledge of the truth and asserted that other Christians spoke falsely (2:22,27).

6. They denied that Jesus was the Christ; thus John classified them as "antichrist."[2]

Biblical teachings related to the person and work of Jesus Christ of

---

[1] A. E. Brooke, *The Johannine Epistles,* ICC (Edinburgh: T & T Clark, 1912), 54–60.

[2] K. Grayston, *The Johannine Epistles,* NCBC (Grand Rapids: Eerdmans, 1984), 76–78. For a more extensive treatment of the false teachers and the reasons for their claims, see p. 79. For a treatment of primitive Jewish apocalyptic myths in correlation with the antichrist concept, see pp. 79-81.

necessity will stand in contrast and opposition to those of antichrists. The word "antichrist" is made up of two words, *anti* and *christos*. The word *christos* translates "Christ" and refers to the concept of Messiah, or the Anointed One of God. *Anti* means either "against" or "in place of."[3] When the word is employed in English as a prefix, it usually focuses more on the concept of *opposition* to or being *antagonistic* of something or someone. In the Greek language, however, it also can carry the idea of "in the place of," something perhaps present in John's usage.[4] This idea would indicate not only opposition but false claim and usurpation. Interestingly, John did not use the term *pseudochristos* meaning "false Christ." This word is found in Matt 24:24 and Mark 13:22.

What is the possible origin of the term "antichrist?" R. Brown has identified what he believes are four different and possible parallel traditions that eventually shape and define the "Antichrist" myth: (1) the sea monster image of ancient mythology (e.g., the dragon Rahab or the sea beast Leviathan); (2) the Satan or angelic adversary of the Satan-Belial motif; (3) the tyrannical, wicked human ruler (e.g., Nebuchadnezzar, Antiochius Epiphanes, Nero) who is the very embodiment of evil; and (4) the false prophet. Brown claims the "false prophet" is the dominant motif in the epistles of John and is perhaps influenced by the Satan adversary tradition.[5]

In a somewhat similar vein A. E. Brooke states, "The idea is undoubtedly taken over from Jewish Apocalyptic thought, to which it is also probable that early Babylonian, or at least Semitic, nature-myths had contributed."[6] The elder in this view refers to a popular tradition only to spiritualize it, being the first then to contribute the term. Alleged mythological creatures like Leviathan and Behemoth are most certainly the stuff out of which the two beasts of Revelation 13 is conceived.

C. H. Dodd says that John "rationalizes the myth." There is "no single antichrist." It is not a person but an idea.[7] The spirit of the antichrist is seen wherever doctrines are taught that undermine the essential truths of the gospel, particularly that Jesus is the one and only Christ come and coming again.[8]

I. H. Marshall provides a more balanced assessment and offers a counterproposal to Dodd: "[John] has not demythologized the figure of the antichrist, nor does he deny the future coming of the antichrist, but he is much

---

[3] C. E. Simcox, "Is Anybody Good Enough to be Antichrist?" *The Christian Century 102* (20) (1985): 582.

[4] R. Yates, "The Antichrist," *EQ,* XLVI, no. 1 (1974): 44.

[5] R. Brown, *The Epistles of John,* AB (New York: Doubleday, 1982), 332–37.

[6] Brooke, *Johannine Epistles,* 51–53.

[7] C. H. Dodd, *The Johannine Epistles,* MNTC (New York: Harper & Brothers, 1946), 48–49.

[8] Yates, "The Antichrist," 43.

more concerned with the present fact of false teachers in the church who have the spirit of antichrist."[9]

It does seem certain that the concept of antichrist was a known part of the apostolic teaching. In 2 Thess 2:1–12 Paul uses the term "man of lawlessness" in describing the coming deception in the last days (2:3). Similarity in teaching between Paul's "man of lawlessness" and John's "antichrist" indicate the same apostolic concept. John's statement that the "spirit of antichrist" is already at work in the world also echoes Paul's statement in 2 Thess 2:7 that "the mystery of lawlessness is already at work." John can say (without contradicting his expectation that the ultimate Antichrist will come) that there are many antichrists who have arisen (2:28). The idea of the personal eschatological Antichrist who is to come is an idea affirmed by both apostles. It also receives additional support in the apocalyptic concept of "the beast" in Revelation 13.

Early commentators took "antichrist" to mean primarily an "adversary" of Christ. The early church Fathers quickly labeled as "antichrists" those who were in active conflict against the truth of Christ and his church. Some said that the 666 of the beast in Revelation 13 applied to the Roman Emperor Nero (A.D. 54–68) and that John had him in mind when he penned Revelation. Christians of the eighth century thought that Mohammed was the Antichrist because his teachings and character so closely fit the description. For the most part, though, commentators would say that these were "types" only.[10]

In the fifteenth century there was great fear that the end of the world was approaching. Antichrist was an ever present thought in German minds. They called him the "Endchrist," that is, the last Antichrist. Some drew out, in detail, descriptions of this soon-to-appear antichrist figure: his appearance, place of birth, timeline of his life, his satanic education, the location of his persecution of Christians, etc.[11]

Other dominant, politically ominous figures throughout history have been labeled "antichrist" as well: for example, the Pope, Napoleon, Hitler, Mussolini.[12] The list continues to grow until the present. Such speculation has proven fruitless and often quite foolish.

Christians developed an eschatology that was informed by the Hebrew Scriptures: specifically Daniel, Ezekiel, and Isaiah. The next great influence was Jesus himself. Parallels between Dan 2:7; 9:24–27; Matthew 24; 2 Thessalonians 2; and Revelation 13; 17 are obvious. "Apocalyptic thought prophesied the coming of a supremely evil antagonist of God in the last

---

[9] I. H. Marshall, *The Epistles of John,* NICNT (Grand Rapids: Eerdmans, 1978), 151.

[10] G. Drach, "Antichrist," *LQ* (1949): 457.

[11] Ibid., 457–58.

[12] W. Barclay, *The Letters of John and Jude* (Philadelphia: Westminster, 1976), 75.

days—the lawless one (2 Thess 2:1–12) or the beast (Rev 13). This figure is certainly opposed to Christ and attempts to emulate his powers."[13] In the epistles of John, however, the concern is of a different sort. The spirit of opposition to God's Christ is already present. In 1 and 2 John we gain doctrinal and Christological content for the concept of the antichrist. We also receive the term.[14]

---

[13] Marshall, *Epistles of John,* 71.

[14] For anyone interested in a detailed, historical study, there are several significant works: R. C. Fuller, *Naming the Antichrist: The History of an American Obsession* (New York: Oxford University Press, 1995); G. C. Jenks, *The Origin and Early Development of the Antichrist Myth* (New York: Walter de Gruyter, 1991); B. McGinn, *Antichrist: Two Thousand Years of the Human Fascination with Evil* (San Francisco: Harper Collins, 1994).

APPENDIX 2

"Welcoming False Teachers into Your Home"

In the early church it was common for traveling missionaries and evangelists to seek shelter and support from fellow believers as they ministered. Travel was quite dangerous, and hotel accommodations were poor and unattractive. Believers were encouraged from the church's inception to receive one another (Matt 10:40; Mark 9:37; Rom 12:13; 15:23–24).

Some believe in 2 John that John is not forbidding personal hospitality but only an official welcoming into the congregation with the opportunity to promote the false teachers' agenda.[1] This may be the case, but it does not address the whole of the issue. In the late first and early second century, it is evident that even entrance into private homes became a problem. For example, the Didache (ca. A.D. 100) states:

> About apostles and prophets, follow the rule of the Gospel, which is this: Let every apostle who comes to you be welcomed as the Lord. But he shall not stay more than one day, and if it is necessary, the next day also. But if he stays three days, he is a false prophet. And when an apostle leaves, let him take nothing except bread to last until he finds his next lodging. But if he asks for money, he is a false prophet. ... But not everyone who speaks in the spirit is a prophet, but only if he has the ways of the Lord. So the false prophet and the prophet will be known by their ways. ... If the one who comes is a traveler, help him all you can. But he must not stay with you more than two or if necessary three days. If he wants to settle among you and has a trade, let him work for his living. But if he has no trade, see to it in your understanding that no one lives among you in idleness because he is a Christian. If he will not do this, he is trading on Christ. Beware of such men.[2]

The context in which we find ourselves today is significantly different from that of the early church. While some find John's instructions too harsh, others have taken his words to mean believers are to have no contact with traveling false teachers who evangelize door to door (e.g., Mormons and Jehovah's Witnesses). Both positions miss the heart of what John intended. We are not to provide physical or financial support to those who bring false teaching. This much is clear. At the same time, it is our responsibility to bear witness to those who are deceived and need to be confronted with the truth of the gospel. Most persons in the church today feel ill prepared to engage cult members in spiritual conversation. They find it more convenient to simply send them on their way. Sometimes this is done in a

---

[1] S. S. Smalley, *1, 2, 3 John*, WBC (Waco: Word, 1984), 333.

[2] E. J. Goodspeed, trans., *The Apostolic Fathers* (New York: Harper & Brothers, 1950), 16, 17.

rude and un-Christlike manner, and the cause of the gospel is harmed.

Is there a strategy followers of Jesus Christ might employ when someone knocks on their door wishing to promote their cult? I believe there is.

First, be kind and gracious. Genuinely love these persons (1 Cor 13). Remember Christ died for these who stand before you.

Second, if convenient and appropriate (a woman alone at home should never invite strangers to enter), invite them in for a brief visit. If the time is problematic, set a future time for a conversation.

Third, establish clear and fair ground rules for the visit. I suggest that you give your guests approximately fifteen minutes to share, without interruption, what they believe. Encourage them to tell you what they believe a person must do to know God, be saved, and go to heaven when they die. After they finish, you then take fifteen minutes and share your testimony. Require that you also speak without interruption. Emphasize the assurance you have of eternal life through your personal relationship with Jesus Christ.

Fourth, when you finish, lead in prayer, asking God to show both of you the truth. In your prayer be evangelistic and gospel oriented.

Fifth, thank the persons for coming and let them know of your openness to visit again in the future.

This strategy is effective because it does not require one to have all the answers or know every detail of theology (theirs or yours). It avoids the tit-for-tat argumentative style in which most cultist are trained. It forces them to think about the testimony of a personal encounter with the Lord Jesus Christ that they do not have. It allows you to share the joy and blessing of knowing you have eternal life through a relationship with Jesus (1 John 5:11–13).

I believe this approach to be biblically sound, evangelistically effective, and in harmony with John's instruction in his second letter. I have found it to be honored by God and offer it as a loving and wise approach of sharing Christ.

Appendix 3: Homiletical Outlines for the Epistles of John

"What a Life"

1 John 1:1–4

I. Examine the Word of Life (vv. 1–2)
   1. He Is Eternal in His Deity (v. 1)
   2. He Is Historical in His Humanity (vv. 1–2)
      They Heard Him with Their Ears (v. 1)
      They Saw Him with Their Eyes (v. 2)
      They Touched Him with Their Hands (v. 1)
      They Shared Him with Their Mouth (v. 2)
II. Expound the Word of Life (v. 3)
   1. With Jesus You Have Fellowship
   2. With Jesus You Have Family
III. Enjoy the Word of Life (v. 4)
   1. Enjoy Salvation (see Ps 51:12; Hab 3:18)
   2. Enjoy the Scriptures (see Jer 15:16)
   3. Enjoy His Strength (see Neh 8:10)
   4. Enjoy Service (see Ps 100:2)
   5. Enjoy the Spirit (see Gal 5:22; 1 Thess 1:6)
   6. Enjoy Soul-winning (see Ps 126:5)
   7. Enjoy Suffering (see Acts 5:41; Jas 1:2–3)
   8. Enjoy Sharing (see 1 John 1:4)

"When Men Call God a Liar"

1 John 1:5–2:2

I. Do Not Deny the Character of God (1:5)
   1. God Is the Proclaimed Light
   2. God Is the Perfect Light
II. Do Not Deny the Consequences of Disobedience (1:6)
   1. Do Not Tell a Lie Concerning Fellowship with God
   2. Do Not Live a Lie Concerning Fellowship with God
III. Do Not Deny the Cure in the Blood of Jesus (1:7)
   1. Jesus Provides Communion for the Saints
   2. Jesus Provides Cleansing from Sin
IV. Do Not Deny the Condition of All Humanity (1:6)
   1. Do Not Be Deceived Concerning the Truth
   2. Do Not Be Devoid of the Truth
V. Do Not Deny the Confession of Sin (1:9)
   1. Confess Your Sins Personally

2. Confess Your Sins Continually
3. Confess Your Sins Confidentially
VI. Do Not Deny the Correctness of God's Word (1:10)
   1. Do Not Defame the Lord
   2. Do Not Be Destitute of His Word
VII. Do Not Deny the Cost of Salvation (2:1–2)
   1. Jesus Is Our Advocate
   2. Jesus Is Our Atonement

"Know and Obey for There's No Other Way"

1 John 2:3–11

I. Obedience Is the Test of Our Confidence (2:3–5)
   1. Enjoy Certainty (2:3)
   2. Escape Hypocrisy (2:4)
   3. Experience maturity 2:5)
II. Obedience Is the Test of Our Confession (2:6)
   1. You have a statement to prove
   2. You have a Savior for a pattern
III. Obedience Is the Test of Our Commandment (2:7–8)
   1. It Is Proclaimed in Conversion (2:7)
   2. It Is Personified in Christ (2:8)
   3. It Is Present in the Christian (2:8)
   4. It Is Perfected in the Consummation (2:8)
     (cf. 1 Cor 13:13)
IV. Obedience Is the Test of Our Communion (2:9–11)
   1. It Affects Our Position (2:9)
   2. It Affects Our Practice (2:10)
   3. It Affects Our Perception (2:11)

"The Love That God Hates"

1 John 2:12–17

I. Worldliness Discourages Our Maturity (2:12–14)
   1. As Little Children, You Are in the Family (2:12,13c)
   2. As Young Men, You Are in the Fight (2:13b,14b)
   3. As Fathers, You Are in the Faith (2:13a,14a)
II. Worldliness Destroys Our Fidelity (2:15–17)
   (cf. Gen 3:6; Matt 4:1–11)
   1. Know That the World Is Treacherous (2:15)
   2. Know That the World Is Tempting (2:16)
   The Lust of the Flesh Appeals to Our Appetites

The Lust of Our Eyes Appeals to Our Affections
The Pride of Life Appeals to Our Ambitions
3. Know That the World Is Temporal (2:17)

The Antichrist(s)

1 John 2:18–27

I. Antichrists Attack Christ (2:18)
 1. Antichrist Has a Period
 2. Antichrist Is a Principle (cf. 4:3)
 3. Antichrist Is a Person
II. Antichrists Abandon the Church (2:19,22–23,26)
 1. Physically They Desert the Fellowship (2:19)
 2. Spiritually They Deny the Faith (2:22–23,26)
 They Reject the Savior
 They Reject the Father
III. They Assault the Christian (2:20–21,24–25,27)
 1. Experience the Anointing of the Spirit (2:20–21,27)
 2. Embrace the Authority of the Scriptures (2:24)
 3. Enjoy Abiding in the Son (2:24–25)

"The Blessings of Abiding in Christ"

1 John 2:28–3:3

I. Be Confident at His Coming (2:28–29)
 1. Be Confident Because of Your Position (2:28)
 2. Be Confident At His Parousia (2:28)
 3. Be Confident in Your Practice (2:29)
II. Be Certain You Are His Child (3:1)
 1. You Have a New Father
 2. You Have a New Family
 3. You Have a New Foe
III. Be Conformed to His Character (3:2)
 1. We Have An Indestructible Position
 2. There Is An Inevitable Revelation
 3. There will be an incredible transformation
IV. Be Committed to Consecration (3:3)
 1. Possess Your Glorious Hope
 2. Pursue Godly Holiness

"Child of God / Child of Satan"

1 John 3:4–10

I. Recognize the Wickedness of Sin (3:4,7,8)
 1. Sin Is Disobedience (3:4)
 2. Sin Is Deceptive (3:7)
 3. Sin Is of the Devil (3:8)
II. Remember the Work of the Savior (3:5,8)
 1. Jesus Delivers Us From Sin (3:5)
 2. Jesus Destroys the Work of Satan (3:8)
III. Rejoice in the Walk of the Saint (3:6,9,10)
 1. Enjoy a New Liberty (3:6)
 2. Enjoy a New Life (3:9)
 3. Enjoy a New Love (3:10)

"It's Love That Makes the World Go Right"

1 John 3:11–18

I. We Have a Message That Commands Love (3:11)
 1. Love Is Essential (From the Beginning)
 2. Love Is Personal (One Another)
II. We Have a Murderer Who Contradicts Love(3:12–15
 1. Do Not Murder By Action (3:12–13)
 2. Do Not Murder in Attitude (3:14–15)
III. We Have a Master Who Compels Love (3:16)
 1. His Sacrifice Proves His Love for Us
 2. Our Service Proves Our Love for Him
IV. We Have a Mission That Calls for Love (3:17–18)
 1. Do Not Be Selfish with Your Possessions (3:17)
 2. Do Not Be Satisfied with Your Profession (3:18)

"Help for a Hurting Heart"

1 John 3:18–24

I. Love Provides Acceptance in His Presence (3:18–20)
 1. Have Certainty in the Faith (3:18–19)
 2. Have Confidence before the Father (3:19–20)
II. Obedience Provides Confidence in Our Prayers (3:21–22)
 1. Be Confident in Your Position (3:21)
 2. Be Confident in Your Petitions (3:22)
 3. Be Confident in Your Performance (3:22)
III. Faithfulness Provides Assurance in Our Position (3:23–24)

1. Confess the Son (3:23)
2. Care for the Saints (3:23)
3. Commune with the Spirit (3:24)

"The Marks of a False Prophet"

1 John 4:1–6

 I. Know Them By Examination (4:1)
   1. They Are Different As to Their Master
   2. They Are Deceptive in Their Message
   3. They Will Depart On Their Mission
 II. Know Them By Their Confession (4:2–3)
   1. Faithful Prophets Declare the Truth About Jesus (4:2)
   2. False Prophets Deny the Truth About Jesus (4:3)
 III. Know Them By Their Identification (4:4–5)
   1. Faithful Prophets Have a Foundation in God (4:4)
   2. False Prophets Have a Congregation of the World (4:5)
 IV. Know Them By Their Corruption (4:6)
   1. Faithful People Hear God's Word and Listen to That Which Is True
   2. False Prophets Hate God's Word and Listen to That Which Is False

"How's Your Love Life"

1 John 4:7–10

 I. Biblical Love Is Specific (4:7)
   1. It Is a Personal Responsibility
   2. It Is a Comprehensive Responsibility
 II. Biblical Love Is Supernatural (4:7–8)
   1. It Shows You Are Born of God (4:7)
   2. It Shows You Know God (4:8)
 III. Biblical Love Is Seen (4:9–10)
   1. God Sent His Son That We Might Live (4:9)
   2. God Sacrificed His Son, Which Proved His Love (4:10)

"The Power of Love"

1 John 4:11–16

 I. God's Love Is Satisfying (4:11–12)
   1. You Have a Motivation to Love (4:11)
   2. You Experience Maturity Through Love (4:12)
 II. God's Love Is Spiritual (4:13–14)

    1. The Spirit Is a Gift of Love (4:13)
    2. The Son Was Sent in Love (4:14)
III. God's Love Is Secure (4:15–16)
    1. Because of Jesus I Know God Lives in Me (4:15)
    2. Because of Jesus I Know God Loves Me (4:16)

"God Is Love"

1 John 4:16–21

  I. God's Loves Provides for Us Communion (4:16)
    We Live in God
    God Lives in Us
 II. God's Love Makes Us Confident (4:17–18)
    1. Be Confident about the Future (4:17)
    2. Be Confident without Fear (4:18)
III. God's Love Gives Us a Command (4:19–21)
    1. God's Love Is Prior (4:19)
    2. God's Love Is Our Proof (4:20)
    3. God's Love Is Our Practice (4:21)

"7 Things Every Child of God Can Know"

1 John 5:1–21

We Can Know:
    I. That We Love One Another (5:1–3)
   II. We Have Overcome the World (5:4–5)
 III. Jesus Is God (5:6–10)
 IV. We Have Eternal Life (5:11–13)
  V. God Answers Prayer (5:14–17)
 VI. Christians Do Not Practice Sin (5:18–19)
VII. That We Know the True God (5:20–21)

"Faith Is the Victory"

1 John 5:1–5

  I. Experience Victory by Believing in Jesus (5:1)
    1. Know Who to Believe
    2. Know What to Believe
 II. Experience Victory by Loving Others (5:1–2)
    1. Love the Father (5:1)
    2. Love the Savior (5:1)

3. Love the Brothers (5:2)
III. Experience Victory by Obeying God (5:2–3)
    1. God's Commandments Are a Blessing (5:2)
    2. God's Commandments Are Not a Burden (5:3)
IV. Experience Victory by Overcoming the World (5:4–5)
    1. You Must Be Born of God (5:4)
    2. You Must Be Believe in Jesus (5:5)

"Why Should You Believe Jesus Is the Son of God?"

1 John 5:6–12

  I. Believe the Witness of His baptism (5:6–8)
 II. Believe the Witness of His crucifixion (5:6–8)
III. Believe the Witness of the Holy Spirit (5:6–8)
IV. Believe the Witness of the Father (5:9,10b)
 V. Believe the Witness in Your Heart (5:10)
VI. Believe the Witness of Eternal Life (5:11–12)

"God Is Listening! What Are You Saying?"

1 John 5:13–17

  I. I Believe Jesus Is the Son of God (5:13)
    1. Know Who You Should Trust
    2. Know What You Have Received
 II. I Believe God Answers Prayer (5:14–16)
    1. Be Confident When You Pray (5:14–15)
    2. Be Careful When You Pray (5:14)
    3. Be Concerned When You Pray (5:16)
III. I Believe Sin Is Wrong (5:16–17)
    1. Sin Leads to Death (5:16)
    2. Sin Is Disobedience (5:17)

"Let Jesus Be Your Teacher"

1 John 5:18–21

  I. Jesus Teaches You How to Live (5:18)
    1. Do Not Continue to Sin
    2. Be Confident in the Savior
 II. Jesus Teaches You Where You Are (5:19)
    1. Some Are Children of God
    2. Some Are Controlled by Satan

III. Jesus Teaches You Whom to Believe (5:20–21)
    1. Affirm the True God (5:20)
    2. Avoid the False Idols (5:21)

"Truth or Consequences"

2 John 1–13

  I. Love the Truth (vv. 1–3)
    1. Embrace the Truth (vv. 1–2)
    2. Enjoy the Truth (v. 3)
 II. Live the Truth (vv. 4–6)
    1. Be Concerned with What You Believe (Creed) (V. 4)
    2. Be Concerned with How You Behave (Conduct) (vv. 5–6)
III. Look for the Truth (vv. 7–11)
    1. Recognize the Deceptive (v. 7)
    2. Resist the Destructive (v. 8)
    3. Reprove the Destitute (v. 9)
    4. Reject the Dangerous (vv. 10–11)
IV. Long for the Truth (vv. 12–13)
    1. Experience the Fullness of Joy (v. 12)
    2. Experience the Fellowship of the Family (v. 13)

"Four Men and Their Reputations"

3 John 1–14

  I. Gaius Is a Commendable Christian (vv. 1–8)
    1. Live Spiritually (vv. 1–2)
    2. Walk Truthfully (vv. 3–4)
    3. Serve Faithfully (vv. 5–6)
    4. Minister Generously (vv. 7–8)
 II. Diotrephes Is a Conceited Christian (vv. 9–10)
    1. Do Not Be Driven By Prideful Ambition (v. 9)
    2. Do Not Display Pompous Arrogance (v. 9)
    3. Do Not Deliver Perverse Accusations (v. 10)
    4. Do Not Dominate with Profane Activity (v. 10)
III. Demetrius Is a Consistent Christian (vv. 11–12)
    1. Pursue a Godly Example (v. 11)
    2. Possess a Good Testimony (v. 12)
IV. John Is a Caring Christian (vv. 13–14)
    1. Desire the Presence of Fellow Believers (v. 13)
    2. Desires Peace for Fellow Believers (v. 14)

Selected Bibliography

Achtemeier, E. R. "Jesus Christ, the Light of the World: The Biblical Understanding of Light and Darkness." *Int* 17 (1963).

Alexander, N. *The Epistles of John: Introduction and Commentary.* TBC. New York: Macmillan, 1962.

Alford, H. *Alford's Greek Testament.* Grand Rapids: Guardian, 1976.

Barker, G. *1 John.* EBC. Grand Rapids: Zondervan, 1981.

Berge, P. S. "The Word and Its Witness in John and 1 John: A Literary and Rhetorical Study." In *Word and World.* Supplement Series 3 (1997).

Black, C. C. II. "The Johannine Epistles and the Question of Early Catholicism." *NovT* xxviii, 2 (1986).

Bogart, J. *Orthodox and Heretical Perfectionism in the Johannine Community as Evident in the First Epistle of John.* SBLD 33. Missoula; Mont.: Scholars Press, 1977.

Boismard, M. E. "Une liturgie baptismale dans la prima Petri." *RB* 63 (1956).

Boyer, J. L. "Relative Clauses in the Greek New Testament: A Statistical Study." *GTJ* 9 (1988).

Breck, J. "The Function of ΠΑΕ in 1 John 2:20." *St. Vladimir's Theological Quarterly* 35 (1991): 203–6.

———. *Spirit of Truth: The Origins of Johannine Pneumatology.* Crestwood, N.Y.: St. Vladimir's Seminary Press, 1991.

Brooke, A. E. *A Critical and Exegetical Commentary on the Johannine Epistles.* ICC. New York: Scribner's, 1912.

———. *The Johannine Epistles.* ICC. Edinburgh: T & T Clark, 1948.

Brown, R. *The Epistles of John.* AB. New York: Doubleday, 1982.

———. *The Community of the Beloved Disciple.* New York: Paulist Press, 1979.

Bruce, F. F. *The Epistle of John.* Grand Rapids: Eerdmans, 1970.

Bruns, J. E. "A Note on John 16.33 and 1 John 2.13–14." *JBL* (1967).

Bultmann, R. *The Johannine Epistles.* Her. Philadelphia: Fortress, 1973.

Burdick, D. *The Letters of John the Apostle.* Chicago: Moody, 1985.

———. *The Epistles of John.* Chicago: Moody, 1970.

Burge, G. M. *The Letters of John.* NIV Application Commentary. Grand Rapids: Zondervan, 1996.

Calvin, J. *The Gospel according to St. John Part Two, 11–21* and *The First Epistle of John.* CNTC. Grand Rapids: Eerdmans, 1988.

Carl, K. J. "The Idea of 'Knowing' in the Johannine Literature." *Bangalore Theological Forum* 25 (1993).

Carson, D. A., D. J. Moo, and L. Morris. *An Introduction to the New Testament.* Grand Rapids: Zondervan, 1992.

Cook, W. R. "Hamartiological Problems in First John." *BSac* (1996).

Culpepper, R. A. *1, 2, 3 John,* Knox Preaching Guides. Atlanta: John Knox, 1985.

———. "The Pivot of John's Prologue." *NTS* 27 (1980/81).

De Boer, M. C. "The Death of Jesus and His Coming in the Flesh." *NovT* XXXII-II, 4 (1991).

de Jonge, H. J. "Erasmus and the Comma Johanneum." *Ephemerides Theologicae Lovanienses* 56 (1980): 385.

de Jonge, M., C. Haas, and J. L. Swellengrebel. "A Translator's Handbook on the Letters of John." *BT* 22 (1): 111–18.

Dericksen, G. W. "What Is the Message of 1 John?" *BSac* 150 (1993).

Dodd, C. H. *The Johannine Epistles*. New York: Harper & Brothers, 1946.

Edwards, M. J. "Martyrdom and the First Epistle of John." *NovT* xxxi, 2 (1989).

Francis, F. "The Form and Function of the Opening and Closing Paragraphs of James and 1 John." *ZNW* 61 (1970): 125.

Grayston, K. *The Johannine Epistles*. NCBC. Grand Rapids: Eerdmans, 1984.

Guthrie, D. *New Testament Theology*. Downers Grove: InterVarsity, 1981.

Hansford, K. L. "The Underlying Poetic Structure of 1 John," *JTT* 5 (1992).

Hengel, M. *The Johannine Question*. Philadelphia: Trinity Press International, 1989.

Hiebert, D. E. "An Exposition of 1 John 2:18–28." *BSac* (1989): 79.

Hiebert, D. E. *The Epistles of John*. Greenville: Bob Jones University Press, 1991.

Hill, J. "A Genre for 1 John." In *The Future of Early Christianity*. Edited by B. A. Pearson. Minneapolis: Fortress, 1991.

Hobbs, H. H. *The Epistles of John*. Nashville: Thomas Nelson, 1983.

Inman, K. "Distinctive Johannine Vocabulary and the Interpretation of 1 John 3:9." *WTJ* 40 (1977–78): 136–44.

Jackman, D. *The Message of John's Letters*. Downers Grove: InterVarsity Press, 1988.

Kistemaker, S. J. *James and I–III John*. NTC. Grand Rapids: Baker, 1986.

Klauck, H.-J. "Internal Opponents: The Treatment of the Secessionists in the First Epistle of John." *Concilium* 200 (1988): 55–65.

———. "Zur rhetorischen Analyse der Johannesbriefe," Zeitschrift für die Neutestamentliche Wissenschaft 81 (1990).

Kotzé, P. P. A. "The Meaning of 1 John 3:9 with Reference to 1 John 1:8 and 10." *Neot* 13 (1979): 68–83.

Kubo, S. "1 John 3:9: Absolute or Habitual." *AUSS* 7 (1969): 47–56.

Kysar, R. *1, 2, 3 John*. ACNT. Minneapolis: Augsburg, 1986.

Ladd, G. E. *A Theology of the New Testament*. Grand Rapids: Eerdmans, 1974.

Law, R. *The Tests of Life*. Reprint, Grand Rapids: Baker, 1979.

Lenski, R. C. H. *The Interpretation of the Epistles of St. Peter, St. John and St. Jude* (Minneapolis: Augsburg, 1966.

Lieu, J. M. "What Was from the Beginning: Scripture and Tradition in the Johannine Epistles." *NTS* 39 (1993).

———. *New Testament Theology. The Theology of the Johannine Epistles*. New York: Cambridge University Press, 1991.

Longacre, R. E. "Exhortation and Mitigation in First John." In *Selected Technical Articles Related to Translation* 9 (1983).

Luther, M. *Lectures on the First Epistle of St. John. LW*. St. Louis: Concordia, 1967.

Marshall, I. H. *The Epistles of John*. NICOT. Grand Rapids: Eerdmans, 1978.

Martin, F. "The Integrity of Christian Moral Activity: The First Letter of John and Veritas Splendor." *Cummunio* 21 (1994).

Metzger, B. M. *A Textual Commentary on the Greek New Testament*, 2nd ed. New York: American Bible Society, 1994.

Minear, P. S. "The Idea of Incarnation in First John." *Int* xxiv (1970): 291–302.

Morris, L. *The Apostolic Preaching of the Cross*. Reprint, Grand Rapids: Eerdmans, 1976.

————. *The Cross in the New Testament.* Grand Rapids: Eerdmans, 1965.

Moule, C. F. D. *An Idiom-Book of New Testament Greek.* 2nd ed. Cambridge: University Press, 1959.

Neufeld, D. *Reconceiving Texts as Speech Acts: An Analysis of 1 John.* Leiden: Brill, 1994.

Painter, J. "The 'Opponents' in 1 John." *NTS* 32 (1986).

Polhill, J. "An Analysis of II and III John." *RevExp* LXVII, No. 4 (1970).

Plummer, A. *The Epistles of S. John.* Reprint, Grand Rapids: Baker, 1980.

Raabe, P. R. "A Dynamic Tension: God and World in John." *Concordia Journal* 21 (1995): 132–47.

Reno, R. R. "The Marks of the Nails: Theological Exegesis of the First Letter of John for Easter." *Pro Ecclesia* Vol. VI, No. 1 (1997).

Shirbroun, G. F. "Life." In *Dictionary of Jesus and the Gospels.* Downers Grove: InterVarsity Press, 1992.

Sweazey, M. "Chiastic Study of the First Epistle of John." Master's Thesis, St. Vladimir's Orthodox Theological Seminary, 1986

Synge, F. C. "1 John 3:2." *JTS* 3 (1952): 79.

Strecker, G. *The Johannine Letters.* Her. Philadelphia: Fortress, 1996.

Swadling, H. C. "Sin and Sinlessness in 1 John." *SJT* 35 (1982): 205–11.

Sloyan, G. S. *What Are They Saying about John?* New York/Mahwah, N.J.: Paulist Press, 1991.

Stevens, G. B. *The Johannine Theology.* London: Richard D. Dickinson, 1894.

Sloyan, G. S. *Walking in the Truth.* Valley Forge: Trinity Press Internatuonal, 1995.

Schnackenburg, R. *The Johannine Epistles.* New York: Crossroad, 1992.

Stott, J. R. W. *The Letters of John.* Rev. ed. TNTC. Grand Rapids: Eerdmans, 1988.

Scholer, D. M. "1 John 4:7–21." *RevExp* 87 (1990).

Schweizer, E. "Zum religionsges-chichtlichen Hintergrund der 'Serdung-sformel' Gal. 4:4f. Rm. 8:3f. John 3:16f. 1 John 4:9." *ZNW* 57 (1966).

Sherman, G. and J. C. Tuggy, *A Semantic and Structural Analysis of the Johannine Epistles.* Dallas: Summer Institute of Linguistics, 1994.

Smalley, S. S. *1, 2, 3 John.* WBC. Waco: Word, 1984.

Smith, D. M. *First, Second, and Third John.* IBC. Louisville: John Knox, 1991.

Sproston, W. E. "Witness to What Was *ap' arches:* 1 John's Contribution to Our Knowledge of Tradition in the Fourth Gospel." *JSNT* 48 (1992).

Talbert, C. H. *Reading John.* New York: Crossroad, 1994.

Thomas, J. C. "The Literary Structure of 1 John." *NovT* XL 4 (1998): 369–81.

Thomas, R. L. "Exegetical Digest of 1 John." © 1984 R. L. Thomas. Used by permission. For a copy of this work call 1-800-GRACE15 or go to www.gbibooks.com.

Thompson, M. M. *1, 2, 3 John.* NTCS. Downers Grove: InterVarsity, 1992.

Tollefson, K. D. "Certainty within the Fellowship: Dialectical Discourse in 1 John." *BTB* 29, no. 2 (1999).

Thompson, M. M. *1–3 John.* Downers Grove: InterVarsity Press, 1992.

van der Horst, P. W. "A Wordplay in 1 John 4:12." *ZNW* 63 (1972).

Van Staden, P. J. "The Debate on the Structure of 1 John." In *Hervormde Teologiese Studies* 47/2 (1991).

van Unnik, W. C. "The Christian's Freedom of Speech in the New Testament." *BJRL* 44 (1961–62).

Vaughan, C. *1, 2, 3 John.* Grand Rapids: Zondervan, 1970.

Watson, D. F.   "Amplification Techniques in 1 John: The Interaction of Rhetorical Style and Invention," *JSNT* 51 (1993).

Watson, D. F.   "An Epideictic Strategy for Increasing Adherence to Community Values: 1 John 1:1–2:29." In *Proceedings: Eastern Great Lakes and Midwest Biblical Societies* 11 (1991).

Wendland, E. R.   "'Dear Children' Versus the 'Antichrists': The Rhetoric of Reassurance in First John." *JTT* 11 (1998).

Westcott, B. F.   *The Epistles of John.* New York: Macmillan, 1905.

Whitacre, R. A.   *Johannine Polemic: The Role of Tradition and Theology.* Chico, Cal.: Scholar's Press, 1982.

Witherington, B. III,   "The Waters of Birth: John 3.5 and 1 John 5.6–8." *NTS* 35 (1989): 160.

York, H. W.   "An Analysis and Synthesis of the Exegetical Methods of Rhetorical Criticism and Discourse Analysis as Applied to the Structure of 1 John." Ph.D. diss., Mid-America Baptist Theological Seminary, 1993.

Selected Subject Index

Person Index

Selected Scripture Index